The Martians of Science

The Martians of Science

*Five Physicists Who Changed
the Twentieth Century*

István Hargittai

OXFORD
UNIVERSITY PRESS

2006

OXFORD
UNIVERSITY PRESS

Oxford University Press, Inc., publishes works that further
Oxford University's objective of excellence
in research, scholarship, and education.

Oxford   New York
Auckland   Cape Town   Dar es Salaam   Hong Kong   Karachi
Kuala Lumpur   Madrid   Melbourne   Mexico City   Nairobi
New Delhi   Shanghai   Taipei   Toronto

With offices in
Argentina   Austria   Brazil   Chile   Czech Republic   France   Greece
Guatemala   Hungary   Italy   Japan   Poland   Portugal   Singapore
South Korea   Switzerland   Thailand   Turkey   Ukraine   Vietnam

Copyright © 2006 by Oxford University Press, Inc.

Published by Oxford University Press, Inc.
198 Madison Avenue, New York, New York 10016
www.oup.com

Oxford is a registered trademark of Oxford University Press

Library of Congress Cataloging-in-Publication Data
Hargittai, István.
The martians of science : five physicists who changed the twentieth century / István Hargittai.
p. cm.

ISBN-13 978-0-19-517845-6

1. Physicists—United States—Biography.   2. Science—United States—History—20th century.
3. Von Kármán, Theodore, 1881–1963.   4. Szilard, Leo, 1898–1964.   5. Wigner, Eugene Paul, 1902–1995
6. Von Neumann, John, 1903–1957.   7. Teller, Edward, 1908–2003   I. Title.
QC15.H27 2006
530.092'2—dc22   2005029427

9 8 7 6 5 4 3 2

Printed in the United States of America
on acid-free paper

For Balazs and Eszter

The twentieth century saw the transformation of science from a gentleman's trade into an industry. It became a major arena of human endeavor, one of whose purposes was the creation of military might. No other institution or group of people symbolized this transformation better than the lives and deeds of the five friends that this book is about:

Theodore von Kármán (1881 Budapest–1963 Aachen, Germany)
Leo Szilard (1898 Budapest–1964 La Jolla, California)
Eugene P. Wigner (1902 Budapest–1995 Princeton, New Jersey)
John von Neumann (1903 Budapest–1957 Washington, DC)
Edward Teller (1908 Budapest–2003 Stanford, California)

These men are often referred to as the "Martians." There are anecdotes about the origin of this label. The essence is that there was some discussion among the participants of the Manhattan Project about the smart and extraordinary Hungarian scientists. Someone suggested that they had come from Mars, but to disguise themselves they spoke Hungarian. The story has several variants, but the conclusion is the same, and nobody ever questioned its trustworthiness. So the label "Martian" was a joke originally; here I use it to refer to the five scientists as a group.

Edward Teller characterized the Martians in the dedication of his *Memoirs* in the following way: "All of them . . . came to the United States during the period that Fascism was gaining power in Europe. All of them played a role in the technical developments of the twentieth century."[1] All five were outstanding scientists dedicated to the defense of democracy, regardless of whether they were considered to be "hawks" or "doves." In their deep concern for the Free World they were willing to act relentlessly, risking even their scientific careers. The Martians as a group were more extraordinary than the sum of them as individuals. This book aims to give readers a better understanding of what made these five scientists so special and to give readers an appreciation of their lives and work.

Occasionally, the label of Martians has been used to refer to others than these scientists. The late Hungarian physicist George Marx's book *The Voice of the Martians* included not only scientists but also chess players and financiers, economists and writers, who had been born in Hungary and had become famous abroad.[2] Marx brought the Martians into the limelight and encouraged the documentation of their origins and achievements. He started writing extensively about them in the 1980s, before the fall of communism, and this explains why he avoided such sensitive issues as Hungarian anti-Semitism. Other authors in Hungary also contributed a great deal to our knowledge about the Martians.[3] Tribute is due to William O. McCagg, Jr., who published his book *Jewish Nobles and Geniuses in Modern Hungary* in 1972.[4] He did his research during the second half of the 1960s when this topic was largely a taboo in Hungary and where the original edition of McCagg's book was not made available. There was a section in his book that directly bears on our subject, "In Explanation of Hungary's Scientific Geniuses."[5]

Shortly after the last Martian, Edward Teller, died, I received an invitation from Oxford University Press to write a book about the five scientists. The more I thought about this challenge, the more natural it seemed to me to take it up. I live in Budapest but spent a considerable amount of time in the United States teaching and doing research in the 1980s and 1990s. I am a physical chemist, and my main research thrust has been in molecular structures, which figured in the science of some of the Martians. I have had a side interest in symmetry, to which I was introduced personally by Eugene Wigner in 1969. I have been interested in the discoveries of twentieth-century science. I have conducted and published interviews with many of its outstanding individuals and wrote a book about the Nobel Prize. I knew two of the five Martians, Eugene Wigner and Edward Teller, personally, and have long admired Leo Szilard. I found some common traits in our origins and backgrounds and I felt as if I knew the Martians better than my scarce interactions with them might have suggested.[6]

My first encounter with Eugene Wigner was especially important because it came early in my career. Wigner received the Nobel Prize in 1963, and in the fall of 1964 I read an article by him in a Hungarian weekly about the limits of science. The article caught my interest, I sent a response to the magazine, and it was published.[7] I was a Master's degree student in Moscow and it was the first time I had seen my writing published. Soon, something of even greater significance happened. I received a long letter from Wigner and some reprints of his papers. He agreed with some of what I had written and disagreed with other aspects, all in his most polite way.

After our first exchange, Wigner and I kept up a correspondence on and off until his last years, but we met in person only once, in 1969. I was spending a year at the physics department of the University of Texas at Austin and he came for a brief visit as a guest lecturer. Our meeting consisted of five one-hour conversations during the week of his visit. We talked about many things. He taught me about symmetry, and this had a long-ranging impact on me. It was fortunate that at that time I was studying one of the most symmetrical molecules, adamantane, $C_{10}H_{16}$, whose name refers to its high stability. Later he sent me his essay book, *Symmetries and Reflections*, in which he had a diagram of the diamond structure, which very much resembled the structure of adamantane. It dawned on me only later how lucky I was that, if only for a few days, I had had Wigner as my mentor in symmetry.

I met Edward Teller in 1996, when my wife Magdi and I visited the Tellers in their home in Stanford, California. First there was a little small talk in Hungarian, and then we recorded a long conversation with Teller in English. He was convalescing after an illness and the conversation started slowly. He was curt, and at one point Mici Teller interjected in Hungarian, "Don't be so unfriendly!" Fortunately, Teller gradually warmed to our questions and became a more and more forceful advocate of his views. He was most vigorous and captivating when speaking about science, and he kept his mini-audience of two in awe. Even his letters to me not long before his death were full of purpose and energy.

In spite of these personal encounters, my knowledge of the Martians has come primarily from the literature, and especially from the following monographs: Theodore von Kármán with Lee Edson, *The Wind and Beyond*; William Lanouette with Bela Silard, *Genius in the Shadows*; Eugene P. Wigner with Andrew Szanton, *The Recollections of Eugene P. Wigner as told to Andrew Szanton*; Norman Macrae, *John von Neumann*; and Edward Teller with Judith Shoolery, *Memoirs*.[8]

The Martians made diverse contributions to science that had both fundamental value and significance for military defense. Their works ranged from aerodynamics to quantum mechanics, from the stored program computers to molecular biology, from the nuclear chain reaction to game theory. In addition to their outstanding science, each took an active part in the defense of the United States in World War II and beyond. Von Kármán was important for developing the U.S. Air Force. Szilard initiated the work on the American atomic bomb, known as the Manhattan Project. Wigner was instrumental in building the first nuclear reactors and was the world's first "nuclear engineer." Von Neumann participated in various defense-related projects, including the use of computers in designing the hydrogen bomb. Teller, best known as the father of the hydrogen bomb and initiator of the second weapons laboratory in the United States, figured prominently in the Strategic Defense Initiative, known also as Star Wars. All were dedicated to democracy and were on the conservative side, with the exception of the leftist liberal Szilard.

All five came from Budapest and ended up in the United States via Germany. All benefited from and were shaped by the sizzling intellectual life of the Hungarian capital around the turn of the twentieth century. They kept up their friendships throughout their lives, regardless of differences in their outlooks on life and politics. All were Jewish, suffered from anti-Semitism in Hungary, and found their new home in Germany, but had to leave that country because of the Nazi takeover. Regardless of whether they had converted to other religions, they never shied away from their Jewishness. They also proudly maintained their Hungarian identity. Some of them were ostracized in Hungary during the communist era, but all were honored—most posthumously—after the political changes of 1989–1990.

The widespread labels attached to most of the Martians warned me to be cautious. Von Kármán has been called the Father of Supersonic Flight, and three of the others have been called the father of something. In particular, their contributions to the American nuclear program have been interpreted alternatively in positive and in negative lights. I offer here two *imaginary* descriptions:

An appreciative one
Szilard, Wigner, von Neumann, and Teller made seminal contributions that accelerated the ending of World War II. Szilard first thought of, and then patented, the idea of nuclear chain reaction and he initiated the famous Manhattan Project with a letter from Albert Einstein to President Franklin D. Roosevelt. Wigner was the world's first nuclear engineer, besides his pioneering applications of symmetry principles to atomic physics. Von Neumann was the father of the modern computer and Teller the father of the hydrogen bomb. The American hydrogen bomb saved the world from the Soviet threat that might have prevailed had the Soviet Union alone developed the hydrogen bomb. This terrible weapon ultimately acted as a deterrent through the possibility of mutual destruction. Star Wars, in whose development Teller played a pivotal role, accelerated the collapse of the Soviet Union.

A damning one
The Einstein letter to President Roosevelt hindered rather than accelerated the development of the American atomic bomb because it doomed the not-yet existing program to wander in the bureaucratic maze. It could have been started much sooner, had it been initiated by people better versed in American conditions. The bomb was finally developed due to the impact of British scientists. If properly initiated, the atomic bomb could have been ready a full year earlier. The Nobel laureate physicist I. I. Rabi stated that "The Germans owed a lot to Szilard."[9] Although he initiated the Manhattan Project, Szilard did little for its successful completion. Teller worked in Los Alamos, but mostly refrained from working on the atomic bomb. Later he pushed the world to the brink of annihilation with his hydrogen bomb program, in which von Neumann and Wigner actively assisted him. Star Wars was not only a hoax, it almost led to the bankruptcy of the United States.

Regardless of whether one appreciates or curses the deeds of these scientists, they were extraordinary, and many people have wondered about the secrets of their success and the similarity of their backgrounds and education. In particular, it has been suggested that the Martians all went to a special high school, but in fact they attended three different high schools. Although some were influenced by enlightened teachers, others found their schooling boring.

Were the Martians a group? The spread of their birth dates is wide, with 27 years between von Kármán and Teller, while those of Szilard, Wigner, and von Neumann formed a small cluster, being born within five years of each other. However, the lives and activities of von Kármán and the rest of the group show so many similarities that it seems as if von Kármán's life was merely shifted to begin a couple of decades before the rest. Similar ages were the least of what connected the Martians; it was their common interests in science and defense and their networking that made them a group. What part did nature and nurture play in their development? How they would have fared, had they lived in a totalitarian society, is an intriguing, if highly unscientific question.

There are other questions that are of interest to pose. Would present-day education (in Hungary, or in the United States, for that matter) be conducive to their respective careers? What was the justification for dealing with the Soviet Union from the position of strength (here, of course, benefiting from hindsight)? What was the impact of the anti-Semitism they experienced in Hungary, Germany, and even the United States when they arrived there? Looking at such aspects and others might provide some hints to the question that must be on the mind of every reader who is interested in the subject matter of this book: Can we expect the occurrence of another group of Martians anywhere, anytime soon?

Learning about the Martians made me better understand the world we live in today. Perhaps this is what I hope most to share with my readers.

A NOTE ON LANGUAGE

Being Hungarian and someone who cares for languages, I invite my readers to trust me by accepting my spelling of Hungarian words and names as correct. I need to make this remark because my spelling in many instances differs from that in much of the existing literature about the Martians. The "accents" deserve a special comment. There is no need to indicate where the stress is in the Hungarian language—and it is never done—because the stress is always on the first syllable. What foreign authors often mistake for accent is the indication of a different letter and a different sound. Thus, for example, the Hungarian word *ver* means beats (the verb) in Hungarian and the "e" in it is pronounced something like the vowel in "get." In the Hungarian word *vér*, meaning blood, the "é" is pronounced something like the vowel in "name."

The peculiarity of the way Hungarian names are written is that the surname comes first and the given name or "first" name comes last. It is perhaps one of the characteristics of Hungarian usage showing the Asian relationship of the language. In this book, to avoid confusion, all names are given in the Western way, that is, the first name first, middle initial if any, and the surname last. The "Martian" names went through some transformations as they moved from Hungary to Germany and to the United States. Thus, von Kármán's first name changed from the Hungarian Tódor to the German Theodor, then to Theodore in English, although his surname remained Kármán, with its exact Hungarian spelling, throughout. (The "von" in his surname is pronounced "fon," while the letter "á" is pronounced in both instances as it is in "car.") Leo Szilard (pronounced "Silard") was Leó Szilárd in his Hungarian period and Leo Szilard later. Eugene P. Wigner (pronounced "Vigner") was Jenő Wigner or Jenő Pál Wigner originally, Eugen Wigner in his German period, and Eugene P. Wigner in his American period. John von Neumann was János in Hungary, Johann in Germany, and John in America. Edward Teller was given the name Ede when he was born.

ACKNOWLEDGMENTS

My first words of thanks go to Magdi, my wife, friend, partner, and critic, for her multilevel assistance in bringing this project to completion.

I have benefited from numerous interviews with scientists who in one way or another were connected with the story of the Martians. Most interviews were not explicitly conducted with this project in mind; rather, they were part of a larger undertaking of conversations with famous scientists published in the *Candid Science* book series. The following conversations are mentioned here in connection with the present book: Alexei A. Abrikosov (2004, Lemont, Illinois); Harold Agnew (2003, Budapest); Sidney Altman (1998, New Haven, Connecticut); Philip W. Anderson (1999, Princeton, New Jersey); Nicolaas Bloembergen (2005, Lindau, Germany); Erwin Chargaff (1994, New York City); Francis Crick (2004, La Jolla, California); Freeman Dyson (2000, Princeton, New Jersey, by M. Hargittai); Richard Garwin (2004, Scarsdale, New York); Walter Gilbert (Indian Wells, California, 1998), Vitaly L. Ginzburg (2004, Moscow); Donald Glaser (2004, Berkeley, California); Maurice Goldhaber (2001, 2002, Brookhaven, New York); David Gross (2005, Lindau, Germany); François Jacob (2000, Paris); George Klein (1999, 2000, Budapest); Nicholas Kurti (1994, London); Benoit Mandelbrot (2000, Stockholm); Matthew Meselson (2004, Woods Hole, Massachusetts); Rita Levi-Montalcini (2000, Rome, by M. Hargittai); George Marx (1999, Budapest); Yuval Ne'eman (2000, Stockholm); Marshall W. Nirenberg (1999, Bethesda, Maryland); George A. Olah (1996, Los Angeles); Wolfgang Panofsky (2004, Stanford, California, by M. Hargittai); Arno Penzias (2001, Stockholm); Max Perutz (1997, 2000, Cambridge, UK); William H. Pickering (2004, Pasadena, California); Kenneth S. Pitzer (1996, Berkeley, California); F. Sherwood Rowland (2005, Lindau, Germany); Glenn T. Seaborg (1995, Anaheim, California); Nikolai N. Semenov (1965,

Budapest); David Shoenberg (2000, Cambridge, UK); Gunther S. Stent (2003, Budapest); Gerard 't Hooft (2001, Utrech, the Netherlands, by M. Hargittai); Valentine L. Telegdi (2002, Budapest, by M. Hargittai); Laszlo Tisza (1997, Budapest); Charles H. Townes (2004, Berkeley, California); James D. Watson (2000, 2002, Cold Spring Harbor); Steven Weinberg (1998, Austin, Texas); John A. Wheeler (2000, 2001, 2002, Princeton, New Jersey, by M. Hargittai); Marina Whitman (née von Neumann, 2005, Ann Arbor, Michigan, by M. Hargittai); and Frank Wilczek (2005, Lindau, Germany).

I am grateful for helpful information and materials to Endre Czeizel (Budapest); Burtron Davis (Lexington, Kentucky); Tibor Frank (Budapest); Richard L. Garwin (Scarsdale, New York); Maurice Goldhaber (Brookhaven, New York); Margit Grigori (Los Gatos, California); Eszter Hargittai (Evanston, Illinois); Tamás Kármán (Budapest); Mária Kolonits (Budapest); László Kovács (Szombathely, Hungary); Arnold Kramish (Reston, Virginia); William Lanouette (Washington, DC); Karl Maramorosch (Scarsdale, New York); István Orosz (Budakeszi, Hungary); Arno Penzias (Menlo Park, California); János Philip (Budapest); Judith Shoolery (Half Moon Bay, California); John Silard (Bethesda, Maryland); Manfred Stern (Halle, Germany); Valentine Telegdi (Geneva, Switzerland); Wendy Teller (Naperville, Illinois); James D. Watson (Cold Spring Harbor, New York); Helen Weiss (Carlsbad, California); Martha Wigner Upton (Hudson, Ohio); and Marina Whitman (née von Neumann, Ann Arbor, Michigan); also to the Budapest University of Technology and Economics and its Public Relations Office; the Dwight D. Eisenhower Library (Abilene, Kansas); the Eötvös Loránd Physical Society (Budapest) and the Photo Archives of its magazine, *Fizikai Szemle*; the Hungarian Academy of Sciences and its Photo Archives; the Hungarian National Museum and its Photo Archives; the Lawrence Berkeley National Laboratory; the Lawrence Livermore National Laboratory; NASA; the Ronald Reagan Library (Simi Valley, California)

I appreciate the comments and suggestions I received on the manuscript at its various stages from Lawrence E. Bartell (Ann Arbor, Michigan); Tibor Frank (Budapest); Balazs Hargittai (Tyrone, Pennsylvania); George Klein (Stockholm, Sweden); Torvard Laurent (Uppsala, Sweden); Arno Penzias (Menlo Park, California); and Valentine Telegdi (Geneva, Switzerland).

I express my thanks for generous support by the Hungarian Academy of Sciences, the Budapest University of Technology and Economics, and Oxford University Press (New York).

CONTENTS

INTRODUCTION

Budapest in the period 1867–1914 was a uniquely fertile site for promoting talent. The first date refers to the so-called Compromise between the Habsburgs and Hungary and the second to the outbreak of World War I. The compromise was called *Ausgleich* in German and *Kiegyezés* in Hungarian. The Habsburgs and the Hungarians had to come to an agreement following the crushed Hungarian revolution and war for liberation of 1848–1849 against Austria. The Habsburgs could not defeat the Hungarians alone and had to call in the Russian czar for their rescue. A period of ruthless terror followed and finally the Austria weakened by lost foreign wars could no longer live with a rebellious nation under her rule. The compromise created a dual monarchy of Austria and Hungary, a personal union under Franz Joseph I. He became the King of Hungary in addition to being the emperor of the rest of the empire. The Austrians and the Hungarians henceforth reigned over smaller nations. Thus, for example, the Kingdom of Hungary included Croatia and Slovakia, which today exist as independent nations. The monarchy had Vienna and Budapest as its twin capitals. Budapest was born from uniting Buda, Pest, and Óbuda (ancient Buda) in 1871, with Buda and Óbuda on the right bank of the Danube and Pest on the left. Buda is hilly and Pest is considered to be plain because its elevation is gradual; its outer districts reach the altitude of the conspicuous Gellért Hill of the Buda side. The city lies in a basin and the air sits over it when there is no wind, turning into smog especially in wintertime.

With 1867, the door opened to unprecedented progress in Hungary, and Budapest became one of the fastest growing cities in Europe. Immigration was encouraged. At the end of the nineteenth century Budapest was one of the main destinations of Jewish immigration in the world, second, perhaps, only to New

York City. According to some, the more well-to-do Jews congregated in Budapest and the poorer went to New York. The Hungarian nobility—and it was a large class, especially those without any land—monopolized the political bureaucracy and the military. It left wide open the professional intellectual trades, which became vastly popular among the recently emancipated Jews, as well as among the Germans and other minorities. There seemed to be a welcome division of labor between Hungarians and Jews with intensifying Jewish assimilation. This assimilation was largely welcomed by the Hungarians and especially by the political elite. This was because the loyal Jewish Hungarians strengthened numerically the Hungarian population that found itself in the minority in large areas of this multiethnic country.

There are opposing views as to the origin of the great possibilities for Jews in fin de siècle Hungary (meaning, of course, the turn of the twentieth century). According to one view, it was because Hungary was so liberal. The opposing view maintains that it was exactly Hungary's backward feudalistic regime that brought about those unique opportunities for Jews in Hungary.[1] In any case, their numbers were swelling because of the absence of persecution. They burst onto this scene after centuries of having been excluded from the professions. They were ready for the new opportunities because their culture valued education.

Budapest of the early 1900s has been the subject of as much scrutiny as admiration because of its extraordinary production of gifted scientists, artists, composers, and playwrights. One-fifth of its population was Jewish, consisting of native Budapesters, incomers from provinces of Hungary proper, and immigrants from all directions. My own ancestors came from the northwest on the paternal side and from the southwest on the maternal side. They spoke German, and soon learned Hungarian.

Many came from the East, from Galicia (see map), and they spoke Yiddish. An early twenty-first-century anti-Semitic utterance by an extreme right-wing Calvinist minister in Budapest referred to Jews as "the nobodies from Galicia." Whether he knew it or not, and it would not have mattered to him anyway, Galicia has produced an extraordinary amount of talent in the Western world, often going through Hungary. This is little known because often these outstanding contributors to world culture had lost their Eastern origins and been regarded as Austrians. A case in point is Erwin Chargaff, the noted biochemist, who lived in the United States from the mid-1930s and whom everybody considered to be the archetypical Viennese, which he was. But Chargaff was originally from Czernowitz, which he describes as "at that time a provincial capital of the Austrian monarchy" and he refers to his father as "a typical old-fashioned Austrian."[2] A look at the map reveals that Czernowitz (called Černovcy today) is about 800 kilometers (500 miles) from the eastern border of today's Austria, east of the Carpathian Mountains and well into today's Ukraine.

Isidor I. Rabi's Nobel autobiography states that he was born in Raymanov, Austria.[3] His biographer writes more precisely that he was born in Rymanow,

Galicia, "then a province of the Austro-Hungarian Monarchy, now in Poland."[4] It is curious that nobody has yet made a compilation of famous scientists who originated from Galicia and more broadly from the strip of area stretching from the Black Sea to the Baltics, much of which used to be called the Pale. It would be of interest to examine the fertility of that region for scientific talent. The task would not be easy because of the masking effects of autobiographies by such people as Chargaff and Rabi. Of our five heroes, at least Szilard's and von Neumann's ancestors had come from Galicia.

For prominent Jews the ultimate sign of assimilation in Hungary was to become a member of the hereditary nobility. And what could have been better evidence of the liberal atmosphere of the Habsburg Empire than the fact that even non-converted Jewish families could acquire such a distinction? In the early 1900s, even some members of the Hungarian government came from Jewish families, with names that sounded genuinely Hungarian. But World War I, known also as the Great War, brought an end to this seemingly idyllic situation. The most forward-looking Jewish families had sensed for some time that the peaceful conditions could not last forever and made sure that their children received a good education that would help them survive in any part of the world. In addition to the traditional approach of placing great emphasis on education, this meant cultivation of modern languages and practical trades.

Von Kármán, Szilard, Wigner, von Neumann, and Teller came from a Budapest upper-middle–class Jewish background and developed like many other children of similar backgrounds. Even their precocity might not have led to extraordinary lives had there not been some special circumstances. Many others experienced similar circumstances but perhaps not in their totality. These included affluence, valuing education and culture, and early exposure to totalitarianism: the short-lived Hungarian "Soviet" Republic and the savage White Terror that followed it in Hungary in 1919–1920. They knew that they had to excel in their immediate environment in order to survive, and they gained experience from early emigration. This emigration was forced upon them not only by anti-Semitism but also by the lack of perspective at home. They all went to Germany, whose economy had suffered from a lost war, but which at the time was a flourishing democracy, the Weimar Republic. Many others followed this path and their destinations included other West European nations as well. My future stepfather was among them.[5]

The most important experience for the Martians in Germany was that they became part of top-of-the-world science. This catapulted them into a different orbit. This experience was the Berlin physics colloquia for Szilard, Wigner, and von Neumann; Werner Heisenberg's Leipzig group for Teller; and, two decades before, Ludwig Prandtl in Göttingen for von Kármán. The five were able to turn this opportunity to their advantage and soon became recognized players in top science. This was a turning point in their lives. That Hungary ejected them so early was also to their advantage as it prepared them for later challenges. Their

The Austro-Hungarian Empire and surrounding areas in (a) pre-1914 Europe, and (b) the same area with present-day political borders.

b

Hungarian existence was the first period of their lives, and their years in Germany the second. The third period started with their departure from Germany and lasted until the start of World War II. There were small variations. For Szilard it was a shorter period, which ended when he realized the possibility of nuclear chain reaction. For Teller it ended when he attended Franklin D. Roosevelt's speech to the scientists that made him realize that he—together with thousands of others— carried a special responsibility.

The fourth period was World War II and within it, conspicuously, the creation of the atomic bomb. This was the time when their political formation was completed. The fifth period was the Cold War, including the development of the hydrogen bomb and, on von Kármán's part, the creation of the modern U.S. Air Force. The hydrogen bomb dominated Teller's and von Neumann's defense-related activities, while civil defense was Wigner's highest concern. Szilard was also deeply involved (although on the other side of the fence) with the struggle to curb the arms race and bring the two superpowers together. Von Neumann died in 1957, von Kármán in 1963, and Szilard in 1964. Wigner carried on. He remained committed to defense, but his activities no longer carried global significance. In this last period, Teller remained alone in his self-determined role as defender of Western civilization, as he saw it, or as a Cold War warrior, as many others saw him. Our discussion will loosely follow this subdivision of their paths.

Of all the five friends, only Teller remained a non-converted Jew, but this had no more significance on his life than the conversion of the others had on theirs. Their Jewishness was not a determining factor per se, but it was an important factor because of the external circumstances. This is basically why they had to leave Hungary, and then Germany as well. Their common Jewish roots and similar backgrounds in childhood and youth contributed much to their friendships and much to their dedication to fight totalitarian regimes. Their being Hungarian and Jewish is interwoven, regardless of whether we consider Szilard and von Neumann, who never stepped onto Hungarian soil after World War II, or Teller, who loved to bathe in Hungarian recognition and admiration after the political changes of 1989–1990. When Teller first returned to Hungary after the fall of the one-party system, he addressed his audience at a rally with something like "My blood brother Hungarians!"[6] This was as bizarre as it was pathetic.

The Martians of Science

CHAPTER ONE

Arrival and Departure

Budapest was filled with fine high schools.
  Eugene P. Wigner

Hungary has no place for you.
  Miksa Teller

This chapter provides some information about Martian genealogy, the circumstances of their growing up, the high schools (*gimnáziums*) they attended, and the circumstances which made them leave their home country to seek their fortunes elsewhere. In 1926, the youngest of them, Edward Teller, left Hungary; he was the last to leave. The discussion will extend a little further into the period when the Martians might have considered returning to their home base, in the 1930s, but that proved unrealistic.

Family Origins and Early Childhood

Where did the ancestors of the Martians come from? What were their family environments when they arrived? Unfortunately, we cannot go back many generations,

because most records have been lost due to wanderings and persecution. Below
is a brief summary of what we know about their immediate ancestors.[1] Much more
is known about their early childhood, which for all of them was spent in comfort
and enlightenment and was conducive to fast intellectual development. In this,
their home environments and high school instructions augmented each other.

Theodore von Kármán

Theodore von Kármán was born in Budapest in 1881 as Tódor Kármán, eight
years after his father Mór Kármán (1843–1915) had changed his surname from
Kleinmann. The family lived in Szeged, where Tódor's grandfather was a tailor.
There was a famous rabbi there at that time, Leopold Löw, who introduced the
Hungarian language into the synagogue. Although Mór caught the eye of the great
rabbi, who wanted him to become one, he preferred secular studies in philosophy and pedagogy at the University of Vienna. After graduation, he went to the
University of Budapest to earn a doctorate. Then he studied the most advanced
systems of education in Germany. Upon his return to Hungary Mór worked out
a reform of secondary education, which has a direct bearing on our story.

The new system removed the control of education from the churches and
established a strong secular system, with high schools called gimnáziums. By "the
churches" I mean the Catholic, Calvinist, and Lutheran churches, which retained
some of their own schools, as did the Jewish community. The denominational
schools continued to be strong academically, and there remained important in-
centives for good teachers to work for them, including higher salaries. The situation could be compared to today's America, where the excellent private schools
serve as driving force for the aspiring public schools. One of the new secular high
schools in Budapest was called the *Minta*, meaning "model."

Mór Kármán's success in reorganizing the Hungarian secondary school system brought him a court appointment in Vienna. He was responsible for the
education of one of the Emperor–King's cousins.[2] Upon its completion, Franz
Joseph I offered Kármán an award, but he told His Majesty that he would rather
have something that he could hand down to his children. Hence he received hereditary nobility in 1907. About ten percent of the population in Hungary belonged
to the nobility at that time, and perhaps because it was not so unreachable, it was
rather coveted. Had it been a minuscule part of the population, people might not
have been concerned with it. The indication that a Hungarian is a nobleman is a
prename in front of the surname, supposedly referring to the geographical location of his estate. This prename for the Kármán family was *szőllőskislaki*, indicating that the family had originated from Szőllőskislak. So our hero's proper
Hungarian name would be szőllőskislaki Tódor Kármán. This was complicated,
and nobody outside Hungary would know from this combination of the nobility
of its bearer. The German equivalent of his name would be Theodor Kármán von

a

d

b

e

c

f

Birthplace buildings of the Martians in Budapest (courtesy of László Kovács, Szombathely, Hungary): (a) Theodore von Kármán: 22 Szentkirály Street (drawing by László Pittman), (b) Leo Szilard: 50 Bajza Street (drawing by Gyula Széles), (c) John von Neumann: 62 Bajcsy Zsilinszky Avenue (drawing by László Pittman), (d) Eugene P. Wigner: 76 Király Street (drawing by László Pittman). (e) The Szilards soon moved to a big house at 33 Városliget (drawing by László Pittman). (f) Birthplace of Edward Teller: 3 Kozma Street (drawing by Gyula Széles).

Szőllőskislak. This could then be conveniently shortened to Theodor von Kármán or, in French-speaking territories, to Theodore de Kármán. His sister is known to have preferred the "de Kármán" version because she had lived in Paris for some years.[3] Another example is John von Neumann.[4]

Apparently, these superintelligent men of Jewish extraction found it prudent to carry on with names that stressed their nobility and, in so doing, implied German origin, even in the citadel of democracy, the United States. For von Neumann, stressing the noble origin of his name may have in part reflected his own efforts to survive. He told and retold a story, with many variations, which he had originally heard from Stanislaw Ulam: A Jewish farm boy, Moyshe Wasserpiss, emigrates to Vienna where, upon becoming a successful businessman, he changes his name to Herr Wasserman. Then he moves on to Berlin, where he becomes yet more successful and changes his name first to Herr Wasserstrahl (water-jet), then to von Wasserstrahl. Finally, in Paris he becomes Baron Maurice de la Fontaine.[5]

Tódor's mother was Helen Kohn (1852–1942), whose ancestors were scholars, and she had the rare distinction that she could trace them back for centuries, to a famous court mathematician in Prague. This mathematician was credited with having created the world's first mechanical robot, the Golem. Kármán's maternal grandfather had taken up agriculture. He rented a large estate, which provided an excellent playground for the Kármán children (five sons and one daughter) during their summer vacations in the country. In the true Hungarian spirit of the landed gentry, when grandfather Kármán's affairs were down financially, he entertained his non-Jewish farmer friends to luxurious feasts of champagne and caviar.[6]

Theodore von Kármán started as a child prodigy, and later felt that he had been destined to become a scientist.[7] However, he was almost diverted from this path. When he was six years old he could multiply six-digit numbers in his head, to the amazement of his family and friends. When his father learned about this, he asked his son never to think about mathematics again. This was not because his father did not care for his mental development; on the contrary, he made his son read geography, history, and poetry. He was only afraid that his son would turn into a freak with a one-sided development, which could not be used for anything but entertaining people. Tódor would turn back to mathematics in his teens, but he never again learned to do fast multiplication. As an adult, even though he could add and subtract in several languages, he could multiply only in Hungarian.

The elder von Kármán was a strong influence on his son, who forever remembered the intellectual curiosity his father induced in him.[8] They would talk about science, politics, and religion, and Mór taught his son that, "If one doesn't sympathize with revolutionaries when one is young, he has no heart. If he accepts their ideas when he is old, he has no brain." By then the elder von Kármán had rejected the teachings of Marx and Engels, but the young von Kármán remained

Theodore von Kármán
(drawing by István
Orosz).

open to them throughout his youth. Their discussions about faith taught von
Kármán to carefully separate science and religion.

Leo Szilard

Leo Szilard's ancestors on both sides arrived in Hungary from Galicia.[9] His
paternal ancestors came in the middle of the eighteenth century, when Jews had
only Hebrew given names. They acquired surnames under the reign of the Habsburg Emperor Joseph II (1780–1790). This explains why they were given German
names and of a relatively small variety. Szilard's paternal ancestors acquired the
surname Spitz (summit), perhaps because they lived in mountainous northern
Hungary, which is Slovakia today. They rented an agricultural estate, which included a fortress-like palace with a drawbridge entrance. They did not do well,
and after a series of misfortunes moved to a town in the region. The grandfather
was a bitter, tyrannical person. After his death his widow moved to Budapest with
her fourteen children.

One of these children became Leo's father, Lajos (1860–1955). He graduated
from the Budapest Technical University in the mid-1880s and founded his own
bridge and railway construction company. He married Tekla Vidor (1870–1939)
in 1896. Her father was a medical doctor specializing in ophthalmology. Lajos and
Tekla had a civilian marriage followed by a wedding in the synagogue, but they

were not religious and assimilation was natural for them. They changed their surname from Spitz to Szilárd ("solid" in Hungarian) in 1900.

Leo was the first child in the family, followed by Béla and Rózsi. Of the three, only Béla had children. He was an accomplished engineer, who changed his name to Bela Silard in the United States, and contributed to William Lanouette's excellent Szilard biography.[10] Szilard was a creative child but somewhat clumsy with his hands. He was a born leader who invented new games and new rules for old games. He consciously accepted being different and did not mind being in the minority. He was stubborn and honest to the extreme and developed a feeling of community responsibility at an early age. Another of his characteristics was that he concentrated on his current tasks and did not dwell on past events. An exception to this was what he learned from his mother; the tales she told him were the source of his values. His childhood experience was the more important for Szilard because he thought that in some way he remained a child throughout his life. This is not so unorthodox a thought as it might seem because Szilard identified "an inquisitive mind, the mind of a scientist" as that with which all children are born. His mother "wanted to inculcate addiction to truth in her children."[11] Szilard remembered a story told him by his mother about his grandfather, of an incident that had happened in his grandfather's school when he was a child: he had to supervise the class in the absence of the teacher and report the violators of order. When the teacher arrived he reported them, including himself, as he was one of the violators. Szilard found his role model in his grandfather.

Szilard's "addiction to the truth was victorious over whatever inclination he might have had to be tactful." When World War I started, Szilard and his family returned from a resort to Budapest. As they were traveling, they met trains moving in the opposite direction with drunken soldiers whose behavior the passengers mistook for enthusiasm. Szilard, however, insisted that they were simply drunk. He saw the situation clearly and did not hide his observation just because it was not polite and tactful. Szilard was sixteen years old at the time and this was the age at which he considered—more than half a century later—that his clarity of judgment was at its peak. He drew a life lesson from the experience, according to which clarity of judgment is not a matter of intelligence. Rather, it "is a matter of ability to keep free from emotional involvement."[12]

Szilard characterized his childhood guardedly, "I couldn't say that I had a happy childhood, but my childhood was not unhappy either." He was often ill until the age of ten, when he started attending high school, which had eight grades and lasted until Szilard was eighteen. His classmates liked him, perhaps because his good grades came easily to him rather than from his trying hard. They liked to have him on soccer teams although he was not a good player. He completed high school while World War I was on and was drafted into officers' school, where, again, he was liked by his comrades. He was lucky to avoid fighting on the front, as well as the Spanish flu epidemic of 1918.[13]

Eugene P. Wigner

Eugene Wigner's paternal grandparents lived in central Hungary. The Wigner name was a simplified version of Wiegner (meaning cradle maker in German), which may have referred to his ancestors' trade. Wigner's father, Antal (1870–1955), was three when he lost his father and sixteen when his mother died. After Antal's father's death, the family moved to Budapest, where Antal soon started to work at the Mauthner leather factory. He completed the Lutheran Gimnázium in night school and moved gradually to a director's position in the leather company. Wigner's mother Erzsébet Einhorn (1879–1966) had the rare distinction among Jewish families of claiming to trace her ancestors back for hundreds of years. Her father was a medical doctor in Kismarton (Eisenstadt in German), on the Esterházy estate in Hungary's westernmost region. The family came from the northwest.

Jenő Pál Wigner was born on November 17, 1902. The family spoke Hungarian and German and he was taught French by a governess. He was a quiet child, started wearing glasses early, and was not very active in sports and games, but he liked long walks. He studied part of his elementary schooling privately at home; then, at the age of eleven he started at the famous Lutheran Gimnázium. Wigner had two sisters, Berta and Margit ("Manci"). Manci divorced her first husband in 1934 and married the physicist Paul Dirac in 1937, who by then was a Nobel laureate; they met when visiting Princeton.

John von Neumann

John von Neumann's ancestors probably originated from Galicia.[14] The paternal grandparents came from a small village in northern Hungary, and had three daughters and three sons. One of the sons was von Neumann's father Miksa, or Max (1870–1929), who came to Budapest in his late teens and married the upper-class Margit (Margaret) Kann (1881–1956). This elevated his social status steeply, and he managed the change superbly. He was a cultured man and saw to it that their three children would get a broad-based education. The maternal grandfather had four daughters and his big house contained five spacious apartments, all occupied by members of his family. Each family maintained at least one German and one French governess.[15] The Kann house became virtually a private educational institution: besides the Neumann children, their numerous cousins also joined in their private lessons. The three Neumann sons were János (called by the nickname Jancsi by everybody), Michael, born as Mihály, and Nicholas, born as Miklós.

Von Neumann's father acquired hereditary nobility in 1913 for his achievements in the economy, and Miksa became margittai Miksa Neumann, or in German, Maximilian Neumann von Margitta. Accordingly, our hero's name was margittai János Neumann or Johann Neumann von Margitta, which was eventually simplified to Johann von Neumann and later to John von Neumann. Margitta was the place whence the family had ostensibly come and where they ostensibly owned land. It is probable that Miksa derived his prename from his wife's given name, Margit. It is consistent with this notion that his coat of arms displayed three marguerites (daisies), again probably as a reference to his wife.

Von Neumann's maternal grandfather Kann was a wizard at arithmetic manipulations and so also became Jancsi. The home surroundings of the von Neumann family were conducive to learning and Jancsi made great use of all the opportunities. They had bought an entire library from an estate and rebuilt one of their large rooms to accommodate it. There, Jancsi read the forty-four volume universal history series in German and remembered it for the rest of his life.

Edward Teller

Teller's father, Miksa (Max) Teller (1871–1950), was born in Érsekújvár in northwestern Hungary (today it is Nové Zámky in Slovakia). Jews could not stay overnight in the town until the early 1800s, but they were active in trade on market days. When they finally gained the right to settle in the town, they brought prosperity to it. Érsekújvár developed early into a railway center, and the arrival of the fast train from Budapest used to be greeted daily with a Hungarian patriotic song by a live gipsy band. Miksa Teller graduated from law school in Budapest, where he opened his practice in 1895. He was successful, and from 1913 co-edited a law magazine with Rusztem Vámbéry, the son of the famous explorer Ármin Vámbéry.[16] Miksa married Ilona Deutsch (1891–1985) in 1904. The Deutsch family lived in Lugos in southeast Hungary (now Romania), where the first Jewish families had arrived at the end of the eighteenth century. Her father was a well-to-do banker and he became Teller's favorite grandparent. The language of the Deutsch family was German, but Ilona learned several other languages as well, including Hungarian.

When Miksa Teller and Ilona Deutsch married, they settled in Budapest and had two children, Emma and Edward, whose original Hungarian name was Ede. Edward left Hungary in 1926. Emma married a successful lawyer, András Kirz. They had one son, János. András Kirz was killed in a concentration camp in 1945. The rest of the family (Teller's parents, Emma, and János) survived in Budapest. After Miksa died in 1950, the Communist authorities deported the surviving family members from their Budapest home to the countryside, ostensibly for Miksa Teller's "capitalist" past. Following Stalin's death in 1953, they returned to Budapest but they had lost their home and hardship followed. János Kirz left Hungary in the wake of the suppressed revolution of 1956, studied physics at Berkeley, and became a professor at the State University of New York. Teller's mother and sister were permitted to leave Hungary in 1959, largely due to Szilard's connections with the Soviet and Hungarian representatives at a Pugwash meeting. Teller's mother died in the United States when she was 94 years old.

Teller's childhood was not a happy one. He liked his family environment but suffered in school from teasing by his classmates. Even eight decades later these memories haunted him. His situation eased when Teller learned to ignore the teasing. He earned some respect by helping others in their studies, and he started making friends. His mother was very protective of him. He did not seem to be very close to his father. Instead, he looked up to his maternal grandfather in Lugos. One of their exchanges became a life lesson for him: Teller asked his grandfather about the validity of laws because he had some doubts. He asked him whether it was right to take "an eye for an eye, a tooth for a tooth?" He never forgot what his grandfather told him:

> Laws must be obeyed without exception. The law cannot make
> everyone a saint. Only a very few people are saints, and obeying the law
> must be possible for all people. If someone knocks your tooth out, you
> have a strong urge to hit back. The meaning of the law is that you must
> never take more than one tooth for a tooth. To forgive is much better.
> But the law cannot forbid the desire for revenge. It can only limit it by
> justice.[17]

According to his long-time co-worker, Judith Schoolery, who co-authored his *Memoirs* with him, Teller never accepted that personal responsibility might override what the law says, even if it worked against one's conscience.[18] He could have never accepted such dissent, although breaking a law that is against one's conscience is an American tradition.

Gems and Less: Gimnázium Experience

The widespread notion is that all the Martians went to the same gimnázium and that it had a miraculous impact on their further careers. Although they did not all go to the same gimnázium, and I contend that the gimnázium did not have a decisive impact on their careers, it was an important enough ingredient in their lives to deserve greater scrutiny. At the beginning of the twentieth century this form of education encompassed eight years, from the ages of ten to eighteen, so the gimnázium had a profound impact with long-lasting consequences on its pupils. It was the single most important influence on the Martians in Hungarian life, outside of their families. After the gimnázium, only von Kármán spent an equal or longer period in Hungary. The fact that they did not go to the same high school does not mean that their secondary educations differed greatly, because the gimnáziums followed a certain established pattern even if with different emphases on different subjects and with different strengths in the teaching staff. A gimnázium would emphasize either humanistic subjects, or mathematics and the "hard" sciences.[19] On a relative scale, the fin de siècle Hungarian gimnázium was far more advanced than the Hungarian university of that era.

The gimnázium as an institution had an important weight in the country's cultural life. Even the architecture signified that importance, as distinguished architects provided magnificent designs for them, often with innovations and artistic value.[20] This is not to say that these designs necessarily served modern education well; thus, for example, little attention was paid to proper gyms for physical education. This obsolete approach to physical education was in contrast to the otherwise growing awareness of the importance of athleticism and sports for the healthy development of the individual.

John Lukacs, a historian of the Budapest of around 1900, noted the rigidity of the requirements in the gimnázium. "In most classes the hour began with recitation, meaning that each student had to be ready for testing and questioning each day." As a consequence, "students were haunted by the fear of being suddenly called on, of being inadequately prepared, and of receiving a consequent poor or failing mark at the end of the semester." Lukacs allows that this approach may have contributed to self-discipline, but he warns that the "almost impossible demands also brought forth . . . an early and youthful realization that cutting corners and disregarding rules, that clandestinity and prevarication were inevitable conditions of survival in a world with rigid, categorical, insensitive and often senseless rules." We might add with some cynicism that in this sense the gimnázium prepared its pupils for real life. Lukacs's conclusion is that, in spite of a lot of good coming out of the education at the gimnázium, "there was no direct correlation between high marks and high character, and sometimes not even between one's scholastic record and one's subsequent career."[21] My experience with the gimnázium came five decades later, but it was sadly consistent with what Lukacs had to say.

It is also true that not all gimnáziums had the same atmosphere and a lot depended on the individual teachers. Good teachers could have an impact in a most direct way on the students. Von Kármán and Teller went to the *Minta*, Wigner and von Neumann to the Lutheran Gimnázium, and Szilard to a lesser known school. An important means of enhancing the intellectual level of education and of broadening their pupils' outlook was the so-called self-improvement circles. They were organized in better schools in various disciplines. Talent and independent study received more exposure in these circles than in the regular curriculum.

The Minta: von Kármán and Teller

Von Kármán called the *Minta* "the gem" of his father's educational theories.[22] It was designed to be a practice school for training high school teachers from the university and it has fulfilled that function ever since. Our daughter Eszter at-

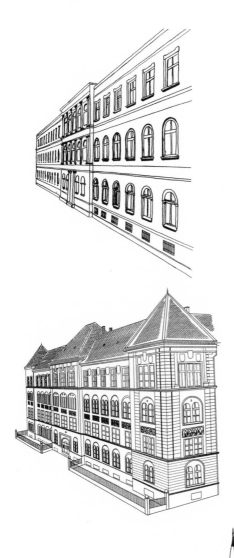

Gimnáziums of the Martians (courtesy of László Kovács, Szombathely, Hungary): (top) Minta Gimnázium (drawing by László Pittman), (middle) Főreálgimnázium of District VI in Budapest (drawing by Gyula Széles), (bottom) Lutheran Gimnázium (drawing by László Pittman).

tended this school in the late 1980s. The teachers in training provide a good experience not only for the would-be teachers but also for the students, by both groups becoming immediate parties to a learning experience. In addition to the two Martians, the school's famous pupils have included Michael Polanyi, who would become Eugene Wigner's "doctor father," and two future British economists of great distinction, Thomas Balogh and Nicholas Kaldor, who eventually became barons (life peers) in Great Britain. Another important future British scientist, the physicist Nicholas Kurti, also went to the *Minta* and so did the 2005 Abel Prize winner mathematician Peter Lax.[23]

Von Kármán found the *Minta* "a great educational experience." It taught a wide range of subjects, for example Latin, mathematics, and history, trying to link them to experience in everyday life. Latin was especially important because it had been the official language in Hungary until 1844. All the speeches in the Hungarian Parliament used to be given in Latin. The language was taught as if it was alive and it came to life in the classroom. Von Kármán was eager to learn mathematics and it, too, was taught in conjunction with practical uses, involving statistics, for example. The pupils prepared graphs and studied the rate of change, which brought them close to calculus. A favored technique of teaching was learning by deriving rules from specific examples. When von Kármán was hired to tutor a student from another school, the student's parents could not believe that such unorthodox approaches might yield results. The student passed the exam, but by then they had fired von Kármán as a tutor.[24] He also noted that the relationship between teachers and students at the *Minta* was more liberal than was the practice in other high schools in the country at that time, which fostered the learning process through informal channels.

In von Kármán's time the national competitions in mathematics among high school students had already started, and he earned first place. The other Martians would also excel in these competitions, which were extended to physics from 1916. Wigner was a conspicuous exception: he considered it a sign of conceit to compete and did not want to seek recognition. He thought that the prizes would seek him out if he deserved them.[25] Szilard and von Neumann found these competitions so useful that, when they were in Berlin, they were thinking of introducing them in Germany.[26] Two Hungarian émigré mathematicians, George Pólya and Gábor Szegő, introduced the Stanford Mathematics Competition for high school students in 1946, first in California and eventually in six more states.[27]

The *Minta* did not undergo any important change from von Kármán's time to Teller's. This is the more remarkable because when Teller joined the *Minta* World War I was being waged, but the outside world barely impinged on the school. Nonetheless, Teller's high school experience was different from von Kármán's. Teller had been educated at home and at a private school before he joined the *Minta* in 1917, when he was nine years old. He studied mathematics, history, Hungarian, German, and Latin, and participated in physical education. The academically uninteresting program was coupled with his being a social outcast who had problems of adjustment during his years at the *Minta*. Teller does not waste much space in his *Memoirs* on his high school experience; it was a painful topic for him. But it lasted eight long years and he underwent some trials during those years. When Teller suggested an alternative solution to a math problem, the teacher (who happened to be the school director) wondered if he was a repeater, which was an insult. When on another occasion Teller showed a simpler solution to the one the math teacher gave on the blackboard, the teacher called him a genius and added ominously that he did not like geniuses. This teacher's rigid disciplinarian approach to teaching Teller's favorite subject "set me back several years," he commented later. His physics teacher even confiscated the book from which Teller wanted to ask him an extracurricular question, and returned the book to him only after he had completed the final examinations. "Challenging students to explore ideas was not a common aim at the *Minta*" was Teller's summary judgment, although he describes some positive experiences with other teachers.[28]

Főreálgimnázium of District VI in Budapest: Szilard

Főreálgimnázium in Hungarian meant a leading school, the adjective "real" referring to the emphasis on sciences. The general emphasis notwithstanding, much depended on the actual teachers and the compositions of the classes as to whether there would be more engineers and scientists emerging from such a school than from one inclined more toward the humanities. Szilard's school was good, but the least known among the schools the Martians attended. It was close to the Szilard home, in the neighborhood of elegant Andrássy Avenue. That whole area was carefully designed and built during the building frenzy of the Millennium of Hungary, at the end of the nineteenth century. The building of Szilard's school was completed in 1898, the year he was born. It was a modern and spacious structure with well-equipped special lecture rooms for the sciences. There were authors of textbooks among its teachers.[29] However, Szilard did not find his high school inspiring and referred to his mathematics teacher as "a complete idiot," whose classes he found boring. Szilard and his two friends organized their own study group for mathematics.[30]

The Lutheran Gimnázium: Wigner and von Neumann

Wigner and von Neumann had outstanding education in the Lutheran Gimnázium. To Wigner, it was the best high school in Hungary, possibly in the world.[31] Their mathematics teacher was László Rátz. He tutored von Neumann and gave books to Wigner to read. Later Wigner stressed modestly that he never expected Rátz to give him private lessons and was grateful for what Rátz offered him. According to Thomas Kuhn, who interviewed Wigner in 1963, the year he won the Nobel Prize in Physics, "Wigner seemed almost to have an inferiority complex toward the dead Johnny."[32] The books Rátz gave Wigner included advanced texts in calculus, analytic geometry, the theory of numbers, geometry, and even statistical mechanics (non-quantum mechanical, to be sure). Wigner kept a photograph of Rátz in his Princeton office and remembered him in his banquet speech in Stockholm following the Nobel award ceremony: "My own history begins in the high-school in Hungary where my mathematics teacher, Rátz, gave me books to read and evoked in me a sense for the beauty of his subject."[33]

László Rátz had studied in Budapest, Berlin, and Strasbourg and was not only a practicing teacher of mathematics but also took an active part in reforming and improving mathematics teaching at the secondary school level.[34] He attended international meetings and received a French award for his achievements. He published his views on teaching and collections of mathematical exercises. He was especially good in recognizing talent and cultivating it, in which he involved university instructors.

Wigner's other notable teacher in the Lutheran Gimnázium was Sándor Mikola, who taught him physics.[35] Mikola published epistemological studies of physics and he had the unique distinction for a high school teacher of having been elected to the Hungarian Academy of Sciences. He placed great emphasis on experimental demonstrations in teaching. Wigner appreciated Mikola but not with the same enthusiasm as he remembered Rátz.[36] He learned a lot of classical physics from Mikola, which was nineteenth-century physics. The teacher restricted his interest to what could be seen and observed directly. Atoms and molecules might have existed, but he did not find them relevant to physics. When Wigner gave a talk to a colloquium of his fellow students on Einstein's theory of relativity, Mikola became genuinely annoyed. He had a conversation with his pupil, the only one they had outside the class. Mikola did not like Wigner's enthusiasm for the theory of relativity and his interest in modern experiments, which were at variance with Newton's teachings. So Mikola's physics was obsolete according to Wigner's standards, but not according to the generally accepted level of high school instruction at the time. When Wigner first signed up for physics courses at the Budapest Technical University, they gave him nothing more than what he had already learned from Mikola.

It was not only Rátz who gave Johnny von Neumann private lessons; with the consent of Johnny's father he arranged instruction for the boy by a succession of university professors. The list of von Neumann's early tutors reads like a mini-Who's Who in Hungarian mathematics of the era. Some then made it to the Who's Who in American mathematics as well. All this was happening while he was carrying on with his regular high school education at the Lutheran Gimnázium. Wigner was one year von Neumann's senior, but as Thomas Kuhn noted, "it must have been a shattering experience to have grown up with von Neumann however bright one is."[37]

*　*　*

It seems fair to say that the high school experience was stimulating for all of the Martians, even if for contrasting reasons, partly because of challenging teachers and partly because of defiance against boredom. This high school experience would not fully explain their future paths, but certainly contributed to their intellectual development.

The Hungarian gimnázium education at the beginning of the twentieth century was an elitist kind of education, rather broad based in its curriculum, with a select group of students, and highly educated and cultured teachers who were members of an appreciated and respected profession. The excellence of the Budapest high schools came partly from the fact that they catered to a small portion of the population—high school education at that time was not yet for everyone. To be a high school teacher meant prestige in society and life at a comfortable level. Something else was also important at the time: it was not only in the secular high schools but also in the denominational ones that religion was not a determining factor in the school accepting a student. The Lutheran Gimnázium had Calvinist, Catholic, and Jewish students in great numbers. For the weekly periods of religious instructions, a local priest and rabbi came to instruct the boys according to their respective religions (it was an all-male school). After the communist takeover, by the 1950s, the Lutheran Gimnázium ceased to exist, only to be revived as part of the political changes four decades later. A few denominational schools remained in operation throughout, but from the 1950s they could no longer accept students outside their faith.

Background in Hungary and First Transition

In addition to family and high school, the broader background in early twentieth-century Hungary, and in particular in Budapest, played a decisive role in the formation of the Martians. It meant there were many positive and some negative aspects. On the positive side was the sizzling intellectual life, the broad interests of the people around the young Martians, and the melting pot character of the Budapest of the time, which brought together various nationalities and vastly different backgrounds. An important feature of this life was the Jewish experience that after long centuries of severe restrictions had received an outlet in the Habsburg Empire. This period lasted from the Habsburg–Hungarian Compromise in 1867 to the beginning of World War I in 1914.

In 1867, new legislation guaranteed civil and legal equality of Jews in Hungary. This not only made life more tolerable for them, but also opened up drastically different possibilities for their advancement and encouraged immigration from neighboring lands where such guarantees did not exist. There was also budding anti-Semitism, to be sure, that would grow into a formidable force after

World War I and the ensuing revolutions. The anti-Semitic outbursts during the period 1867–1914, however, did not disturb progress significantly, and would show the strength of the system in resisting it. There was the case of a young Christian peasant girl allegedly killed by the Jews as part of their religious ritual in Tiszaeszlár (a village in eastern Hungary). A trial followed, with divisive impact on Hungarian society at large. However, "Respectable opinion, including most of the aristocracy and the gentry, rejected anti-Semitism."[38] Thus Hungary fared better on this occasion than France did in the Dreyfus case.

Although Wigner lamented the absence of Jewish participants in Hungarian political life, according to Lukacs's count there were 16 Jewish members (out of 413) in the Hungarian Parliament around 1900.[39] In that period, "it seemed that the compound of the older Hungarian and the newer Jewish aspirations had fused into something inseparable and lasting."[40] This soon proved, though, to be illusory. The contrast between the stability and peace of the period before World War I and the period of revolutions and the bloody right-wing terror that followed in 1919–1920 added to the hopelessness as the young Martians pondered their futures in Hungary. This lack of opportunity for gifted Jewish youth in the Hungary of the early 1920s was a determining factor in their lives and encouraged them to leave the country. Ironically, this was a positive step for their overall future careers.

Fin de siècle Budapest was conspicuously characteristic of an era even worthy of a best-selling work of literature, *Budapest 1900*, by John Lukacs. "Foreign visitors arriving in that unknown portion of Europe, east of Vienna, were astounded to find a modern city with first-class hotels, plate-glass windows, electric tramcars, elegant men and women, the largest Parliament building in the world about to be completed."[41] This description is characteristic at more than one level. It refers to the progressive state of technology in Hungary at that time, but it also conveys the perception of ambition as well as pretension. Budapest was like a younger brother to Vienna. As it was catching up with a phase shift, technological innovations could be added to its constructions. The Elizabeth Bridge was completed in 1902 and at that time it was the largest single-span bridge on earth. It still stands today, but completely rebuilt because it was—as all the other bridges of Budapest—blown up by the retreating Germans in 1945. The city had become a world-class metropolis by around 1896, the Hungarian Millennium, and 100 years later it was still the progress of that time that made Budapest attractive—including the Castle Hill, which is now recognized by UNESCO as a World Heritage site. The first subway on the European Continent was built in Budapest, initially horse-drawn, later changed to electricity-run.

The period of peace that lasted from 1867 to 1914 witnessed a prosperity in many areas. Budapest became a banking center for the broader region. There was considerable technological innovation and a large-scale industrialization in Hungary, with Budapest leading the rest of the country. Modernization was more conspicuous in Budapest than in most other great cities in Europe because in many areas it was not just the new gradually replacing the old, but the new being created where nothing had existed. Having lacked industry in many areas before, it could start with the most modern concepts and constructions. The Ganz factory developed and built the first electric railroad engine in the world. Soon after introducing the telephone system in Budapest, the city also initiated a telephone news and entertainment service, a forerunner of radio. The period witnessed an unprecedented growth in educational and cultural opportunities, never approximated since. New buildings went up for the university, the Technical University, the Music Academy, and many other institutions. During the period 1867–1914 Budapest was the fastest-growing city among the major cities in Europe, and might have been the fastest growing in the world, save for Chicago. The fast growth included fast expanding services. Toward the end of the period there were increasing signs of the social illnesses that accompany such growth.

Budapest had close to one million inhabitants by the time World War I arrived. That meant that roughly one in every twenty people in Hungary lived in the capital city, which was considered to be a healthy proportion. In comparison, with a decreased population in what is a smaller country today, and Budapest's inflated population of close to two million, one in every five inhabitants in Hungary currently lives in Budapest. Part of the progress was the development of the school system, due to which parents expected their children to outdo them in all facets of life. In addition to the old, landed aristocrats, a new aristocracy emerged, the financial aristocrats, and there was a well-defined division of influence between them. This division was bridged on occasion by intermarriage between aristocratic sons and the daughters of rich, often Jewish, members of the financial aristocracy.[42]

By the end of the nineteenth century, the members of the once-landed gentry class of the country had lost their land and largely congregated in Budapest, gaining positions in the civil service regardless of their qualifications. They would have found it beneath their pride and dignity to deal with commerce, finance, industry, or any kind of business. There is some resemblance to the English attitude so intimately reflected in Jane Austen's novels, but this was being played out a hundred years later. The Hungarian gentry formed the so-called "Christian gentlemanly middle class," which remained characteristic through World War II. The label stressed Christian to signify the exclusion of Jews from their ranks and this echelon was a brewing place for future anti-Semitism. The sons of this class went preferentially into the army and law and seldom studied to become medical doctors and engineers. Lukacs enumerates the division between the two strata, which was the "division between the urban and the populist, between the commercial and the agrarian, between the cosmopolitan and the nationalist," that is, between the Jewish Hungarian and the non-Jewish Hungarian culture.[43] In the period of growth and prosperity, the animosities seldom came to the surface, but this would change later when things went sour.

Although a conspicuously large proportion of the financial aristocracy was Jewish, the Jewish population was much larger than this thin top layer. There was strong Jewish immigration into Hungary both from the West and from the East.

Its primary target was Budapest, but there was considerable immigration to the rest of the country as well. This is why the deportation of the country Jews, including those from Hungary's regained territories, to Auschwitz in May–June 1944 could amount to half a million people. By the outbreak of World War I, about twenty percent of the inhabitants of Budapest were Jewish. Nobody knows the proportion today, but it would not be higher than five percent, and it would be close to zero in the rest of the country.

The period 1867–1914 accorded the best chance for Jewish assimilation in Hungary. The Jews wanted to identify themselves as Hungarian and the Hungarian ruling classes welcomed them into their ranks, even if only on the surface, either by recognizing their values or for increasing the relative share of the Hungarian population in this multinational kingdom. Although the great majority of the Jewish population was not politically active, there was a vocal and visible layer of it. Especially after World War I, they were conspicuously among the former prisoners of war returning from Soviet Russia, who wanted to change the social system, taking their example from Lenin's revolution. The bourgeois democratic government of Count Mihály Károlyi, which came about at the end of the war, in October 1918, folded under the pressure of the Western Allies' demands for the dismemberment of Hungary. Under the dangers of an attack from neighboring countries, Károlyi handed over the government to the communist Béla Kun and his comrades in March 1919, and an ill-fated and ill-managed communist rule of 133 days followed. Kun was Jewish, as were the majority of his people's commissars.

By the time Admiral Horthy entered Budapest on a white horse, the relationship between Hungarians and Jews had changed drastically. The peace treaty of June 4, 1920, signed in Trianon (a palace in Versailles), dismembered historic Hungary. It gave independence to Croatia and Slovakia in the new Yugoslavia and Czechoslovakia, respectively. It also carved out large chunks of the country to add them to Romania and some territory even to Austria. There was no longer any need for assimilated Jews to enhance the Hungarian population. In Hungary proper there were hardly any sizeable minorities, whereas Hungarians were trapped by the millions in the neighboring countries.

But in the "happy peace time" of 1867–1914, the Hungarian–Jewish coexistence prospered and the Jews in Hungary spoke Hungarian and German; only a few spoke Yiddish. Conversion to Christianity helped Jewish careers, but in many professions non-conversion did not constitute a barrier. The von Neumann family had not converted at the time of their elevation to nobility. In fact, the family would not do so until after Miksa von Neumann, the father, died in 1929. By then John von Neumann no longer lived in Hungary. Even though some professions did not open up for Jews between 1867 and 1914—and this was not explicitly spelled out, either—there was a tremendous opening up in opportunities for the Jewish middle class, and even recently arrived immigrants, that was unimaginable a few decades before. The unprecedented growth of the country and enhancement of opportunities was matched by the thirst for such opportunities among the heretofore suppressed Jewish population and other minorities as well. The outcome was spectacular. Its impact was magnified in the decades to come because much of this talent would leave and find self-fulfillment abroad, initially in Germany, and ultimately in the United States. The Martians were not unique in this respect. In addition to scientists, Hungary ejected significant playwrights and composers, artists and film directors, musicians and mathematicians, economists, and many others into the international scene.

What followed World War I, the failed revolutions, and the humiliating Trianon Peace Treaty, was the White Terror and vicious anti-Semitism in the early 1920s. Miklós Horthy became the Regent of Hungary, the head of state in the absence of a king in the Kingdom of Hungary, and so remained until 1944. Legislation was introduced in 1920, known commonly as *numerus clausus*, which severely limited the number of Jewish students admitted to higher education. This law had the dubious distinction of being the first anti-Jewish legislation after World War I in Europe. The weight of this legislation might be better appreciated if we compare the estimates of the Jewish proportion of the country's population at about five percent and the Jewish proportion of the country's medical doctors and some other professionals at well over fifty percent. The law always had authority in Hungary, and there could be little doubt about the political alignment of the Hungarian judicial system. When Horthy and his troops came to power, a bloodbath followed. Many of the victims were summarily executed just because they were Jews. Eventually, some of the mass murderers were brought to trial; one of them was the infamous Mihály Francia Kiss. Predictably, he was acquitted and the presiding judge parted from him with a most friendly farewell, "God be with you, Mihály."[44] This episode could be taken as emblematic of the regime that ruled Hungary between the two world wars.

How and to what extent the Hungarian experience affected the Martians' lives is an interesting question. George Marx was especially interested in what they might have gained from their Hungarian experience for their later careers:

> Cultures met and collided in Hungary in the twentieth century and
> Hungary was one of the focal points of history. Wars started here,
> political regimes and systems of ideology changed here, especially
> around the times of the two world wars. A young person, a teenager, if
> open to the world, experienced a change in the truths of the grownups
> from year to year, and this made him willing to survive and follow the
> trends rather than seeking universal truth.[45]

Marx's next comments refer to the relatively large Jewish proportion among the outstanding Hungarian scientists:

> I prepared a graph in which I plotted the school years of these out-
> standing scientists and the peaks appear during the years of the two

world wars. My interpretation is that hard times provide a good condition for inducing creativity. However, at hard times the scale of values lost its authenticity, and one had to guess the nature of the next regime and its ideology because that gave a direction whether to choose adaptation or escape. This was so for everybody, but especially for Jews for whom the current of history was faster than for others and for whom the time scale was further compressed. It is difficult to live through drastic changes in the conditions under which we have to operate yet from it one gains valuable experience. This is the advantage of Jews in handling the rapid changes of historic eras.[46]

Von Neumann was also interested in the question of why so much talent had come from the regions on both sides of the Carpathian Mountains, whose representatives first moved to Budapest before later immigrating to America. He said that "it was a coincidence of some cultural factors . . . an external pressure on the whole society of this part of Central Europe, a feeling of extreme insecurity in the individuals, and the necessity to produce the unusual or else face extinction."[47] According to the Hungarian–Swedish tumor biologist George Klein, it was partly the Jews' high regard for learning combined with important environmental factors: "in Budapest . . . the middle-class Jews . . . got the drive and the ambition with mother's milk. You either became successful or you were going to end up in the gutter."[48]

Eugene Wigner mused toward the end of his life about the question that he had been asked repeatedly, "Why was his generation of Jewish Hungarians so brilliant?" Wigner gave credit to "the superb high schools in Budapest," and ascribed an even greater share in this to forced emigration:

> Emigration can certainly be painful, but a young man with talent finds it stimulating. Outside your own nation, you lack a ready place. You need great ingenuity and effort just to find a niche. Hard work and ingenuity become a habit. Often they are enough to earn you a place above natives of your adopted country quite as talented as you.[49]

Commenting on the success of most of the young Jewish refugees from Nazi Germany in their new countries, Walter Laqueur noted that for them it was "swimming or sinking." They "had to start from scratch, because there was no helping hand, no money, no connections, no safety net."[50]

The medical doctor turned chemist turned social scientist Michael Polanyi was probably the closest to the five Martians among the rest of the outstanding Hungarian scientists.[51] He could have been a Nobel laureate, but he was not. Two of his former pupils won the Nobel Prize, Eugene Wigner and Melvin Calvin. By the time his son John C. Polanyi won the Nobel Prize in Chemistry, Michael Polanyi was no longer alive. Polanyi had a strong political stance—he was an anti-

Marxist liberal—but he was not a participant in political or defense-related activities. His impact extended to several fields, not only within science but beyond it as well.

Early on, Michael Polanyi reflected on the fact that so much talent had left Hungary. I quote here two paragraphs from one of his writings in 1929 in which he contrasts the conditions in Germany and Hungary. First he characterizes the situation in Germany in the 1920s, and then he refers to his departure from Hungary:

> In Germany the professors grab the student's hands, if he is supposed to be gifted. They are like art collectors whose obsession is discovering talent. They educated me and gave me a position where I could address myself to my abilities. They gave me everything and demanded nothing of me. They trust that who gets to know the joy of scientific work, will never leave it as long as he lives. . . .
>
> . . . Looking back, I see the depth from which I was rescued by helping hands, the lucky one out of many. Looking back, I see other Michael Polanyis bogged half-way down and disappearing, I see them in my good friends, who stayed behind, I see them in unknown poor boys, by the dozen, like me and worthier, cast out of the university, thrown to the ground in front of the barbed wires of *numerus clausus* and other restrictions—onto a heap of invalids.[52]

To understand the puzzle of the relationship of the Martians and other Hungarian émigrés with Hungary in the twentieth century, I offer here a brief discussion. A Hungarian writer published an essay after the political changes of 1989–1990 in which he stated that the experience of 1944–1945 had made Jewish alienation irrevocable. His statement might have been a matter-of-fact reflection of the sad reality. However, his formulation called for strengthening this separation of Jews from true Hungarian life. There has been no decisive response to such calls because Hungarian society has not yet faced the realities of the history of Hungary between the two world wars and the history of the Holocaust. Lately, the apathy and silence has been giving way to a falsification of this history.

An expression of this falsification is the attempt to exonerate Horthy and his regime and to ascribe all the terrible crimes of violent anti-Semitism to the Arrow-cross movement which took over the rule of Hungary with a Nazi-type putsch on October 15, 1944. The Arrow-cross may have killed as many as a hundred thousand Jews, mainly in Budapest, during their short-lived reign of less than half a year. By then, however, Horthy's Hungary had deported half a million Hungarian Jews to Auschwitz and elsewhere, following years of anti-Jewish legislation and anti-Semitic propaganda at the highest level of the official Hungarian State. By ascribing all the bad deeds to the Arrow-cross movement, a rewriting of history is being carried out, which contributes to canning this most shameful period of Hungarian history rather than facing it.

It would be interesting to conduct a sociological study of the tremendous loyalty of the Hungarian Jews to, and their identification with, Hungary in spite of the hardships imposed on them by official Hungary.

This could also be observed in the Martians' expressions of their Hungarian patriotism, no matter what. A case in point is when Wigner downplays the beatings he suffered for his Jewishness from fellow Hungarian students. The Martian behavior toward Hungary is recognition and appreciation of the cultural heritage that they experienced, absorbed, and lived intensively. This Hungarian heritage fortunately augments the Jewish heritage and the two are irrevocably interwoven in the Martians' lives and personalities.

Theodore von Kármán

Theodore von Kármán lived a greater portion of his life in the period of the "happy peace time" of 1867–1914 than any other Martian, and he was the only Martian who completed his university education in Budapest.[53] He enrolled in the Royal Palatine Joseph Technical University of Budapest (in short, the Technical University) in 1898 and graduated in 1902.[54] The education was largely descriptive; hydraulics, electricity, steam engineering, and structures were taught without invoking nature's laws. There were happy exceptions, though, that called for independent studies. The university had famous mathematicians as teachers. Kármán enjoyed geometry best, which challenged his imagination, like the task of drawing a statue and determining the length and position of its shadow at various hours of the day. Kármán also took humanities like history and literature.

He had his first taste of research at the Technical University. His mentor was Donát Bánki, who had studied at the same university but had spent the first part of his career in industry.[55] He designed motors and improved the carburetor. His employer, the Ganz Works in Budapest, the largest company for building engines and generators in the country, produced Bánki's motors for decades. He had many patents and was the first to use water injection in internal combustion engines to protect their walls from overheating. Von Kármán noted in his autobiography that the jet engines in the Boeing 707 would later use water injection. In 1899, Bánki became professor of mechanical engineering of the Technical University, where he continued both his creative work and the filing of patents about his innovations. Some of his turbines are operational even today. There is a bust of him at the university campus and a Hungarian stamp was issued in his honor.

Bánki's approach to engineering was different from the way engineering subjects were being taught by his colleagues. He tried to find explanations for things on the basis of phenomena in nature. Von Kármán's first piece of research came from a practical problem: Why do the valves in engines sometimes oscillate and make a clattering noise? Von Kármán concentrated on this research problem, shutting out everything else, and this kind of complete dedication would become his trademark. He did experiments and found that clattering appeared when the engine shaft reached a certain number of revolutions.[56]

The young scientist's first paper appeared in 1902, for which he received an award.[57] Upon graduation and after having served a year in the artillery of the Austro-Hungarian Army, he became an assistant professor under Bánki. Assistant professors in the German-type university system, which was also the Hungarian model, were not independent researchers and teachers as they are in the American system today. Rather, they were subordinated to elder professors. As Bánki continued his involvement with the Ganz Works, Kármán joined him there for three years, until he outgrew Bánki's theoretical interest and scope of activities.

When he was only twenty-four years old, von Kármán found a problem that was his alone and that was to play an important role in his early career.[58] The problem was the buckling of columns. A column withstands a certain amount of weight, but if more is loaded onto its top the column becomes unstable, bows out, and buckles. The great Leonard Euler had been interested in this problem and had given a solution for it supposing an elastic structure for the column. Von Kármán addressed himself to a more general and thus more practical problem and succeeded in expanding Euler's solution. It is only fitting that he started his career as an independent researcher following the path of Euler, who was himself an internationalist and a scientist of broad interests. Von Kármán published his results in an obscure Hungarian engineering magazine, where it did not initiate much interest.[59] However, it sufficed to convince the elder von Kármán about his son's engineering acumen and he suggested to him that he continue his studies abroad.

At this point the younger Kármán had no desire to leave Hungary. He did not have his later disillusionment with Hungarian life. However, his father had had some. Although on the outside he was a successful member of the Establishment, he had also become a bitter man. He had had other ambitions than to be a policy maker of education. His true interest was in the philosophy of history and he felt himself bogged down by petty university politics. He did not want his son to spend his career in such an atmosphere and suggested to him strongly to seek his fortune abroad.[60]

Theodore von Kármán's first departure from Hungary in 1906 was supported by a two-year scholarship from the Hungarian Academy of Sciences. He went to Göttingen, where he knew about Professor Ludwig Prandtl, who was interested in problems similar to those that interested him. Von Kármán's education gave him a broad world view and a familiarity with what was happening in Western Europe in the fields that interested him. He called Göttingen "the prince of German universities." Germany was at the time the most attractive place not only for Hungarian scientists, but also for many young Americans, to come and perfect their education.

There was then a second and shorter period of von Kármán's life in Hungary, with a much more dramatic exit than the first.[61] His participation in World War

I will be briefly mentioned in the next chapter. When World War I was over von Kármán returned to Budapest and wanted to go back to Germany and to his science as soon as possible. However, being a reserve officer, he could not leave the country until a peace treaty was signed. In the meantime the revolutions came in 1918 and in 1919, which have already been alluded to in our narrative.

A former associate of his father involved von Kármán in the Ministry of Education of the democratic revolution in October 1918. When it changed into a communist administration in March 1919, von Kármán stayed on. He had a high position in the ministry and he considered his involvement in the national education project, regardless of the nature of the revolutions, to be an opportunity to accomplish his father's legacy. He wanted to modernize university education, to bring research onto an equal footing with teaching, and to introduce modern biology, psychoanalysis, and atomic physics into the curriculum. The old professors who were not involved in research had sabotaged previous attempts in this direction. Von Kármán worked out further reforms that were put into practice later, including one that made it possible for women to study at the Technical University. When the stillborn Hungarian "soviet" Republic collapsed, von Kármán went into hiding. His reforms were quickly annulled and the association of Hungarian engineers expelled him from its ranks because he had "served and morally supported" the Soviet Republic.[62] As he was informed that his appointment in Germany was still in effect, he left Hungary for the second time. This time he was leaving happy that he was able to go, and this time he left for good.

Not much information is available about von Kármán's activities during the revolutionary times in Hungary. Apparently, his involvement with the communist government in 1919 caused no difficulties for him in the United States. However, there were extensive investigations into his past in the early 1950s.[63] The first task for the investigators was to identify Theodore von Kármán, one of the world's leading aerodynamicists, holder of the U.S. Medal of Merit, and chairman of the Scientific Advisory Board of the Commanding General of the Air Force, having an office in the Pentagon, with a Todar (sic) Kármán, who had a conspicuous role in the communist government of Hungary in 1919. Information on him was so scant that when the investigators discovered that *Time* magazine had published a photograph of him, their copy was repeatedly referred to as a prized possession in the secret reports. They alleged that von Kármán had joined the Hungarian Communist Party in 1918 and served as deputy commissar of Cultural and Educational Affairs in charge of higher education. They further asserted that he fled Hungary after the fall of the communist government and escaped to Germany, where his party membership was transferred to the German Communist Party. They had no information about any communist affiliation by him in the United States. Von Kármán did not mention his Communist Party membership in his visa application to the United States in 1930, which may have been a cover-up, or it may have been because he might have never been a member of the Communist Party.

Theodore von Kármán was the first among the Martians to visit Hungary after World War II. An occasion arose as early as 1945, when he was attending the celebrations of the 250th anniversary of the Soviet-Russian Academy of Sciences. He decided to go to Budapest and with some adventures he did. This visit was primarily to see his brother. Soon after this, in 1947, he was approached by a professor from the Budapest Technical University with an inquiry.[64] He asked von Kármán whether he might be interested in taking over the chair of aerodynamics and fluid mechanics. The letter did not entertain any illusion that what they could offer would be on a par with von Kármán's other opportunities, but it was a gesture. The letter thanked von Kármán for some publications, which means that von Kármán was helping his Hungarian colleagues in catching up with the literature after the devastating war. Von Kármán then returned to Budapest in 1962 to receive his honorary doctorate from the Technical University. This was before any other Martian would have visited Budapest since the end of World War II. It was on this occasion that von Kármán had a memorial tombstone erected on his beloved father's grave in Budapest.[65]

Leo Szilard

Szilard was eighteen years old when he graduated from high school, as the vast majority of Hungarian students are. The Martians did not jump classes, whereas it is not a rare phenomenon in American schools even for not-so-great talents. The level of Szilard's performance can be judged by the fact that—with no preparation—he earned second place in the national competition for high school graduates in physics. This was in 1916, the first year that a physics competition was held. Only fourteen students participated, and Albert Kornfeld (later Kóródi) came third.[66] Kóródi later became the engineer who worked on the realization of some of Szilard's inventions, including the Einstein–Szilard refrigerators.

Szilard was interested in physics but determined that "there was no career in physics in Hungary."[67] A little later Wigner would come to the same conclusion. Physics was not a common profession in other countries either during the first decades of the twentieth century. The American Charles Townes, future inventor of the laser and Nobel laureate physicist, for example, did not know that physics could be a profession when he was choosing his direction of study in the 1930s.[68]

For Szilard, chemistry would have been a viable alternative, but some of his family urged him to study engineering and he succumbed; it was one of those rare occasions when he could be influenced by others. His engineering studies eventually helped him in working on the nuclear reactor and on the numerous patents he submitted over the years. Finding a use for his engineering studies was another parallel with Wigner. Szilard first went to study at the Technical University in Budapest. There, he almost perversely concluded that "the poor quality of the teaching . . . furnished stimulation to independence of thought and originality."[69] Szilard joined the university in the mechanical engineering division in the academic year 1916–1917.[70] He soon had to interrupt his studies because he was drafted into the army: World War I was going on. For such an independent person, he tolerated the military service surprisingly well. It is not known whether the temporary character of barrack life agreed with his nature, or whether this experience helped him in later life to limit his possessions so as to be ready to move at short notice.

Szilard realized the unreasonable character of the war, and he made the prescient, though seemingly bizarre prediction that it would end with the defeat of Germany and Austria–Hungary, as well as Russia.[71] The Central Powers and Russia were on opposite sides in the hostilities, yet Szilard's predictions proved correct. In 1936, John von Neumann would predict correctly about World War II that Russia was to be Germany's main enemy and that France would not amount to much in hindering Germany's advances.[72] This was at a time when many did not yet believe that war was coming soon.

After World War I, Szilard continued his studies, but they did not satisfy him and he participated in Budapest's intellectual life with zest. He was attracted to socialist ideas but not to the Communist Party because even then he disliked Soviet Russia. His independence found its expression in his and his brother Bela's forming their own Hungarian Association of Socialist Students. Its sole purpose was the distribution of their pamphlet about how to cure Hungary's problems.[73]

He did not view the communist takeover in 1919 with sympathy and anticipated its defeat, along with increased anti-Semitism. On both counts he proved to be right. He decided to move to Germany and continue his studies at the Technical University of Berlin. Before that, he took the practical step of converting and became a Calvinist. Conversion was widespread in Hungary after the revolutions that followed World War I. It was a matter of convenience for protection against the rising anti-Semitic repression. This was the second wave of conversion. The first was around the turn of the century when it was more for facilitating assimilation. Yet another wave would come in the 1930s—however hopeless those conversions were to prove—as the country was rapidly moving with ever expanding anti-Jewish legislation towards the Holocaust.

A less traumatic experience in Budapest in September 1919 sufficed to move the Szilard brothers in the right direction. When Leo and Bela wanted to enter the Technical University, they were stopped and kicked down the stairs of the university by nationalist students. Although the Szilards protested, the papers about their conversion did not make any difference to those students. This was the end of Szilard's connections with this school.[74] As Szilard was leaving Hungary on a Danube steamer at Christmas time in December 1919, an old visiting Hungarian émigré told him, "As long as you live you'll remember this as the happiest day of your life!"[75]

Eugene P. Wigner

Wigner told his father that he would like to become a physicist. To his father's question about how many jobs for physicists existed in Hungary, he exaggerated and said four. The jobs for physicists would be university professorships, and there were two such in Budapest and one in Szeged at the time. Wigner's father then asked him whether he could hope to get one of those scarce jobs. Although there is no precise record of what the young Wigner answered, he could not have realistically hoped to do so. He accepted his father's suggestion to study chemical engineering, with an eye on a future managerial job at the Mauthner leather factory. He started attending the Budapest Technical University, where he spent one year. He found his physics course merely repeating what he had learned from Mikola in the Lutheran Gimnázium. Then, again on his father's advice, he moved to Berlin.

Eventually, though, conditions in Hungary consolidated and there was about a decade of more relaxed political atmosphere between the mid-1920s and mid-1930s. By then, Wigner and many other Hungarian youths were studying or working in Western Europe. At this time, an ambitious minister of education, Kuno Klebelsberg, recognized the value of the talent that would be lost to Hungary if it was left abroad forever. He made attempts to bring back scientists and a prominent gain from his policies was Albert Szent-Györgyi's return to the University of Szeged. Szent-Györgyi would then become the only Hungarian scientist to go to Stockholm to pick up his Nobel Prize while working in Hungary. None of the Martians returned, though, and there is no record of any attempts to attract them back.

In fact in 1929, years after Wigner's departure from Hungary, there was a vacancy for a physics professor's job at Szeged University. The former occupant of the chair, Rudolf Ortvay, had moved to the University of Budapest and he recommended inviting three prominent Hungarian scientists, among them Eugene Wigner and John von Neumann, to apply for the job. The third was Cornelius Lanczos, who had moved from Hungary to Germany in 1921. He was not considered to be a viable possibility because he had been Einstein's assistant for a while and he could not be expected to be interested in moving to Szeged.[76] Ortvay enumerates the scientific achievements of his nominees and stresses that all three of them are internationally recognized scientists. However, the faculty members of Szeged University showed no interest in offering the job to Wigner (or to von Neumann).[77] On his part, Wigner did not think that he would have a real chance of getting the job. He also recognized that Szeged was rather isolated from the scientific world and lacked a "scientific atmosphere." He was apprehensive of going to a place where his future colleagues would not want him and where he and the conditions of his work would be at the mercy of ministerial bureaucracy.

John von Neumann

Von Neumann graduated from the Lutheran high school in 1921 and won the national Eötvös competition in the same year. Kármán and Szilard had won or taken second place in previous competitions, and Teller would win a later one. Von Neumann's father consulted the elder von Kármán about his son's further education. Pure sciences did not seem practical, and it was decided that von Neumann should study chemical engineering in Berlin. After four semesters he transferred to Zurich to the Federal Institute of Technology (ETH), where he graduated after six semesters. At the same time, he signed up for his mathematical studies at Budapest University and completed them in 1925, having attended the university only infrequently. It caused him no difficulty to carry out studies in two different subjects at two different universities at the same time.

Von Neumann was no ordinary student and published independent studies in mathematics during his university years. These helped him write his dissertation for a university doctorate in 1926, a mere eight months after his final university examinations. His dissertation was on the topic of the axiomatic development of general set theory.[78] His main subject was mathematics and the two secondary subjects were experimental physics and chemistry. In all three he received the highest qualification, summa cum laude.[79]

The von Neumann family took it for granted that John would continue his studies abroad. For the next degree, the habilitation, he went to the division of mathematics at the Faculty of Philosophy of the Friedrich Wilhelm University of Berlin (today, Humboldt University). Habilitation is a higher doctorate in the German system, certifying one's ability to teach at a university, and it implies an accumulation of independent research findings and publications. In order to become a professor, habilitation was (and is, and also in Hungary) a necessary condition.

Looking ahead, apart from the vacancy of a physics chair in 1929 in Szeged, mentioned above, there was only one more vacancy, seven years later, for which von Neumann might have been considered. It was again in Szeged, but he was not a candidate and had he become, he wrote to his physicist friend Rudolf Ortvay, he would have not considered it as a viable possibility.[80]

By the mid-1930s, all the Martians had settled in America.

Ortvay kept his eye on the international developments. He realized the value of physicists and mathematicians like Wigner and von Neumann, and the loss that Hungarian science suffered by their absence. In 1938, Ortvay informed von Neumann that he had tried to see whether von Neumann's nomination for membership in the Hungarian Academy of Sciences might be successful, if attempted.[81] It seemed unrealistic, though, and Ortvay and others did not go ahead with it. By then von Neumann had been elected to the National Academy of Sciences of the U.S.A.[82] He was the first among the five Martians to have been accorded this honor. The election of the rest followed: von Kármán in 1938, Wigner in 1945,

Teller in 1948, and Szilard in 1961. Half a century after von Neumann's election to the U.S. Academy of Sciences, the surviving Martians, Wigner and Teller, were elected as honorary members of the Hungarian Academy of Sciences, in 1988 and 1990, respectively.

Edward Teller

Teller did not enjoy high school, which he completed in 1926. Some of his few positive experiences came from tutoring others. He determined that the best of all professions was being a professor, a view that was partly formed by an experience he had when he was ten years old.[83] His father took him to Leopold Klug, a retired professor of projective geometry in Budapest. It was a highly specialized subject, yet Professor Klug was the only grownup Teller ever met in his childhood who obviously enjoyed what he was doing. However, aiming at a professor's career was not a practical goal for Teller in the Hungary of the 1920s, and in his *Memoirs* he refers to this repeatedly. As a teenager, he had known that Budapest could not be a place for his career and for his future life. Over the years, "anti-Semitism had, if anything, grown worse."[84] His father and his especially revered grandfather urged him to continue his studies abroad, preferably in Germany, which was then living in a golden age of physics—although his father and grandfather could not have been aware of it.

Teller had received the greatest pleasure in his high school years from meeting "three young men from the Jewish community in Budapest," Eugene Wigner, Johnny von Neumann, and Leo Szilard.[85] They were his seniors by five to ten years and all were doing physics in Germany. Teller met with them during summer vacations and they represented role models for him. Teller had doubts in himself, which were alleviated at least partially when he won the national physics competition alone and shared the first prize with three others in mathematics.

Because of his mother's worries, it was decided that Teller should start his studies in Budapest at the Technical University and, when he reached eighteen years of age, continue his studies in Germany. The question of what to study had been decided before. Teller would have opted for mathematics, but it was as impractical at the time as physics. So Teller settled for chemistry—a convenient compromise for him as it had been for others.

Teller last saw his closest friends in Budapest on a visit in 1936. By the time he returned more than half a century later, as if to underscore the judgment of Teller's father that "Hungary has no place for you,"[86] he found that none of them were alive. Most had perished in Nazi concentration camps.

CHAPTER TWO

Turning Points in Germany

It is a joyful thing to know that you are truly a physicist. What
else besides love can compare with it?

Eugene P. Wigner

The Martians arrived in Germany to seek university education and higher scientific degrees and eventually employment that corresponded to their aspirations. They found much more: top science, about which they had not dreamed in Hungary. They soon recognized their potentials and became participants in this top science among the world's players. This was a turning point in their lives. Their contributions were appreciated, and they became respected members of their professional communities. The more they found their homes in Germany, the more traumatic it was when they realized that it was all built on quicksand, and that they had to embark yet again to find a new home and build up new careers.

Theodore von Kármán

Von Kármán found scholarly elegance and culture when he first came to Göttingen in October 1906, which "was pleasing to my Hungarian soul."[1] But the place could be cold and depressing. There was social segregation between professors and students, which he compared to the relationship between officers and enlisted men in the military. In addition, there was discrimination against Jews and Catholics: they could not join the student dueling societies. It was not the drinking and singing that von Kármán missed, and he might have not even noticed this discrimination had he not come from the Hungary of the "happy peace time."

The professor who attracted him to Göttingen in the first place, Ludwig Prandtl, had enormous authority in his field. He was alternately referred to as "the father of fluid mechanics" and "the father of aerodynamics." Prandtl's most important discovery was the boundary layer in flow. His discoveries greatly contributed to the progress of manned flight. He was also interested in the theory of structures, and that was initially von Kármán's interest, too. Von Kármán was Prandtl's doctoral student, but he was more independent than most. Although Prandtl let him choose from among fifteen topics, von Kármán told him that he had already set his eye on a problem of his own, the theory of nonelastic buckling. Prandtl informed von Kármán that someone else had already worked on the problem, although without fully solving it. At first von Kármán was dismayed, but he soon realized that "Exaggerated concern about what others are doing can be foolish. It can paralyze effort, and stifle a good idea. One can find that in the history of science almost every problem has been worked on by somebody else. This should not discourage anyone from pursuing his own path."[2] This attitude showed both self-confidence and a broad view on his part.

At the beginning Prandtl disappointed von Kármán because the famous professor did not care for practical problems at that time. Modern industrialists, such as the managers of the Krupp Concern, soon realized von Kármán's value and provided support for his projects. They built equipment for his experiments, and he started investigating the properties of various materials. Prandtl soon warmed to his new pupil's approach, who even at this young age wanted to penetrate beyond superficial observations of phenomena and base his designs on scientific principles. He completed his thesis work within two years, his Hungarian stipend lasting just long enough for the project.

After completing his doctoral work von Kármán went to Paris. He attended lectures at the famous Sorbonne, where Marie Curie was among his lecturers. In Paris, as everywhere, he had Hungarian connections, and this would be characteristic of the other Martians as well. He met Margit Vészi, a reporter for a Budapest paper who had just divorced the famous Hungarian–American playwright Ferenc Molnar.[3] This meeting brought von Kármán an experience that influenced him for the rest of his life. Persuaded by Vészi, he witnessed a historic event in a suburb of Paris: the first two-kilometer (1.3 mile) airplane flight in Europe.[4] The flight made a big impression, not only on him but on the French, too. The Americans and the Germans were more advanced in flying than the French at that time. Von Kármán remembered this when observing the American reaction to Soviet advances in space travel after Gagarin's historic flight in 1961.[5]

Although von Kármán was considering going back to Hungary after obtaining his doctorate, he received an attractive offer to work for the Zeppelin project that made him stay in Germany.[6] In his work, he used the wind tunnel built at the suggestion of Prandtl to test the airship model. This experimentation had an enormous impact on his future activities.

Göttingen University hired him. He received permission to teach, but aside from that he was working for his higher doctorate (habilitation). For this he made an excursion into geology. He performed experiments to find out why the sheets of rocks in the depth of the earth did not buckle under the enormous pressures created during the cooling of the earth's crust millions of years before. He reasoned that the sheets of rock would buckle if they were free to move; however, these sheets were contained in areas surrounded by walls. Under these circumstances the sheets became plastic rather than buckling. This study was related to his earlier interests in the strength of materials. He designed an experiment which proved his theory correct.

His work was greatly assisted by the research seminars in Göttingen, which he called "the transmission belt of the newest scientific ideas."[7] Even today, the research seminars are the single most important ingredient in the life of a research university. They introduce the beginning researchers to new ideas, broaden their horizons beyond the research group they are working in, and make it possible to meet scientists from other schools, including international scholars. It is the seminars where researchers observe how questions are formulated, how scientific debates are initiated and conducted, and how to defend their views—how to interpret experimental results and how and when to quit and realize and admit error. At the research seminars, scientists can measure their knowledge and understanding and have their performance tested in the least painful way. In the research seminar, scientists can start by asking innocent questions and request clarifications and gradually gather the courage to contradict even their elders and enter debates. There is no better way to gain an understanding of research life than at the seminars of a good school.

Many young people attended the research seminars in Göttingen, where they met Felix Klein, David Hilbert, Hermann Minkowski, Hendrik A. Lorentz, and even the greatest of all, Albert Einstein, when he came from Berlin. These seminars helped von Kármán to be widely informed about the latest developments in fields ranging from atomic theory to the study of the motion of sand in the desert. He ascribed his broad interests in science, rather than becoming narrowly focused in specialized problems, to these seminars. Two giants overshadowed the rest in Göttingen: Klein and Hilbert. Von Kármán met Hilbert through a Hungarian friend, the mathematician Alfred Haar. Von Kármán and Hilbert became close friends in spite of their twenty-year difference in age. Hilbert taught von Kármán that "The descriptive or qualitative way of viewing Nature, . . . could be replaced, or at least strengthened, by a quantitative method." This convinced von Kármán that Nature was inherently mathematical. This conviction remained with him for the rest of his life and "led me throughout my life to search for mathematical solutions in areas where practical men saw only insurmountable chaos." Most engineers, though, did not care about the scientific basis of their constructions. A mathematician put it bluntly, "Kármán, of all the applied idiots I think you are the only one with the possibility of being educated."[8] Aviation was increasingly becoming von Kármán's favorite field, and in this area scientific knowledge and technological applications progressed in parallel.

Von Kármán was a scientist of broad vision, not only interested in new developments but also in earlier achievements.[9] An example is the Englishman Frederick W. Lanchester, who discovered the connection between the circulatory motion of the air and lift. He submitted a paper in 1897 in which he outlined the theory of lift, years before everybody else. He recognized the importance of aeronautical research for modern warfare, a field in which von Kármán extended Lanchester's ideas when he worked for NATO in the early 1950s.

By 1904–1905, the elements of lift were well understood. The next phenomenon to be understood was drag, the air resistance which opposes motion. The description of air friction appeared too complicated to allow it to be applied to the design of an airplane wing. Prandtl came up with a great idea about the tip vortices that led to the design of wing configurations which would minimize the loss of energy. Von Kármán was curious and he eventually became deeply involved in studying vortices. The result was his best known scientific paper, about the drag that occurs when the air stream fails to stick to the shape of the body and breaks off behind it into a wake. This phenomenon, which became known as the Kármán Vortex Street, consists of a series of vortices. The drag can be calculated, and with this information engineers can minimize its impact by creating the most appropriate form: streamlining. It also explained some previously puzzling phenomena, such as the so-called singing propeller of submarines. Another, later application was in providing the explanation for the collapse of the Tacoma Narrows Bridge in 1940 (see below).

"This theory whose name I am honored to bear," von Kármán used to say, because he considered the discovery to be more important than the discoverer. When about twenty years later a French scientist, Henri Bénard, claimed priority for the discovery of the vortex streets, von Kármán did not protest. Rather, with characteristic humor he suggested that the term "Kármán Vortex Street" be used in London and "Boulevard d'Henri Bénard" in Paris.[10] He stressed that he did not discover vortices—they had been around for ages. Von Kármán went on to become the foremost figure in a broad field, aerodynamics and the science of flight, and eventually he would be called "the father of modern aerodynamics." His principal strength was "the understanding of the mathematics of aerodynamics."[11]

His scientific interests spread even more broadly as a consequence of the seminars in Göttingen. He also benefited from his interaction with Max Born, who was to become one of the founders of quantum mechanics, and who would receive a belated Nobel Prize in Physics in 1954 for his fundamental research in quantum mechanics.[12] But this was now 1911, just as atomic theory was coming to the forefront in physics. This was in spite of the predictions towards the end of the nineteenth century that there was very little left for physicists to discover.

Max Born came from Breslau (then Germany, now Wrocław in Poland) and obtained his doctorate in Göttingen in 1907. He and von Kármán were also Privatdozents at the same time. Together they worked out an important problem, namely, the specific heats of solids, related to the atomic vibrations in the crystal lattice.[13] Originally Einstein had described the atomic vibrations in crystals; there were, however, small discrepancies between theory and experiment. Von Kármán and Born tried to eliminate these discrepancies by taking account of the whole spectrum of lattice vibrations. Today it is school material, but in 1911 the crystal lattice was not yet an experimentally established fact (it came, though, soon enough, in 1912). Von Kármán and Born relied on group-theoretical considerations (of which Wigner would become a great master a decade and a half later). Peter Debye anticipated von Kármán and Born's results by a few weeks using a simpler approach, which did not make use of the concept of lattice. For a long time Debye's theory was more popular, but von Kármán and Born's more detailed work proved to be of longer-lasting value.[14]

The von Kármán–Born cooperation came out of a casual interaction and shared interest without any formal ties. They were introduced to each other by Alfred Haar. For Born, Haar and von Kármán became "great friends of mine. Both were Hungarian Jews and mathematicians."[15] Born mentions other important names, too, who also had the position of Privatdozent in Göttingen, and says that he owes them a great deal, but that he owes even more to Theodore von Kármán.[16] For a while, Born and von Kármán lived in the same house and had daily discussions of physical problems.

Both Haar and von Kármán greatly influenced Born's scientific development, Haar by his love of the beauty of mathematical construction and his rigor and von Kármán by being an applied mathematician. Born noted that von Kármán was not very interested "in things which had no practical application in natural science or technology." Born could observe at close hand how von Kármán was working on his theory of vortices in a liquid flowing around a cylindrical object. He wrote admiringly about the beauty of von Kármán's theory and especially about the practical demonstration of its validity by convincing photographs. Von Kármán dispersed a powder on the surface of water, which made the formation of the vortices visible. Born learned the essentials of mathematical physics from von Kármán: "to regard the problem in its right perspective, to estimate . . . the order of magnitude of the result expected before going into detailed calculations, to use approximations adapted to the accuracy needed, . . . and to be constantly aware of all the facts."[17]

Originally though, von Kármán's approach of looking for approximations appeared to Born as carelessness. Von Kármán was used to dealing with enormously complex systems where approximations were the order of the day, whereas the physicists dealing with the most fundamental principles of the structure of matter tried to be as rigorous as possible. This difference in scientific culture was the reason why Born sensed a basic contrast in the way they handled information. About their actual cooperation, Born noted, "I enjoyed very much working with you, and as a physicist I profited by following your way of solving theoretical problems. But fortunately for me I did not adopt your carelessness in handling data."[18] Von Kármán was obviously bothered by Born's remark and years later found some consolation in spotting some errors in their joint paper in the mathematical descriptions for which Born was responsible. The Born–von Kármán interaction demonstrated von Kármán's prowess in attacking problems quite outside his field.

A further episode in which von Kármán was involved concerned the discovery of the Bohr atom.[19] It was yet another area that laid outside his immediate expertise. He met Niels Bohr in 1912, when Bohr was already working on a new theory of the atom. According to the then-existing theory by Ernest Rutherford, an atom is made up of electrons, which orbit around the nucleus on fixed trajectories. When the atom is given energy, the electrons move faster and give off light. However, if the atom loses energy by radiating light, the electrons should orbit around the nucleus more slowly, and eventually they should plunge into the nucleus. But no changes in the atomic structure consistent with such a scenario were ever observed. Bohr came up with the solution in 1913: when the electrons give off light, they jump from one orbit to another of lower energy. Conversely, when the atom absorbs energy, the electron would jump back to an orbit of higher energy. The new model was consistent with observations.

Von Kármán had also come up with the idea of the energy levels of electron orbits, but not with the idea of the electron emitting radiation when it jumps from an orbit of higher energy to another of lower energy. He found such a scenario too radical, and from the episode he concluded that "in science you must be a radical in order to find a new truth."[20] Of course, there should be a balance between being cautious and bold in pursuing scientific discoveries. The atomic model referred to a branch of science that was not von Kármán's immediate field of expertise, and it is to his credit that he kept up with recent developments in physics.

After four years (1909–1912) as Privatdozent, von Kármán's opportunities for academic advancement in Germany seemed to be in doubt. His mother urged him to return to Hungary because "the austere Prussians would never learn to appreciate the impassioned Hungarians."[21] It was, however, more than that. Years later, Max Born confessed to von Kármán in a letter that when the possibility of von Kármán's professorship in Göttingen came up, nobody—including Born— was willing to take up the issue. Born writes "I had to decide if I wanted to carry the fight for you against the enemies of Israel."[22]

His father, however, urged him to stay in Göttingen and keep waiting for a professorship. Von Kármán became somewhat restless and in 1912 he applied for a professorship in Selmeczbánya, Hungary (now Banská Štiavnica in Slovakia), about 100 kilometers north of Budapest. The position was the chair of applied mechanics at a mining academy. He won the position and took up residence in Selmeczbánya in the fall of 1912. Alas, the school was outside the mainstream and the place was a backwater, which would be a dead end for von Kármán as a scientist. He soon returned to Göttingen. The interlude proved to be beneficial, though, because it brought his frustration with his position into the open and helped him win a professorship in Germany: the chair of aeronautics at the Technical University in Aachen in northwestern Germany, right on the Belgian and Dutch borders. He arrived in Aachen in February 1913 and stayed there for the next 16 years, with some interruptions for World War I and the ensuing revolutions in Hungary.

Aviation was a subject of secondary importance in Aachen at the time of his arrival, but he was set to change that. As a faculty member, it was now up to him to make Aachen into a top institution. Fortunately, there were some foundations to build on. Hugo Junkers had been a professor in Aachen until he had given it up to devote himself completely to his research. He later became one of Germany's biggest airplane manufacturers and one of von Kármán's important clients. From the start, Junkers involved von Kármán in designing his airplanes, and the one they designed in 1914–1915 was in use as late as 1955. Von Kármán provided the mathematical foundations for Junker's designs and they became the standard for military and commercial transport in Germany until the jet era. This was not the only connection von Kármán had with the German Air Force. Some of the pilots asked him to teach them the theory of flight in exchange for them teaching him to fly. Hermann Göring, later to be Nazi air marshal, might have been among them, but von Kármán subsequently learned, much to his relief, that Göring served in another squadron.

World War I brought science and war close for von Kármán. First he had to report back in Budapest and was engaged in preparations for the artillery defense of a (highly unlikely) Russian attack on the city. Eventually his expertise in aviation was discovered and he was transferred to Vienna, where the Ministry of War set up a department of aviation for the Austro-Hungarian Army. He joined the Austro-Hungarian *Luftarsenal* in 1915, which became the start of his life-long association with military aviation. He liked to compare himself to Archimedes, who held off the Romans for three years with his engines, to Leonardo da Vinci, who invented many weapons of war, and to Tartaglia, the Renaissance scientist who first applied mathematics to the science of artillery. A major project was to find out how to equip the planes with a machine gun that would fire through a revolving propeller. At one time, the aerial machine gun was a "more frightening weapon developed by the Germans in the First World War than poison gas."[23]

Von Kármán contributed to the success of the aerial machine gun against the Allies and wrote with obvious pride about it. From this work he became friends with Anthony Fokker, known popularly as the Flying Dutchman. The fighting plane emerged, and the approach of the military to aviation changed overnight. When it became obvious that Germany was losing the war and a siege of Berlin was in sight, von Kármán was ordered to Berlin to help with its defense, which was using helicopters to provide supplies for the city. It proved hopeless and he returned to Budapest, where a democratic revolution greeted him upon his arrival in October 1918. His adventures in revolutionary Hungary were mentioned in the preceding chapter.

Von Kármán arrived in Germany from Hungary for the second time in 1919, after five years of absence and thirteen years after his first entrance. There were differences between the two arrivals. This time, it was not Imperial Germany but a country ravaged by a devastating lost war. And it is also important to consider whence he arrived. When he left Hungary in 1906, it was a flourishing country. Now, in 1919, it had lost a war, had gone through two failed revolutions, and was being raped by an extreme-right power infested with ruthless and state-sponsored anti-Semitism. Germany, on the other hand, was embarking on the uncertain yet hopeful democracy of the Weimar Republic. Von Kármán jumped into fervent work in rebuilding the school in Aachen that had offered him a respectable position before, and which was now relying upon him to help it become strong and important again.[24]

Von Kármán's zest in rebuilding his institute was infectious, and not only the German students but even the Belgian occupiers gave him a helping hand. The Belgians warned him, though, about the prohibitions of the Versailles Treaty concerning motor-flying in Germany. The same treaty also forbade the design and construction of aircraft, but "the German students could not be held down for long by treaties."[25] They formed the Aachen Association for Aeronautical Sciences,[26] a small but enthusiastic group that included many ex–war-pilots. Von Kármán knew that it was more than sport, yet he assisted them, first in building a glider. Looking back, he wrote "I had no way of knowing, of course, that I was inadvertently helping to lay the base for what was to become an important part of the German aerial machine in World War II."[27]

The gliders became an essential ingredient of military aeronautics, and of all people von Kármán should have known this. The students and those who helped them knew that what they were doing was illegal, and they worked in secret. Beside the later military significance of these activities, there was something else: "It was the symbol of independence, a reminder that even though Germany was beaten in war, the nation could still excel in something." When the glider had to be transported (von Kármán proudly described it), their operations were truly clandestine, cheating the Allies. Von Kármán and Prandtl held joint seminars about the gliders in Aachen. One of the attendees was W. Messerschmitt, then a student and part-time draftsman and later one of the most famous designers of German military aircraft in World War II. Anthony Fokker also participated. "Throughout the 1920s, the glider craze swept Germany and spread the fame of Aachen," von Kármán noted.[28]

Von Kármán was not very apologetic about helping German gliding to flourish; on the contrary, when he writes about the Nazis utilizing gliders, he accuses the Allies of having been short-sighted when they banned motor-flying in Germany after World War I. His reasoning is that the ban stimulated the development of German aviation. The German Ministry of Transportation[29] established a branch of aviation in the charge of Adolf Bäumker, a professional Army officer although it was a civilian branch. The question was how to channel money from this Ministry to scientific research in Aachen. The Allies were very sensitive to possible violations of the Treaty of Versailles. To overcome the obstacles, Prandtl, Bäumker, and von Kármán set up an advisory board of renowned scientists to screen the projects and summarize their purpose for the Allies. What was this if not a smokescreen to camouflage the military significance of their work? In this light, it is puzzling that he asserts, "If there was secret German rearmament in the early 1920s I had no direct evidence of it."[30]

Von Kármán helped Germany alleviate the damages caused by the war in more than one way. One of the negative consequences of the war was Germany's isolation on the international scientific scene. In 1922, he organized the first international conference in mechanics in Innsbruck, Austria. The meeting was a great success; it broke the ice after World War I and brought together winners and vanquished. The series of conferences that followed became an established institution.

Von Kármán's success and authority in his field could not have been characterized better than by his engagement in a friendly though fierce competition with his old teacher Prandtl.[31] Incidentally, Prandtl was only six years older than his former pupil. At stake was solving the problem of turbulence. They wanted to understand—and accordingly describe in simple mathematical terms—the laws governing turbulence. It was an unfolding scientific drama. Prandtl was a gentlemanly competitor, who shared with von Kármán his lieutenant, Frank Wattendorf, and even his unpublished data. Von Kármán and Wattendorf reduced the data in a number of ways and plotted them on graph paper, looking for a straight line that would be the clue to the mathematical evidence for a law. At one point they had run out of the variations on how to reduce the data, and von Kármán suggested a different approach: they should vary the paper on which they were plotting the data. It was just another experiment to direct them to simplified relationships among the variables. Using graph paper with a logarithmic scale showed a relationship which seemed manageable and provided a formula consistent with von Kármán's original basic concept of turbulence.

There is an anecdote about Niels Bohr having a conversation with a colleague at a streetcar stop in Copenhagen: the conductor would not signal departure until Bohr had concluded the conversation. The story illustrated Bohr's enormous authority in his native land. Von Kármán had a similar story. In this case, he and Wattendorf had worked together in von Kármán's home until late in the evening, but Wattendorf did not want to miss the last tram home, so they walked together to the tram stop to use some extra minutes for their discussion. They were still not ready when they reached the tram stop, and though the tram had to leave they kept on talking. The conductor warned them that the tram should start, while the scientists kept pleading with him for another moment and for another moment, and the tram kept waiting for Herr Professor Dr. von Kármán to finish his conversation. This was an unambiguous sign of his authority, and there is no doubt that he enjoyed it enormously. Incidentally, von Kármán and Wattendorf completed their solution overnight. Von Kármán was soon ready to deliver a decisive blow in his competition with Prandtl, who admitted defeat by saying that von Kármán had once again exercised "his well-known talent for skimming the cream off the milk."[32] We will see similar comments about von Neumann by his colleagues that were not always complimentary.

In 1921, von Kármán's mother and his sister Josephine, nicknamed Pipő, joined him in Aachen. However, they set up their household across the border, in Holland. The ladies did not care for Germany, yet Pipő was later characterized ridiculously as pro-Nazi in one of the FBI files. It was on the Aachen background that von Kármán started his interactions with American science, which would eventually lead to his departure for the United States. This was not only due to the very tempting offers but also to the clouds of Nazism gathering over Germany. Nonetheless, Germany retained a soft spot in von Kármán's heart and some mistook these sentiments for pro-Nazi manifestations. In 1941–1942, J. Edgar Hoover, the director of the FBI, personally issued directives to investigate von Kármán in connection with his visa application. He was not only considered to be a Nazi sympathizer but also a potential spy. At the same time, other reports asserted to his being anti-Nazi, a reliable citizen of the United States, and "one of the top-ranking men in the field of aeronautical science." The FBI investigation seems to have started from scratch; for example in one of the early reports he was "*alleged to be a Hungarian Jew*" (italics added).[33]

After World War II, von Kármán again helped in reorganizing German science. And when he led an American task force to Germany, his former colleagues opened up to him more than they might have to a stranger. From the mid-1950s, von Kármán was showered with German decorations.[34] In his old age, he would spend more and more time in Europe, including Aachen, where he died of a heart attack in 1963.

Leo Szilard

Szilard arrived in Berlin early in January 1920 and became a student of the Technical University, called *Technische Hochschule Berlin*. His favorite subject was physics, but practical considerations made him go for engineering. However, he soon became dissatisfied with the technical subjects and wandered around not only in his own university but also in the science university.[35] There he found what he subconsciously might have been looking for: the physics colloquia at the university. From his very first encounter, he religiously attended them. Joining the physics colloquia at the University of Berlin was a turning point in Szilard's life.

In the early 1920s, Berlin was the capital of modern physics. At the university were people such as Max Planck, Max von Laue, Walther Nernst, Fritz Haber, Gustav Hertz, and James Franck. Einstein was based at the Prussian Academy of Science and at the Kaiser Wilhelm Institute in Berlin-Dahlem, not the university, but he was a regular visitor to the colloquia. These scientists were already great authorities in their fields. They were, or would soon become, Nobel laureates, and there were other bright people around them, including future Nobel laureates Wolfgang Pauli and Werner Heisenberg (the latter when he was in town). Joining this circle of people transformed Szilard's life. Suddenly he was catapulted onto a scene of frontier science in the field that he coveted most. Everything else, including the Technical University, dwarfed in comparison.

These colloquia were not seminars where the participants would make presentations of their own work; rather, they were more like the American journal clubs where people reported on recent publications from the literature. Those who attended these colloquia knew what was going on in physics in those days. Von Laue was the organizer and he was always looking for volunteers to review current papers for the next colloquium. For graduate students, it was the thing to do. There was a considerable degree of democracy present, brought about by the extraordinary concentration of talent, even genius, at these gatherings. For the young participants it was also wonderful to see that every now and then even the great men could make silly mistakes.[36] Once, the famous Erwin Schrödinger suddenly stood up in the middle of a discussion on the spectra of triatomic molecules and suggested that the calculations could be simplified under the assumption that the three atoms are in the same plane. There was a stunned silence, followed by an outburst of laughter (three atoms cannot but be in the same plane).

The atmosphere at the Berlin colloquia was unique at the time. Two generations later, a future Nobel laureate, Sidney Altman, experienced a similar atmosphere at the Laboratory of Molecular Biology in Cambridge, England, when he was there as a postdoctoral fellow in 1969–1971.[37] There, it was not at the colloquia but at the daily tea in the laboratory canteen where the discussions allowed even beginners to participate with the gods of molecular biology. The notion of comparing a Berlin colloquium in the 1920s with a Cambridge gathering in 1970 shows how forward-pointing those physics seminars were, where Szilard suddenly found himself. He did not even have his doctorate, yet it was possible for him to communicate with the gods of physics.

Ordinary mortals might have been intimidated, but not Szilard. He told the great Planck, "I only want to know the facts of physics. I will make up the theories myself."[38] This was in November 1920, that is, the year he had arrived in Berlin. And consider who Planck was at that time: the revered great physicist and highly positioned administrator of German science; a Nobel laureate. He was the pioneer who had introduced the quantum into the science of the twentieth century, thereby making one of the most important and most original contributions to physics.

Szilard took a large number of courses during his first semester at the University of Berlin, October 1920 to March 1921, as if making up for lost time. He was still only twenty-two years old. In addition to the various subjects in physics, he continued taking philosophy and ethics courses. The physics colloquia and seminars remained the focus of his activities and life. The atmosphere on those afternoons was very special, with those gods chiding each other and discussing the frontiers of their science. Szilard was fast developing his future famous "impertinence." He asked Einstein to give a course on statistical mechanics and Einstein did. It was not Einstein's favorite field, but he accepted the challenge and taught the course in the winter of 1921–1922. In addition to Szilard, Wigner and von Neumann signed up for it, and Szilard invited a few other very bright students, Dennis Gabor among them. Szilard developed a close relationship with Einstein. He talked with him, made suggestions, walked him home, and often visited him at home.

According to Wigner, the seminars on statistical mechanics made Szilard feel inadequate in higher mathematics.[39] In this case, Wigner thought, Szilard underestimated himself. Szilard did not take up Wigner's suggestion to work jointly on some problems connected with quantum mechanics. It was perhaps that Szilard did not want to settle on specific problems, especially not on problems that he did not initiate and in which he might not be the prime mover.

The Berlin colloquia had a well-defined protocol: the front row, with Planck, von Laue, Einstein, the middle rows, and the back rows, which seated the students like Szilard, Wigner, von Neumann, Dennis Gabor, and others. But Szilard gradually moved from the back row toward the front and talked with those in the front row after the colloquia were over. Not everybody took advantage of this opportunity, but no one took greater advantage of it than Szilard. The Berlin physics colloquia were a decisive point, not only in Szilard's career but also in those of Wigner and von Neumann, just as for Teller the sojourn with Werner Heisenberg and his group in Leipzig was a decisive moment. It might be put this way: in order to become a Martian, one needed to have experienced a turning point in Germany to be among the great pioneers of physics (or to be with Prandtl of aerodynamics, in von Kármán's case). However, this was only necessary, not sufficient. Eventually, they all became deeply involved in the defense of the Free World.

Others had very different careers. A case in point was Dennis Gabor, also from Budapest and from Jewish background, who would stay on in Britain after having been forced out of Germany. Even in Britain, he could have become part of defense efforts, but did not. Rudolf Peierls, a German–Jewish physicist, stayed in Britain, too, and he did play a role in defense.[40] He eventually had to move to the United States with other members of the British contingency to participate in the

Manhattan Project. Another example is George von Hevesy, who also had to leave Hungary after the extreme-right takeover in 1919; he moved to Germany, where his career peaked similarly to von Kármán's. He had also been abroad for periods prior to World War I. He was older than the younger Martians, but younger than von Kármán. He received his Nobel Prize in 1944 (for 1943) for his work using isotopes as tracers in the study of chemical processes. So his field was related to nuclear science, yet he did not participate in defense-related work. When von Hevesy had to move out of Germany, or at least when he felt he did—nobody in his Freiburg environment knew about his Jewish roots—he went to Denmark. When the Nazi danger was engulfing Denmark, he moved to Sweden. Otto Robert Frisch was also a refugee in Denmark from Germany, and he moved to Britain where he became engaged in the atomic project along with Peierls.[41] Von Hevesy did not consider such an option.

What about the important German physicists who became refugees from Germany and moved to the United States? What was the difference between them and the Martians? The Martians had already experienced one forced departure when they had moved from Hungary to Germany; they were better prepared to be alert and feel responsibility for affairs beyond their narrow surroundings; they were less occupied with reestablishing their lives in their new country because they had done so before. Also, von Kármán, Wigner, and von Neumann arrived in the United States before the bulk of the refugees. Teller came later, after having spent some time in England, but he was also invited in order to take up a job (thanks to George Gamow) rather than having to hunt for one. Szilard was seldom invited or appointed to jobs, but he was not eager to settle in an ordinary appointment in the first place. This is now running ahead in our narrative, but it is important to see the significance of the German experience for the Martians in perspective.

In Berlin, Szilard was experiencing "the most creative period in my life, where there was a sustained production of ideas."[42] He was now writing his doctoral dissertation, officially under von Laue, but on a topic of his own choice, with Einstein's encouragement. Von Laue had suggested a project, but Szilard could not make headway with it and remained unconvinced that it had a solution. His dissertation was related to the Second Law of Thermodynamics.[43] He recognized an application of this law that was broader than what had been thought possible before. What he developed formed in his head during his long walks, seemingly without any effort. Before submitting the work to von Laue, he showed it to Einstein, who first listened to Szilard in disbelief but then grasped the ideas within minutes.

Armed with Einstein's approval, Szilard handed his paper to von Laue, who accepted it overnight as Szilard's doctoral work.[44] Within about half a year Szilard had prepared another paper about the operations of the so-called "Maxwell's Demon, who guesses right and then does something, thereby violating the Second Law of Thermodynamics."[45] It was about how more ordered structures could arise in a closed system without being in violation of the Second Law, which would prescribe simultaneous energy decrease and entropy increase. The solution included information transfer, although the term itself was not mentioned, as it was not yet in usage as a mathematical concept.[46] In the early 1950s, John von Neumann referred to Szilard's work in his research on automata. This research had military significance, including the determination of the reliability of missiles. Von Neumann suggested that error estimation be treated by thermodynamic methods, just as Szilard treated information.[47] Szilard's second paper served as the dissertation for his habilitation, and in the 1950s and 1960s it came to be regarded as the earliest known paper in the field of information theory. As one of Szilard's friends noted, "Thinking generates entropy."[48] Information theory was also a link with John von Neumann; this was yet another example of the professional and personal affinities that existed between the Martians.

In any case, within two years of beginning his studies in Berlin as an undergraduate, Szilard had a doctoral dissertation. These distinctions were not as clear-cut in the Berlin of the 1920s as they are, for example, in a modern American school. It was not unusual for a student to attend lectures for years at the university, and at the end write a thesis and get a doctorate. Szilard's studies and dissertation procedures took place at the Faculty of Philosophy of the University of Berlin; they were in the specialization of physics, to be sure, yet the specializations were not as distinct then as they are today. In addition to noted physicists, there were noted chemists in Szilard's Habilitation Committee, including two recent Nobel laureates, Fritz Haber and Walther Nernst.[49]

Szilard did everything fast, and Einstein's and von Laue's openness helped him move ahead. The fact that he wrote a brief but revolutionary paper to serve as a dissertation was not so extraordinary. In 1948, C. N. Yang provided a proof to an unproven statement by Edward Teller and Emil Konopinski about the relationship between the angular momentum changes and the angular distribution of the products in a nuclear reaction.[50] Yang, who had arrived in the United States from China just two years before, walked into Teller's office at the University of Chicago one day in 1948 and showed the proof. Teller suggested that he write it up for a PhD dissertation, which Yang did. He brought it back to Teller. It amounted to three pages. Teller felt a little uneasy and subsequently made two suggestions to expand the work, which finally grew to eleven pages. At that point Teller was satisfied; Yang became a PhD and went on to a brilliant career in physics, including a Nobel Prize within a decade.

Szilard did not follow up the two papers related to his dissertations; he was too restless for that. He often did not write up his findings for publication, and the two papers had served practical purposes, gaining him his degrees. Rather than pushing for papers, he preferred taking out patents from time to time. This was characteristic not only of his German period but of his entire life. When he attended James D. Watson's first announcement of the double helix structure of DNA, to his Cold Spring Harbor audience in 1953, Szilard's response to the talk was not an academic one. He asked Watson, "Can you patent it?"[51] Szilard's patenting habits could be a little annoying to colleagues because they sensed material motives behind his actions.

In 1928 Szilard formulated his ideas about a linear accelerator, before Rolf Wideroe, and in 1929 about the cyclotron, before E. O. Lawrence. Szilard was a bona fide inventor during his German period.[52] Of course, there were also material motives in his patenting because he would have liked to receive income from his patents, but it was more than that. Once he had submitted a patent, he could leave the topic behind. Also, he assigned his most important patent, on the nuclear chain reaction, to the British Admiralty, with little hope of income. Further, Szilard freely and liberally gave away his ideas, and many benefited from them. Moreover, even when he was involved in a work manually (a rare occasion), he might decline to participate in publication. In 1938, Szilard was collaborating with physicist Sidney Barnes at the University of Rochester. When their work was completed, Szilard told Barnes to publish the paper under his name alone because he was "not interested in credit, just in getting things done."[53]

In Berlin, Szilard was developing many of the trademarks that would characterize him throughout his life. He was bursting with activity. He took it upon himself to ensure that the students and visiting scholars met all the people they needed to meet at the university. His informal relations with Planck, Einstein, and others demonstrated that he could play this role that fit his personality and interests.[54]

Lanouette quotes Szilard's brother, Bela Silard, saying that "Leo would pick up people, suck them dry of ideas, and like an empty orange peel, toss them aside."[55] Here, there is another similarity with von Neumann, who was known to run away with peoples' ideas, and people resented this because he did not let them work them out at their own pace. However, science is not necessarily done in a most considerate way. Szilard was known to be very generous with dispensing ideas, but when he, like an inquisitor, interrogated people about their research, it was inevitable that he brought ideas from one person to another, which might also elicit resentment. In any case, Bela's above description is rather negative. Nonetheless, if a researcher felt a little uneasy when either von Neumann or Szilard appeared in his vicinity and started asking him about his work, his nervousness was understandable.

Without the Berlin colloquia Szilard and Wigner might have just become competent professionals. Their attending these colloquia and attending the Einstein course that Szilard initiated strengthened their friendship. Von Neumann was the third member of this inner circle within the Martians. There was much that brought them close together, although not too close. They had a common background of well-to-do middle-class Jewish families that converted; Szilard became a Calvinist, Wigner a Lutheran, and von Neumann, after his father's death, a Catholic. They shared not only their pasts and roots but also their present worries; the news from Hungary; the growing anti-Semitism. They became friends, as only people who understand each other's half-words can, but still they kept some distance between them, as rational people whose measure of everything in life was reasonableness.

There were other people around, but less intimately connected with them, like Szilard's brother, Bela Silard, like Dennis Gabor, and like Michael Polanyi. Polanyi was a little older, but only seven years older than Szilard, whereas Szilard was five years older than von Neumann. Teller, in turn, was ten years younger than Szilard yet they forged a lasting friendship. The Martians had other friends, but none ever shared the closeness that they had between themselves. Polanyi might not have been as close to the Martians as he became, because he had acted as thesis advisor to Wigner, but Szilard befriended Polanyi and eventually so did Wigner. Szilard also made friends with Herman F. Mark.[56] In the 1920s, Mark was a research director in one of the chemistry institutes of the Kaiser Wilhelm Society in Berlin-Dahlem. If Szilard was not intimidated by Planck and Einstein, of course, he did not feel any restraint when discussing scientific projects with Mark and Polanyi. These researchers were at the time investigating the structure of fibers using X-ray diffraction. Szilard told them that they should rather use their experiments for probing into the nature of X-rays. His authoritative approach in the research institutes of the Kaiser Wilhelm Society earned him the nickname of *Generaldirektor*.

Szilard and the other Martians came across several important physicists while in Germany who would eventually end up in the United States. Szilard's record is especially impressive in meeting influential people, including non-scientists. I single out Arthur Koestler, the journalist and writer, from among them; his novel *Darkness at Noon* would influence Edward Teller in developing his anti-communism.[57] Szilard also knew Lev Landau, the Soviet physicist, Erwin Schrödinger, with whom he jointly taught courses, and the Indian scientist Satyendranath N. Bose, with whom he discussed relativity and quantum mechanics. Szilard taught a course with Lise Meitner at the Kaiser Wilhelm Institute in Berlin-Dahlem, which was part of the research institutes of the Kaiser Wilhelm Society (today it is the Max Planck Society and its institutes).

When von Neumann gave a seminar in quantum mechanics, which was an extension of the physics colloquium in Berlin, Szilard and Schrödinger attended along with the students, and they developed a lively exchange. The three would also teach one or other course together, and they would pair off, in a variety of ways, teaching more courses. Szilard always participated in the discussions in the colloquia and seminars. Schrödinger characterized his participation as "to whom one always listens with great interest, for what he had to say was always of profound and original kind. He very often points to an important point or to a view of the subject matter that would not occur to anybody else."[58] Also as an extension of the physics colloquia, Einstein held gatherings in his home; Polanyi and Mark often went and Szilard appeared every time.

Einstein had a special place among Szilard's friends.[59] Although he could be rude to others he revered Einstein, even though he could be impolite with him as well. Einstein must have enjoyed Szilard's wit, with which he made connections between seemingly disparate events, and he tolerated well his friend's occasional irreverence. Who else could have turned to Einstein and told him during a colloquium, "But, Herr Professor, what you have now said is just nonsense."[60] By then, Szilard had eased himself into the front row during these colloquia.[61] The interactions between Szilard and Einstein had very practical aspects as well; they jointly devised and patented refrigerators without moving parts, and a Hungarian engineer, Albert Kóródi, directed the constructions of their joint inventions.[62] These were not found suitable for manufacturing and marketing, but the principles were later utilized in the nuclear reactor called the breeder. They filed German patents jointly for their electromagnetic pump and related parts.[63] The two shared other interests as well, including cosmology and religion. They agreed in that "As long as you pray to God and ask him for something, you are not a religious man."[64] They wanted to understand Nature and how it was created; they wanted to know God's thoughts when he created it. Once they knew these thoughts, it would be their task to figure out the rest. Szilard and Einstein shared an interest in and admiration for Spinoza, the seventeenth-century Dutch philosopher. This is how Einstein characterized Szilard: He "is a genuinely intelligent man, not generally inclined to fall for illusions. Perhaps, like many such people, he tends to overestimate the role of rational thought in human life."[65]

Szilard asked Einstein on more than one occasion to write letters of recommendation on his behalf to help him secure his American visas. Einstein's letters always worked. However, he never asked Einstein to help him get a job. It was perhaps that Szilard did not want to test Einstein's friendship in such a manner. It may also be that it was out of reverence toward Einstein, because Szilard was never really sure whether he wanted a particular job or not. He might not have wanted to "waste" Einstein's assistance in something that he thought was of ambiguous value in the first place. However, Michael Polanyi did ask for Einstein's recommendation for Szilard's appointment to the Institute for Advanced Study, which was then, in 1932, being formed in Princeton. However, Einstein did not recommend Szilard for such an appointment, which would have been in mathematical physics. He thought that technical sciences and experimental physics would be more suitable for Szilard.[66] Perhaps Einstein understood Szilard better than most of his other friends and perhaps Szilard sensed this.

Lanouette called Szilard an "intellectual vagabond."[67] He lived with two suitcases, always ready to go, and had no family or other obligations. He moved around a great deal, not only in Berlin, but also frequently traveled to various other cities. His brother, Bela, helped him with the ordinary chores of life. Szilard had small, temporary appointments, which were nevertheless prestigious, like being consultant to Herman Mark's laboratory or von Laue's assistant, or giving courses at the

University of Berlin. Publications which contained important ideas trickled out haphazardly from some of these engagements. Thus, for example, Mark considered Szilard to be a founder of non-equilibrium thermodynamics. At one point, Szilard suggested to Dennis Gabor that he build a microscope with electrons because Gabor was studying the electron beam, following the first electron scattering experiments on solids in 1927. Gabor thought that it was too early, but soon an electron microscope was built, alas, not by Gabor. In 1931, Szilard filed a patent application for a simple variation on the electron microscope. In the same year, Ernst Ruska operated the first electron microscope, for which more than half a century later he received the Nobel Prize.[68] Szilard, on his part, considered his contribution closed with the patent application; he did not follow it through, as he did not follow through many of his other ideas. Gabor immortalized his own name by inventing holography, for which he received the Nobel Prize in Physics in 1971.[69]

It cannot be said that Szilard was taken by surprise when the Weimar Republic collapsed. He predicted its fall as early as the mid-1920s. Many others made similar predictions, but not many did it so early. According to Szilard, the Weimar constitution yielded "entropy of governance."[70] He was shocked when in 1929 the president of the German Reichsbank declared that Germany could not pay reparations prescribed by the peace treaties after World War I unless she got back her former colonies. Szilard found it ominous that Germany's leading banker thought that he could get away with such an effrontery, which he did. Szilard's reaction was to transfer all his savings from Germany to foreign banks.[71] Szilard was increasing his political awareness and activities with the increasing Nazi dangers in Germany. He was pushing for an organization called the Bund (not to be mistaken for the German Bund); it had two important features, both pioneering. One was that it included boys and girls without sex discrimination. The other was that it was international, in contrast with the increasing nationalism around him. Szilard's attempts to organize the Bund were a forerunner of his later attempts to organize the intellectual elite for national and international leadership. Szilard was ready for war or any other change. In 1930, he became Privatdozent and received German citizenship. However, he recognized the instability of the political situation in Germany and started thinking about moving to the United States.

Eugene P. Wigner

Similarly to Szilard, for Wigner the move from the Budapest Technical University to Berlin set him on a course that would see him leave Europe, help fight World War II, and work for a government (the American government, that is). Wigner could not have imagined such a career when in 1921 he left Hungary for Germany.[72] At first, he merely experienced Berlin as a haven for studying. Although Wigner's father planned a job for his son at the Mauthner tannery in Budapest, Wigner envisioned a career as a professor of physics in Germany or Hungary.

He diligently studied chemistry and consciously performed all the laboratory exercises in order to be admitted to the examinations. At one point he remarked that in his time inorganic chemistry was more concerned with materials and properties than with electrons orbiting the nucleus.[73] This indicates that Wigner must have learned a good deal of real chemistry, which he later utilized in his work on reactors. He took special instruction that would help him work in the tannery.[74] He was a reliable student but not especially remarkable. He felt fascination only for physics and this is why he started attending the physics colloquia at the University of Berlin.

At the beginning he hardly understood a word; he knew that his role was a silent one; he was there to listen rather than to speak. Eventually he also volunteered to report on papers. It gave him a great feeling when he saw that not even the greatest physicists could solve all the problems alone, that even his contribution was needed and appreciated. It gave him the feeling that Albert Einstein personally needed him. This was encouraging. Otherwise, Einstein and the other greats did not provide any direct encouragement for the young people. They behaved with them as if they were their equals, and this in itself was an indirect expression of appreciation. One of the lessons Wigner learned from these colloquia was about the importance of theoretical physics; he instinctively preferred theory over experiment. He found it conspicuous that nothing besides pure physics was ever discussed at the colloquia—no politics or world affairs.[75] The colloquia were followed by a visit to a coffee house where they continued their discussions of physics.

Going to the physics colloquia and taking up additional subjects were taxing Wigner's time, but he did even more. From his third year, he arranged to work for eighteen hours weekly at the same Kaiser Wilhelm Institute that was mentioned above in connection with Szilard. It was in a suburb, Berlin-Dahlem, which Wigner compared, looking back, to the Institute for Advanced Study in Princeton. First he did his diploma work (Master's thesis) at this institute and later his doctoral dissertation. For his diploma thesis he chose crystallography and worked under the supervision of Herman Mark on the structure of a sulfur crystal modification, the rhombic sulfur.

Herman Mark has already been mentioned as one of Szilard's contacts in Berlin.[76] He was an Austrian, Jewish on his Hungarian father's side, whose family converted to Lutheranism. Mark grew up in Vienna, and after leaving Berlin moved to work in industry in Ludwigshafen. He returned to Vienna in 1932 because I. G. Farbenindustrie let him go due to the anticipated Nazi threats. He had to leave Vienna when Austria became part of Germany with the *Anschluss* (annexation) in 1938. At that point, he went to the United States, where he had a distinguished career at Brooklyn Polytec. He initiated a new technique of molecular structure determination, but he was best known for his polymer chemistry.[77] Mark did not become as close to Wigner as his mentor for his doctoral dissertation, Michael Polanyi, was to become.[78] Wigner ranked Polanyi immediately after his parents and László Rátz in considering his great influence on his life. It is curious that Wigner meticulously recorded the Jewish roots of Mark and Polanyi in his *Recollections*. He took remarkable notice of this aspect of people's backgrounds, in spite of his repeated assertion that he paid scant attention to this question.

Polanyi encouraged Wigner in his research: "he was truly an artist of praise."[79] Wigner needed this praise, whose absence he sadly noted when referring to the physical colloquia at Berlin University. This is noteworthy, because if even an intellect as great as Wigner's felt need for such praise, how much more may ordinary mortals need it? Polanyi, however, was unusual in any case because he fraternized with his student. Wigner noted that Mark, although he was younger than Polanyi, kept a distance and failed to show the enthusiasm with their work that Polanyi showed. In Wigner's City Hall Speech in Stockholm in 1963, he paid tribute to Polanyi, and singled out the inspiration he received from his mentor. Polanyi taught him that "science begins when a body of phenomena is available which shows some coherence and regularities, that science consists in assimilating these regularities and in creating concepts which permit expressing regularities in a natural way."[80]

Wigner lived his own inner life in the Berlin of the 1920s, and much of what was going on around him did not meet his notice. He met only with physics students and physics professors, and with some people of other fields, such as chemistry. One of the few things he noticed was inflation. In 1922 there were 4500 marks to the dollar, and a year later it was 4 trillion marks to the dollar. This he could not help but notice, but he did not observe what he, looking back, described as "deep trouble in the social and political currents of Germany." Wigner was not, by any stretch of the imagination, a radical from the point of view of society. However, he did consider himself a radical in regard to physics and how he embraced quantum mechanics, which radically transformed this traditional field. The kind of comparison Wigner used to characterize the changes that physics was undergoing in the 1920s is telling. Traditional physics was so obsolete for him that it invoked the image of man hunting wild beasts for his dinner.[81] He was happy to register, though, that things were moving very fast in physics.

Max Planck pioneered quantum theory around 1900, when it was truly revolutionary, but by 1925 it was in trouble because it could not explain the behavior of electrons and nuclei within the atoms and molecules. Wigner noted, "A new kind of mathematical physics was needed." Nonetheless, even for Wigner, "the discovery of quantum mechanics was a nearly total surprise." Wigner was not one of its discoverers, although two of the principal characters were just as young as he was. One of them was Werner Heisenberg, and when Wigner read his article about the radical new idea of his uncertainty principle, he felt the need to share the news with someone. He called Leo Szilard and told him, "The problem is solved."[82] It was not the only time Wigner needed to confide in someone, and on such occasions he would call Szilard or von Neumann. The other young man was the British Paul Dirac. He had the distinction that he wrote his papers in English rather than in German, which was the language of physics in the 1920s, and people were suspicious of them because of both the science and the language. The third, and somewhat older, principal contributor was Erwin Schrödinger, who became especially famous for his ingenious equation.

The new physics was of probabilistic nature and that was rather alien to the great Albert Einstein, who pointedly declared that "*He* does not play dice," meaning God. Einstein did not like dice throwing and he said, "The Lord God is subtle, but malicious he is not."[83] But the creation of quantum mechanics brought great relief to Wigner and many others because they had not been sure whether humanity would be able to grasp quantum theory, and quantum mechanics gave them hope that it would.[84]

Wigner met Einstein through Szilard, and they developed a friendship. Einstein invited Wigner to his home, and they talked not only about statistical mechanics, which was the subject of Einstein's seminar course, but also other areas of physics, and about social and political problems. Even in his lectures, Einstein would sometimes turn philosophical. Wigner remembered him musing about time being infinite, compared with which our finite lifespan was negligibly short. "The probability that I am alive today is zero," Einstein said, but then added that "In spite of this, I am now alive." From this, Einstein concluded that "after the fact, one should not ask for probabilities."[85] Wigner benefited from Szilard's friendship in Berlin in other ways as well. After one discussion, for example, Szilard told Wigner to have his remarks printed and Wigner appreciated Szilard's encouragement.

After taking his chemical engineering degree at the Technical University of Berlin, Wigner returned to Budapest and started working at the tannery in 1925.[86] He was a conscientious worker, learning everything he could at the tannery and visited other tanneries to learn more about the processes he was using. Even decades later he proudly displayed his knowledge of the chemistry of various processes in leather treatment: some leather is prepared for the bottom of the shoe, some for the upper part of the shoe, and some other leather is prepared for travel bags.[87] Yet in Budapest, in 1925, he missed physics, and to ease the pain he subscribed to a German physics journal, *Zeitschrift für Physik*. It was a godsend when, in 1926, he received an invitation to return to Berlin to work with a crystallographer named Karl Weissenberg at the Kaiser Wilhelm Institute.[88] The invitation was the work of Michael Polanyi, who knew that his friend and former pupil belonged to science.[89]

Weissenberg's interest was in crystal structures, and he suggested that Wigner read up on group theory, which is the mathematical means to handle symmetries. This proved decisive for Wigner's further development. Weissenberg prodded Wigner to find more elegant solutions to the problems he was trying to solve. Wigner was making good progress and the discussions with Weissenberg encouraged him to go deeper and deeper into the applications of group theory. When he felt he had bumped into some unsolvable problems, he asked von Neumann for help. Their interests fortunately augmented each other.[90]

The application of group theory to quantum mechanics became Wigner's specialty. Quantum mechanics had been created without him; now group theory gave him a chance for originality.[91] This is why it is even more curious that he did not give more credit to Weissenberg when he enumerated those to whom he owed his development. He attributed his success to hard work, willpower, and patience rather than to being gifted. He said it was nothing brilliant, just good instinct and good luck. It may well be that growing up in the shadow of von Neumann from his high school days made him under-appreciate himself. It did not help, either, that several of his great contemporaries did not much value group theory: Wolfgang Pauli called it "die Gruppenpest" in German, which is something like "that pesty group business."[92]

Again, von Neumann came to Wigner's help, saying that "In five years, every student will learn group theory as a matter of course."[93] Thus von Neumann helped Wigner not only with his difficulties in mathematics but also in a human sense. In the late 1920s, there was no good textbook on modern group theory. Hermann Weyl had written one, but Wigner did not find it clear enough. Weyl was fifteen years Wigner's senior, almost a member of the previous generation. At this point, Szilard encouraged Wigner to write a book about group theory. Szilard believed that, by writing a new text, Wigner would establish his priority claim on the subject. Finally, Wigner devoted two years to writing *Group Theory and Its Application to the Quantum Mechanics of Atomic Spectra*, which came out in 1931 in German.[94]

Wigner went farther in his symmetry studies than just showing the utility of this concept in quantum mechanics. He had the notion that the laws of nature had symmetries. He, in his modest and polite way, did not disagree when some of his peers and some of his seniors declared it to be foolish to devote so much attention to his symmetry studies. He "did not mind playing the fool" because he got a lot of pleasure out of these studies. Concerning physical symmetry he said, "My favorite physical theorems might lack the full beauty of a great poem or the wit of a first-rate joke, but they had a special tricky charm." Wigner did not mind that, to some, his projects appeared to be trivial. With no modesty this time, he stated that: "eventually this work had quite fundamental applications. It spread the basic truth that laws of nature have simple invariance properties. It even influenced the basic design of nuclear reactors."[95]

More than half a century later, Steven Weinberg, a much respected Nobel laureate physicist—and not a friend of Wigner as far as their politics were concerned —stressed the pioneering character of Wigner's contribution. According to Weinberg, "Wigner realized, earlier than most physicists, the importance of thinking about symmetries as objects of interest in themselves."[96] In the 1930s, physicists talked about symmetries in the context of specific theories of nuclear force. "Wigner was able," Weinberg continues, "to transcend that and he discussed

symmetry in a way, which didn't rely on any particular theory of nuclear force."
Gerard 't Hooft, another Nobel laureate physicist, traced back to Wigner the
notion that symmetry can break in many different ways and that "Both symmetry and symmetry breaking are examples of patterns that we see in Nature."[97]

In April 1995, the American Physical Society held a memorial symposium for
Eugene P. Wigner in Washington, DC. He was called "a towering figure of modern
physics," and David J. Gross (Nobel Prize 2004) summarized his legacy in the applications of symmetry in physics.[98] He drew a simple diagram that expressed the
essence of the relationship among the symmetry principles, laws of nature, and
physical phenomena. This was eloquently described in Wigner's Nobel lecture: the
symmetry principles are independent of specific dynamics and they "provide a structure and coherence to the laws of nature just as the laws of nature provide a structure and coherence to a set of events," the physical phenomena.[99] In this, Wigner
worked out fundamental relationships of profound importance.

Symmetry principles → Laws of nature → Physical phenomena

Even in his Nobel lecture Wigner showed modesty when he formulated the principal task of physics. He stressed the limitations in the ambitions of physics and
physicists:

> [P]hysics does not endeavor to explain nature. In fact, the great success
> of physics is due to a restriction of its objectives: it only endeavors to
> explain the regularities in the behavior of objects. This renunciation of
> the broader aim, and the specification of the domain for which an
> explanation can be sought, now appears to us an obvious necessity. In
> fact, the specification of the explainable may have been the greatest
> discovery of physics so far. . . .
>   The regularities in the phenomena which physical science endeavors
> to uncover are called the laws of nature. The name is actually very
> appropriate. Just as legal laws regulate actions and behavior under
> certain conditions but do not try to regulate all actions and behavior,
> the laws of physics also determine the behavior of its object of interest
> only under certain well-defined conditions but leave much freedom
> otherwise.[100]

Wigner's work on symmetry, and in particular the applications of the symmetry
concept in nuclear physics, earned him his Nobel Prize, but much later, in 1963.
However, his views did not change over the intervening decades and continued
to be his leitmotif.[101] The immediate personal consequence for Wigner was in
convincing him that he had to be a physicist. He sounded like a romantic poet
when he declared: "It is a joyful thing to know that you are truly a physicist. What
else besides love can compare with it?"[102]

Wigner had a series of jobs in Germany. After having spent his time in Göttingen, formally as David Hilbert's assistant, he returned to Berlin and the Technical University in 1928. By now he was a Privatdozent working with Richard Becker, one of the more senior regulars at the physics colloquia. Wigner taught quantum mechanics and was not a good lecturer. Later, when he experienced difficulties in teaching at Princeton it was not only his English that hindered his communicating physics effectively in the classroom. Weinberg took his course and noted that "He was not a very good teacher because he was obsessively worried that there might be someone in the class who didn't understand him." This made his lectures exceedingly slow, yet, Weinberg added, "he was still very profound."[103] Wigner also felt that most physicists did not know quantum mechanics as well as they knew classical physics; the new physics was not "at their fingertips."[104] He not only complained about this, but also tried to find a remedy, and, teaming up with von Neumann, they co-authored a series of papers. They wanted to put quantum mechanics at the physicists' fingertips, although the papers were rather technical.[105]

In October 1930, years before Hitler's accession to power, there was a dramatic opening in Wigner's life.[106] He received a very attractive offer from Princeton University for a visiting position at a fabulous salary seven times higher than what he was being paid in Berlin. He thought that Princeton wanted him because the United States needed to improve its standing in physics. He suspected even more that Princeton had asked him because it wanted to make its invitation to von Neumann—the man Princeton wanted in the first place—more attractive. This is characteristic of Wigner's modesty, but there might have been some truth in it, too. Initially von Neumann and Wigner were invited to Princeton for one term, and, before it was over the university offered to extend their visiting appointment, on a half-time basis, for the next five years. This seemed to be an ideal solution, to benefit from both worlds, the United States and Europe, and they accepted the offer. The Princeton appointment helped Wigner to get a teaching job for the other half of his time at the Technical University in Berlin.

In spite of Wigner's international engagement and outlook, Hitler's accession to power found him unprepared because he had not previously paid any attention to politics. When Hitler told the German people that they were better than the others, his political rivals did not dispute it because, as Wigner noted, "in national politics the truth is often less popular than a clever lie."[107] Not only Wigner, but also most Germans, were unconcerned with Hitler, and Wigner thought that people were hungry both for power and for having someone to hate and that the new Führer and his vicious anti-Semitism satisfied both. Wigner did not foresee the Nazi danger, and the fact that he had established himself in Princeton by the time he had to leave Germany was not due to foresight; it was only due to the early invitation from Princeton University. However, when after the war people demonstrated shock and disbelief about the Nazi crimes, Wigner was not shocked and did not find it difficult to believe what he learned. He

Eugene P. Wigner
(drawing by István
Orosz).

maintained that Hitler had already revealed himself in the early 1930s to anyone who cared to see his and his regime's true face. The gas chambers and Auschwitz were only the technical means of carrying out what he had been preaching all the time. Thus Wigner was defiant against Hitler and against those who supported him and who were blinded by him.

John von Neumann

Szilard, Wigner, and von Neumann were a subgroup within the Martians, tied by the closeness of their ages and the many similarities in their backgrounds. They overlapped in Berlin and often saw each other at the physics colloquia and other seminars. However, for von Neumann, Berlin was only one of two bases during this period; the other was Zurich. The von Neumanns charted John's education with great care. Although mathematics was his favorite, it was decided that he should study chemical engineering as well. So in this case the more practical chemical engineering was not a substitute for something less practical; rather, it was an addition.

Von Neumann was a student in Berlin and in Zurich, and at times he had to study hard, especially for entrance examinations at the ETH. Lest we underestimate his smooth sailing through these examinations, let us remember that more than two decades before, in 1895, Albert Einstein failed them. Tough requirements, however, did not set von Neumann behind in his other engagements; he progressed in each of them as if the other had not existed. As early as 1922, he already had a draft of what would become his doctoral dissertation on the axiomatization of set theory, having only completed his high school studies at the normal age of eighteen in Budapest in 1921. So he had his work for his doctorate mostly done before he sat for the entrance examination for the ETH in 1923.

Von Neumann simultaneously received his diploma in chemical engineering and his doctorate in mathematics in 1926. When the draft of his dissertation was sent to a professor in Marburg, who was also one of the editors of a mathematical journal, he recognized in the young von Neumann the lion from its claw, "*ex ungue leonem*," using the expression once used about Isaac Newton. Von Neumann came across great men of science both in Berlin and in Zurich. Although he was studying chemical engineering in Zurich, he had interactions with one of the shapers of mathematics of the first half of the twentieth century, Hermann Weyl, who would later be his fellow professor in Princeton. Weyl quickly recognized the prowess of the young student and on occasion asked him to substitute for him as lecturer during Weyl's travels.[108]

Von Neumann did not limit his presence to these two hubs of modern science. He also frequented Göttingen, especially for visiting David Hilbert, who appreciated von Neumann's advances in the areas of mathematics where Hilbert had been a recognized leader. Von Neumann joined Hilbert in his attempts to demonstrate that the entire body of mathematics was consistent and free of contradiction. Von Neumann developed in the 1920s the basic mathematical tools that would serve him in attacking the most diverse physical problems. He did not merely employ his techniques to satisfy the physicists' needs. Rather, he immersed himself into their world in the process. This approach became his trademark later, during his involvement in the physics of weaponry. He also developed a way of presenting his findings that was esthetically pleasing and attractive. He was an artist of presentation and he was truly successful.[109]

Others may have resented his success and were jealous. In addition, von Neumann's ability for quick problem-solving manifested itself early on. He became known not so much for raising problems as for solving them, and this did not always endear him to his peers. Conversely, when he had original ideas—and he had many of those, too—he did not always work them out to the fullest. Others eventually had to work through these problems in detail, but then they had to refer back to von Neumann's pioneering contributions—if they were well informed and versed in the literature. Macrae characterized him as "flashing like a meteor," for his original contributions. Others were less kind, accusing him of "skimming off the cream."[110] We have already seen such a characterization for von Kármán. At the same time, von Neumann developed into a rather charming personality, which softened the hard feelings against him. Also, he did not mind when others extended his ideas and were appreciated for it, even though they were sometimes not even aware of his prior contributions to the topics.

There seems to be less information about von Neumann's life during the 1920s than about the other Martians, except that his scientific production was extraordinary. He went to Göttingen after he had completed his formal education, and soon found a task to solve. Although Heisenberg had invented quantum mechanics in 1925, others criticized it, notably Schrödinger, and von Neumann found an elegant way to describe the new science in the language of mathematics that the others accepted.[111] It was especially appreciated by mathematicians.[112] He seemed to be settling down in Germany; he was appointed Privatdozent at the University of Berlin in 1927 and Privatdozent at the University of Hamburg in 1929, with better prospects for a full professorship. By the end of 1927, he had published twelve major papers in mathematics. Then, in 1928 and 1929, he added ten papers each year to his production. His papers were often physics-related, so he became well known both among mathematicians and physicists. His papers included some on spectroscopy, co-authored with Wigner. Their close interactions invited the comparison that "Although Johnny instantly leapt an average of five blocks ahead of most people who brought suggestions to him, he could leap only about one block ahead of Wigner."[113]

There was no doubt that Johann von Neumann had found his home in his second adopted country and would be happy to chart his career and life there. However, this notion was rapidly losing its base in the uncertainty of the political atmosphere in the whole of Europe, and in particular in Germany. Across the Atlantic Ocean, in the meantime, von Neumann was not only noticed for his outstanding abilities and achievements, but was also recognized as a possible factor in the modernization of American mathematics. This was bound to happen if America wanted to play the role that was destined for it in world science. It was this double development that would soon bring von Neumann from Europe to Princeton.

Edward Teller

As soon as Teller turned eighteen, he embarked on a trip to Germany, leaving behind his family, his sweetheart (his future wife), and his three best friends. In 1926, he went initially to Karlsruhe, where he studied chemistry, and there he first came across modern science: Herman Mark gave a guest lecture on quantum mechanics. By then, Mark had left Berlin and joined I.G. Farbenindustrie, which was not far from Karlsruhe. Teller also became acquainted with P. P. Ewald, whose doctoral work in theoretical physics in Munich in 1912 served as the impetus for Max Laue (as he was then) to initiate X-ray crystallography. Ewald might have shared the 1914 Nobel Prize in Physics, which was, however, given to Max von Laue alone. Ewald would eventually move to the United States and his daughter Rose would become Hans Bethe's wife. The Tellers and the Bethes would become close friends, only to later experience a rift, following which Bethe would become Teller's bitter critic. Teller's engagement with chemistry in Karlsruhe lasted two years and created a good foundation for his future successes in physical chemistry and chemical physics.

In 1928, he went to Munich and enrolled in physics under the legendary physics professor Arnold Sommerfeld. However, Teller did not like Sommerfeld, whom he characterized as "very correct, very systematic, and very competent." One of Teller's fellow students was a future Nobel laureate, physicist John H. Van Vleck.[114] Upon his joining the group, Van Vleck went through a series of greetings when he saw Sommerfeld, from "Guten Morgen, Herr Sommerfeld" to, finally, "Guten Morgen, Herr Geheimrat." First, he received hardly an acknowledgment; finally he earned praise for the improvement in his German. *Geheimrat*, meaning something like a secret councilor, was a high distinction on the civil servants' ladder, much coveted by title-conscious Germans, and Sommerfeld's vanity was not at all a rare phenomenon.

In Munich, Teller lost a foot in a streetcar accident, but his strong will and determination had him walking again with a prosthesis within a few months. When his recuperation in Budapest was over, he did not return to Munich but went instead to Leipzig and joined Werner Heisenberg. His new mentor was the opposite of the pompous German professors. He had a spirit of youthful competition and he was a true pioneer of modern physics. Teller developed a respect and admiration for Heisenberg that would last to the end of his life, notwithstanding Heisenberg's questionable behavior during World War II.

Heisenberg never became a Nazi and even had difficulties with the Nazis because he would not join in their ridicule of the physics of Einstein and other Jewish scientists. However, he stayed in Germany, lived alongside the Nazi crimes, and became head of the Nazi nuclear program. He did not mind the deployment of slave laborers when he urged a speedier production of materials for his program, and called the infamous super-Nazi Hans Frank his friend.[115] It was the same Frank that others labeled the "butcher of Poland." Heisenberg paid visits to occupied countries. The most controversial of these visits was to Copenhagen, where he engaged his former mentor, Niels Bohr, in a conversation whose character has remained a matter of controversy ever since.[116] After the war, Heisenberg had the nerve to claim moral superiority for himself for his failed nuclear program over those scientists who participated in the Manhattan Project, which was originated out of the fear of Hitler's acquiring the atomic bomb before the democracies did.

Teller's bias was not shown only to Heisenberg. One of his colleagues in Leipzig was the anti-communist Carl Friedrich von Weizsäcker, the elder brother of the man who later became president of the Federal Republic of Germany. An excellent physicist, and later philosopher, he became a close friend of Teller, and they studied together in Leipzig and Göttingen. Then, in Copenhagen, they lived in the same house. Von Weizsäcker was not only anti-communist; he also leaned toward the Nazis well before Hitler acquired power, although he never joined the Nazi party.[117] Under the Nazis, von Weizsäcker's father was undersecretary in the Foreign Ministry. He is known to have signed the deportation order of the French Jews.[118] Toward the end of the war, von Weizsäcker Senior was the German ambassador to the Vatican. After the war, the Americans sentenced him to years in prison, but he didn't have to serve much of it. His son, Teller's friend, while on a postwar visit to America, told Teller that the Americans had every reason to be angry, but what they did to his father had nothing to do with justice. Teller quoted him, saying, "If the Americans had come in and shot every tenth German, I could have understood it, I could have called it justice."[119] He was not quite alone in such views because some British would have liked to shoot all the Nazis during the first six weeks and then forget the whole thing.[120] Teller considered Carl Friedrich to be his friend to the end. However, von Weizsäcker surprised even his loyal friend when on a later visit he was actively looking for ways for the German government to help rehabilitate former Nazis.[121]

There was a stellar collection of physicists around Heisenberg in Leipzig. Friedrich Hund was a staff member. His is an important name in molecular orbital theory, which is a cornerstone in modern structural and computational chemistry. There was Rudolf Peierls, then German, later British, who eventually played a pivotal role in the British efforts to develop the atomic bomb. There were the Americans, Van Vleck, Boris Podolsky, and Robert S. Mullikan, also a future Nobel laureate. Mullikan and his wife visited Teller in Budapest, at which time Teller was a mere twenty-year-old student and Mullikan thirty-two. The future Nobel laureates Swiss Felix Bloch and Soviet Lev Landau were also there. In spite of Landau's then-communist politics, Teller and Landau became friends. They also had some scientific interactions. What has become known as the Jahn–Teller effect should have been called, according to Teller, the Landau–Jahn–Teller effect.

After his sojourn in Western Europe in 1929–1931, Landau went back to the Soviet Union. First he worked in Kharkov in the Ukraine, then in Peter Kapitsa's institute in Moscow, and soon became strongly disillusioned with communism. In 1938, he was arrested. He behaved courageously in jail; he maintained silence for two months and declared a hunger strike. He was released as a result of Kapitsa's protests and put under his responsibility, with Kapitsa acting as guarantor of his good behavior. By the time Kapitsa fell into disfavor with the authorities after World War II, Landau had become indispensable in the Soviet nuclear bomb program. Landau felt that he was a "learned slave" and considered the Soviet regime to be fascist.[122] He detested the political system for which he was diligently building the devastating bombs. His participation in the bomb project was his shield from the authorities.[123] After Stalin's death he no longer felt its necessity, and he quit the program.

Teller, who was to become one of the most rigid and most well-known anti-Soviet anti-communists of the Cold War era, maintained that during his stay in Germany he had an open mind about communism and about the Soviet Union. As evidence, he liked to mention not only his friendship with Landau, but also his friendship with Laszlo Tisza.[124] All of what he said in this connection, Tisza corroborated.[125] Teller and Tisza met in Budapest as winners of the national science competition. Tisza, like Teller, continued his studies in Germany. At Teller's suggestion, he also joined Heisenberg in Leipzig. When Tisza returned to Hungary, his communist friends persuaded him to get involved in their clandestine activities. As a consequence, Tisza was imprisoned for a year. Teller continued working with him and visited him in prison during his brief stays in Budapest. When Tisza was arrested, he had already completed his doctoral thesis. On one of his visits to Tisza in prison, Teller brought Tisza's Hungarian thesis to him and offered to take back the German translation to Germany if Tisza would prepare it. Tisza worked feverishly on the translation in prison, which Teller took to Germany and had published for his friend.

When Tisza was released from prison, he could not find employment and Teller helped him to get a position with Landau, who was then in Kharkov. The disillusioned Tisza left the Soviet Union during Stalin's purges in 1937. Again with Teller's help, he secured a fellowship at the College de France in Paris, where he stayed until the German occupation. Then he went to the United States, where he became a professor at the Massachusetts Institute of Technology. Upon his arrival, the FBI debriefed him; by then he had abandoned his leftist politics. Although his past was known, he experienced no difficulties in the United States even in the dark years of Senator Joseph McCarthy. Tisza's name came up recently in connection with the 2001 Nobel Prize in Physics, which was awarded for the experimental realization of the Bose–Einstein condensation.[126] Tisza had written about this phenomenon while working in Paris, but only half a century later would it become reality.[127]

It took just over a year for Teller to prepare his doctoral dissertation under Heisenberg. When he arrived in Leipzig, Heisenberg gave him a paper by Wigner on group theory, and he had to report about it at the next seminar. Heisenberg maintained a seminar program that was similar to the Berlin colloquia. Later, Landau would emulate these seminars in Moscow.[128] Teller's doctoral thesis was on the physics of the hydrogen molecular ion (the system of two protons and one electron), and he completed his doctorate in January 1930. He was not yet twenty-two years old. For the young doctor, Heisenberg offered an assistantship, which was a great honor and a sure sign of Heisenberg's being happy with Teller's performance. During Teller's final months in Leipzig he turned to chemistry, working on the structure and vibrations of polyatomic molecules.

Teller's excursions into the science of molecules are less well known than his involvement in nuclear physics. Yet these studies would have amounted to a full career in science. This is the field that occupied him in his last period in Germany. He carried it over to Britain, and it was still his specialty at the beginning of his American career. A few examples will suffice to characterize the scope and importance of these studies, some of which continue being used and built upon at the dawn of the twenty-first century. In the early 1930s, Teller studied the internal rotation of atomic groups with respect to other atomic groups around a chemical bond as axis of rotation in the molecule. All initial studies assumed free rotation, that is, that no energy barrier hindered such a motion. Teller and Bryan Topley, however, decided that there was a real problem for ethane, $H_3C–CH_3$, in which the rotation of interest is that of the two methyl groups relative to each other around the carbon–carbon bond. They suggested that a barrier to internal rotation might be the solution. Although they did not pursue this study, it remained a pioneering contribution to the understanding of the structure of molecules.[129]

Another example is the discovery of the Jahn–Teller effect, mentioned above, which is when a high-symmetry molecule happens to be unstable because of some properties of its electronic structure and increases its stability by lowering its symmetry.[130] To the present day the Jahn–Teller effect is an important tool in understanding the structure of numerous materials. The third example is about multilayer adsorption. The formula named B.E.T., after Stephen Brunauer, Paul Emmett, and Teller, has long served to describe effective surface areas in physical chemistry.[131] Teller was probably the proudest of this contribution among his results pertaining to chemistry. His later interactions in chemistry involved the famous British chemist Christopher Ingold, with whom he studied isotope shifts of vibrational frequencies upon isotopic substitution. Their interests overlapped in the vibration of polyatomic molecules, but they did not publish together.[132] Teller never completely detached himself from chemistry, and his contributions were appreciated by chemists.[133]

When Heisenberg gave Teller Wigner's paper, Teller had had only some superficial acquaintance with Wigner from Budapest, as one of those somewhat older scientists with whom he had so much savored a budding friendship. Now he could join Wigner's company on more equal terms. Teller liked to retell the story of his walking with Wigner in the Berlin Zoo after an Einstein presentation, which he could not follow. He complained about his own stupidity to Wigner, expecting some consolation. Wigner, however, surprised as well as pacified him with his response, "Stupidity is a general human property."[134]

In 1930, Teller went to Göttingen to work for Arnold Eucken and for James Franck, who was already a Nobel laureate. He stayed there until 1932 and also collaborated with others, among them Gerhard Herzberg, a future Nobel laureate. They worked together on the vibrational spectroscopy of molecules, which became Herzberg's life-long occupation. During his Göttingen time, Teller traveled to other places, and spent a few weeks in Enrico Fermi's laboratory in Rome. This was before Fermi's discovery of slow neutrons.

The year 1932 is often called the miracle year for physics, with many important discoveries. It was followed by Hitler's accession to power in Germany in 1933. In his *Memoirs*, Teller recalled fondly his time in Germany: "My years as a young scientist in Germany were the most satisfying years of my life." Then the shock of what followed was the graver, when "at twenty-five years old, I painfully discovered that the community of German physicists was also closed to me."[135]

CHAPTER THREE

Second Transition: To the United States

Why should we stay in a part of the world where we are no longer welcome?

Wigner, quoting John von Neumann

I would rather have roots than wings, but if I cannot have roots I shall have wings.

Leo Szilard

This chapter covers the period that began with the departure of the Martians from Germany in the early 1930s and ended when they joined American defense projects in their new country in the late 1930s. They had two advantages over many other refugees. One was their fame, due to which they were in demand even before Hitler came to power. The other was their experiences in departures and in starting new lives.

In their second transition, the Martians were in a large group of exceptional people. Hitler and the Nazis purged Germany of many of her greatest minds. Hitler declared, "If the dismissal of Jewish scientists means the annihilation of German science, then we shall do without science for a few years!"[1] Wigner noted that "Hitler's campaign against the Jews cost him most of the greatest people I had studied with."[2] Wigner singled out Erwin Schrödinger (who was not Jewish, but left anyway), Victor Weisskopf, Max Born, Michael Polanyi, Leo Szilard, Dennis Gabor, Walter Heitler, Fritz Haber, James Franck, Hans Bethe, Edward Teller, the Italian Enrico Fermi (whose wife was Jewish), and, above all, Albert Einstein. Wolfgang Pauli lived and worked in Zurich, but he did not find Switzerland safe enough and also moved to America. Herman Mark first went to his native Austria, and then to America after the *Anschluss*. Paul Ehrenfest in Holland took his own life at least partly because of the threat of the Nazis.

At first, it seemed as if the Martians would continue their lives in the United States as they had lived them in Germany. Von Kármán, Wigner, and von Neumann moved directly to America, and the transition was gradual, following invitations and preliminary stays. Teller initially went to Great Britain, but moved to the United States when it became clear that there were few prospects for him in Britain. Szilard's transition was different from the others. It was as if he was moving in two different orbits. One was his own life, which took a back seat at times of calamity and emergency. In the other, he busied himself in finding temporary support and, ultimately, jobs for other refugees. One could have thought that he was comfortably off and secure, but of course he, too, was a refugee.

For the Martians there were many differences between the German and American scenes. In Germany, they had arrived as students and found themselves in the company of the giants of their fields. In America, they were asked over partly because the Americans wanted to develop important research and educational centers. Once again, Szilard will be an exception from many points of view, but none of the differences between him and the rest of the Martians makes him any "less" of a Martian. For von Kármán, there were other differences as well.

Theodore von Kármán

Von Kármán's problems in Germany started well before Hitler's accession to power. He was sensitive to early expressions of anti-Semitism, as he was criticized for being a foreigner and thus lacking German patriotic feelings.[3] When a new building was to be inaugurated for his institute, he invited seventy specialists from all over the world for the celebration. He wanted to use the occasion to award honorary doctorates to five scientists of former belligerent countries. The German nationalists were unhappy about these actions.[4] This was still during the period of the democratic Weimar Republic. Then, slowly, von Kármán had to face the fact that his activities were becoming more and more related to German military revival (see the discussion of von Kármán's activities involving the German gliders in chapter 2). In the midst of this, von Kármán received invitations and offers from California. Robert Millikan, who was instrumental in building up the world-class California Institute of Technology (Caltech) from the backwater Throope College in Pasadena, sent an invitation to von Kármán for the first time in 1926. Millikan wanted to start an aerodynamics laboratory with money from the philanthropist Daniel Guggenheim, who had stipulated that somebody from Europe should establish the scientific side of the new laboratory.[5] Millikan offered von Kármán the directorship of the new Guggenheim Aeronautical Institute, but he declined.

In July 1929 Millikan repeated his offer, outlining the exceptional work opportunities, and von Kármán, his mother, and his sister left for Pasadena in December 1929. At first, he only took a leave of absence and spent some time in Aachen in 1931 and 1932. Further developments in Germany then made him resign his appointment in Aachen. In his letter of resignation he wrote to the Ministry of Education, "I hope that you will be able to do for German science in the next years as much as you accomplished in this year for foreign science."[6]

Von Kármán made a visit to Germany in 1934, after his resignation and even after Hitler's accession to power. By then there was an Air Ministry, headed by Hermann Göring, which invited him to return to Germany and work as a "consultant." Göring had declared that "I decide who is a Jew," but even he could not have given von Kármán a university job.[7] The offer von Kármán received was not unique: the Nobel laureate Otto Warburg, in spite his Jewish ancestry, remained in Germany and continued his research into the cure of cancer under Göring's protection.[8] It is supposed that Göring's fear of cancer influenced his ruling. Officially Warburg was said to have only one-quarter Jewish ancestry, but even that one-quarter barred him from a teaching job. This he did not mind; he was completely dedicated to his research. His colleagues in the West, though, did not appreciate his staying in Germany.

When von Kármán attended the Fifth Volta Congress in Rome in 1935, aviation was already an important issue in world politics and in the military preparations by the Fascist nations.[9] It was expected that war would begin in Europe within a few years, but in fact it began much earlier in the Far East and Africa. By the time of the congress, Air Marshal Göring had confessed publicly to the existence of the German *Luftwaffe*, in open defiance of the Treaty of Versailles. This came as no surprise to the big powers, nor to von Kármán in view of his experience in Germany in the 1920s. The Italians and Soviets were also busy building military planes, while the Japanese were not only building planes but also deploying them against Manchuria.

At the Volta Congress, a delegation of the participants visited Mussolini. As senior statesman, von Kármán headed the delegation to the Duce's headquarters, the Palazzo Venezia in Rome, and later described his impressions of the visit.[10] They walked down a long marble corridor and stopped in front of a pair of massive doors. When the doors were thrown open, they entered a small, carpeted reception room, which led into a huge chamber. There, at the end of a large and empty space, was Mussolini's small table and chair. The visitor, in order to reach him, had to walk about thirty meters (a hundred feet). The dictator was sitting in semi-darkness to enhance the effect. By the time he reached Mussolini, the visitor had been sufficiently humbled. In 1935, it was not yet so extraordinary for the Italian dictator to receive a Jewish scientist. The Duce's regime was slow in catching up with anti-Semitic legislation, which would come in 1938, after Fascist Italy irrevocably tied itself to Nazi Germany.

Von Kármán tried to stay aloof from politics and restrict his actions to the activities of a scientist/engineer who does not get involved. Even when later he became actively associated with the U.S. Air Force, he projected himself in such a light. He was not a political person like Edward Teller.[11] However, this aloofness toward politics carried him to the extreme when he testified in a dispute between the Nazi regime and several U.S. firms.[12] The dispute concerned a Junkers patent controversy. Although by then the anti-Nazi Junkers himself had been kicked out of the business, the Nazis continued manufacturing planes of Junkers' design. The U.S. firms were accused of infringing Junkers patents. For von Kármán this was a technical question, and he testified so successfully for the Germans that the U.S. firms had to pay Germany dollars that Hitler desperately needed. There were people who would have liked von Kármán to testify for the Americans. Of course, he could not do so against his knowledge, but it was a mistake on his part to get involved in the case in the first place. As he reminisced about the trial, he took obvious pride in having been asked and was thrilled to have won it, regardless of for whom he had won it.

At the same time as the Caltech people were prodding von Kármán to move to the United States, he started receiving invitations from Japan.[13] Admiral Yoshida of the Japanese Embassy in Berlin conveyed to him the invitation from the Kawanishi Machinery Manufacturing Company in Kobe. They wanted von Kármán to spend six months with them and to establish the first major Japanese research laboratory in aeronautics. Von Kármán did not want to accept the invitation, but found it impolite to reject it outright. Rather, he asked for double the sum the Japanese had offered. By doing so, he thought, they would be discouraged, but the Japanese accepted his condition. Such a trivial demand could have not discouraged the Japanese, especially, as von Kármán himself supposed, the Japanese Navy was behind the Kawanishi interest.[14]

Reluctantly, von Kármán accepted the position and started to build the first Japanese wind tunnel, which was completed in 1928. In retrospect, he understood the consequences because the independent aircraft company which Kawanishi set up "became the key manufacturing facility of the Japanese Imperial Navy during World War II, turning out gun turrets, sea-planes, and fighters." While in Japan, von Kármán advised the Japanese to seek originality instead of restricting themselves to copying Western design—although they produced excellence there, too, as they chose the best to copy. There is false modesty in von Kármán's following statement: "I do not wish to take too much credit—or perhaps in this case, blame—but I believe that I was also the man who introduced Japan to metal airplane propellers."[15]

The Japanese clearly benefited from their association with von Kármán. Well into the 1930s, when he was already settled in America, he was still monitoring European developments in aviation for Kawanishi.[16] And if he was monitoring European development from the United States, it would have been strange for him not to be monitoring American developments at the same time. Had this been the case, it would have been a sadly questionable activity.

It would be wrong, however, to believe that von Kármán's bias in favor of the Japanese went beyond practical considerations. He was also ready to help potential enemies of the Japanese, including the Chinese and the Soviets. In 1937, he paid a visit to China and Russia. The China visit was charged with military urgency, and he met with air force leaders and Generalissimo Chiang Kai Shek and Madame Chiang. At Tsing Hua University, his former student Frank Wattendorf was director of the department for aeronautical engineering. The Chinese lacked a good railway system and so wanted to jump immediately into the aviation age. They had started to build up the Chinese Air Force and wanted von Kármán's advice. On his previous visit to China, in 1929, he had suggested starting an aeronautical engineering course, and by his second visit there was already a whole department devoted to it.[17] The Japanese had attacked China as early as 1932, and von Kármán's visit to the Far East in 1937, which included Japan, took place with the two countries on the verge of renewed hostilities.

We have already commented that von Kármán was either naïve or calculating in his reaction to the first Japanese invitation. Similarly, was he naïve or calculating when he bought some vases for his sister on his visit to China and complained to one of his main hosts that the one he really liked was too expensive for him? Of course the next day it was delivered to his hotel room, compliments of his high-ranking Chinese host.[18]

Von Kármán was a student of local customs and conditions. He noted that professors were revered as just one step removed from God, both in Germany and Japan, whereas in the United States they were regarded as ordinary people. He wished that the Americans had it rather somewhere in between.[19] Nonetheless, the informality of the student/professor relationship in the United States suited him well. He built friendships with his pupils, who in turn adored him.[20]

On his way to China, von Kármán was invited to make a stopover in Moscow. He praised the level of training in the Russian engineering schools, which he thought "was fairly high even by the best European standards." Noteworthy is his praise for secondary school training (his father's specialty) in mathematics and science. He thought that "the Russians were beginning to turn out research engineers, grounded in the fundamental sciences. This was near my heart since it was the message I had learned from Felix Klein at Göttingen, and which I hoped I had brought to America."[21]

The United States was rich in resources, and economizing in materials was not a priority. This was very different from Germany. For this reason, the scientific approach to practical applications, in which von Kármán was such a master, did not seem to be important in America. In this the Soviet Union had some similarities with the United States at the time of von Kármán's arrival. Under the Soviet system, performance was often judged by the amount of materials that went into production, which implicitly encouraged the overuse and waste of resources.

Von Kármán made interesting comparisons between the American and German students, and these could also be applied to scientists.[22] The Germans were seldom gifted with mechanical ability; the Americans, on the other hand, were better at handling machines and materials due to their love of automobiles, with which they often had to tinker. The American high school placed a lot of emphasis on manual arts. The Americans were not as good as the Germans in mathematics, which von Kármán ascribed to the difference in high school education. This experience would later prompt von Kármán to change the curriculum of his students at Caltech, introducing more mathematics and less measurement and observation. In later years, von Kármán regretted that the spread of the computer made mathematics seemingly not so much needed by engineers. For von Kármán mathematics served not only as an engineer's tool, it also taught him a way of thinking.

Von Kármán made himself useful in civilian projects in the United States that went beyond his teaching and research.[23] He contributed greatly to the improvement of steam turbines for General Electric in the 1930s, and continued his interactions with its Research Laboratory in Schenectady, New York. He helped to build the water pumps on the Colorado River and assisted with the civil engineering for the Los Angeles Metropolitan Water District in Southern California. When dust storms ravaged the country in 1933, he brought up plans for a 5,000-mile-long "shelter belt," consisting of rows of trees stretching across the United States. This was to be part of the grandiose New Deal program by the new American president, Franklin D. Roosevelt. The administration wanted to break the force of the winds, thereby saving and strengthening agriculture, which, it was hoped, would help bring the country out of the Depression. There were important questions that needed to be answered. For example, how far apart should the trees be spaced for maximum efficiency, what are the dynamics of dust blowing, and what are the mechanism with which air lifts soil? A lot of modeling went into the project and von Kármán and his colleagues, Frank Malina and Martin Summerfield, designed a sand-blowing tunnel and a soil-blowing tunnel. By the time they made their proposals, however, the dust storms had abated and the government's interest declined. War was approaching, but the research added to the understanding of the dynamics of wind erosion and the natural barriers that tree lines made against heavy windstorms.

Another example of von Kármán's conspicuous involvement in civilian projects was his troubleshooting on the Grand Coulee Dam. The dam had developed cracks, and although von Kármán did not know much about dams, he declared that the "dam is a structure that has to be designed according to scientific principles, and scientific principles are my business."[24] The problem boiled down to the question of the ratio of the thickness of the dam to its overall width, and whether it could be reduced to something resembling the buckling problem of columns that von Kármán had solved at the start of his scientific career. Another project was the development of windmills to generate electricity in 1939. He designed a new form of propeller and in 1941 the new windmill started operations. Eventually this initial project was abandoned but the progress that had been made proved valuable.

The project that gave him the greatest publicity was related to the collapse of the Tacoma Narrows Bridge in 1940 in the State of Washington.[25] The mile-long suspension bridge, with the fanciest single span in the world, connected the Olympic Peninsula with the rest of the state over the narrowest section of Puget Sound. Its collapse was a tragic sensation. Von Kármán used some rudimentary modeling and determined that the cause was the Kármán vortices he had discovered many years before. These vortices developed when the bridge started to oscillate with the same frequency as the rhythm of the air movement caused by the wind. The new bridge was built taking the Kármán Vortex Street into account, after careful experiments in the Caltech wind tunnel. Other suspension bridges were investigated, including the Golden Gate Bridge in San Francisco, but were found to be safe. Von Kármán's interest in bridges was noted in secret documents about his activities, and an informant reported that he kept many maps of bridges in the United States at home. A clandestine investigation, however, determined that von Kármán possessed the maps "legally and rightfully."[26]

The examples mentioned above show the significance of von Kármán's activities for civilian purposes. They were, however, only a prelude to what was to come, when America needed him in World War II and in the Cold War that followed it.

Leo Szilard

In 1931, Eugene Wigner engineered an invitation for Szilard to spend a year in Princeton doing research in mathematical physics. Upon his arrival in New York, Szilard expressed his doubts that New York City would still be standing in the decades to come.[27] The terror attacks of September 11, 2001 now give his words a chilling effect. At the very beginning of 1933, Szilard foresaw the deterioration of the situation in Germany and urged Michael Polanyi to leave. Polanyi had been offered an appointment at the University of Manchester, but he could not imagine highly cultured Germany falling for the Nazis. In a few months' time, however, he could, and he moved to Manchester with his family. Polanyi's case is of special interest because—as we have seen—he had eloquently justified his departure from Hungary, yet he found it difficult at first to justify a similar departure from Germany. He did not have Szilard's foresight in anticipating political developments, although he was an observant thinker. Szilard evaluated the meaning of seemingly insignificant things. He noticed that "the Germans always took a utilitarian point of view" in which moral considerations played very little role. It was not so much that Hitler was so strong, rather that the resistance to him was so weak.[28]

The British were very good at welcoming the refugees, and even though at the outbreak of World War II many of them were deported as enemy aliens, their treatment was always humane.[29] There were few dissenting voices, but there was an interesting if atypical aspect in Polanyi's reception in England. The oldest Fellow of the Royal Society protested against Polanyi's employment, stating that he was "against the importation by Manchester of a physical chemist from somewhere in the Balkans."[30] On another occasion, the same person raised his voice "against the appointment . . . of a gentleman who is not an Englishman nor in any way connected with us."[31] The author was a notorious protester, and his stand subtracts nothing from the selflessness of many others. However, reservations occurred in the United States as well. The mathematician George D. Birkhoff was afraid that the refugee immigrants from Europe would shake his position as "the unquestioned leader of American mathematics" and that the refugees would take away academic jobs. In Birkhoff's words, "If American mathematicians don't watch out, they may become hewers of wood and carriers of water."[32] He suggested that the new arrivals should take lesser positions, which in fact they did in most cases, as compared with their qualifications and prior positions.

During a brief visit to Budapest in early 1933, Szilard tried to convince his brother and parents to get out of Europe, but they thought that he was exaggerating. He also warned a friend, Alice Eppinger, again to no avail.[33] After World War II Szilard helped her; the Nazis had killed her husband and one of their daughters. The European situation was hopeless, but it was compounded by the Depression in the United States following the stock market crash in October 1929. The Americans and the Germans responded to their respective crises in very different ways. The Americans elected Franklin D. Roosevelt as their president in 1932. He was inaugurated on March 12, 1933, and he brought the reforms of the New Deal with him. The Germans elected the Nazis in great numbers to the Reichstag and Hitler became chancellor. Roosevelt and Hitler were in power for the same duration at the same time.

In Germany, Jewish professors started losing their jobs even before the promulgation of racial laws, because "timid academic councils forced them out of their positions fearing a rising wave of anti-Semitic policies."[34] The Nazis used the Reichstag fire—which they themselves engineered—as a pretext for curtailing and suspending civil liberties. Again, Szilard saw the situation more clearly than Michael Polanyi: "Do you really mean to say that you think that the Secretary of the Interior had anything to do with this?", Polanyi asked him. To which Szilard responded, "Yes, this is precisely what I mean."[35] The Reichstag fire signaled the opening of the road to the Nazi dictatorship, ending the democratic Weimar Republic virtually overnight. No wonder that some people, especially those with European experience, were frightened about the possible consequences of the September 11, 2001 terror attack on civil liberties in the United States.

Although the Nazis opened their first concentration camp on March 20, 1933, in Dachau, with unprecedented speed and efficiency, they did not start killing people right away. One of their first measures was to allow Jews to be admitted "to universities and to the professions of attorney and physician" only in proportion to their numbers in the German population, that is, less than one percent. It is noteworthy in regard to the Martians that Hungary introduced such measures thirteen years before Germany (the *numerus clausus* in 1920). Szilard saw what was coming, even if not in precise terms, but even he could not have foreseen the extent of the horrors that would be unfolding in a few years' time. For many people, though, the gradual nature of the worsening situation worked as a sedative.

The Nobel laureate physicist Arno Penzias, himself a Jewish child refugee from Nazi Germany, wondered why more people did not leave when the Nazis came to power or soon afterwards.[36] Most ordinary people found such a departure virtually impossible: giving up one's trade, language, and livelihood, and carrying the responsibility of providing for one's family figured heavily in the equations. And there were often insurmountable difficulties stemming from the reluctance of countries that might potentially take refugees. Under the Nazis, every new rule looked as if it was the final rule, after which there could be nothing worse. In addition—Penzias noted—there were some remnants of rationality even in the most irrational laws that made people believe they could tough it out. For example, when the Germans occupied Holland, the Jews in Amsterdam were restricted to using public transportation during specified daytime hours, but there was an exception for those who went to work. Similarly, Jews were restricted in their shopping to certain hours, but there was an exception for drug stores. People did not know about the extermination camps at that point.

Even though Szilard could not have imagined Auschwitz, he warned everybody who would listen to him to leave. He left Germany on March 30, 1933, crossing the border into Czechoslovakia on March 31. The next day Germany closed her borders to would-be refugees, and from then on it was much more difficult to leave. This was a close call that Szilard considered a lesson for the rest of his life: "If you want to succeed in this world you don't have to be much cleverer than other people; you just have to be one day earlier."[37]

Szilard arrived in Vienna, but rather than worrying about his own fate he immediately began helping academic refugees find places to work outside Germany. This shows, perhaps more than anything else, his human greatness. Of course, such operations could not be started too early. One of Szilard's colleagues predicted that once the flood of refugees started, "the French would pray for the victims, the British would organize their rescue, and the Americans would pay for it."[38] Szilard devised realistic schemes and proposed the formation of an Academic Assistance Council (AAC). This came to life and Szilard electrified others as well: Esther Simpson left a job in Geneva for one with the AAC in London for one-third of her Geneva salary. The AAC was to stay around.[39] In 1957, when George Olah was on his way from Hungary to North America as a refugee after the crushed revolution in 1956, it was the AAC and the same Esther Simpson that helped him find a job.[40]

Szilard had no position or support but found it prudent not to ask for assistance and was paying for all his AAC-connected travel out of his own pocket. Referring to Szilard's frantic activities, Bethe said: "We were convinced that Szilard could be in two places at the same time." The AAC had placed more than 2,500 refugee scholars by 1939.[41] In judging the performance of the AAC, one has to remember that Hitler's rise to power and the dismissal of Jewish and other "undesirable" intellectuals took place en masse at the height of the Depression, so the difficulties were "enormously increased by financial conditions, collective and individual, in the academic institutions of all countries alike."[42] Szilard's activities stand out even against the background of all other rescue operations.[43]

How could Szilard, with his scientific prowess, devote so much time and energy to non-scientific matters in his thirties, when he had no position and when he should have been securing his future career? Szilard himself gave the answer in a letter to Eugene Wigner in 1932. Here are some excerpts from the English translation of that letter after Lanouette:

> When the knowledge that right now we have more noble causes than to do science, when this knowledge has entered our blood, then I am afraid this knowledge cannot be distilled out of it. . . . .
>
> Thus once one is devoted to some work that so far has not yet been done and for which, therefore, there are no institutions yet, there is no justification for a complaint that such institutions do not yet exist. . . .
>
> . . . [I]f one does not succeed in becoming financially independent, thereby getting into a situation that makes one a free man, then one must try to get a job that leaves one enough time and permits a sufficient amount of attention for the things that one considers more important. . . .
>
> Up to the time when such a "position" would offer itself, I could not, without having a bad conscience, devote myself to science.[44]

Szilard thus made his priorities very clear. Financial independence would, of course, have greatly helped Szilard in his endeavor; alas he did not have this, so eventually he had to look for a job. But as he was trying to explain in his letter to Wigner, he wanted a job that "leaves one enough time and permits a sufficient amount of attention for the things that one considers important."[45] In another letter, of August 11, 1933 (addressee unknown), he says: "I am spending much money at present for traveling about and earn of course nothing and cannot possibly go on with this for very long. At the moment, however, *I can be so useful that I cannot afford to retire into private life*" (italics added).[46]

Szilard's job situation came up from time to time. His supporters and friends did not quite see what he so clearly explained in his letter. Wigner was worried about his friend and thought of two possibilities; one was that Szilard might work as a consultant for a large company, the other that he might work for a publisher. When the question of recommendations for an appointment in Britain came up, the responses were enthusiastic: Von Laue and Schrödinger responded jointly. Max Volmer (Berlin Technical University) wrote about Szilard: "capable and many-sided . . . unites in a rare fashion a complete understanding of the development of modern physics with a capacity for dealing with problems of all fields of classical physics and physical chemistry . . . unique in his independent, original, and inventive attitude toward all problems." Einstein described Szilard as a "versatile and able physicist," found him creative, with ideas on the experimental and technical levels, and felt that he "keeps his focus on the theoretically substantive matters." Paul Ehrenfest wrote that Szilard was "a very rare example of a man because of his combination of great purely scientific acumen, his ability to immerse himself in and solve technical problems, his fascination and fantasy for organizing, and his great sensitivity and compassion for people in need." He also found Szilard "extremely original, versatile, and innovative." Ehrenfest captured some very characteristic traits in Szilard when he pointed out how he immediately dropped everything else when he felt that refugees needed his help, whereas he would long for the opportunity to "quietly contemplate those questions that interest him most." In a second letter, Schrödinger lavishly praised Szilard and described him as "absolutely truthful and truly altruistic."[47]

Szilard felt happy in London and especially liked the reserve of the English. He met with Archibald V. Hill, who had begun as a physicist and then changed to physiology, where he earned a Nobel Prize. Hill, who encouraged Szilard to take up biology, was at one time President of the Academic Assistance Council. This was the same Hill who would give Francis Crick advice when he was choosing his career after World War II.[48] Crick had also earned his first degree in physics, but switched to molecular biology after the war. Hill thought that Szilard could learn biology by starting to teach it right away. Szilard seriously considered the move and found some of his readings in this direction inspiring.[49] He read Paul de Kruif's widely popular *Microbe Hunters*, which has encouraged many future Nobel laureates to embark on a lifelong career in science.[50] He also read Niels Bohr's essay, "Light and Life" and H. G. Wells' *The Science of Life*.[51] However, his attention was diverted away from biology by some developments.

Rutherford gave a lecture about nuclear physics on September 11, 1933, and he issued a warning, "to those who look for sources of power in atomic transmutations—

such expectations are the merest moonshine."[52] Szilard read about Rutherford's lecture and was irritated by the great physicist's categorical statement, "because how can anyone know what someone else might invent?" On June 4, 1934, Rutherford received Szilard, who told him about his idea regarding a nuclear chain reaction, but his host was upset by learning that Szilard had already patented the concept of the nuclear chain reaction, and he threw him out.[53] Later in 1934, Teller attended another lecture by Rutherford, who was still angry from his encounter with Szilard. He declared that those who believed that the energy in the atom could be liberated and utilized were lunatics.[54] Rutherford was not alone in his negative opinion. Einstein, the discoverer of the matter/energy equivalence, compared the feasibility of transforming matter into energy to "something akin to shooting birds in the dark in a country where there are only a few birds."[55] Szilard, though, remained undeterred. He told Teller of his idea "that a critical mass of material would retain sufficient fraction of neutrons and produce an extremely powerful explosion."[56]

The circumstances in which Szilard came to the idea of the nuclear chain reaction have become a legend. One day in 1933 he was walking along Southampton Row in London, when possibly the change in the traffic lights made him stop, and he suddenly realized that "if we could find an element which is split by neutrons and which would emit *two* neutrons when it absorbed *one* neutron, such an element, if assembled in sufficiently large mass, could sustain a nuclear chain reaction" (italics in original).[57] In fact Szilard came to two concepts: the nuclear chain reaction and critical mass. Here it is important to delineate Szilard's contribution from those of others. The concept of chain reactions had been known in chemistry. Even such specialized reactions as the branched chain reactions that lead to an explosion had been discovered by Nikolai Semenov and his co-workers in Moscow, for which Semenov would later be awarded a Nobel Prize.[58] Szilard recognized that a nuclear chain reaction would also be possible. However, there remained many unanswered questions, about which of the elements was capable of doing this, how one could go about finding it, and what techniques should be used once the element was identified.

In any case, the idea of atomic energy and the atomic bomb was moving from fantasy to possibility. For Szilard, not having a job bogging him down was a great advantage, as was, in his view, the absence of family responsibilities. He could spend any amount of time thinking; he could visit any laboratory; he could question any scientist—and he interrogated them "often with the precision of a prosecuting attorney."[59] He had the great advantage of being an outsider, and there are many examples in the history of science where outsiders make seminal discoveries because they are not bound by the existing dogmas of their fields.[60] Szilard concluded, from what he had learned, that Rutherford was wrong. This was not too much of a shock for Szilard, who had proved other great scientists wrong before. He had read H. G. Wells' *The World Set Free*, whose author predicted some important discoveries in physics, including the creation of the atomic bomb and its deployment in a big war.[61] This book and some other considerations prompted Szilard to think about entering nuclear physics; he had never considered this before, but it was to become his major area of activities during the next decade.

As soon as Szilard understood the potential of nuclear physics for destruction, he knew that he had found a worthy task for himself and it "became a sort of obsession" with him.[62] His sense of responsibility, and experience concerning political implications, made him uniquely qualified to take up this problem. Although he had failed with Rutherford, Szilard continued his quest of contacting big names to alert them to the potentials of nuclear physics. There was, though, an unfortunate ambiguity in his quest. On the one hand, he wanted to alert people; on the other hand, he wanted to keep secret those things about which he wanted to alert them. He might have been more successful had he been less secretive. However, he wanted to avoid the Germans learning about his concept. His scientist contacts included George Paget Thomson and Patrick M. S. Blackett, both future Nobel laureates in physics. Blackett told him that it would be easier to mobilize resources in Russia than in the West.

In 1934, Szilard filed for a patent for the nuclear chain reaction. He also saw the need for some further experiments, and he enlisted Lise Meitner in Berlin to perform them. In some measure this was innovation, because at that time international cooperation was not as common as it became later. However, this action also seemed to be a breach of his concern for keeping his findings secret from Germany. It is hard to imagine that Lise Meitner's experiments could have been kept from German officialdom even if Meitner had been willing to participate in such clandestine actions, which is doubtful.

Even though his secretiveness hindered Szilard's effectiveness, there were some willing to help him, or let him work in their laboratories. Thus Szilard was allowed to experiment in St. Bartholomew's Hospital, a teaching institution.[63] It was stipulated, however, that a staff member should be participating in Szilard's experiments. This brought about a cooperation between Szilard and a young physicist, Thomas A. Chalmers. Their joint work led to a simple method of isotope separation, published in *Nature*.[64] They started the work in August 1934 and published their first paper in September. It is known as the Szilard–Chalmers Effect and became widely used. A decade and a half later Willard Libby suggested a follow-up project to the Szilard–Chalmers Effect to his graduate student F. Sherwood Rowland.[65] Both later became Nobel laureates for independent and unrelated discoveries. The work at St. Bartholomew's was Szilard's entry into nuclear physics; he was still an amateur outsider but now there was something attached to his name.

Lanouette quotes the hospital director, F. L. Hopwood, warning Szilard that he should not violate regulations about the use of isotopes. He wanted to underline the importance of adhering to the rules, and to make Szilard aware of the fact that when he looked out the window, he saw walls that "have been standing here for over five hundred years." Szilard was not someone to be impressed easily by such a warning, considering his disregard for the past. Now, he had the added weight of the anticipated war. He responded to Hopwood that "these walls may not be standing here ten years from now."[66] Sadly, Szilard was proved right: the walls were destroyed by German bombing in World War II. Szilard and Chalmers' experiments at St. Bartholomew's Hospital progressed well, and there was soon a second paper in *Nature*.

In the meantime Szilard continued building his network of influential people. He visited Oxford and met the low-temperature physicist Francis Simon, who was also a refugee scientist. In spite of the fleeting acquaintance between Szilard and Simon, the latter gave a penetrating if brief assessment of Szilard's problems with finding a permanent job by quoting someone: "there are quite a few people who are dying to converse with you for a few days but none who would like to offer you a job."[67] Szilard had clarified his intentions regarding jobs to Wigner, but to most he gave the impression that he was looking for a position.

Through Simon, Szilard met Frederick Lindemann, who was later to become Winston Churchill's scientific advisor under the name Lord Cherwell. Szilard continued to keep an eye on events taking place in the wider world. When in 1934 Peter Kapitsa was detained in the Soviet Union, Szilard wanted to organize protests and was even contemplating schemes to free Kapitsa.[68] For many years Kapitsa had lived and worked in Cambridge, spending his summers in the Soviet Union. At some point he was urged to return to the Soviet Union for good, but declined. Kapitsa was very successful at the Cavendish Laboratory and was elected Fellow of the Royal Society.[69] He was given substantial funding for the costly equipment he was using to investigate the impact of very strong magnetic fields on materials. At first he took his Soviet detention badly, but his initial lethargy soon gave way to renewed energy, and he built up an exceptionally strong institute for physical research in Moscow. The Soviet government shipped his Cambridge equipment from the Cavendish Laboratory, and delivered it to him. He was a somewhat tyrannical figure for his co-workers, but he also had the courage to stand up to the authorities, even to Stalin.[70]

Also in 1934, Szilard attempted to mobilize Nobel laureates to protest against the Japanese attack in Manchuria. To encourage them to join, he stipulated that the protest would take place only if eighty percent of all laureates joined. The protest would amount to a scientific boycott of Japan and Japanese scientists.[71] Recruiting Nobel laureates to a cause has since become a popular way of expressing political protest.

In 1935, at the Washington physics meeting, Szilard met physicist Gregory Breit of the University of Wisconsin, who helped Szilard land an appointment at New York University. Breit was also instrumental in getting Wigner appointed at Wisconsin. Among the other prominent physicists that Szilard met in Washington were Hans Bethe, George Gamow, Edward U. Condon, then of Princeton University, and Ernest O. Lawrence of the University of California, Berkeley.

By the mid-1930s Szilard had realized that the atomic weapon might play a decisive role in the coming war. His thinking was pregnant with this tremendous responsibility. This may also be why he schemed in an overcomplicated way. He called for secrecy but could not fully explain why, and at the same time took out a patent for the nuclear chain reaction that he was secretive about and which did not yet exist. He himself realized the situation he was in and compared it to somebody trying to rescue some jewelry from a fire but being caught with it while running from the scene to take the jewelry to safety.[72]

Szilard was commuting between Great Britain and the United States during the second half of the 1930s, but in 1935 he correctly predicted to Michael Polanyi that he would return to England until "one year before the war." By the time Szilard arrived in New York in the spring of 1937, he had filed for immigration to become a U.S. citizen. The Munich Agreement between Nazi Germany and Great Britain and France was signed on September 30, 1938. That made Szilard decide to stay in the United States rather than travel to England, which he should have done according to an agreement with Oxford University. World War II broke out on September 1, 1939, and once again Szilard's foresight had proved to be prophetic.

Eugene P. Wigner

Wigner had had an association with Princeton University since 1930, having a shared appointment between Princeton and Berlin. In 1934, he spent six months in Manchester with Michael Polanyi. His Princeton/Berlin appointment might have continued for some time, because as a Hungarian citizen he would not have been subjected to the German anti-Jewish legislation. However, Wigner realized that he and Germany would have to part sooner or later. He compared Europe to a ship which was sinking and even had qualms about abandoning a sinking ship.[73] In 1935–1936 Princeton made him a full time professor and the other half appointment in Berlin became superfluous. At Princeton, Wigner had superb doctoral students in solid state physics.

His first graduate student was Frederick Seitz, awarded his PhD in 1934, who was to become an important figure in American science politics. At one time Seitz was the President of the National Academy of Sciences of the U.S.A. His most important position was the prestigious presidency of Rockefeller University. Wigner's second graduate student was John Bardeen, who took his PhD in 1936. Bardeen went on to an exceptionally brilliant career in physics, becoming the only scientist, to date, with two Nobel Prizes in Physics. Wigner's third graduate student was Conyers Herring, who himself became a mentor of other important physicists.[74] Wigner's sophisticated mathematical background fortunately combined with his acute interest in practical problems. This resulted in excellent research projects for his students, involving real solids and their structures and properties. They were exceptional students, who became the first three truly solid-state physicists in the United States. The most important lessons Wigner taught his students were how to choose and attack research problems, how to decompose them, and how to solve the essentials by understanding their physics. In Princeton Bardeen took instructions not only from Wigner but also from von Neumann, and of all his professors, Bardeen was "most stimulated by the two young Hungarians." For Seitz, working with Wigner was "one of the most remarkable experiences of my life." Years later, Bardeen and Seitz were invited to participate in the Manhattan Project. Seitz joined Wigner's nuclear reactor group in the fall of 1943, whereas Bardeen continued in his previous assignment at the Naval Ordnance Laboratory.[75]

In spite of his success with students, Princeton did not renew Wigner's appointment in 1936; at least, this is how Wigner remembered it. He even gave the perceived reason for his dismissal: "My appointment had apparently aroused the jealousy of others who felt they deserved my job." While Wigner praised the Princeton University of that time, he did not mince words when he described its physics department. It was behind the times, did not care about quantum mechanics, yet it felt superior to other and better departments like Columbia or Chicago; it behaved like Göttingen without any foundation. One of his complaints was that the department head at Princeton could not tell von Neumann and Wigner apart even six months after they had arrived there.[76] Fellow physicist and science historian Abraham Pais was puzzled by Wigner's story and had the Princeton University files investigated.[77] According to the records, the university proposed a reappointment but not to a position that Wigner had expected to get. This prompted him take a leave of absence from Princeton.

The "dismissal" hurt Wigner and shook his self-confidence. He felt that maybe he was not good enough and maybe Princeton was right to "fire" him, but he resented the way the university had treated him. In his despair, Wigner turned to Gregory Breit, who was then at the University of Wisconsin. Wigner had done some work with him at Princeton, when Breit was at the Institute for Advanced Study, and they had published an important paper together about the spectra of chemical reactions. Breit was a Russian immigrant who liked to speak German. He was the opposite of Wigner in that he could be abrupt and wild, but he was a loyal friend and helped Wigner secure a job at Wisconsin.[78]

Wigner liked Wisconsin and its people, both ordinary folk and his physicist colleagues. He felt that it was in Wisconsin that he became an American, to the extent that he would ever become one. He fell in love with a young Jewish woman, Amelia Z. Frank, who was the only female graduate student in physics.[79] They married in 1936, but she fell ill and died in 1937. Wigner was devastated, and when Princeton called him back in 1938, he swallowed his pride and returned.[80] He was appointed to a named professorship, a position that he had expected, but failed to get, in 1936.[81] Wigner contributed greatly to the physics department of Princeton University becoming a world leader in the field.

Left: Young Theodore von Kármán. (Courtesy of the Archives of the Hungarian National Museum, Budapest.)

Below: Leo Szilard, first row, third from the right, with his graduating class in 1916. (Bela Silard Collection; courtesy of John Silard.)

Right: Leo Szilard's portrait in a Hungarian document with his signature. (Courtesy of the late George Marx.)

Below: Eugene Wigner in the graduating class of the Lutheran Gimnázium in Budapest, 1919; Wigner is the second from the right, first row. (Courtesy of the Archives of Fizikai Szemle, Budapest.)

Left: John von Neumann at the time of graduation from the Lutheran Gimnázium. (Courtesy of Ferenc Szabadváry, Budapest.

Below: The teachers at the Lutheran Gimnázium; László Rátz is first on the right in the front row. (Courtesy of the Archives of Fizikai Szemle, Budapest.)

Above left: Theodore von Kármán with his mother and sister. (Courtesy of Roger Malina.)

Top right: Edward Teller at the time of his graduation from the Minta. (Courtesy of Wendy Tellerand Paul Teller.)

Bottom right: Young Eugene P. Wigner with his parents. (Courtesy of Martha Wigner and the late George Marx.)

Above: Edward Teller with Robert Mullikan and his wife, Budapest,1928; between them is Béla Pogány of Budapest Technical University. (Courtesy of Wendy Teller and Paul Teller.)

Left: Theodore von Kármán lecturing at the California Institute of Technology. (Courtesy of Roger Malina.)

Above: Eugene P. Wigner
and his second wife,
Mary Wheeler, John von
Neumann and his first
wife, Mariette Kövesi, with
friends in Princeton in the
mid-1930s. (Courtesy of
Marina Whitman.)

Right: Leo Szilard with
two future Nobel laureate
Norwegian scientists, Odd
Hassel and Lars Onsager,
in Berlin-Lichterfelde,
1924. (Photo by Johan P.
Holtsmark; courtesy of the
late Otto Bastiansen.)

Above: Theodore von Kármán with (from the left) Martin Summerfeld, Frank Malina, Walter Powell, and Paul Dane in California in the early 1930s. (Courtesy of Roger Malina.)

Left: Theodore von Kármán writing on the body of an airplane in the company of Frank Malina and others. (Courtesy of NASA.)

Above: John von Neumann. (Courtesy of Marina Whitman.)

Right: Edward and Mici Teller, 1940. (Photo by Harold Argo; courtesy of Wendy Teller and Paul Teller.)

Above: Eugene P. Wigner and Werner Heisenberg in the 1930s. (Courtesy of Martha Wigner Upton and the late George Marx.)

Left: John von Neumann and his second wife, Klára Dán, at their Princeton home. (Courtesy of Marina Whitman.)

Above: Eugene P. Wigner with Michael Polanyi and his son John (Nobel laureate in 1986) in Manchester, England, 1934. (Courtesy of John C. Polanyi.)

Right: Eugene P. Wigner and Leo Szilard. (Courtesy of the late George Marx.)

Left: John von Neumann and his daughter Marina. (Courtesy of Marina Whitman.)

Below: Eugene P. Wigner with his son and daughter. (Courtesy of Martha Wigner Upton and the late George Marx.)

Above: John von Neumann
(second row, partially
hidden) and others in
Albert Einstein's company
in Princeton. (Courtesy of
Marina Whitman.)

Left: The three scientists of the B.E.T. equation, Paul Emmett, Stephen Brunauer, and Edward Teller, on the occasion of a later reunion. (Courtesy of Wendy Teller and Paul Teller.)

Below: Eugene P. Wigner (in back) with workers of the Budapest tannery. (Courtesy of Martha Wigner Upton.)

Above: John von Neumann (first from the left, second row) at the award ceremony of honorary doctorates at Harvard University. Sitting in the middle is James B. Conant, President of Harvard University. On his right is Dean Acheson, President Truman's Secretary of State. (Photo by Walter R. Fleischer; courtesy Marina Whitman and Harvard University Archives.)

Right: Participants of the Theoretical Physics Conference at George Washington University in 1937. Wigner is on the far left of the third row; Teller is fourth from left in the fourth row. (Courtesy of Martha Wigner Upton.)

John von Neumann

Oswald Veblen was professor of mathematics at Princeton. He wanted to modernize American mathematics and in the 1920s he traveled throughout Europe, Budapest included, looking for talent. He wanted to bring people like Hermann Weyl and John von Neumann to Princeton. Weyl spent the academic year 1928–1929 there, but when it was over he returned to Europe. Weyl would later come back to Princeton where, in addition to his mathematics, he gave a famous lecture series, which was published as *Symmetry* and became a classic.[82] Princeton was considering inviting von Neumann next; the university wanted to make him happier there than Weyl was, and so decided to also invite his friend and frequent co-author Eugene P. Wigner. The invitations arrived in the fall of 1929, for the spring 1930 semester. Just before leaving for Princeton, von Neumann went to Budapest and married Mariette Kövesi at the very end of 1929. She was Catholic and the von Neumann family had converted to Catholicism in 1929. By then von Neumann's father had died. Mariette, who was five years younger than John, came from the converted family of a wealthy Budapest doctor. Their daughter, Marina, was born in 1935, and the marriage broke up in 1936.[83] John and Mariette got a divorce in Reno, Nevada, in 1937 after she had spent six weeks there. Marina was to live with her mother until high school, then live with her father. In 1938, von Neumann went back to Budapest to marry Klári Dán; he was to be her third husband. By then von Neumann had become a naturalized citizen of the United States but retained his Hungarian citizenship as well. However, Hungarian law did not recognize the validity of the Nevada divorce. Hence he had to renounce his Hungarian citizenship and marry Miss Dán as an American citizen.[84]

Von Neumann fell in love with America on the day of his arrival, according to Wigner. To von Neumann, the Americans were "sane people, less formal and traditional than the Europeans and a bit more commercial. But a great deal more sensible too."[85] The adjustment, though, was not made without problems. When the von Neumanns and Wigner were invited to a dinner party, they suffered from all kinds of mishap.[86] By the time they arrived, forty minutes late according to the old Hungarian custom, dinner was almost over. Wigner was bald—he had shaved his head to make his hair grow thicker, but it hadn't worked. Von Neumann's wife appeared in a backless dress: this was the latest Parisian fashion, but one that had not yet reached provincial Princeton. And von Neumann himself was formally overdressed.

Adolf Hitler was appointed Germany's chancellor in January 1933 and at about the same time the Institute for Advanced Study was established in Princeton.[87] Von Neumann was appointed as one of its lifetime professors. The arrangement allowed him to spend half of each year in Europe. As his half-year in Berlin was coming up, he noted that Europe was "relapsing into the dark ages." So he did not go to Berlin in the summer of 1933, but went back to Princeton in September. However, he waited quite a while before, in April 1938, resigning "in gentle German" from German academic institutions, tying his resignation to the Nazi atrocities and expressing the hope that the "German professors would do more to help" the victims.[88]

The von Neumanns gave memorable parties, which were meeting places for bright conversation and for helping European refugees to find employment. Theodore von Kármán attended the parties when he was in town. Von Neumann quickly adapted to the American lifestyle, and his love of automobiles fitted in well. As the number of vehicles increased and traffic jams occurred more often, he declared that the "cars in America are no good for transportation any more, but they make marvelous umbrellas." He had the ability to package even serious statements into jokes, referring to a Gothic university chapel, for instance, as "our one million dollar protest against materialism."[89] Although Princeton was a provincial town, it was fast becoming a lively academic center. The many distinguished visitors helped in changing its image, and von Neumann brought in some of the most distinguished, Paul Dirac among them. It was in Princeton that Dirac met Wigner's divorced sister, Manci, who had come from Budapest. She was Wigner's guest, but because of his sparse accommodation she was staying in the von Neumanns' spacious home. Alan Turing was another illustrious visitor in the 1930s and von Neumann would have liked him to stay at the institute. However, Turing opted for returning to Manchester, England, and became a valued decoder of German ciphers during World War II.

Von Neumann was horrified by the idea of communism, whereas many of his colleagues appeared to be left-wing and preferred to ignore the frightening news of poverty and tyranny from Soviet Russia. It was Depression time in America and this helped them to take a tolerant view of the Soviet Union. Von Neumann was patient and magnanimous, at least outwardly, although some of the practices of his American colleagues worried him. He noticed their eagerness to file patents at the slightest provocation, and he found it equally strange to see some of his colleagues jealously guarding their little ideas from others. Von Neumann was known to pick up other people's problems and to run away with them by bringing them to quick solutions. He "believed the only way science could progress was by scholars picking up each other's work and improving it."[90]

For the Institute for Advanced Study, von Neumann became a great success story. On the institute's sixtieth anniversary, three outstanding achievements were singled out. One was the mathematician Kurt Gödel's work on the continuum problem; another was C. N. Yang and T.-D. Lee's discovery of parity violation, for which they received the Nobel Prize in Physics for 1957; and the third was von Neumann's activities. From the point of view of von Neumann's publications, his initial years at the institute were his second most productive period. In Germany, he published a paper almost every month. In the period 1933–1942 he published thirty-six papers, and during the remaining years of his life, another thirty-nine.[91] As the years went by, the time he devoted to his other activities kept increasing.

John von Neumann
(drawing by István
Orosz).

Edward Teller

Teller's first stop on his way from Germany to America was Copenhagen, in 1933–1934, on a Rockefeller fellowship.[92] Niels Bohr's international group was a good medium for transition and Teller was now with some scientists he had come across in Germany. The Rockefeller Foundation was Teller's authority figure now and his relationship to it showed how Teller related to authority. The foundation did not encourage scientists to marry while on its fellowships, so Teller postponed his marriage. When James Franck heard of this he scolded the foundation, and it agreed not to be an obstacle. However, Teller was supposed to write a letter requesting permission to marry. He did so, but he also wanted Bohr's approval, who, as Teller's host, was yet another authority figure. Teller spent three weeks chasing Bohr before finally cornering him and receiving his approval. Only then did he post the letter to the foundation. This episode might be interpreted as another example of Teller's perseverance and stubbornness, but it might also be seen as a sign of his concern for winning the goodwill of the powers that be.

The stay in Copenhagen signified important changes in Teller's life. He arrived there single, but left married; he arrived feeling solidly versed in quantum mechanics but was unsure when he left that he would ever become an expert in this field. Niels Bohr had an ambiguous impact on Teller. Bohr loved paradoxes, and while Teller understood his paradoxes, he did not understand Bohr. He understood Heisenberg and could imagine himself in his place, but never in Bohr's place. He became acquainted with Bohr as a physicist but they never met as human beings.

Teller was rather apolitical during these years. Politics gradually caught up with him, and being forced out of Germany played a role in his awakening. What he was leaving behind in Germany was his second home and perhaps the most carefree and wonderful period of his life. He had two offers to come to England, but the appointment he accepted turned out to be transitory.[93] There were invitations from the United States, and he opted for the one from George Washington University in Washington, DC. It was initiated by George Gamow, whom he had first met in 1930 in Copenhagen. Gamow was Landau's friend, but the two Russians were also each other's opposites. Landau was satirical and reserved and often expressed deep concern about politics; Gamow was jovial and impetuous and did not much discuss politics.[94]

Gamow liberally dispersed his ideas and he was magnanimous with assigning credit. He was a vivacious personality, he lived for physics, but even physics was a big joke for him; however, he took jokes very seriously. Gamow did early and important work in nuclear physics. His most remarkable scientific contribution—the Big Bang explanation of the origin of the universe, came after World War II. Later he pioneered ideas in connection with the genetic code in molecular biology. Teller developed a close friendship with Gamow; they traveled in Denmark on Gamow's motorcycle in 1931.[95] Then Gamow returned to the Soviet Union and Teller to Göttingen. Gamow describes his and his wife's subsequent escape from the Soviet Union in his unfinished autobiography.[96] Eventually, he moved to George Washington University, where he became instrumental in organizing a full professor's job for Teller. They jointly ran an annual conference on theoretical physics, which was meant to boost physics at George Washington University. Gamow and Teller were both at one time visiting professors at Berkeley, where Gamow "did not notice that Teller associated preferentially either with more liberal or more conservative elements of the faculty."[97]

There is an interesting comparison between Gamow and Teller, which throws more light on their interactions at George Washington University. Merle Tuve wrote a letter in response to an inquiry from the University of Chicago about whether to invite Teller to be a professor there. Tuve noted that "If you want a genius for your staff, don't get Teller, get Gamow. . . . Teller is something much better. He helps everybody. He works on everybody's problem. He never gets into controversies or has trouble with anyone. He is by far your best choice."[98] Tuve's letter referred to Teller's happiest period in the United States, which was in great contrast to his standing in the community of physicists in the Cold War era. Clearly, his life took a bizarre turn away from projecting the character described in Tuve's letter.

The Tellers moved to Washington in 1935. An official of the Rockefeller Foundation gave him this advice: "You are Jewish. One terrible thing about Jews is that they have only Jewish friends. Don't do that." In his *Memoirs*, Teller took stock of his friends in the United States. He did not consciously take the advice of the Rockefeller official in choosing his friends, but he was nonetheless conscious of who was and who was not Jewish among his friends: his non-Jewish friends included George Gamow, Merle Tuve, Luis Alvarez, and several of his former students at George Washington University.[99] Maria Mayer had one Jewish grandfather, and her husband, Joe Mayer, was not Jewish. All his Hungarian friends were Jewish, and so were Bethe, Bloch, and Weisskopf. For someone who did not care about the origin of his friends, he knew their backgrounds remarkably accurately.

In order to sail to America, the Tellers applied for a visa and there were some problems with quotas. But a former *Minta* pupil, the famous economist Thomas Balogh, helped them. At George Washington University, Teller had a light teaching load, lecturing on quantum mechanics three times a week to a small group of adult students. These were scientists who wanted to learn about the new physics. They included another Hungarian, Stephen Brunauer of the Brunauer–Emmett–Teller, or B.E.T., equation. Teller's main occupation was to test the fantastic ideas that Gamow came up with daily.[100] Most of them were nonsense, but Gamow did not mind being told so. On the rare occasions when Teller did not find fault with one of Gamow's ideas, they wrote a joint paper. They got along very well and with their wives they went together to Florida. There Gamow's vocal anti-Semitism came to the surface: although he was a friend of both Teller and Landau, he blamed the Jews for Communism in Russia and was disturbed by the wealthy Jews in Miami.

Gamow prompted Teller to make forays into nuclear physics, but molecular structure and spectroscopy still dominated Teller's research, for which he earned the nickname molecule inspector. One of his most curious contributions was in connection with Linus Pauling's theory of resonance of molecular structures.[101] The problem started in the late nineteenth century when August Kekulé suggested a structural formula for the benzene molecule of a six-member ring with alternating single and double carbon–carbon bonds. However, there may be two ways of describing such a structure—that is, there are two possible structures, equivalent but unable to exist separately. Pauling's resonance theory overcomes this difficulty, but it is more a convenient model than a reflection of physical reality. It uses the two structures, representing two extreme cases, with the real structure emerging from resonance between the two extremes. Teller provided a plausible interpretation of Pauling's theory on the basis of spectroscopic evidence. Such a confluence of scientific interest and support should have brought the two scientists together; alas, by then (in the 1950s) their political differences had proved stronger than the overlap in their scientific interests, and no direct scientific interaction developed between them.

In view of Pauling's leftist politics, it was an ironic twist that there should be, in the early 1950s, a big scandal about his theory in the Soviet Union. Some backward but politically ambitious chemists saw more in Pauling's theory than a convenient model and ascribed it to foreign bourgeois ideology. It soon became a political issue.[102] Some excellent chemists lost their jobs as a consequence (but not their lives), which was sometimes the tragic result of similar "ideological struggles" in biology. Physics was spared such a fate due to the nuclear weapons program, by then underway in the Soviet Union.

The Tellers had extensive interactions with friends and colleagues in the United States in the 1930s. Their car was a great help in this and they both learned to drive. They visited the Bethes, Hans and Rose, in Ithaca, New York, where Bethe was a physics professor at Cornell University. Teller met Fermi again, who came to a conference at Stanford University; Fermi and his family would later immigrate to the United States. The Tellers and the Bethes traveled together in the Tellers' car to Stanford and back to the East after the meeting. It was a close friendship. In addition to Fermi, Teller met with Robert Oppenheimer, who invited him to give a seminar at Berkeley, and with Ernest Lawrence, who took him for a motorboat excursion. The Tellers introduced Fermi to von Kármán in Los Angeles. Mici's parents had known von Kármán back in Budapest, and Fermi was much impressed by the famous Hungarian's Hollywood acquaintances. This was in 1937.[103]

There is no doubt that Teller was not only part of a large and growing network of friends and colleagues but that this network included the top layer of his profession. At the end of March 1939, while Niels Bohr was visiting Princeton, there was a meeting in Bohr's Princeton office.[104] Bohr, Szilard, Teller, Wigner, Weisskopf, and John A. Wheeler were present.[105] By then, nuclear fission had been discovered, and the consequences, further work, and the need for secrecy were discussed. Those with experience of German physics argued for secrecy, except for Bohr, who argued against it. Bohr thought that separating uranium-235 (i.e., the fissionable isotope of uranium) from the rest was impractical. He argued that the whole country would have to be turned into a giant factory to produce enough uranium-235 for the bomb. At that point it sounded a convincing argument against considering nuclear weapons, but in a few years' time such a barrier would not hinder the success of the Manhattan Project. As far as secrecy was concerned, the participants understood that if they decided on secrecy others would have to be convinced as well. Teller was delegated to ask Fermi to join in their efforts.[106]

This development showed that Teller was gradually becoming involved in science that affected world politics, if not yet in world politics itself. It was at that time that Heisenberg came for a visit and Teller asked him why he did not stay in the United States, given the conditions in Nazi Germany. Heisenberg's response should have sobered Teller, if not then, at least later. Heisenberg said, "Even if my brother steals a silver spoon, he is still my brother." How much more did that brother do than steal a silver spoon! Teller could not at that time (or any time after the war, either) "find a way to present my argument that would have fit our relationship" to Heisenberg.[107] This was uncharacteristic for Teller because he was usually ready with a forceful argument when he needed one.

At this stage it was not yet clear whether Teller's future would be connected to powerful weapons or whether he would go on with his ideal life as a university professor. Then a speech was announced, to be delivered by President Roosevelt in May 1940 to the Pan-American Congress. Teller decided to attend.[108] It became a turning point in his attitude towards defense matters. Roosevelt spoke about human rights, the blessings of democracy, and the progress made by science: "I believe that . . . you and I, if in the long run it be necessary, will act together to protect and defend by every means at our command, our science, our culture, our American freedom and our civilization." Teller felt as if the president was speaking directly to him. Among the thousands of scientists who heard the speech he might have been the only one thinking of the atomic bomb when the president said that they should be "using every knowledge, every science we possess."[109] From then on, he felt that his path had been charted.

CHAPTER FOUR

"To Protect and Defend": World War II

We five were survivors of a shipwreck and found a lifeboat. Of
course, we were eager to protect it against all dangers.
  Edward Teller

The Martians were alert to the dangers of Nazism and were determined to defend
the Free World from it. When they experienced the ineptness of American politics
and the unconcern of their own colleagues, they threw themselves into activities
that were aimed at making America better prepared for the coming war. Following
Einstein's famous letter (see p. 99), there was a presidential initiative for an atomic
bomb project, but unfavorable circumstances hindered an efficient start. Although
Einstein understood the physical possibility of liberating atomic energy and its military implications, the politicians and the military understandably regarded the fantastic promise by a few foreign scientists with reservations, to say the least. Another
ingredient of the slowness may have been that President Roosevelt was making war
preparations with utmost caution. Although he was an anti-Fascist and recognized
the inevitability of America's participation in the coming war, there was considerable opposition in America to any involvement in yet another "foreign conflict." It
would be futile to speculate about other road maps that Szilard and his colleagues
might have followed in a more efficient way. They did what they thought was best.

In the war, von Kármán became involved with the U.S. Army Air Corps (there was no separate air force until after World War II) and the rest of the Martians became active members of the atomic bomb project, with von Neumann participating in several other projects as well. Although the initiators of the atomic bomb project were foreign-born scientists, they seldom appeared among the people put in charge of its programs. Their activities were at times viewed with suspicion. At one point, a company that was deeply involved with the engineering tasks of the atomic bomb project asked A. H. Compton "about the trustworthiness of recommendations made by recently arrived émigrés." Rather than simply assuring the company people of the competence of the scientists involved, Compton repeated the calculations and verified their results before responding to the inquiry.[1] Szilard held strong views in connection with discrimination against foreign-born scientists: "If authority is not given to the best men in the field"—because, say, they are foreign-born—"there does not seem to be any compelling reason to give it to the second-best man and one may give it to the third- or fourth- or fifth-best men." The judgment will then be made "on purely subjective grounds."[2] The Martians contributed decisively to the war efforts, regardless of whether they had administrative positions or not. They made a difference, and they emerged from the war years as transformed scientists and personalities.

Theodore von Kármán

The activities of von Kármán that were related to military applications of science did not generate direct public interest; he did not invite controversy among his colleagues, and he was never a subject of public controversy. Enormous as von Kármán's projects were, they did not measure up to the scale of the Manhattan Project or that of the hydrogen bomb. When von Kármán did not get what he wanted he remained quiet and applied himself to other tasks, whereas both Teller and Szilard would only intensify their efforts in such a situation. Von Kármán was no less effective than the others, though, because in most cases those who had turned down his suggestions eventually came around. When he felt discouraged, he remembered the old axiom, "Good judgment comes from experience, but experience comes from bad judgment."[3] Von Kármán consistently refused to voice his political opinion in military matters; he never played for the galleries; and he did not testify before congressional committees. Both Szilard and Teller were very determined and impatient; they were politically motivated and they voiced their political opinions. However, von Kármán's impact on defense should not be underestimated. The co-author of his memoirs noted that no other scientist in the twentieth century "wielded as much intellectual power over a military department as von Kármán did over the U.S. Air Force in the years just before, during and after World War II."[4]

Von Kármán's first connection with the American air force occurred as early as 1926, when, on his first visit to the United States, he lectured to the National Advisory Committee for Aeronautics and the air force. From 1932, when he was at the California Institute of Technology (Caltech), he started attracting graduate students from the Navy, some of whom later became generals in the air force. He was always ready to embrace innovations, introducing scientific meteorology into the military, for example, via a course at Caltech to which the Army Air Corps sent officers.[5] Not only the United States military but those of other countries, too, made use of von Kármán's expertise at various times during his career. It started with Germany and Austria–Hungary, and continued later with Japan, China, and Italy.

In the 1930s, Italy had the lead in some military uses of aviation, and there were even discussions about rockets and hints about the possibility of using atomic energy for interplanetary spaceship propulsion. The Italians had a modern wind tunnel for supersonic experiments, designed by a Swiss scientist who was then a consultant to the Italian Air Force.[6] In 1935, von Kármán went to Washington, DC, to alert the U.S. government to the progress of high-speed flight (the topic of the Volta Congress he had attended) and what it might mean to the development of aviation. He mentioned the high-speed Italian Air Force squadron, which was unique at that point, and the research developments in Germany, Italy, and Switzerland. He came away from these meetings with the impression that the U.S. military did not appreciate the importance of high-speed flying.[7]

In the meantime the Germans were building the first Heinkel turbojets, in 1935 and 1936, with the full support of the Air Ministry, and the first successful flights were in 1939. The Germans had long-range plans and vision, and they took full advantage of the coming jet power in their aerodynamic designs. In 1937, after another trip to Europe, von Kármán made one more unsuccessful attempt to convince the American administration to build a modern supersonic wind tunnel. The situation changed when General H. H. (Hap) Arnold and von Kármán got together. They first met in 1936 at Caltech, but at that time Arnold was not in a position to make use of von Kármán's abilities and aspirations. Their decisive meeting took place in 1938; Arnold had just been appointed chief of the Army Air Corps, and they discussed rockets as a means of assisting bomber take-off. Von Kármán had a great supporter in General Arnold, and a fruitful and lasting association developed between the scientist and the U.S. Air Corps. This is how von Kármán characterized General Arnold: "he was the greatest example of the U.S. military man—a combination of complete logic, mingled with a farsightedness and superb dedication." Arnold was instrumental in bringing jets to the arsenal of the U.S. Army. Shortly before America entered the war, the general saw turbojets fly in England, in 1941. He immediately ordered jets built in the United States and his order marked the beginning of U.S. activity in jet propulsion. The supersonic wind tunnel that von Kármán had dreamed about and had argued for was finally built in 1944.[8]

Arnold believed that the Army Air Corps could not reach the top in aviation and stay there without doing experimental work to advance the art. He wanted to rely fully on von Kármán's advice, and the advice was eagerly delivered. Von Kármán wanted a wind tunnel large enough to contain a full-scale airplane engine installation that should be capable of generating winds of at least 400 miles per hour. Arnold immediately authorized its construction, a 20-foot wide and 40,000-horse power wind tunnel at Wright Field in Ohio. By then, some rivalry had developed between the National Advisory Committee for Aeronautics (NACA) and the Army Air Corps, which, ironically, also facilitated support for von Kármán's experiments. His industrial relationships continued, and they were inseparable from military applications. Thus, von Kármán helped design what was the largest American industrial high-speed wind tunnel at the time, which was instrumental in developing such fast bombers as the B-47, B-52, and, later, the KC-135 and KC-707. Boeing kept receiving huge orders for the bombers.[9]

The serious interest of the U.S. military in supersonic flight began in early 1943: it wanted an airplane that could fly at 1,000 miles an hour. Von Kármán had been involved with such projects since the turn of the century. Finally, theory and technology were together and the practical need also appeared. The major decision to go ahead with it occurred only after the war, in 1946. The concept of supersonic flight made von Kármán consider the almost philosophical question of ever-increasing speeds. Such things need be considered from the point of view of both cost *and* benefit. He posed the question: Was it justified to seek higher and higher speeds from a human point of view? His answer was an enthusiastic yes, "High speed has its uses. It brings people closer together and in time that may work its own magic." However, he added a personal note that he preferred a slower pace: "I like nothing better than to think of myself riding through the Paris boulevards as my parents did in old Budapest—in a fiacre with a coachman and two horses."[10]

When von Kármán became a member of the Advisory Committee of the Army Bureau of Ordnance, he suggested building a supersonic wind tunnel and made several formal proposals to this effect, starting in May 1939. His proposal had important supporters in army research organizations as well as in the special committee of the National Academy of Sciences advising the Bureau of Ordnance. However, higher authorities in the army turned his proposal down. In 1942, General G. M. Barnes, chief of Ordnance Research and Engineering, visited England and learned that the British were building a supersonic tunnel to study guided-missile behavior. Barnes immediately ordered that such a tunnel be hastily built in the United States. As von Kármán remarked, this was the military method, first no, then maybe, and finally yes, but quickly.[11] Of course, by then the United States had entered the war. This was a good example of von Kármán doing his best to push his projects, but then waiting for further developments if and when he did not get through.

Paying attention to detail and learning from it was another von Kármán trademark. The following story illustrates that he knew the importance of naming heretofore unknown phenomena when they are finally recognized.[12] At some point von Kármán and his co-workers noticed some erratic behavior by bombs when they went through the speed of sound. There was, however, no term to describe the region of airflow in which the phenomenon occurred. Von Kármán and his friend, Hugh Dryden, by then the director of NACA, decided to invent one. They wanted something in between subsonic and supersonic to indicate that the body travels across the speed of sound and back. The word trans-sonic seemed appropriate and the correct spelling was with two s's. However, von Kármán wanted it with one s ("transonic"), and when Dryden argued that logic required two s's, von Kármán referred to Goethe, saying that some logic is desirable, but to be always logical is horrible.[13]

Openness and supporting innovation were characteristic of Theodore von Kármán. For instance, in 1936 a Caltech graduate student, Frank J. Malina, and two of his colleagues, a chemist and an engineer, wanted to start a rocket program at Caltech.[14] They had no support and no backing, but von Kármán tried to help them. The three men knew of von Kármán's perceptiveness for innovation; the professor himself dreamed about space exploration. However, at that time rockets were not considered to be promising business and it was advisable even to avoid using the word rocket lest their aspirations be ridiculed. There is another intriguing question here, of semantics. Von Kármán did not care for the word Astronautics because it refers to travel between the stars. Cosmonautics is better because it refers to travel in the cosmos and the cosmos is that part of the universe bounded by one star, our sun. But as the Soviets had taken over that word the Americans stuck to Astronautics, and astronauts versus the Soviet cosmonauts.[15]

Malina and his colleagues started with modest aims and financed their project themselves with their own little savings. It did not occur even to von Kármán at that time that the military might be interested.[16] This situation changed abruptly in May 1938 when General Arnold visited Caltech and was fascinated by the rocket work; he realized its potential for the military. The first contract was for $1000 and the next for $10,000. By the time von Kármán was working on the manuscript of *The Wind and Beyond*, it was more than five billion dollars a year. He was actively involved in the program, and in particular in rocket propulsion, from 1939. In World War II, they applied their rocket technique to assisting the takeoff of heavy airplanes, and were looking for the appropriate propellant to provide a controlled thrust.

Initially, von Kármán did not work directly for the military. His participation was through the National Academy of Sciences (NAS), which, by its charter, is obliged to advise the American government on issues they are approached about. For national defense, NAS was asked to give advice on the effects of blasts on structures like hangars and other buildings. In its turn, NAS invited von Kármán to a meeting in its headquarters in Washington, and asked him to consider the problem. This time von Kármán traveled by train, and on his way back, while he was being entertained by people in the club car, suddenly an idea struck him. He retired to his compartment and, oblivious to his surroundings, worked out the problem. Typically, no noise or other conditions distracted him and he could have missed his station had it not been so far away. He did not distinguish between a train compartment, his Caltech office, and his home where work was concerned. Many of the decisive staff meetings took place in his home. This particular example showed yet another characteristic feature of his method of working. The problem of blast had been attacked by others, assuming elasticity. However, von Kármán introduced the possibility of a considerable inelastic component in the consequences of the blast. This came to him when remembering his work on his doctoral thesis. The ability to connect seemingly widely separated fields characterized his approach.[17]

He often had to face the dilemma of being forced to choose between practice and theory. He considered it to be another "victory for engineering science" when he decided once again "to follow the thin song of mathematics and not the heavy voice of experience." However, he was not an ordinary engineer and the problems he faced were not the usual engineering problems. This is why experience had limited value for him. He notes that others, at the same time or even earlier, had worked out the same problem and had come to the same solution, for example, in Germany or in Russia.[18] Certain solutions became ripe at about the same time in different places and, in this case characteristic of wartime, the militaries faced similar problems in different countries.

Jet-Assisted Takeoff (JATO) could considerably shorten the runway needed for heavy bombers. The technology had high military value because it made possible the use of those bombers in makeshift airports during frontline advances. However, the rockets had to use appropriate fuels and this required a lot of experimentation. This and numerous other projects involved scientists and engineers from many different disciplines, including chemists and materials scientists, and von Kármán appeared to be at ease working with representatives of so many fields. He was always ready to work out the mathematical equations for a problem, but did not hesitate to call in experts to help him solve complex problems. He also knew that "making records and being first are not enough from a long-range point of view."[19]

The JATO project also took von Kármán into the business world. At Malina's suggestion, six members of their group set up a company to sell JATO units to the armed services. Each of them contributed $200, raising a total of $1,200. They incorporated the company in March 1942 as the Aerojet General Corporation. By the time von Kármán was writing about it, its annual business was seven hundred million dollars, with a staff of nearly 34,000 people and a key role in the defense of the United States. In the meantime, the Jet Propulsion Laboratory had also come into existence.[20] Von Kármán thought that if the United States had given their early work in rockets more support, they would have had a better V-2 than the Germans and a satellite in space ahead of the Soviets. As early as 1945, Malina and Summerfield described a rocket that actually went into operation in 1958 when

America's first satellite, Explorer I, was launched. But the United States did not feel a need for long-range rockets at the time.

In the spring of 1944 there was a decisive moment in von Kármán's life, and for the development of the American Air Force.[21] General Arnold had a secret meeting with him on the general's way to the Quebec meeting between Roosevelt and Churchill. The soldier and the scientist met at La Guardia Airport in New York City. By then, the forward-looking general was no longer interested in World War II. He wanted to talk about the post-war period and about the future of air power and aerial warfare. He wanted to know everything about the significance of new devices, jet propulsion, rockets, radar, and other electronic devices. He invited von Kármán to the Pentagon to set up what became the Scientific Advisory Group (SAG; and later the Scientific Advisory Board [SAB]) to chart a blueprint for air research for the next fifty years. He was convinced that America's survival depended on superiority in the air. This approach was vastly different from American unpreparedness before World War II.

As on many other occasions, von Kármán took up the challenge, and again, in his characteristic way, he collected the people who had been around him for many years. There was a strong and mutual loyalty between him and his men. He never fired anybody; even when he wanted to get rid of a co-worker or student, he made sure he had found a position for the man before they parted. In this way he never made an enemy. He gathered people from many different places, including future physics Nobel laureates E. M. Purcell and Norman Ramsey, future Caltech president Lee DuBridge, and others.[22]

Early on von Kármán went to see General Leslie Groves, then military commander of the Manhattan Project, and asked him to designate someone to give the air force advice about nuclear bombs. The air force wanted to be prepared to carry and deliver the atomic bombs of the future. They also thought about airplanes operated by nuclear fuel. Groves was rude to von Kármán, and the general informed the Pentagon that if they wanted information from him, they should send somebody whose English he understood. This was especially unfair from Groves, who had had experience with strange accents at Los Alamos and elsewhere in the Manhattan Project. It was jealousy: Groves was an army man, and this was not the first time, nor the last, that von Kármán experienced inter-service rivalry. He relates an anecdote whose existence points to the general's unpopularity among scientists: "General Groves and Robert Oppenheimer are in an atomic shelter watching the first A-bomb explosion. 'What did you see?' a reporter asked. 'I saw the end of the world,' Oppenheimer replied. 'And I saw a third star,' said the two-star General." For the initial interactions between the nuclear project and the air force, eventually Norman Ramsey became the liaison man. When the group von Kármán had gathered for the advisory work at the Pentagon met for the first time in 1944, Arnold told them that he envisioned a man-less air force. Whereas the air force used to be built around pilots, he said, the future air force was to be built around scientists.[23]

It is impossible to overestimate von Kármán's contribution to the Allied victory in World War II; yet it is also apparent that his contributions were in response to challenges set up by people like General Arnold. His part was not the initiation of new projects, although he was instrumental in initiating new solutions and new approaches when the challenge arose.

Von Kármán was the only Martian who gained direct experience with the horrors of World War II. In the final months of the war he was leading a group of experts in the wake of the American troops in Germany. One of the places they visited was Nordhausen in the Harz Mountains, some fifty miles south of Braunschweig, where work on V-2 rockets and production of Junkers engines for Messerschmitt jet fighters was going on, all with slave labor.[24] The Nazis executed their prisoners by controlled starvation: the prisoners worked in factories, and the Nazis determined how long each prisoner should be allowed to live. Their rations were then gradually reduced in accordance with this death sentence, so that they would die of hunger at the end of the time allocated to them.

Leo Szilard

Szilard made many attempts to involve people and companies in developing the commercial potentials of the nuclear chain reaction without revealing the details of his ideas. Neither financiers nor companies trusted his promise of cheap energy, since they had no way of knowing if there was any solid foundation to his claims. In desperation and disappointment, Szilard resigned his claim to the patent on the nuclear chain reaction, but when the news about the discovery of nuclear fission reached him, he withdrew his withdrawal. The British Admiralty appeared patient and understanding.[25]

One of the people who showed a special affinity for Szilard and who developed a long-standing friendship with him in spite of their later political differences was Lewis L. Strauss.[26] Strauss, who had broad interests, started as a volunteer for Herbert Hoover, as his personal secretary, and later worked on behalf of the disadvantaged and refugees. He built up his wealth by working in the financial world. In World War II, Strauss served in the U.S. Navy. After the war he was involved in national politics and in particular in nuclear matters, rising to become commissioner of the Atomic Energy Commission, then chairman, when von Neumann was one of the commissioners. Strauss made many friends and many enemies during his career.

Szilard and Strauss first met in 1937 when Szilard and another physicist refugee were looking for support for an experiment.[27] Strauss helped them, both financially and through his contacts with many influential people. Szilard was impressed by Strauss's ability to take action and he kept Strauss informed about various developments in nuclear science over the years. The next time their interests intersected was after the discovery of nuclear fission.

This scientific breakthrough was a pivotal point in Szilard's life and in his apprehensions of world events. It also strengthened his fears about Germany's potential for the atomic bomb. Of course, nuclear fission did not yet mean nuclear chain reaction. For that, the number of neutrons produced had to be greater than the number used for bombarding the uranium atoms. The French soon showed that this was indeed the case, but it became clear that only the rare uranium-235 isotope was fissionable, and thus suitable for the chain reaction. Szilard, in a letter to Strauss dated January 25, 1939, stated that such a chain reaction "might lead to a large-scale production of energy and radioactive elements, unfortunately also perhaps to atomic bombs."[28] Other players in nuclear physics did not have Szilard's foresight in this matter, not even the great Niels Bohr.

A lucky breakthrough for Szilard and the nuclear story was Fermi's coming to Columbia University. Joint experiments soon started, involving Fermi, his assistant Herbert Anderson, and Szilard.[29] Isidor I. Rabi, who was to become one of the world's most revered physicists and mentor to future Nobel laureates, was also at Columbia. Szilard was just as tactless with him as with everybody else, instructing him in which experiments to do and so on. Rabi suggested to Szilard that he should be doing his own experiments. When Szilard prodded him too much for new experiments, Rabi asked him to leave and take his many ideas with him.

Money was needed for the experiments at Columbia University that would confirm the possibilities of the nuclear chain reaction. The first private money appeared when Szilard borrowed $2,000 from Benjamin Liebowitz in the spring of 1939. At the end of the same year, Szilard asked Liebowitz to write the loan off as a bad debt. In spite of many disappointments, Szilard seems to have always found the right person to ask for help. Incidentally, years later Szilard repaid his debt to Liebowitz.[30] But looking back to 1939–1940, it is difficult to imagine the general atmosphere in which Szilard was operating as the first and, for a while, only person in the world who had envisioned the nuclear chain reaction.

Fortunately, Szilard did not seem to mind being in a minority of even one; rather, he took pride in belonging to "the sensitive minority among men of science."[31] He constructed an experiment at Columbia University to confirm the recent French finding about the extra neutrons being produced during the fission of uranium. When they found them, Szilard hastened to inform Teller on the phone with a simple Hungarian sentence, "I have found the neutrons."[32]

Szilard took practical steps, not only in the laboratory, but outside as well, to facilitate the work. He established the Association for Scientific Collaboration (ASC), mainly as a recipient of money for people who wanted to provide financial assistance for the nuclear experiments. Teller and Wigner joined immediately. Szilard was concerned with the uranium-235 separation and prepared a detailed memorandum about it, showing once again that he was not just daydreaming about the utilization of the chain reaction, but also working on its realization. He was trying to find the best moderator for the chain reaction. Ordinary water was not suitable because its hydrogen atoms captured the neutrons. Graphite was a possibility, and so was heavy water. However, Szilard was unable to get more funding. The Anderson–Fermi–Szilard team carried out the last experiment with uranium and water at Columbia University in late spring 1939, and then everything stopped.

Although few shared his feeling of urgency, Szilard knew that they had to hurry. The Czech uranium ores came under the rule of Nazi Germany in March 1939 and the Germans banned the export of uranium. Germany was the first country where the military took steps to investigate possible utilization of nuclear physics. Nothing was going on in the United States as it was only the Hungarian group that believed that the danger of war was imminent and that nuclear weapons might play a role in it. They also believed in secrecy lest Germany benefit from their research. On the other hand, and this is a recurring theme, being secretive did not help them in their efforts to convince others about the need for immediate action. Fermi was cooperative, declaring that if the others adhered to secrecy, so would he, but the French were less amenable, and when they broke the supposed code of self-restraint, the Americans had no reason not to publish their findings, too.

There was no well-established way of alerting the government other than by soliciting minuscule support from low-ranking military officials. When on one occasion Szilard, Wigner, and Fermi were discussing the potentials of the nuclear chain reaction for military purposes, Wigner suggested informing the American government.[33] Fermi was going to be in Washington, and it was arranged that a committee of naval representatives would receive him. However, they did not find Fermi and his story credible.

The international situation continued to deteriorate. Szilard, Wigner, and a few others knew that the expected German invasion of Belgium would have serious consequences in nuclear matters, in view of the vast uranium ores in the Belgian Congo. Their first thought was to alert the Belgian government about the possible strategic importance of the uranium ores. They remembered that Einstein had good connections with the Royal Family of Belgium, and he might be willing to write to them directly. Then they began to wonder if it would be proper to contact a foreign government without the approval of the State Department. This was an important question for the law-abiding Hungarians. Gradually the idea crystallized that Einstein should send a letter to the American president.

On July 12, 1939, Szilard and Wigner drove to Peconic, Long Island, where Einstein was vacationing. They explained to him the physics and the dangers of the nuclear chain reaction following uranium fission in a critical mass of uranium sufficient to be utilized for an atomic bomb. Einstein understood everything in no time at all and expressed his amazement: "I haven't thought of that at all."[34] Until then Einstein had not believed that nuclear energy would be utilized in his time, although all the physics involved was based on the famous equation $E = mc^2$, which he had formulated in 1905. In this equation, E is the energy, m is the mass, and the constant c is the speed of light. This equation established the equivalence between mass and energy, and for the first time gave a hint of the enormous energy locked inside matter. With the nuclear chain reaction, the possibility had arisen of liberating this energy, for good or evil.

Szilard and Wigner's story must have greatly impressed Einstein because it showed the power of science in practical terms. He also saw that, for the first time, energy could originate from a source other than the sun. The political implications were equally dramatic, and obvious, and the conclusion reached by Szilard must also have been reached by the physicists in Germany. This was enough to make Einstein abandon his pacifism. With nuclear weapons in their possession, the Germans would conquer and enslave the world. Einstein was a lucky choice for contacting the president: he was the physicist who, although not involved directly in nuclear physics, was primarily responsible for the development of modern physics. Einstein was a fierce anti-Nazi, he commanded a tremendous respect, and he was well known by millions. Wigner later remembered though that "the idea to approach Einstein and altogether to approach the government originally went against Szilard" because he did not want the project become bureaucratized.[35] Later critics charged the Hungarian physicists with naiveté about how democracy works, in view of the very slow beginning of the atomic bomb project.[36] Szilard simply noted that "we were all green. We did not know our way around in America."[37]

Having agreed on the principles, they decided on a second meeting, at which a letter to the President of the United States would be signed by Einstein. They met on August 2, again on Long Island. This time Wigner was away and Teller drove Szilard to see Einstein (Szilard could not drive). Einstein's letter has become a famous historical document. It is quoted as document 55 in *Leo Szilard: His Version of the Facts*.[38]

Albert Einstein
Old Grove Rd.
Nassau Point
Peconic, Long Island
August 2nd, 1939

F. D. Roosevelt
President of the United States
White House
Washington, D.C.

Sir:
Some recent work by E. Fermi and L. Szilard, which has been communicated to me in manuscript, leads me to expect that the element uranium may be turned into a new and important source

of energy in the immediate future. Certain aspects of the situation which has arisen seem to call for watchfulness and, if necessary, quick action on the part of the Administration. I believe therefore that it is my duty to bring to your attention the following facts and recommendations:

In the course of the last four months it has been made probable —through the work of Joliot in France as well as Fermi and Szilard in America—that it may become possible to set up a nuclear chain reaction in a large mass of uranium by which vast amounts of power and large quantities of new radium-like elements would be generated. Now it appears almost certain that this could be achieved in the immediate future.

This new phenomenon would also lead to the construction of bombs, and it is conceivable—though much less certain—that extremely powerful bombs of a new type may thus be constructed. A single bomb of this type, carried by boat and exploded in a port, might very well destroy the whole port together with some of the surrounding territory. However, such bombs might very well prove to be too heavy for transportation by air.

The United States has only very poor ores of uranium in moderate quantities. There is some good ore in Canada and the former Czechoslovakia, while the most important source of uranium is the Belgian Congo.

In view of this situation you may think it desirable to have some permanent contact maintained between the Administration and the group of physicists working on chain reactions in America. One possible way of achieving this might be for you to entrust with this task a person who has your confidence and who could perhaps serve in an inofficial capacity. His task might comprise the following:

a) to approach Government Departments, keep them informed of the further development, and put forward recommendations for Government action, giving particular attention to the problem of securing a supply of uranium ore for the United States,

b) to speed up the experimental work, which is at present being carried on within the limits of the budgets of University laboratories, by providing funds, if such funds be required, through his contacts with private persons who are willing to make contributions for this cause, and perhaps also by obtaining the co-operation of industrial laboratories which have the necessary equipment.

I understand that Germany has actually stopped the sale of uranium from the Czechoslovakian mines which she has taken

over. That she should have taken such early action might perhaps
be understood on the ground that the son of the German Under-
Secretary of State, von Weizsäcker, is attached to the Kaiser-
Wilhelm-Institut in Berlin where some of the American work on
uranium is now being repeated.

Yours very truly,
A. Einstein

Szilard added a technical memorandum to the Einstein letter, with details of how
to build the nuclear reactor and about its possible military and other uses. It
reflected current knowledge about building a reactor. The production of extra
neutrons was possible with neutrons, which had to be slowed down with a moderator. On August 15, Einstein's letter and Szilard's memorandum were given to
Alexander Sachs, a friend of the president, but it was not until October 11 and 12
that Sachs delivered them personally to Roosevelt.[39]

World War II started on September 1, 1939, but the United States remained
neutral for more than two years. Nonetheless, the U.S. Congress soon repealed
the arms embargo provision of the Neutrality Act, and this made it possible for
America to sell arms to belligerent countries.

Szilard's main concern now was to obtain tons of highly pure graphite, because even small impurities might absorb rather than only slow down the neutrons. The Germans had also tried to use graphite as a moderator, and their
experiments failed. They did not know that their graphite was impure, and they
had to resort to heavy water. The Americans, thanks to Szilard, went ahead and
used graphite. This was an example of Szilard's meticulous attention to the mi-
nutest detail, and it paid off. This may have been the decisive difference between
the German and American nuclear efforts.[40]

When Roosevelt finally saw Sachs and received the Einstein and Szilard documents, he created an Advisory Committee on Uranium and wrote to Einstein that
"I have found this letter of such import that I have convened a board . . . to thoroughly investigate the possibilities of your suggestion regarding the element uranium."[41] The head of the new committee was the director of the National Bureau
of Standards, Lyman J. Briggs. Szilard, Wigner, and Teller were also members.
The Briggs Committee held its first meeting on October 21, 1939. The most memorable event was the exchange between Colonel Keith Adamson of the army and
Eugene Wigner.[42]

Adamson told the scientists that it usually took two wars to develop a new
weapon. It was the morale of the civilian population rather than new weapons
that brought victory. Wigner did not miss his chance: he challenged the colonel
to distribute the military's funding among the civilian population to boost their
morale. The military representatives quickly agreed to grant the scientists' request
for $6,000 for uranium research. It was the first government money for the atomic
bomb project, but it took a while to reach the scientists. Looking back in 1973,

Wigner gave more credit then to Adamson than he did at the actual meeting, agreeing that "the morale of the civilian population is decisive."[43]

In the meantime, both Wigner's actual studies and Szilard's efforts continued. Szilard organized meetings, wrote memos, and encouraged physicists to refrain from publishing their results. He described the necessary experiments and stressed that even negative results would be valuable, that is, if it could be proved unequivocally that the sustained nuclear chain reaction was impossible. Fermi and Szilard designed the uranium–graphite reactor, which they called a pile.

Still nothing had happened by February 1940; the money had not been delivered, and Szilard turned again to Einstein.[44] They decided that Szilard would describe the uranium–graphite reactor for *Physical Review* and then ask the government if it wanted the paper withheld from publication. This was a role reversal of government and scientist, and could even be called blackmail, to force government action, but Szilard was angered by the administration's ineptness. He was also angered because Joliot in Paris had published a report about a chain reaction that stopped because neutron capture did not make it possible to sustain it. The French coined a name for it: convergent chain reaction. Accordingly, Szilard labeled his chain reaction divergent because it did not stop; the neutrons were not captured, only slowed down by the moderator. Szilard's first reference in his report was to Wells' *The World Set Free*, in which the writer envisioned what would later be called the atomic bomb.[45] Szilard asked the editors of *Physical Review* to withhold publication of this manuscript and another of his papers, subject to government clearance.

At the same time, there were reports from Germany about efforts to utilize nuclear power for military purposes. Szilard was alarmed, and he and Einstein decided that there should be a second letter to the president. It was dated March 7, 1940, and mentioned the German efforts and the Szilard papers that might appear in *Physical Review* unless the government took action. Szilard continued writing memoranda, and he raised the possibility of supplying the navy with nuclear fuel that might be especially useful in a war with Japan. This was twenty months before Pearl Harbor, again demonstrating Szilard's foresight. As a consequence of Einstein's second letter, the $6,000 was promptly delivered, the experiments started, and Fermi became very active in them. Szilard continued his crusade for secrecy. Fermi resisted, but Szilard raised the possibility of a publication about the importance of graphite purity, which might have set the Germans on the right track. Fermi also saw the importance of secrecy in this matter, and from that point secrecy was on. In 1954, in his testimony at the Oppenheimer hearing, Fermi spoke appreciatively about Szilard's leadership role in deciding on secrecy.[46]

In the spring of 1940, Louis A. Turner had the important idea that neutrons converted uranium-238 into the next element, plutonium-239, which did not exist in nature, but which was highly fissionable.[47] It was to be an important raw material for atomic bombs. Following this up, Szilard made another highly original suggestion for a new type of reactor, eventually called a breeder, in which fast neutrons from a radioactive core would bombard a surrounding uranium blanket, turning uranium-238 into plutonium-239.[48] Turner submitted his manuscript to *Physical Review* and asked if he should have it withheld. His finding had tremendous military value, but there was still no mechanism in place, apart from voluntary action, for deciding whether manuscripts should be withheld from publication. Lyman Briggs set up a new committee, the Advisory Committee on Nuclear Physics, with Szilard, Wigner, Teller, and Gregory Breit, the editor of *Physical Review*, among its members. Things started getting organized in the United States. A National Defense Research Committee (NDRC) was established under Vannevar Bush to direct scientific work for military use and censorship was finally introduced.

Ironically, as a result of the security measures which Szilard had advocated in such a forceful way, the military and government organization nearly barred Fermi and Szilard from working on atomic research. According to army intelligence reports, Fermi was "undoubtedly a Fascist" and Szilard was "very pro-German," and the conclusion about both was that "Employment of this person on secret work is not recommended." Szilard, however, seemed unstoppable. He was impatient because his mind was always racing ahead and sometimes he used his savings to buy supplies when an experiment would have been delayed by waiting for the official procurement. He became very good at finding the necessary materials. At one point he involved two co-workers, Feld and Marshall, and their report was signed by Feld, Marshall, and Szilard. This resulted in the joke that he had been promoted from *Generaldirektor*, the label he earned in Berlin, to *Feldmarschall* (Field Marshal) Szilard.[49]

It is almost unbelievable that between June 1939 and the spring of 1940 no work was going on in the United States in connection with the nuclear chain reaction and the uranium project in general. Szilard again mobilized Einstein, and again through Sachs they contacted the president. Roosevelt then suggested yet another meeting and Briggs called it; but when Sachs asked Briggs about inviting Szilard and Fermi to the meeting, Briggs said, "Well, you know, these matters are secret and we did not think that they should be included."[50] There are, of course, multiple ironies in this. First, it was Fermi and Szilard who had invented the secret matters. Second, they had pushed for secrecy to prevent the Germans from learning about their results. Third, they, and in particular Szilard, had pushed the American authorities to do something about their inventions. Eventually, however, the atomic bomb project became operational and there was the necessary secrecy without the exclusion of Szilard, Fermi, and the other "foreigners." There was one aspect of secrecy in particular that Szilard always found harmful, and that was compartmentalization. It meant that scientists working in different laboratories on different parts of the program were not supposed to know about each other's work. Szilard complained to Vannevar Bush that compartmentalization "crippled this work from its very beginning."[51] He compared the set-up to a secret society, but found it worse in that "unlike as in secret societies, we do not have a group in the center who knows everything." A sad consequence of keeping the scientists in the dark about the overall project is that "they no longer consider the overall success of this work as their responsibility."[52] Szilard estimated that the way their work was organized "led to a loss of from four to eight months."[53]

Things started moving faster, though, and the NDRC held a meeting on December 6, 1941, which decided to accelerate work on the nuclear chain reaction. The next day saw the attack on Pearl Harbor, and on December 8 the United States officially became a belligerent party in World War II. The Chicago physicist Arthur H. Compton became head of the atomic bomb project at this point. Even about him there were reports claiming a lack of reliability, but Vannevar Bush did not accept the verdicts of the security people; he directed them to continue their investigations and give Compton clearance. By the time he was finally cleared, the task of the Metallurgical Laboratory (see below) in Chicago had been completed.[54]

The final touch of the initial phase of the program took place in September 1942 when General Leslie R. Groves was put in charge of the whole Manhattan Project, more fully, Manhattan Engineering District.[55] Beginning in 1913, he had studied at the University of Washington, the Massachusetts Institute of Technology, and West Point, graduating in 1918. Groves later graduated from three more army schools and was involved with army construction projects, most notably of the Pentagon, before joining the Manhattan Project. He headed it almost from its inception through 1946, before it became part of the newly established Atomic Energy Commission in 1947. Initially he was made responsible for the construction works of the Manhattan Project, but eventually he was charged with the whole atomic bomb project.

The leader of the British team of physicists in the Manhattan Project, James Chadwick, expressed the view of many when he declared, "Without Groves, the scientists could have never built the bomb."[56] Once Arthur Compton asked Groves, "whether, if it came to a matter of choice, he would place the welfare of the United States above the welfare of mankind." They were both the sons of ministers and both were God-fearing. Groves answered that he "must put the welfare of man first," adding that the United States was the best agency "for the service of man." There was, however, an obvious difference in opinion and attitude between Groves and the scientists. Groves complained to Compton that the scientists "don't know how to take orders and give orders."[57] According to Teller, "between 1943 and 1945 General Groves could have won almost any unpopularity contest in which the scientific community at Los Alamos voted."[58]

Groves was a great believer in compartmentalizing the work in the Manhattan Project. His biographer, Stanley Goldberg, saw a certain symmetry—which was, rather, anti-symmetry—between the general and the scientists.[59] Both sides brought their own experiences to the project and both believed that the other hindered performance efficiency. Groves had had industrial experience, where people concentrated on their immediate tasks, whereas scientists have learned to benefit from the broadest possible interactions and from viewing the whole picture rather than just its details. There was no question, though, that in the Manhattan Project Groves had the upper hand over Szilard and the others.

Szilard's role in the atomic bomb project had in any case started diminishing, and by sticking his head out he was perhaps making himself even more of a target for being pushed aside by the military than he might otherwise have been. In Chicago, he was a visiting research associate, and later chief physicist at the university's Metallurgical Laboratory (Met Lab).

Just to avoid confusion, let us briefly enumerate the main components of the atomic bomb project. The project belonged to the NDRC, whose head was Vannevar Bush and vice head James B. Conant. When Bush created and became head of the Office of Scientific Research and Development (OSRD) to oversee the development of all new weapons, Conant was named head of the NDRC. Bush had done research for the navy during World War I, had taught at MIT, was president of the Carnegie Institution in Washington before World War II, and had acted in various capacities as scientific advisor to the American government. As head of the OSRD Bush reported to the president, and Conant reported to Bush.

The contiguous United States with the principal locations of the laboratories of the Manhattan Project.

The Manhattan Project would eventually have the following sites for its subprograms:[60]

Metallurgical Laboratory at the University of Chicago, whose task was to build the first uranium–graphite nuclear pile and to show that plutonium would work; Arthur H. Compton was in charge (and initially he was the head of the whole atomic bomb project). Two other university laboratories were also involved. One was at Columbia University, under Harold C. Urey, where scientists were working on a gaseous diffusion method of separating the uranium isotopes. The other was at the University of California at Berkeley, under Ernest O. Lawrence, where they were working on an electro-magnetic method of separating the uranium isotopes.

Clinton Engineer Works in Oak Ridge, Tennessee, where they separated U-235 from U-238.

Hanford Engineer Works in Hanford (close to Pasco), Washington, where scaled up uranium–graphite piles were built in which U-238 was bombarded by neutrons to produce plutonium-239.[61]

Los Alamos Laboratory in New Mexico, the secret site for building the first atomic bombs; Robert Oppenheimer was its scientific head; it collected brainpower from the Met Lab and elsewhere, uranium-235 from Oak Ridge, and plutonium from Hanford.

Sometimes Oppenheimer is assumed to have been the scientific head of the whole Manhattan Project. Of course, when it became operational, the work at Los Alamos was the overwhelming portion of the project, but he was never the overall scientific man in charge. Formally, it was James Conant, Vannevar's Bush's deputy at the OSRD, and in this capacity he was advisor to General Groves. At Conant's suggestion, there was yet another advisor, Richard C. Tolman of Caltech, and a vice chairman of the NDRC whose chair was Conant (and before him, Bush).[62] When Oppenheimer was recruiting his co-workers, he was given a letter signed by Groves and Conant that was supposed to boost his confidence and that of those he recruited.[63]

There can be little doubt that Bush and Conant and their organizations were instrumental in launching and carrying out the efficient operations of the American atomic bomb project. The United States was gradually but surely getting onto wartime footing. It was as if President Roosevelt were waiting for a signal to join the anti-Fascist coalition. That signal was Pearl Harbor. The American atomic bomb project was given an important stimulus when American officials learned about the British advances, primarily by two refugee scientists, Otto Frisch in Liverpool and Rudolf Peierls in Birmingham.[64] They had shown that the atomic bomb was a possibility. The British experience greatly enhanced the American resolve to assign manpower and resources to the development of nuclear weaponry. Szilard stressed the importance of the British contribution to the atomic bomb and did not think that due credit was given "to those responsible for the British contribution in its official histories."[65]

A British contingent of scientists was soon to join the Manhattan Project because it was foreseen that a similar plan could not be accomplished in wartime Britain. The contingent was led by Chadwick, the Nobel laureate discoverer of the neutron, and Mark Oliphant, both formerly close associates of Rutherford. Frisch and Peierls were among the members and so was Klaus Fuchs, another German refugee who would be unmasked as a Soviet atomic spy after the war. Fuchs was a non-Jewish German Communist who became a refugee because of his political affiliation.

Oliphant had been instrumental in supporting the initial British studies and bringing them to the attention of Churchill's government. In the early years of the war the British had a better system for giving the government scientific advice than the virtually nonexistent American system. Both the attack on Pearl Harbor and British involvement made a difference in American resolve to further the atomic bomb project. Whereas in an October 1941 decision President Roosevelt gave no explicit instructions about nuclear research and ordered Bush not to proceed, in January 1942 the president signed a letter formally approving the development of the atomic bomb.[66] Without Einstein's letter to the president and without the feasibility studies at Columbia University, the Manhattan Project could have not taken off in the way it did. In hindsight, though, various estimates have appeared that up to a year could have been gained had the American government and military recognized the possibility, the merits, and the importance of the atomic bomb when it was initially brought to their attention.[67] However unwise it might be to contemplate such scenarios, one cannot but shiver at the thought of what might have happened had the atomic bombs been ready for deployment against Germany by the summer of 1944.

As the organization for creating the atomic bomb was becoming established, Szilard started thinking about the postwar role of nuclear weapons and about a possible race among the winners of the war. Other scientists shared his worries, before there was even a bomb. In 1942, he drafted a memorandum about "winning the peace" after the war with Germany. He built the title of Imre Madách's play into his text, which shows how much it was on his mind. He wrote that "when the war is won or lost, the history of this chapter of *The Tragedy of Man* may perhaps be pieced together."[68] Thinking about the postwar world, Szilard considered international controls, and even the possibility of preemptive war, to prevent the proliferation of nuclear weapons. He proposed controlling the world's uranium deposits. He foresaw that the coming peace would be an "armed peace" if several countries acquired nuclear weapons.[69] His expression of "armed peace" corresponded to what eventually would become the Cold War.[70]

As Szilard looked at the broader picture, he realized that he was a thorn in the sides of those who were concentrating on the immediate task before them. It was a rare occasion when he tried to explain his own way of going about things: "I am, as a rule, rather outspoken, and if I do not call a spade a spade I find it rather difficult to find a suitable name for it." He even found it appropriate "to apologize to all members of our group for my outspokenness and to ask them to consider it as one of the inevitable hardships of the war." He noted that there was every reason to be happy, but his feeling of responsibility dictated that he follow an alternative. This was to "take the stand that those who have materially contributed to the development [of this terrible weapon], have, before God and the World, the duty to see to it that it should be ready to be used at the proper time and in the proper way."[71] At this point Szilard was still fully for making the bomb and making it fast. He was in constant fear during the first years of the war that the Germans might be ahead in the race for the atomic bomb. It was during that early period that Szilard told a colleague that "he was going to write down the facts, not for publication, just for the information of God. When his colleague remarked that God might know the facts, Szilard replied that this might be so, but 'not *this* version of the facts.'"[72]

Szilard and Groves took a quick dislike to each other and Lanouette sees in their struggle the conflict of the scientist and the soldier. It was also more than that: today it would be unthinkable for a U.S. general to be openly anti-Semitic as Groves was – and get away with it. Lanouette quotes Groves saying, "I am not prejudiced. I don't like certain Jews, and I don't like certain well-known characteristics of theirs, but I'm not prejudiced." In Groves's eyes, Szilard was pushy and arrogant and tried to prevent the atomic bombs being used against Japan. He accused Szilard of having served in the German army in World War I, of never having done any work, not even teaching, and of spending all his time just learning. While he acknowledged that without Szilard the proposal for what later became the Manhattan Project would never have reached the president, even here Groves was negative because he ascribed Szilard's success to his pushiness. Groves would have liked to have had Szilard off the Manhattan Project, would have liked to have had him interned, but others, ultimately War Secretary Stimson, did not let him have his way. Groves stated that "If this were a country like Germany, I should say there were a dozen [scientists] we should have shot right off. And another dozen we could have shot for suspicion or carelessness."[73] It was to this extent that Groves did not understand democracy and that they were fighting against Germany for exactly what he so much envied. On the other hand, Szilard thought that Groves's way of compartmentalizing information slowed the making of the atomic bomb by a whole year, which was a serious accusation.

Groves's reflections about Szilard quoted above came from Lanouette's diligent compilation. Hans Bethe simply concluded that "General Leslie Groves hated Szilard."[74] In his own book the general is more careful than he was elsewhere, and makes only two references to Szilard by name.[75] In one he mentions "the brilliant Hungarian physicists Eugene Wigner and Leo Szilard;" in the other, he mentions Szilard in connection with a technical question. However, he makes repeated mention of some scientists, mostly European by birth and training, who would have preferred to have control of the entire project. It would be hard to imagine that he did not include Szilard among them. Groves also brings up the question of patents and admits that they "did not show any enthusiasm toward speedy financial adjustment for these claims."[76] To characterize the enormity of this problem during the operation of the Manhattan Project, suffice it to mention that the section responsible for patents had to review 8,500 technical reports, examine 6,000 notebooks, and look into 5,600 inventions.[77]

The first nuclear pile was built in a squash court of Stagg Field at the University of Chicago. It went operational on December 2, 1942. When it proved successful, Szilard said to Fermi, "this day would go down as a black day in the history of mankind."[78] Fermi, on the other hand, "was not dwelling on the significance of what had just been done," he simply directed his associates to close down the pile and return next morning for further experiments.[79] The non-Jewish Arthur Compton noted in his memoirs that December 2 was the eve of the kindling of the Chanukah lights of freedom that year. It was also the day on which the State Department reported that two million Jews had already been killed by the Nazis and that, in its estimate, five million more were in danger.[80]

In March 1943, Szilard became a naturalized U.S. citizen. FBI agents constantly followed and investigated him, on General Groves's initiative. His security file described him as "of Jewish extraction, has a fondness for delicacies . . . speaks occasionally in a foreign tongue, and associates mostly with people of Jewish extraction."[81] The FBI must have spent a fortune and a tremendous amount of manpower on covering Szilard through the entire war. Szilard ridiculed his shadows, inviting them into his cab and offering them a cup of coffee or his umbrella when it rained heavily (the agent preferred, though, getting thoroughly wet). Szilard compared Groves's methods to those of the Nazis.

Szilard had also other troubles with the army because he started actions to protect his patent rights concerning the nuclear chain reaction and the atomic reactor. These activities would greatly curtail his participation in the later stages of the development of the atomic bombs. While the inventions made in government service belonged to the government, those that had been made before government support started belonged to the scientists. The principal invention was the chain reaction on unseparated uranium. Szilard was willing to take out a patent in his name or jointly in his name and Fermi's.[82] Szilard took the issue seriously and he saw a conflict of interest between being on the government payroll and fighting the government in connection with his patent rights. Accordingly, he left formal government service for the duration of this fight, but continued working on the atomic bomb in Chicago.

The government could own the patent for a symbolic fee of just one dollar. Szilard resented the symbolic solution and requested real payment. He remembered a story from World War I, about a poor, little tailor who is drafted into the Austro-Hungarian Army. He is a reluctant warrior, but on one occasion his vigilance saves the lives of many people. His commander asks him whether he would prefer to receive a decoration or a money reward in the amount of a thousand crowns. After some deliberation, the tailor asks the commander about the cash value of the decoration. Although the commander tells him that its high moral value is difficult to put a price tag on, the tailor insists, so the commander tells him that the decoration costs five crowns. The tailor then asks whether he might receive the decoration *and* nine-hundred-ninety-five crowns.[83] This is how Szilard characterized his situation. Eventually, Fermi and Szilard were awarded $50,000 for the nuclear pile (nuclear chain reaction) patent. It came after Fermi had died.

By the time atomic bomb development had reached the stage where their deployment became realistic, the threat of a German bomb was no longer around. Accordingly, Szilard no longer wanted the bombs to be used and made three attempts to stop their deployment, all unsuccessful. In a new memorandum to the president, he not only warned about a postwar arms race with the Soviet Union, he also raised the possibility of small atomic bombs being smuggled into United States cities for later detonation. With this, Szilard did not necessarily foresee modern terrorism but rather some of its potential operational means. He also projected the vision of atomic bombs being carried by rockets over long distances to attack American cities. Again, it was a potent prediction, and the danger of such weaponry arose very soon after World War II. In this connection, Szilard warned of the possibility of a preventive war, into which the countries possessing atomic bombs would be tempted. Szilard came to the conclusion that the only way for the world to avoid this debacle would be by creating a worldwide system of controls.[84] Szilard again enlisted Einstein for assistance. However, at this stage Szilard did not ask Einstein to sign the memorandum, only to supply a letter of introduction to accompany it. This was a step towards freeing himself from a dependence on Einstein's fame, and eventually he would just write and send his own letters to world leaders.

In his letter of introduction, Einstein noted something that later became very important, namely, scientific advising for the president.[85] According to Einstein, Szilard was "greatly concerned about the lack of adequate contact between scientists who are doing this work and those members of [Roosevelt's] Cabinet who are responsible for formulating policy." In his new memorandum, Szilard noted that using the atomic bomb "will precipitate a race in the production of these devices between the United States and Russia."[86] He was also worried that the current course of the United States might lead to it losing its initial advantage. This complaint about the stagnation of American preparations sounded like Teller's arguments years later in connection with the hydrogen bomb. Szilard's memorandum never reached Roosevelt, who died on April 12, 1945. This ended Szilard's first attempt. Harry Truman became president and everything had to be started from scratch, because when he had been vice president Truman had had no information about the Manhattan Project.

The former vice president was an unknown quantity for Szilard, but that did not stop him. He decided that there must be someone in the atomic bomb project from the Kansas region, Truman's home base, who could be a link to him. Szilard found such a person, but his initial contacts with the new administration were not very successful. He did not make a good impression on James Byrnes, to whom Truman directed him and who would soon become his Secretary of State. Szilard wanted to give advice, but his persuasive style repelled Byrnes, a southern gentleman, who thought that Szilard wanted to participate in policy-making, which he did not welcome. Szilard was disappointed; he thought that the world would have been better off if Byrnes had been born in Hungary and studied physics, and Szilard had been born in the United States and become influential in American politics.[87]

Szilard was not a person to give up easily, and especially not if the subject of his trials was of such fundamental nature as the future of nuclear weapons and energy. His third attempt was a petition to the new president. In the meantime, the new administration set up an interim committee for nuclear affairs, which recommended the use of atomic bombs against Japan. Szilard and his supporters could not have had much hope of preventing this after the decision of the interim committee, but they wanted at least to go on record with their opposition to such use.[88] This was an important moment in the history of the Manhattan Project, because the person who is credited with initiating it went on record as opposing the deployment of the bomb. However, this was not really a change of heart by Szilard because by then the hostilities had ceased in the European theater, and it had been his wish to counter the danger of Nazi Germany that had started Szilard on this course years before.

In the first formulation of Szilard's petition, he had ignored the fact that a large number of Americans would die in an invasion of Japan. He thus revised his petition and approved the use of atomic weapons "after giving suitable warning and opportunity for surrender under known conditions."[89] Whereas very few scientists were willing to sign the petition in its first formulation, sixty-seven signed the revised version, which Szilard gave to Arthur Compton to take to Washington. Many supported Szilard's petition, but many opposed it, too, especially on the grounds of saving American lives.

The petition of July 17, 1945, makes it clear that until recently there had been a fear that the United States might be attacked by atomic bombs.[90] But the defeat of Germany eliminated such a danger. Incidentally, by then at least those in the American administration who had access to intelligence reports must have known that the Germans had never even come close to developing an atomic bomb.[91] Further, the petition states that an atomic bomb attack "on Japan could not be justified, at least not until the terms which will be imposed after the war on Japan were made public in detail and Japan were given an opportunity to surrender."[92] It is important to notice in this formulation that Szilard and his colleagues did not exclude the possibility of a justified atomic bomb attack against Japan under certain conditions. Again, the moral considerations are stressed in the petition with a warning about the vulnerability of American cities after the war, when others would also develop atomic weapons. The petition had no impact, and by then the preparations for the nuclear attack against Japan had gone into their final phase. The petition itself was dated one day after the world's first nuclear explosive tested successfully in Trinity, near Alamogordo, New Mexico.

At Los Alamos, Teller had his own personal dilemma about the petition and we will return to its fate there later in this chapter. When the first bomb was dropped over Hiroshima, Szilard wrote to his future wife, Gertrud (Trude) Weiss, "Using atomic bombs against Japan is one of the greatest blunders of history."[93] Szilard's stand against this action has earned sympathy in Japan in spite of his part in starting the Manhattan Project.[94] Szilard's actions during those summer weeks in 1945 should be assessed against the background of the atmosphere at the time, rather than from the perspective of six decades later when it is so much easier to condemn the use of atomic bombs. Again, we will return to this question towards the end of the chapter. Here suffice it to mention that Szilard took frantic actions, including contacting church leaders immediately after the bombings, among them Chicago's Roman Catholic cardinal. The cardinal's response was: "God has locked up the energy in question so securely that only after thousands of years has it been unlocked. Surely, there was a reason for this long delay." When Szilard asked him about the reason, the cardinal replied that "The Church will consider the matter and in due time will make a statement about it."[95]

The Manhattan District soon published the Smyth Report about the project.[96] Szilard resented it because his involvement made him a "war criminal" in the eyes of the world.[97] He had his own dilemmas with respect to the deployment of the first atomic bombs. While he condemned their use from a moral standpoint, he also found using or at least stockpiling them during World War II to be rational, and even mandatory. In his letter of January 14, 1944, to the head of the Office of Scientific Research and Development, Vannevar Bush, he elaborated:

> If peace is organized before it has penetrated the public's mind that the potentialities of atomic bombs are a reality, it will be impossible to have a peace that is based on reality. The people of this country clearly will not be willing to pay the price that, in the face of the existence of atomic bombs, is a prerequisite for a stable peace. Making some allowances for the further development of the atomic bomb in the next few years which we may take for granted will be made, this weapon will be so powerful that there can be no peace if it is simultaneously in the possession of any two powers unless these two powers are bound by an

indissoluble political union. It would therefore be imperative rigidly to control all deposits, if necessary by force, and *it will hardly be possible to get political action along that line unless high efficiency atomic bombs have actually been used in this war and the fact of their destructive power has deeply penetrated the mind of the public* (italics added).[98]

With this, Szilard—with tragic precision—charted the fate of nuclear weaponry at the conclusion of World War II as well as in the Cold War. Also with tragic precision, he predicted—what he resented later so much—that it was inevitable that atomic bombs would be employed in World War II, having the postwar world in mind.

By the spring of 1945, however, Szilard's position had changed and with all his power he opposed dropping the atomic bomb on Japan. He thought that doing so would incite the Soviet Union to start developing her own atomic bomb. In 1945, Szilard did not know that the Soviets were already working on nuclear weapons and that they were engaged in extensive and successful espionage to tap the American nuclear project for crucial information. When he talked about this in 1960 he realized that not deploying atomic bombs against Japan would not have gained much time for the United States in the nuclear arms race.[99] Nonetheless, Szilard suggested that if the United States had not dropped the bombs on Hiroshima and Nagasaki, the nuclear arms race might have been avoided.

In 1945, there were also other considerations in deciding about the deployment of the first atomic bombs. Looking back to 1945, Luis Alvarez noted in his memoirs, published in 1987, shortly before he died:

> What would Harry Truman have told the nation in 1946 if we had invaded the Japanese home islands and defeated their tenacious, dedicated people and sustained most probably some hundreds of thousands of casualties and if *The New York Times* had broken the story of a stockpile of powerful secret weapons that cost two billion dollars to build but was not used, for whatever reasons of strategy or morality?[100]

By the time Alvarez wrote these words, public opinion about the deployment of atomic bombs had become divided, although other war actions had had more severe consequences, for example, the fire bombings over Tokyo, which people tend to forget.[101] According to an estimate quoted by Arthur Compton, in a single bombing raid, and the firestorm it generated in Tokyo, on March 9, 1945, eighty thousand people died, sixteen square miles of the city were devastated, and a million and a half people lost their homes.[102] In this connection it is interesting to quote yet another Nobel laureate physicist, Philip Anderson, from a conversation in 1999. He had been vocal against the hydrogen bomb as well as against the Strategic Defense Initiative, but did not take an apologetic attitude with respect to the atomic bombs of 1945:

I'm not one of those who feel guilt about dropping them on Japan. The one thing that emotionally influences me is that I knew about something which most Americans don't, because, having been there, I knew about the fire bombing from my Japanese friends. The fire bombing of Tokyo was so close to genocide, killed so many people, that it seemed to me much more of a horror than the atom bombs. Another thing I was conscious of, and I don't know why so few Americans are conscious of it, is Nanking. Nanking and the Japanese behavior in China and Korea was a horrible thing, unbelievably savage. I don't think I have any complaint whatsoever about the atom bombs. And I'm not sympathetic to the Germans about Dresden. The old saying is absolutely right, "He that soweth the wind shall reap the whirlwind." That's what both the Germans and the Japanese did. The bombs left them with no illusions about being defeated.[103]

Hans Bethe had no regrets, either, about deploying atomic bombs to hasten the end of the war. He thought that Szilard's protest against their use was based on an incomplete understanding of the situation. According to Bethe, things were so uncertain, confused, and urgent that even Szilard's foresight was insufficient to understand the consequences of taking or not taking certain actions in connection with the atomic bombs.[104]

As to whether the atomic bombs over Japan did make a decisive contribution to the cessation of hostilities, see later in this chapter.

Leo Szilard (drawing by István Orosz).

Eugene P. Wigner

The significance of the discovery of nuclear fission at the end of 1938 was not lost on Wigner. Together with Szilard, he understood that the discovery opened up the possibility of the nuclear chain reaction and the atomic bomb. And the danger was greatly enhanced by the discovery having been made in Nazi Germany, with its aspirations to conquer the world. Although Wigner was a theoretician, he did not refrain from practical work, and he realized at once the necessity for experiments. Wigner was also an overpolite person, and when he tried to enlist his colleagues to carry out some experiments in nuclear physics, he appeared persuasive. So they told him that he was "pleasantly disagreeable."[105] Of course, Wigner was not only a theoretician; he had studied chemical engineering and was well versed in materials. His studies with Michael Polanyi on the mechanism of chemical reactions also proved useful in other branches of science, and Wigner was willing and ready to help when he could be of any use.

In 1939, John Wheeler was working on the detailed theory of nuclear fission in Princeton, together with Niels Bohr, who was visiting. Wheeler turned to Wigner with some questions and here is how he remembers their interaction:

> We had to understand this new nuclear phenomenon, fission. . . . Our Hungarian friend, Eugene Wigner helped us out. He ate some oysters in downtown Princeton and got sick and was in the hospital on the campus. I went to see him at the hospital to get some help. The questions that Bohr and I were dealing with were like a chemical reaction. Uranium breaking up is like carbon monoxide breaking up into carbon and oxygen. I remembered that he had worked in that field with Michael Polanyi. And he helped us.[106]

Bohr and Wheeler's paper appeared in *Physical Review* on September 1, 1939, the day Germany invaded Poland and World War II began.[107] Wigner was not much surprised by the German attack on Poland, whereas he found it difficult to alert the Americans to the dangers of Nazi Germany. He met with even greater hurdles in trying to alert the Americans to the dangers of nuclear warfare. It was partly because of the distrust of foreigners. Even though Wigner considered himself to be politically mild in being anti-Nazi, many Americans labeled him as "a European extremist."[108]

Wigner was active in recruiting scientists to think about and possibly work in nuclear physics. He and Szilard consulted Enrico Fermi. When the young Richard Feynman gave a talk at Princeton while still a graduate student, Wigner made sure that such luminaries as John von Neumann, Wolfgang Pauli, and Albert Einstein were on hand. He persuaded Robert Wilson, the man who many years later would head the accelerator laboratory, Fermilab, in Batavia, Illinois, to join him. There was no government money involved yet, but there was also no restriction in what Wigner and others could do, and they could talk freely about their work. This is not to say that they did not realize the importance of secrecy, but it was not easy to get the work started on the atomic bomb. They were just some crazy foreigners with some crazy ideas.[109]

The story of how they enlisted Einstein's help was told above briefly. Here we note only that Wigner went with Szilard on the first visit to Einstein's summer residence in Peconic, Long Island, in Wigner's car with Wigner driving. They only knew Einstein's general address and lost their way. When they asked various people for directions to Einstein's house, nobody seemed to have heard of him. Finally, they found a child who gave them the proper directions.[110] Teller described the same adventure as if it had happened to him, which just shows that the first Szilard–Wigner visit had become a legend.[111] By the time Teller drove Szilard to his second visit, Szilard knew exactly where they had to go.

The original idea was to warn the Belgians about the value of uranium in the Belgian Congo and to inform the U.S. State Department about it. Not only was Einstein better known than Szilard, he was also a friend of the queen of the Belgians. Then it dawned on them that the United States should start an atomic bomb project and they decided that Einstein should write a letter to President Roosevelt. Einstein dictated a letter in concise and precise German, and Wigner scribbled down his words. They then went back to Princeton where Wigner translated Einstein's letter into English, so he was mainly responsible for the wording of the famous document, although Szilard introduced changes before the actual signing took place. Szilard and Teller returned to Peconic to have the letter, which was dated August 2, 1939, signed by Einstein. By then Wigner had left the northeast for a trip to California by prior arrangement.

As we have seen, things developed slowly, but on October 21, 1939, there was a meeting at the National Bureau of Standards (NBS) in Washington, with Lyman Briggs chairing the Uranium Committee.[112] Gregory Breit was a member, the same man who was instrumental in securing a job for Wigner in Wisconsin. We have already commented upon the meeting at the NBS where Wigner felt compelled to contradict an army colonel who tried to convince the scientists that wars are won by civilian morale rather than by new weapons.

The years 1939–1941 were frustratingly slow. The vision of Germany making progress at the same time was disturbing. There was another meeting at the NBS on April 27, 1940, with the same people and with similarly disappointing results.[113] Wigner found, though, that Gregory Breit and Harold Urey were constructive and they, along with other scientists, hastened the matter. Breit, in particular, chaired a committee which reviewed all fission-related papers to see if their publication would reveal sensitive information. If it did, the committee withheld their publication in scientific journals.

Amid all these events, there were important changes in Wigner's private life, particularly his second marriage in Princeton in 1941 to Mary Wheeler, a physics professor (and no relation to John A. Wheeler). They were to have two children, David and Martha, in a happy marriage that lasted until Mary's death in 1977.

Finally, things started moving with the nuclear project and Arthur Compton set up the Metallurgical Laboratory in Chicago.[114] After a few months, Wigner moved to Chicago to direct a theoretical group of about seven young physicists. He had known of Arthur Compton and he had utilized the Compton Effect when he was working in Berlin. Compton described their meeting, at which Wigner urged him "almost in tears" to help America build the atomic bomb.[115] Compton called Wigner again on December 8, 1941—the day after the Japanese attack on Pearl Harbor—to tell him that the Uranium Project was being reorganized and that they had decided to build a graphite–uranium reactor at the University of Chicago. Work that had begun on building such a reactor at Columbia University was being transferred to Chicago. The Columbia group also went there, including Fermi, as did the Princeton group, including Wigner. Most of the participants were foreigners or recently naturalized Americans. Wigner and his wife moved to Chicago in April 1942. From then on their problem was, in Fermi's words, "not too little money, but too much."[116]

It was not only the money situation that went through such a drastic transformation. Although initially Szilard and Wigner advocated the need for secrecy, once the military took over there was too much of that as well. The army was obsessed with secrecy, which was partly understandable but it made work less efficient. It was very beneficial that initially the uranium work was not considered classified. Szilard also noted this in connection with the work that had begun in England.[117]

The main task of the theoretical group directed by Wigner was the design of the nuclear reactor in Hanford, Washington, which was to produce plutonium-239. One of the two bombs dropped on Japan would be a uranium-235 bomb (Hiroshima), the other a plutonium bomb (Nagasaki). The work progressed smoothly in Chicago but the atmosphere for Wigner was nightmarish in that he constantly worried about possible German progress in making an atomic bomb. The impression from reading his *Recollections* is that he was not sure of an eventual Allied victory. When the American security service took fingerprints of all the participants in the Manhattan Project, he refused.[118] He feared that if the Germans won the war they would execute everybody in the Manhattan Project. Fingerprints would make it so much easier to identify and round them up. It was a naïve thought: he forgot that as a Jew he would be rounded up and executed anyway. He was concentrating on his work in the project, and 1943 was the first time in twenty years that he did not publish a single scientific paper; he might have had new results but they were classified.

Wigner and his co-workers, and in particular Gale Young, had made a rough design for a 100,000-kilowatt nuclear reactor by July 1942.[119] The reactor was to be made of uranium lumps in a graphite cylinder and was to be cooled by water; its improved design would serve for the Hanford nuclear reactor. Not only physics was involved but also what is today called materials science, including metallurgy. Within five weeks of the demonstration of the nuclear chain reaction on December 2, 1942, Wigner and his associates had submitted plans to build a reactor for plutonium production. The plan was carefully reviewed and then passed on to the Du Pont Company.[120] Its engineers foresaw some difficulties, but accepted Wigner's plan as a basis for the design of the production plant for plutonium. In his work with the engineers there were some unpleasant situations for Wigner: some of the engineers felt that he was invading their territory. But nobody owned any territory because nuclear engineering was uncharted waters. In fact, the engineers received directions from the best qualified person at that time in the world. Alvin Weinberg called Wigner "the first nuclear engineer."[121] According to Arthur Compton, Fermi, Glenn T. Seaborg, and Wigner were "supreme" in the laboratory, where what counted was "originality, technical knowledge, and skill in exploring the unknown."[122]

Much has been made of Wigner's bottle of Chianti, the well-known Italian red wine, which he produced to celebrate the successful test of the first-ever nuclear reactor. It was indeed a sign of Wigner's confidence in the project, his dedication to it, and a demonstration of his foresight. From experience, he knew that such items as Italian red wine would disappear under war conditions. It was not only chemical engineering but also how to handle war conditions that he had learned in Europe.[123] "It had required more foresight to buy the Chianti before imported Italian wine became scarce than to predict that the bottle would be needed before 1942 was out" (i.e., that the nuclear pile would become operational).[124]

Compton was aware of the importance of Wigner's background in chemical engineering. He also saw the difficulties in the cooperation between Wigner and the Du Pont engineers. It was difficult, according to Compton, "for Wigner to believe that anything good could come from cooperation with a great industrial organization such as Du Pont. Such companies, he had been taught in Europe, were the tyrants of the American democracy."[125] In this Compton may have been mistaken because such ideological considerations were of no importance to Wigner. What was important to him was that he did not find Du Pont's performance satisfactory and he talked about this in his *Recollections*.

The Du Pont people were "mostly men of practical rather than theoretical experience."[126] They were also "inclined perhaps to be skeptical of the usefulness of anything Wigner and his research team would turn out." Szilard saw the difficulties in Wigner's interactions with Du Pont.[127] When Wigner asked the engineers what they wanted from him, they told him that they only wanted him to answer their questions. This caused Wigner to give a biting response wrapped in polite formulation: "If you know what questions to ask, you will find the answer to any question which you might ask and which I can answer in my files. All I have to do, then, is give you the key to my files, which I shall be very glad to do." The engineers did not understand that the main thing was to figure out the right questions in such a principally novel project. They had to learn to cooperate, and they did, although at one point Wigner even tendered his resignation to Compton. In the end, though, it worked. Compton noted that "underneath there remained a state of tension that caused continual concern to those responsible—that is to Compton—for the success of the undertaking."[128]

Lest we underestimate the enormity of Du Pont's task and especially its responsibility, it is worth remembering that engineering, unlike research in physics, is not an excursion into the unknown but the accomplishment of well-defined plans, which the Manhattan Project was not. Neither was the construction of the Hanford reactors, with which Du Pont was charged. Also, a company like Du Pont had multiple responsibilities, including to its shareholders. Once General Groves had convinced the leadership of Du Pont that they had to participate in the project, the final word lay with the company's board of directors. The challenge was not only that Du Pont was being asked to accept an enormous undertaking without prior experience, but also that it was a classified project.

Groves described the crucial board meeting, when the directors entered the room and "were asked not to look at the faced-down papers on the table in front of them."[129] They were informed about the magnitude of the task and that it had the highest military importance but were told no more because secrecy was necessary. Nonetheless, they were told, if they wished, they could turn over the papers and read them before voting. None of the directors turned the papers over, and they unanimously voted their approval. Let me add a footnote to the story: Du Pont accepted the assignment, which called for reimbursement of expenses without profit; nonetheless, for legal reasons, it was determined that a one dollar fee should be paid to Du Pont upon the successful completion of the contract. Upon Japan's capitulation Du Pont was paid the one dollar fee, but the government auditors found that the contract had not been quite fulfilled, and Du Pont was asked to return thirty-nine cents to the government.[130]

Looking back on his contribution to the atomic bombs and considering the horrors they caused, Wigner would have liked to say that he regretted working on them, just to please his questioners. In reality, however, he did not regret it, neither intellectually, nor emotionally.[131] He felt strongly that the bomb should have been created sooner, while Germany was still in the war, or at least in time to influence the Yalta meeting of the Big Three (Roosevelt, Churchill, and Stalin), to lessen the hardship of Eastern Europe and to ease Soviet domination. But Wigner never wanted to have the bombs dropped on Japan and he did not expect it to happen. However, he understood that the army had developed the atomic bomb and the army was eager to use it, to demonstrate its power. He thought that it probably saved a lot of lives and without it many more American and Japanese lives would have been lost, because America would have had to invade the Japanese islands.

As Wigner remembered it in 1984, there was a point during the Manhattan Project, when Germany had been defeated, when he thought:

> [T]hat it was not necessary to continue the work on the bomb, but the government was not of that opinion. General Groves also wanted to continue and he said that we could use it against the Japanese and it would shorten the war.
>
> We proposed then to demonstrate the bomb in the presence of some Japanese scientists and military leaders. Groves once again disagreed and said that we should demonstrate it on a city. And that is what happened, but we were against it and were quite unhappy. We thought that many Japanese lives could have been saved if the bomb had been demonstrated on an uninhabited territory. But, apparently, I must admit, and I will admit, we were probably mistaken. Much later, I read in a book that the demonstrations in Hiroshima and Nagasaki may have saved many, many Japanese lives. Since I thought that a demonstration over an uninhabited territory in the presence of Japanese scientists and politicians could have sufficed, I went around and asked my Japanese friends about it. And with one exception, they said, "No, such a demonstration would have had no effect on the Emperor." According to all my Japanese friends, with one exception, "It would not have had the same effect; it was very good that you demonstrated it this way." Maybe that was the way to do it, but I did not think so at that time. Of course, they knew the Japanese politicians, the Japanese Emperor, and the Japanese military leaders much better than we did. But I was very surprised. They thought that many Japanese lives were saved this way even though it led to the extinction of many Japanese lives. Apparently General Groves was right and the bomb had to be demonstrated the way it was.[132]

For reflecting on the mood at that time we may turn again to John A. Wheeler, who was called the most versatile physicist of the twentieth century and whom we met above. Wheeler was a participant in the Manhattan Project and did not hesitate in naming his contribution to developing the atomic bomb as his most important achievement. He recalled the many American troops who came up to him saying that those two bombs saved their lives. "All those American troops on the island of Okinawa in the fall of 1945 were ready to invade Japan—they knew that the Japanese were ready to die rather than to give in." Wheeler often wonders, "how many more lives could have been saved, had we done the bomb a year or so sooner." The question had a painful personal relevance to him, because he had a younger brother who was killed in action in October 1944 in Italy. Shortly before, Wheeler received a letter from him in which he wrote: "hurry up!" Apparently, his brother guessed that Wheeler was involved in war work. Wheeler estimated that "had the war ended a year earlier; in mid-1944 instead of mid-1945; possibly 15 million lives would have been saved. A heavy thought."[133]

Alvarez wondered whether the emperor of Japan had been prompted to the unconditional surrender by the atomic bombs or not.[134] The emperor gave a speech on radio, a few days after the second bomb had been dropped, on Nagasaki, in which he announced the Japanese surrender. He talked about a new and most cruel bomb and its incalculable damage. Fifty years after Hiroshima and Nagasaki, Hans Bethe thought that the enormity of the impact of the atomic bombs made them appear "supernatural." This may have provided the emperor with a convenient excuse for surrendering without "losing face."[135] Curiously, there was not much news coverage in Japan about the damage after the first bomb over Hiroshima. Apparently, it took the second bomb to bring the message home.

For determining the yield of the bombs, Alvarez built a device to measure the pressure. It was parachuted from a plane accompanying the plane that dropped the bomb.[136] The device sent back the data as radio signals to the second plane. When the Nagasaki bombing was being prepared, he attached a letter to the measuring device in which he warned the Japanese that if they did not surrender, there would be a rain of atomic bombs in fury. It was a private action by Alvarez and two of his colleagues. The letter was addressed to a former colleague, the Japanese Ryokichi Sagane, who had been a visiting professor at Berkeley before the war. The Japanese found the letter and forwarded it right away to the Japanese High Command. Whether and to what extent the Alvarez letter played a role in the quick Japanese surrender after Nagasaki, we may never know.

According to another noted physicist, Maurice Goldhaber, the atomic bombs over Japan were used too late because the Japanese were already losing the war.[137] He thinks that the atomic bomb gave the Japanese leadership a convenient excuse to give up, but they might have given up anyway because of the raids. Although Goldhaber realizes that public opinion credits (or used to credit) the atomic bombs with saving many Americans who would have gone to Japan to conquer it, there may not have been a need to go in. He thinks that the bombs speeded up the process only slightly, but there is little evidence to support such a view. In contrast, Winston Churchill was one of those who ventured to estimate what might have been the human cost had the Allies had to invade the Japanese islands: he put it at more than a million Allied soldiers and two million Japanese.[138]

The timing of the atomic bomb's appearance was almost as important as its creation, from the point of view of World War II. Wigner was greatly concerned with this aspect of the usefulness of the bomb. He was less concerned with the postwar period, which was, of course, a different story. The atomic bombs were then strategically aimed at the Soviet Union and it was not in the interest of the United States to reveal their existence too soon because that would induce the Soviets to double their efforts to develop their own bombs. In reality, the Soviet Union was well informed about what was going on at Los Alamos.

John von Neumann

World War II brought new challenges for John von Neumann that he was happy
to take up. In 1937, he became a naturalized American citizen. He soon sat for his
examinations to become a lieutenant in the reserve of the ordnance department
of the U.S. Army.[139] He passed all the exams, but as by then he was past the age
of 35 years, his application was declined. This may have been a narrowly focused
bureaucratic decision by the army, but it had positive consequences for the
American war effort.

Although many in Europe were in euphoria after the Munich Agreement of
September 30, 1938, concluded by the British and French prime ministers with
Hitler, von Neumann knew that there would be war in Europe in 1939.[140] His
conclusion was the same as Szilard's. He went back to Budapest to urge his family to leave, but there was false optimism around and they did not follow his advice. The other purpose of his Budapest visit was to marry his second wife, Klári
Dán. She then made one more attempt, just before the war started, in the summer of 1939, to get their families out of Hungary to America. Klári's parents went,
but her father soon committed suicide and her mother returned to Hungary. She
survived the Holocaust and then spent her last years in England with Klári's sister.

Von Neumann was ready to go to war before the United States was, but he was
convinced that America would enter the war soon, and he considered Germany
and Russia to be America's two enemies throughout. The two totalitarian powers
first concluded a nonaggression pact, but later they became mortal enemies; one
became an ally of the United States and the other an adversary. Nonetheless, von
Neumann's position in considering both countries as enemies resembled the young
Szilard's assertion at the beginning of World War I; he had lumped together the
Central Powers and Russia, anticipating that they would both be eventual losers,
although they were standing on opposite sides of the dividing line.

As the war preparations and then the actual war intensified, von Neumann's
connections with the American military became increasingly tighter. In September 1940 he moved from being a consultant to becoming a member of the
scientific advisory board of the Ballistic Research Laboratory at Aberdeen. Other
members included George Kistiakowsky, Isidor I. Rabi, and Theodore von
Kármán; the board met a few times a year. According to von Neumann, "America's
organization of research had proved at least as good as any of the belligerents,
and better than most of the big ones."[141] One of the questions to the advisory
board came from von Kármán himself, about the process of reaching equilib-
rium in shock waves. Bethe, Teller, and also von Neumann became interested
in the problem.

Von Neumann's wartime engagements included the following appointments:
from September 1941 till September 1942, he was consultant and then member of
Division 8 of the National Defense Research Council (NDRC); he was also the
principal scientist in a contract between the Institute for Advanced Study and

the Office of Emergency Management. Von Neumann was involved with the so-called shaped charges for torpedoes and antitank weapons. These charges had a well-defined geometrical shape and were used to "modify, concentrate, or limit the physical effects of detonations."[142] After America entered World War II, von Neumann's fame as a practical designer of explosive weapons spread.

Because of his many different engagements, von Neumann had to be especially concerned with secrecy, but he took this with good humor. As he was traveling a lot, he was accompanied by two "gorillas." He met with Stanislaw Ulam on the Chicago railway station and recruited him for the work at Los Alamos. However, von Neumann could not reveal the exact nature of work, nor the location. He could only tell Ulam that it was in the southwest. Ulam told him: "I know you can't tell me, but you say you are going southwest in order that I should think that you are going northeast. But I know you are going southwest, so why do you lie?" This is after an old Jewish story about two men on a train in Russia. The conversation goes like this:

> "Where are you going?"
> "To Kiev."
> "You liar, you tell me you are going to Kiev so I would think you are going to Odessa. But I know you are going to Kiev, so why do you lie?"[143]

In fact, when Ulam did learn that they were going to New Mexico, he checked out some literature from the library about the region and found that previous patrons who had checked out the same guidebook were people who had already disappeared from the University of Wisconsin, supposedly for war-related classified work. This was a good example of the difficulty of keeping secrets. The story is similar to the one about all the volumes related to uranium suddenly disappearing from the library in Berkeley at the start of the Manhattan Project when the work on uranium was becoming classified. The result was that anybody who might have been interested could have deduced that uranium was involved in classified work.

In September 1942, von Neumann resigned from the NDRC because he had accepted an appointment with the navy. Eventually, though, he rejoined the NDRC without leaving the navy. He had the ability to do lots of things at the same time. He worked for the navy's mine warfare section in the new field of operational research. He was asked, for instance, to determine mathematically the patterns according to which the Germans planted their mines along the convoy routes between America and Britain. He spent considerable time in Britain as part of his navy assignment. He was richly decorated for his services. In July 1946, he was awarded the U.S. Navy's Distinguished Civilian Service Award and in October of the same year, he received President Truman's Medal for Merit. The citation asserted that John von Neumann "was primarily responsible for fundamental research by the United States Navy on the effective use of high explosives, which has resulted in the discovery of a new ordnance principle for offensive action."[144] The citation gave emphasis to his contribution to the enhanced effectiveness of the atomic bomb dropped over Hiroshima.

He was recalled to the United States from Britain in mid-1943 to participate in the atomic bomb program, and it was he who showed that the bomb would be most effective if it exploded well above ground level.[145] It is curious that von Neumann was not recruited into the atomic bomb project when the other Martians were. The explanation is that he was a mathematician rather than a physicist. Also, he provided immediate solutions to many immediate problems and was treasured for that in many different undertakings, whereas the development of the atomic bomb was a longer-range project. For him it was probably also fitting not to dedicate himself to one particular project full time. But in the fall of 1943 he was already engaged at Los Alamos, in addition to his many other assignments.

An example of von Neumann's "picking up other people's work and leaping blocks ahead of them" was the design of the implosion device for detonating the plutonium bomb at Los Alamos.[146] Szilard's idea for the nuclear chain reaction, and accordingly the fission bomb, was to start from one neutron and let it multiply. After sufficient neutron multiplication, a few pounds of fissionable material would liberate a huge amount of energy. In order to produce an explosion, all this has to take place quickly, within about one-millionth of a second, because otherwise the material would fly apart, with much less energy being liberated. So the task was to assemble the amount of fissionable material needed for a self-sustaining chain reaction to start (it is called the critical mass) but in such a way that the chain reaction started only when the bomb was detonated. One possibility was to prepare the critical mass in two halves and suddenly bring the two parts together.[147] This was called the gun method but it involved various practical problems; the especially serious one was that it could not be used for plutonium because of the danger of spontaneous fission.

Seth Neddermeyer suggested another method, to use high explosives to produce shock waves that would implode the plutonium into a critical mass. His suggestion received little attention until von Neumann showed up at Los Alamos at the end of summer 1943. He made calculations and proved that the implosion method would be faster than the gun method and also that it would produce higher pressures that would compress the fissionable material, and thus less material would be needed. In the implosion bomb a hollow sphere of a fissionable material (plutonium) is surrounded by a layer of high explosives. When the explosives are detonated, they compress the fissionable material into a ball and thus produce the needed critical mass. Many credit von Neumann alone with recognizing that the compression of the fissionable material by implosion had additional advantages. Edward Teller remembered it differently.[148] According to his story, he and von Neumann were discussing the implosion technique, and von Neumann first did his calculations with the assumption of noncompressibility. He calculated the enormous pressures produced and that gave Teller the idea of compression; he had some background in geophysics and knew that under the tremendous pressures in the core of the earth even iron is compressed. Therefore, he suggested this possibility. Taking compressibility into account in the calculations was too much even for von Neumann, and this is when he suggested that computers be used. Some of the features of the implosion solution were originally suggested by Richard Tolman, and he was aided by Robert Serber.[149] Then Neddermeyer got involved, and other people, including some of the British arrivals, made some input, and Hans Bethe, too, but it was von Neumann who finally came up with the right solution with some lenses.[150]

In the precomputer era, von Neumann was a living computer. However, even his exceptional arithmetical prowess reached limitations when weapons research encountered problems of hydrodynamics. This prompted him to turn to the budding area of developing computers, where he then left his decisive mark over the years during and especially after World War II.[151]

Jacob Bronowski, who became famous in the post–World War II era for popularizing science in Great Britain, was attached to von Neumann while he was in Britain studying mining patterns. This is how Bronowski characterized him: "endearing and personal . . . the cleverest man I ever knew, without exception . . . a genius . . . , but not a modest man."[152] Apparently, von Neumann was not interested in being praised; he knew that he was right. He told Bronowski that he did not need praise, and asked only that he tell him when he was wrong. Bronowski did not think that this was vanity, because from von Neumann it came naturally.

Concerning the deployment of the atomic bombs, von Neumann took a practical approach. He did not think that inventing the murderous bomb was sinful and he denied that the only reason for it was to be ahead of Nazi Germany. Furthermore, he did not think that nuclear weaponry should be internationalized after the war. According to Macrae, by late 1943 von Neumann hoped that the United States would get the atomic bomb before "either of our two enemies" did.[153] Significantly, he meant Germany and Russia (rather than Japan). By the end of 1943, he expected the European war to end within the foreseeable future, but he was "100% pessimistic" about Russian relations. So he was preparing himself and his adopted country for the postwar conditions of the world.

Von Neumann did not have any qualms about the deployment of the atomic bombs over Japan. He wanted to save American lives and, as we have seen, it was expected that the Japanese would have defended their islands at any cost if the Americans had invaded. In the aftermath of Hiroshima and Nagasaki, Oppenheimer's reaction was characteristic of the mood of some of the scientists. He quoted the Hindu scripture "Now I am become Death, the destroyer of worlds." Von Neumann considered this hypocrisy and it irritated him. His comment was, "Some people confess guilt to claim credit for the sin."[154]

Edward Teller

In 1941 Teller and his wife, Mici, became American citizens.[155] In the same year, Teller was lured away from George Washington University by Columbia University, ostensibly to teach, but in practice to work on the uranium project. From Columbia, those working on the project went to Chicago, and from Chicago to Los Alamos. He never rejoined George Washington University; the worry-free period of his life in the United States was over.

Ever since President Roosevelt's speech, Teller had been fired up to take part in the American war efforts and was disappointed to see that the Americans did not have the same anxiety about Hitler and Mussolini as he and the other immigrants did. A case in point was Robert Serber, a former student of Robert Oppenheimer's. Serber was an outstanding physicist and later an important participant in the Manhattan Project, but in May 1940 he was not interested in the war because he thought it was "a clash between capitalist interests."[156]

A fateful discussion for both Teller's and America's future took place some time in 1942 between Teller and Fermi, during which Fermi asked whether "an atomic explosion might be used to produce a thermonuclear reaction."[157] In a thermonuclear reaction two elements are joined together, producing another, larger element. Obviously, for this reaction to occur, enormous energies are needed to overcome the repulsions of nuclei, and the idea was that a fission bomb might produce such large energies. Gamow and Teller had discussed the thermonuclear process occurring in the stars. Fermi suggested that deuterium would be much better for this reaction than simple hydrogen in order to get greater efficiency. Teller thought about Fermi's question and came to the conclusion that at the very high temperatures practically all the energy produced by the atomic bomb would go into radiation and might not initiate a thermonuclear reaction, that is, fusion. Fermi accepted Teller's explanation and they shelved the idea of thermonuclear explosion for the time being.

But it was for a short time only. The topic next came up in spring 1942 at the Metallurgical Laboratory of the University of Chicago. Teller and his colleague, Emil Konopinski, had nothing to do for a few days, so Teller decided to explain to Konopinski why fusion would not work. According to his recollections, the more he tried to explain this the more he became convinced that he was not right and that the fusion bomb might work.[158] There was to be a meeting of physicists in the summer of 1942 in Berkeley, California, and the Tellers and Bethes went together. Teller and Bethe talked about the possibility of thermonuclear reaction and by the end of the trip Bethe was convinced of its feasibility.[159] During the meeting in California, Oppenheimer left and went north to meet with Arthur Compton to alert him to the possibility of the thermonuclear reaction and to the danger that it might ignite the oceans and the atmosphere. Teller and the others only learned of this in 1945, when the worry again arose about whether atomic bombs might be capable of blowing up the whole planet.

Teller's first practical involvement in the preparations for the atomic bomb project (that is, apart from his helping Szilard with the Einstein letter) was at Columbia University, where he worked together with Fermi and Szilard.[160] It was at this early stage that Edwin McMillan and Glenn Seaborg in California discovered two transuranic elements, neptunium and plutonium, and they predicted that plutonium would be fissionable. The discovery was the more noteworthy in the light of Fermi's earlier mistaken discovery of ostensibly transuranic elements.

As we have seen, when the United States became a belligerent in World War II, it changed the character of the uranium project. When it was decided to transfer it to Chicago, at first Teller was not invited to join. Although he was already a U.S. citizen, part of his family lived behind enemy lines. However, Oppenheimer managed to get clearance for him. Later there would be an ironic twist in their relationship in this respect. Several weeks before the July 1945 test of the plutonium bomb, Fermi revived the question of whether the atomic bomb might ignite the ocean and the air, and Teller and his group were charged with providing the answer. The calculations in 1945, as well as more accurate later calculations, indicated that there was no danger of igniting the atmosphere and the oceans, yet the fact that the possibility had occurred in the scientists' minds showed the gravity of the problem.[161]

The early hesitations of the American atomic bomb program were in great contrast with the later swift and all-out efforts. As we have seen, the first nuclear reactor started up in Chicago in December 1942. Then in March 1943, the first settlers arrived at Los Alamos, including Teller. When Oppenheimer had become head of the weapons design group, he had suggested building a separate laboratory, which became Los Alamos. Oppenheimer assigned Teller the job of briefing new arrivals. Earlier, Teller had helped him to recruit scientists for Los Alamos. Oppenheimer also charged Teller with organizing weekly seminars. From the beginning, Teller was more interested in the possibility of thermonuclear explosion than in the fission bomb, because the latter had already been solved from a theoretical point of view. This may be looked at from two different angles. One is that the immediate task of Los Alamos was the creation of fission bombs and Teller did not sufficiently contribute to this development. The other is that his abilities could not have been best utilized for such work, because at this stage the necessary theoretical work had been mainly reduced to doing calculations, at which he was not very good. It seems that Teller did not devote himself with the expected enthusiasm to whatever tasks there were to further the production of the fission bomb. On the other hand, one might argue that he was preparing the ground for later projects. Teller may have been led by Oppenheimer to believe that the hydrogen bomb was an important part of their current work.[162]

Hans Bethe was head of the theoretical group in which Teller worked. They approached physics differently. Bethe liked to work on what Fermi called "little bricks," and Teller characterized Bethe's work style as "methodical, meticulous, thorough, and detailed." How, then, did Teller characterize his own style in physics?

"Although I have made a few tiny little bricks, I much prefer (and am much better at) exploring the various structures that can be made from brick, and seeing how the bricks stack up." Here, Teller also characterizes Oppenheimer: "Oppenheimer also approaches physics in a manner more like a bricklayer than a brick maker." When Oppenheimer named Bethe to head the theoretical division, Teller "was a little hurt." The collision came when Bethe wanted Teller to work on the detailed calculations for the implosion scheme. Teller did not want to be bogged down with such work, doing detailed calculations, and he did not take up the task. It was the beginning of the end of their friendship according to Teller. Oppenheimer let Teller continue the variety of programs he had been involved with. There was an added task, travel; Teller went to discuss work progress with the people at Columbia University. Other people were dispatched to Hanford, Oak Ridge, and Chicago.[163]

The Los Alamos period was important for Teller's political development as well. He read Arthur Koestler's *Darkness at Noon* there in 1943 and it was a "major milestone" in his thinking.[164] Teller said that, as late as 1937, he was still open to at least considering what might be the best course for the Soviet Union to take. The Hitler–Stalin pact was a big blow, not only for Teller but also, and especially, for communists worldwide. For Teller, the primary concern was defeating Hitler, but he also viewed communism increasingly unsympathetically. As for Koestler's book, he declared, "I don't believe I have ever been more fascinated with a book than I was with *Darkness at Noon.*" In any case, Teller stressed that his becoming an anti-communist was not an overnight event; rather, it was the result of a painstaking process. He considered himself an anti-communist "of the school of Koestler."[165]

Teller met Koestler through von Neumann. He felt a deep kinship with Koestler and not only because of the similarity in their upper-middle-class Budapest Jewish backgrounds. There was a more profound reason in that when Koestler had changed from being a communist to an anti-communist, he lost many of his dear friends. "Eleven years later," Teller writes about 1943 to 1954 in his *Memoirs,* "I began to understand that loss better, because, in a minor way, I went through a similar transformation." Here "in a minor way" is an understatement. Also, the parallel is flawed. Koestler changed his philosophy and lost his former friends. Teller testified against a fellow physicist—which is a less noble cause—and lost his former friends. But Teller ascribes his separation from many of his friends to his gradual but determined turning into an anti-communist at Los Alamos.[166]

In the late fall of 1943, British physicists arrived at Los Alamos: Chadwick, Peierls, Fuchs, and others. Bohr also came; it was like an international reunion of physicists. Von Neumann, who spent short periods of time at Los Alamos, brought the first computer there in the spring of 1944; it was electrical rather than mechanical.[167] Teller also moved around. He went on trips in his role of keeping in touch and recruiting, and kept in contact with Wigner, who worked in Chicago and transferred later to Oak Ridge. On his trips east, Teller often visited von Neumann in Princeton. In addition to his other tasks, Teller spent about a third of his time working on the possibility of a thermonuclear bomb, which became known as the "Super" (for super bomb). His group had, on average, twelve people.

In June 1945, preparations for the bomb were in full flow; uranium-235 was scarce and it was decided that the uranium bomb would be deployed without testing, as there was not enough of the isotope for a second bomb. For the implosion bomb of plutonium, one was to be tested and a second to be used. It was at that point that Teller received a letter from Szilard, together with a petition to the president. Szilard was asking for Teller's help in getting signatures to the petition, which opposed the deployment of the atomic bomb. Szilard asked Teller to "give every member of your group an opportunity for signing." The reasoning of the petition was acceptable to Teller and he was ready to sign it, but he also thought that he should talk to Oppenheimer about it. This was but another example of Teller not wanting to act solely on the basis of his own opinion and seeking the approval or guidance of others, primarily his superiors. Oppenheimer brushed the petition aside: he told Teller that the authors did not see the complete picture and that the leaders in Washington took everything into account. Teller was taken aback by Oppenheimer's harsh tone, but he "accepted his decision and felt relief at not having to participate in the difficult judgments to be made."[168]

This was an opportunistic attitude, shifting responsibility to others and following his superior's judgment. Teller wrote to Szilard and declined to fulfill his request, but did not mention his consultation with Oppenheimer. Teller also sent a note to Oppenheimer, hoping for approval of his response to Szilard. Teller made matters worse when, half a century later, he concluded that Szilard had been right, because the scientists who worked on the bomb had special responsibility.[169] Oppenheimer was also right because the scientists did not have enough knowledge about the political situation. In later interviews, Teller blamed Oppenheimer for his own failure in not supporting Szilard's petition and felt that the technical conditions for a demonstration of the bomb should have been provided, to give the president an alternative to using it. [170]

Back in 1945, Teller did not know that four scientists had been asked for their opinions about dropping the atomic bomb. This was the interim committee, consisting of Compton, Ernest Lawrence, Oppenheimer, and Fermi. Lawrence held out the longest in favor of the demonstration, but finally all four agreed that the bomb should be dropped. The Trinity test took place on July 16, 1945, followed by Hiroshima and Nagasaki. The Japan surrendered on August 15, but Teller "continued to regret that the bomb had not been demonstrated."[171] He was asked many times whether he ever regretted that he had worked on the bombs, and his answer was always an emphatic "no," firing back the question: What if he hadn't worked on them? They did not know then that the Germans were not seriously working on the bomb.

There could also be a different question: What would have happened had the bomb been ready one year earlier? Teller contemplated such a scenario: It could have been if Groves had chosen to produce uranium-235 by the centrifugation technique, as suggested by Urey.[172] Having a bomb available by the summer of 1944 would have meant, among other things, the escape of millions of Jews from Auschwitz, including hundreds of thousands of Hungarian Jews. In addition, millions of Eastern–Central Europeans would have escaped Soviet domination for decades. To be sure, though, Eastern and Central Europe would have suffered atomic bomb damage.

After the mid-July 1945 test, Oppenheimer reorganized Los Alamos: he gave greater emphasis to the fusion bomb work and put Fermi and Bethe in charge. Teller apparently welcomed this increased focus on the fusion bomb. In reading his *Memoirs*, however, this does not sound convincing, because previously Teller had been disappointed when Bethe was made boss of the theoretical division, and here he was being made boss of Teller's pet project.[173] Nevertheless, Teller must have been satisfied indeed that the thermonuclear project was gaining in importance. How much greater, then, was his disappointment when, after the Japanese surrender, Oppenheimer declared that work on the hydrogen bomb should be discontinued? After having seen pictures from Hiroshima, Oppenheimer was determined that Los Alamos should vanish.

CHAPTER FIVE

To Deter: Cold War

You cannot preach international cooperation and
disarmament from a position of weakness. My *Old Testament*
faith tells me that to get one's point across it is best to have a
big stick. You don't have to use it, but you're freer to talk
without interference.

    Theodore von Kármán

World War II ended officially in 1945, with VE Day marking the Allied victory in
Europe and VJ Day the surrender of Japan. But the dividing line between the war
and the ensuing peace was blurred because preparations for peace had started
long before the war ended. Germany's defeat did not slow the work on the atomic
bomb at Los Alamos, but the target was no longer only its deployment in World
War II, even though the first atomic bombs would explode over Japan. All those
who thought ahead also had the relationship with the Soviet Union in mind when
pushing for the speedy completion of the bombs. This was in spite of the fact that
many of the scientists who participated in the Manhattan Project, including Eugene Wigner, questioned the necessity of further work. Their dedication to the
project had originally stemmed from their fear of a German atomic bomb, but
only one scientist left the project upon Germany's defeat.[1]

The war transformed the relationship between the scientists and the elected leaders of the United States. People who were often timid foreigners or recently admitted new citizens before the war now emerged as esteemed advisors for the most powerful decision-makers. This brought a profound change in the status of the Martians. Whether they were testifying before congressional committees (Szilard, von Neumann, Teller), presiding over advisory boards at the Pentagon (von Kármán), gaining membership in the prestigious General Advisory Committee of the Atomic Energy Commission (Wigner, von Neumann), or being appointed to the powerful position of Commissioner of the Atomic Energy Commission by the president (von Neumann), what a change it was compared with their experiences in Hungary and Germany. Even in the United States some of them had been considered at times to be unruly foreigners with crazy ideas and impossible accents. After the war, foreign accents became respectable when scientists had them.

How might the Martians have felt about their change of status? A story by former *Minta* pupil and noted physicist Nicholas Kurti gives us a hint.[2] Kurti was forced out of Germany and ended up at Oxford University in England. Eventually, he was elected Fellow of the Royal Society (London), at one time serving as a council member, and it is while he was on the council that the following episode happened. A new fellow stands before the president at a ceremonial meeting and is formally admitted to the Royal Society. On one such occasion, Kurti had to fill in for the president. As he was speaking the official sentence, he thought of the story of the great Orientalist, Ármin Vámbéry, who had come from a poor Hungarian Jewish family. He had had a hard life, but he was very gifted and became a professor in Budapest and a member of the Royal Geographical Society in London. He helped the British Government to gather intelligence on the Ottoman Empire. On one occasion Vámbéry was invited to Windsor Castle to have dinner with Her Majesty (Queen Victoria). After the dinner he was shown into his beautifully decorated bedroom. He put on the fancy night gown that came with the room, stood in front of a huge mirror, and said to himself: "Haschele Wamberger, das hast Du gut gemacht."[3] The Martians also had every right to tell themselves, in the years following the war, "Well done."

Something also changed for science in general: government support for research increased tremendously compared with its prewar level. John von Neumann liked a story that Stanislaw Ulam told him, which went as follows. One of the mathematicians in Lemberg (today Lviv in the Ukraine), the town where Ulam had been born and spent his youth, came to an ingenious mathematical idea, and was daydreaming that some American reporters might come and announce that he should receive one hundred thousand dollars. He wanted to name what seemed to him an improbable amount of money. It proved prophetic, because within a few years' time the representatives of the armed forces in the United States were giving such amounts to mathematicians and scientists in the form of defense contracts.[4] Von

Neumann was amused by the story, not only by its general merit but also because it even anticipated the sorts of sums that actually were paid.

Von Kármán was instrumental in setting up and modernizing the United States Air Force in the years immediately following World War II. Eventually his activities slowed down, but they never completely stopped until his death in 1963. Szilard remained very active and a champion of a variety of worthy causes, especially arms control and easing East–West tensions, until the very end of his life in 1964. A collection of his letters, speeches, and other documents from the era has been published, introduced by a concise and richly documented biography.[5] Wigner contributed much to the design of nuclear reactors and advocated the importance of civil defense, but his was a supporting role to Teller's. Von Neumann succumbed to a killer cancer at the height of a busy life devoted to the defense of the United States and to improving computational possibilities. Teller became the most conspicuous Martian in the Cold War period. He was credited with creating the hydrogen bomb and initiating the second weapons laboratory in the United States, and he led a crusade for the Strategic Defense Initiative. Even as an octogenarian Teller was a factor in national politics with international consequences.

Theodore von Kármán

World War II was still being waged in the European theater when von Kármán and his associates appeared in Germany to assess progress in aviation science and technology. They discovered a secret institution at Braunschweig. It had been started in 1937 and the director was Adolph Bäumker, von Kármán's old colleague from the German Ministry of Transportation. From what he saw and learned, von Kármán drew the conclusion that "the Germans could have prolonged the war, and could have possibly even won it, if they had been more skilled at organization."[6] He was surprised that the German military had been unable to utilize its scientists sufficiently.

The British had learned from their bitter experience in World War I, when they had not used their scientists according to their skills. The most tragic reminder of this was Henry G. J. Mosley, who was killed at Gallipoli after Rutherford tried, but failed, to secure him for science. Mosley was one of the most promising young scientists who had made his name during a research career of just four years. Among his achievements was the establishment of the atomic numbers of the elements, which provided an explanation for the periodic table on the basis of the structure of atoms. In World War II, the scientist-turned-author Charles P. Snow was advisor on scientific personnel to the Ministry of Labor and, later, Civil Service Commissioner. He was engaged in creating a registry of British scientists and using them to the utmost of their abilities.

No scientist in Germany had anything like the close liaison with the military that von Kármán had with the U.S. Air Force. According to von Kármán, the German military regarded scientists as unrealistic intellectuals who were not to be told too much about military affairs. His impression from a visit to Moscow was that the Soviet military relied more on their scientists than the Germans did on theirs.[7] As soon as Nazi Germany attacked the Soviet Union in 1941, "blood-thirsty Stalin, who openly despised and hated intellectuals, was clever enough to issue a special decree forbidding the call-up of scientists for war service."[8]

Von Kármán and his party found some intelligence in Germany that was later to prove useful in the United States: for example, test data that were instrumental in designing the B-47 airplane, the first U.S. swept-back bomber. Von Kármán wrote up a report on his findings with the title "Where We Stand." It compared scientific aviation in Germany and the United States and gave an estimate of what the Americans could do for further development. The key finding was that the United States was capable of building ballistic missiles with a 6,000-mile range. Later in 1945, von Kármán was back in Europe to augment his previous findings, from which he prepared yet another report: "Toward New Horizons."[9]

The second report ascribed the main factor in Germany's defeat to the Allied, especially American, air power, and in general remarked on the technological character of modern war. It discussed the decisive contribution by "organized science" to the making of effective weapons, and made forecasts and recommendations. It paid special attention to the importance of meteorology. The report examined the effects of the development of guided missiles on the future of the U.S. Air Force. There was an interesting general warning in the report that complete security did not exist anymore. This was fully consistent with Edward Teller's conclusion when he assessed the consequences of nuclear weapons at about the same time.[10] Von Kármán stressed that "the men in charge of the future Air Force should always remember that problems never have final or universal solutions. Only a constant inquisitive attitude toward science and a ceaseless and swift adaptation to new developments can maintain the security of the nation." Von Kármán prided himself that "Toward New Horizons," together with a companion volume, "Science: The Key to Air Supremacy," was "the first exhaustive report of its kind in the history of the American military forces." It pointed to the air force being the major means of defending the United States. It also stressed that science and technology should be continuously tapped for progress. Von Kármán believed that his vision guided the creation of modern air power in the United States, which was not only strong, but also scientific.[11]

The recommendations of "Toward New Horizons" were not immediately implemented. Von Kármán had to argue for the usefulness of even the Scientific Advisory Board of which he was chairman. The wartime supreme head of scientific research, Vannevar Bush, declared that the American military should not be engaged in developing new weapons; rather, it should restrict itself to perfecting the existing systems. This reserve with regard to the development of new weapons was reminiscent of Colonel Adamson's initial attitude at the first meeting of the Briggs Committee in 1939. However, the creation and success of the atomic bomb should have alleviated such reservation. There was strong protest and Bush soon had to recant his statement. Nonetheless, in the immediate postwar years it took a while before national defense again became a public concern. This was a difficult period for the air force; it was being separated from the U.S. Army to form an independent force and a rivalry began. The aviation industry was not enthusiastic about the air force conducting its own research and development. They wanted the air force to spend money on planes rather than research. The first Secretary of the Air Force, Stuart Symington, however, gave importance to scientific research and long-range planning. He was a fighter, so von Kármán did not have to fight.[12]

Von Kármán had a strong interest in the future of nuclear weapons because the air force would have to deliver them. He sought information from the Atomic Energy Commission (AEC), but such information was not forthcoming. Instead of arguing, von Kármán decided to circumvent the AEC and created a Nuclear Weapons Panel for the Air Force Science Advisory Board. He appointed John von Neumann as chairman, and the members included Edward Teller, Hans Bethe, Norris Bradbury, the new director of Los Alamos at the time, and George Kistiakowsky of Harvard University, who would later become President Eisenhower's science advisor. It was a strong body, but not without problems. In time Teller would succeed in creating a second weapons laboratory at Livermore, and he and Bradbury did not see eye to eye on the question of developing new weapons or perfecting existing ones. Then, in 1954, the Oppenheimer hearing introduced yet another line of division among the panel members. Von Kármán did not immerse himself in the deliberations of the panel but counted on von Neumann's skills to hold it together. The panel found that the hydrogen bomb was feasible even if it had to be delivered by intercontinental ballistic missiles (ICBMs). This assessment was timely because the Soviet Union was showing an unexpected vigor in advancing into the nuclear age. The activities of von Neumann were instrumental in creating the first American ICBMs, even though he did not live long enough to see their successful launch in 1959. The air force needed more experts, but rather than going to universities and the industry for ideas, it established a think tank in 1948. This was the RAND Corporation and the Science Advisory Board relied on its recommendations extensively.[13]

It is interesting to ponder whether von Kármán's tremendous impact on the American military preparedness was in any way hindered by the long and meticulous FBI investigation into his past. There is no evidence that he was even aware of the investigation, and no evidence that, even in the dark years of McCarthyism, any open accusation could have been made against him. Such accusations had been made against others on lesser charges than could have been made against him, given his political past in Hungary.

The more interesting case is that of Hsue-shen Tsien, one of von Kármán's best students, who eventually returned to China amid stormy conditions and became China's leading missile scientist.[14] It seems that Tsien fell victim to the McCarthy-led communist witch hunt. One of Tsien's problems was his former association with the alleged communist Sidney Weinbaum in Pasadena. Tsien refused to testify against him, just as he refused to testify against his other friends. This turned the investigators' attention to Tsien himself. The hassle resulted in Tsien eventually leaving the United States, but not before he had suffered long years of humiliation. Incidentally, in an unrelated investigation, when the FBI could not put together a credible case against Linus Pauling it turned against Weinbaum, a Pauling associate for many years.[15] Senator McCarthy's communist phobia and the threat represented by Stalin's Soviet Union came together in a confluence of fear.

It was a shock when the Americans realized that the Soviet Union had acquired the potential to attack the United States and use atomic weapons from the air. This realization came after the first Soviet nuclear explosion in 1949. From then on there was enhanced emphasis on defending the North American continent against such attacks. The answer was an early warning radar system, the research for which took place in the Lincoln Laboratory in Cambridge, Massachusetts. Experience such as that gained fighting against the MIGs in Korea finally convinced the air force to give research equal importance with operations.[16]

In 1953, the air force asked von Kármán to prepare another report, like the one of 1945.[17] When he expressed reluctance, saying that the complexity of the matter could not be accommodated in a single report, the air force turned to the National Academy of Sciences for such a report. A series of studies resulted from informal summer meetings at Woods Hole. What was considered bold in 1945 appeared modest in 1953. In fact, at this time the air force encouraged the scientists to let their imaginations go. Curiously, space was an exception; it was not considered to be a strategic area, but the situation changed abruptly when the Soviet Sputnik went up in 1957. It would be difficult to overestimate the beneficial consequences of the Sputnik for American education, scientific research, and military preparedness.

Von Kármán was a strong believer in the supremacy of individual performance over collective efforts. There was a characteristic debate between him and a Midwestern industrialist, whom he visited on one occasion. There were two pictures on the wall in his host's office: one showed five jackasses pulling a bale of hay in five directions, the other showed the five pulling the bale in one direction. For the millionaire this proved the superiority of teamwork over individual work. Yes, von Kármán remarked, but people are not jackasses. Nonetheless, he changed his views somewhat over the years and came to see a lot of merit in teamwork, especially when representatives of different fields had to cooperate. Yet, he still thought that "the finest creative thoughts come not out of organized teams but out of the quiet of one's own world."[18]

International cooperation was always high on von Kármán's agenda, and he had an international network of students and associates in spite of the classified nature of much of his involvement in U.S. defense work. He advocated not just cooperation but actually working together. In this he also recognized the danger of what we today call brain-drain, as he came from a small country where scientists had restricted opportunities. He felt that an international center of science would enhance the self-esteem of small nations and would help to diffuse the tension that contributed to the outbreak of World War II. He did not find organizations like the United Nations and its specialized agency for education and culture, UNESCO, to be the proper vehicles for such international cooperation. He convinced the U.S. Department of Defense to support a research project for the North Atlantic Treaty Organization (NATO), in aeronautics.[19] Even though the implementation of his proposal was held up for a while by navy/air force rivalry, he was to play an important role in advising NATO, and he happily spent considerable time in the NATO headquarters in Paris, and returned to his base in Pasadena for short periods only.[20]

In spite of his moving in high circles of military command and planning, von Kármán never abandoned his direct interest in scientific matters. When he attended a meeting in Algeria, he became interested in describing scientifically the beautiful ripple formations on flat sand surfaces.[21] He connected it with his research on the dust storms and planned shelter belt in the United States in 1937. Von Kármán's ability, interests, and scope were wide-ranging, and he constantly found new areas for research. One venture, for example, led him into the study of the mechanisms of burning and flame and the chemistry of combustion.

Von Kármán had a legendary ability to accomplish his plans and dreams, and to get support for his schemes. He found it most important to establish "the right point of view." He illustrated this with a story of a Jesuit and a Dominican priest. They both liked to smoke and were unhappy that they were not supposed to during the hours of meditation. They decided to consult higher authority about their rights. The Dominican asked for permission to smoke during meditation and was denied it. The Jesuit asked whether it was all right to meditate while smoking, and nobody would prohibit him doing that.[22]

Was von Kármán an activist in raising issues for strengthening the defense of the United States, or did he just go along with what was needed and help to the best of his abilities? He held the view that scientists as a group should not try to persuade governments; they should only analyze a given situation and establish the true picture by scientific methods. Science should provide alternatives from which to choose. It was his view that: "A scientist should be neither a Teller nor an Einstein insofar as public affairs are concerned." Within these limits he found his close ties with the military to be a natural state of affairs. For him the military was the most comfortable group to deal with in that it had the spirit and the funds to advance science rapidly and successfully. Since he found the world to be increasingly dependent on arms, he thought that the scientist should make the most of military backing to advance science. Von Kármán did not share the positions of idealistic and pacifist scientists like Max Born and Niels Bohr, although he had great respect for them. He believed that their way of thinking would be feasible only if all threat of war could be removed from the Earth, hence his biting statement that: "Nothing in my view is so pathetic as an idealistic man talking of situations which he doesn't have the strength to control."[23]

Leo Szilard

After World War II, the continuation of the atomic bomb program came into question. The general nuclear research program was also put under scrutiny, and especially who should control it. The military had this control and wanted to retain it. A joint U.S. House–Senate bill was introduced to this effect by Representative Andrew J. May and Senator Edwin C. Johnson, both Democrats, who wanted to hasten the bill through the two houses of Congress without public hearings. However, a senator from Connecticut, Brien McMahon, was in favor of civilian control. Ideas were floating around about international cooperation and the participation of the United Nations. It was also a question of how long the United States would be able to maintain a monopoly over the atomic bomb and whether the period of this monopoly should be used for international negotiations. At a conference on atomic energy in Chicago in September 1945, Szilard predicted that the Soviets would soon catch up. He presented two alternatives: one was negotiation and agreement with the Soviets, the other was relocation of tens of millions of people from large cities in the United States to sparsely populated areas.

As early as 1945 Szilard was concerned with the problem of how to verify any agreement the United States and the Soviet Union might reach. He proposed "to guarantee immunity to scientists and engineers everywhere in the world in case they should report violations of the [arms-control] agreements."[24] However unrealistic it was, Szilard saw the possibility for an ambitious "permanent" peace in creating a world government. He also saw a more realistic possibility for "durable" peace if an international agreement could be reached *not* to stockpile atomic weapons.

Listening to Szilard's proposals, some people thought that he was joking, and he admitted that even he did not know for sure when he was kidding. He often used the technique of shocking his audience with wild suggestions. Those who were less polite about Szilard thought that he was a slightly mad scientist. He was an activist, a doer, and he vowed to fight the original May–Johnson bill. In opposing it, Szilard was joined by many of the scientists who participated in the Manhattan Project, especially in Chicago. Szilard started getting involved with congressmen and other politicians, visiting them and presenting his views.

In October 1945, President Truman proposed to Congress the creation of a civilian Atomic Energy Commission (AEC), which would have total control over all matters of atomic energy and the power to oversee all military and civilian operations. He also suggested cooperation with Britain and Canada.

Szilard was asked to testify before the May Committee in the House of Representatives on October 18, 1945. The committee was not very friendly to him, but that the hearing was even taking place was a victory for Szilard. He presented detailed plans for the organization of the American nuclear energy project. This was his first appearance before a congressional panel, but he did not seem at all intimidated. He felt free to advise the congressmen on how to reorganize the atomic energy project and took it as natural that he should be the one telling them what to do. In the House, Szilard continued his activities: he managed to convene a meeting of interested representatives, to which more than seventy came. He briefed them and posed his two alternatives: reach an international agreement or undertake the massive relocation of city populations. His remarks appeared in the *Congressional Record* and were reported by *The New York Times*. [25]

Szilard was immersed in public relations activities: he gave radio and newspaper interviews, was featured in major publications, and delivered speeches; even his engineering of the Einstein letter to President Roosevelt was written about. In his interviews Szilard would mention Madách's *The Tragedy of Man* as a book that had influenced him since early childhood.[26] He was very active and very visible, and there were colleagues who sometimes resented his approach of doing everything independently of them but nonetheless criticizing them when they did something themselves.

At Senator McMahon's suggestion, the Senate created a new committee to write atomic energy legislation. On December 10, 1945, Szilard testified before the McMahon Committee in the Senate, an occasion very different from his appearance before the May Committee in the House. [27] In the Senate he was on friendly ground and was greeted as a pioneer of nuclear science. He discussed the production of uranium and plutonium, his invention of the breeder reactor, and the economic, political, military, and international consequences of the nuclear program. He also discussed the dangers of an arms race with the Soviet Union and that he was dedicated to preventing that race.

Finally, control over atomic development in the United States was given to a civilian authority, although an amendment ensured access to all its business by a permanent Military Liaison Committee. In any case, Szilard played a leading role in shaping legislation for the Atomic Energy Commission.

While Szilard was a celebrity for a short while, his longer-range view of what to do with himself was murky. In addition to having kept him under surveillance during the war, the FBI conducted another investigation in 1946, looking into his association with liberals and his outspoken support of the internationalization of the nuclear program. Szilard did not let himself be intimidated and he was brave in handling the anti-communist hysteria of the McCarthy period. But he was outraged that nobody spoke up against McCarthy and the House Un-American Activities Committee in the 1950s. For him it was a reminder that nobody had spoken up against Hitler and the Nazis at the German universities in the 1930s.[28] Those who lived through the McCarthy period carry scars and deep-rooted fears about American society.[29] However, Szilard was an activist in the 1930s as well as in the 1950s, and he raised money to support the victims of anti-communist discrimination.

Time and again, Szilard lost a cause or a crusade. He was a good loser: he cherished democracy and was always ready for a new battle. He never criticized the American system of democracy and paid attention to its rules even in his wildest actions. Although he was investigated by the FBI repeatedly and for long periods of time, he was not investigated for un-American activities in spite of his very critical approach to McCarthyism.

Szilard received support from the chancellor of the University of Chicago, Robert M. Hutchins, himself a maverick, who had introduced innovations at the university from the 1930s. In the fall of 1946 he appointed Szilard to be half-time professor of biophysics and half-time advisor in the social aspects of atomic energy. He was placed in one of the three newly established institutes, the Institute of Radiobiology and Biophysics.[30] Szilard called this "one of the best positions that exists at any university in the United States," and his affiliation with the University of Chicago then lasted to his retirement. [31]

He did not concentrate on a single topic for long; his interests spread, which was also beneficial because it helped him to make unexpected connections between seemingly unrelated fields. He liked to crisscross the country and visit various people and institutions. In spite of the Chicago appointment, Szilard continued to be without a permanent appointment. He did not want to be bogged down by a real job and dreamed of other solutions; one would have been a "roving professorship" permitting him to work occasionally at six different institutions.[32] It may sound fantastic, but anybody who gets to know Szilard's life story feels that he should have had such a position. And it may be less fantastic than it appears at first sight. When Alfred Nobel created the Nobel Prize in his will, part of his intention was that it would free outstanding scientists from financial worries. Another example is the stipend that some science academies provide to their members regardless of formal employment: the stipend that the peripatetic mathematician Paul Erdős received from the Hungarian Academy of Sciences during the last years of his life provided him with some financial security.

Szilard had few personal belongings, and he mailed his important papers to Gertrud (Trude) Weiss, whom he married in 1951, although they continued to live separately for some time. Erdős, similarly, mailed all his papers to his mother and then, after her death, to a colleague at Bell Labs.[33] Szilard kept his two suitcases ready to go in case of emergency. In spite of his eccentricities, for example, not cleaning the bathtub, he was warm-hearted, kind and helpful to secretaries and other assistants, and particularly kind to children, without being condescending. Szilard cared for the well-being of his colleagues, dispensing good advice whether sought or not. He often gave it in the form of instruction rather than advice, perhaps to mask his shyness, but this made him appear "cold in personal relationships."[34]

Although the FBI was never able to come up with open accusations against him, it could have prevented him from doing classified work and he might have had little hope of getting a government-sponsored position. He might have sought employment with a non-governmental organization involved with nuclear physics, for example the new Institute for Nuclear Studies at the University of Chicago. However, Fermi, did not want him in the institute. Szilard had already become interested in biology before the war; now he turned to this fast developing field.

He was not the only physicist to do so: Erwin Schrödinger had published a small but influential book in 1944 called *What Is Life?* and there were physicists who saw biology as the new frontier and, like Szilard, wanted to be part of it.[35] Others hoped that research in biology might open new vistas to heretofore unknown laws of physics.[36] Max Delbrück was such a scientist. He had followers, and together they formed the phage group, which studied the simplest viruses that attack bacteria, now called bacteriophages.[37] It takes exceptional scientists to move easily from physics to biology, but if there is anything that helps such a move, in addition to talent, it is being educated broadly.[38] This is what Hutchins of the University of Chicago had suggested.

Once one makes the change to a new field, there are enhanced chances for new discoveries because the newcomer is not bound by the existing dogmas of the field.[39] When on one occasion a biologist wanted to explain something to Szilard, he asked Szilard what knowledge he should assume on his part. Szilard's reply was, "Assume infinite intelligence and zero prior knowledge."[40] In an interview in 1962, Szilard commented upon his transition to biology: "What I brought into biology . . . was not any skills acquired in physics, but rather an attitude: the conviction that few biologists had at the time, that mysteries can be solved."[41]

Szilard had scientific interactions with leading molecular biologists and other biologists, including such luminaries as James Watson, François Jacob, Rita Levi-Montalcini, and George Klein.[42] These contacts were beneficial to the biologists in that he cross-fertilized their ideas and findings, gave them suggestions, and participated in a selfless way in their developing their concepts. They appreciated his suggestions, which contributed to the Nobel Prize-winning research of Jacob and Jacques Monod.[43] There was a particularly close friendship between Monod and Szilard.[44]

It rarely happened that Szilard did not grasp a new idea, but this was the case when the young Marshall Nirenberg was looking for a sponsor to have his paper published in the *Proceedings of the National Academy of Sciences of the U.S.A.* (*PNAS*). Members of the academy can publish papers in this periodical, but other authors may do so only if their work is sponsored by a member. Nirenberg was not a member, but Szilard was a recently (April 1961) elected one. Nirenberg, with Heinrich Matthaei, had just made a seminal discovery at the National Institutes of Health, one that would enter the annals of science history as the first step in cracking the genetic code, and they wanted to publish their finding in *PNAS*. At that time Szilard lived in the Dupont Hotel at Dupont Circle in Washington, DC, and Nirenberg visited him there. As he was explaining his discovery to Szilard, various visitors who wanted to confer with Szilard kept interrupting them. His "office" was in the hotel lobby and Nirenberg spent the whole day telling him about what he and Matthaei had done and what the implications were. At the end, Szilard said, "It's too much out of my field. I'm sorry, I can't sponsor it." [45] Seven years later, Nirenberg received a share of the 1968 Nobel Prize in Physiology or Medicine for the discovery. James D. Watson had a similar experience with Szilard.[46] Watson told him about the evidence on messenger RNA (ribonucleic acid), but Szilard did not believe it; he was very much occupied with the treatment of his cancer at the time.

In spite of these lapses, Szilard had an exceptional integrating mind and he made good use of it. He did not have a personal agenda for his own advancement, only science's agenda, to advance science. He interrogated his colleagues about their work and followed their progress. In the words of François Jacob, who met him for the first time in 1953 at a Cold Spring Harbor symposium, "He took me to a corner, took out a notebook, and began asking me questions. He forced me to answer him in his own wording. He had a special way of talking, which probably came from physics." When they met next time, it may have been years later, Szilard took out his notebook again and checked with Jacob whether his previous statements were still valid. Jacob imagined Szilard as ideally having "a special job of a bumblebee in a communication system whose task would be talking with people and getting and disseminating news."[47] This was very similar to the job Szilard envisioned for himself when he applied for support to the National Science Foundation in 1956:

> At present certain branches of biology in which I am interested are in
> rapid progress. The problems of protein synthesis, the role of RNA and
> DNA, and the general problem of self-reproduction, differentiation
> and aging are rapidly becoming open to attack by means of new
> techniques. . . . As a Senior Scientist-At-Large it should be possible for
> me to acquire intimate knowledge of experiments conducted with a
> great variety of biological material and diverse techniques, and thereby
> to be in a position to try to function as "theoretical biologist.[48]

Szilard's postwar excursion into biology commenced when he established a partnership with Aaron Novick in 1947 at the University of Chicago. Together they attended a course on the bacteriophage organized by Max Delbrück at the Cold Spring Harbor Laboratory. In Chicago, lacking lab space, Szilard and Novick arranged for their own space in a synagogue at an abandoned Jewish orphanage owned by the university. They bought everything necessary, in most cases very rudimentary equipment. They made methodological innovations and created the chemostat, as a continuous source of bacterial population. It was so novel that the National Institutes of Health turned down their request for support because the reviewers could not imagine that it would be feasible. They also worked out a methodology for accurately measuring the rate of mutation of bacteria. In their studies of the regulation of gene expression, Szilard and Novick discovered the phenomenon that became known as feedback inhibition, which is decisive in the intracellular processes of metabolism and growth. These were worthy discoveries and made them partners with the most important researchers in biology. According to Novick "Szilard had become a biologist, although I suspect he always continued to think of himself rather as a physicist interested in biology."[49] The excursion into biology showed Szilard's ability to work in the laboratory in a field very different from nuclear physics. Nonetheless, within a few years' time he returned to giving most of his attention to political questions.

He drafted proposals about important issues, some of which came to fruition only toward the end of his life or after his death. These included the Salk Institute for Biological Studies, the Pugwash Conferences on Science and World Affairs, and the National Science Foundation. Szilard was the recognized initiator of the European molecular biology organizations, which came about from a bizarre event.[50] During the Cuban missile crisis (see below), Szilard and his wife fled the United States and went to Geneva where, at the European Laboratory for Particle Physics (CERN), he declared himself to be the first refugee from World War III. He suggested the formation of an international laboratory of molecular biology. During the following weeks and months he did a lot of organizational work, and within a few years the European Molecular Biology Organization (EMBO) and the European Molecular Biology Laboratory (EMBL) had come to life. Szilard was such a master of persuasion that Max Perutz, who never before or after agreed to serve on committees, acted as the first chairman of EMBO for six years.[51]

Other problems about which he cared, but which came to be recognized as important only much later, included overpopulation, poverty, pollution, the buildup of carbon dioxide in the atmosphere, issues of alternative food supply, and even the dangers of cholesterol. He also proposed a full exchange of information on fusion energy with the Soviets, a proposition that became formalized in the early 1990s. One more example of his forward-thinking was the concept of information and entropy, on which he had worked in the 1920s. At that time he and von Neumann had taught a course together at the University of Berlin, and eventually von Neumann took up the topic. Much later, when it was rediscovered, Szilard received some belated credit for his pioneering work. Szilard liked a discovery for the discovery's sake, although he sometimes did not appear so altruistic to his peers because of his extensive patenting activities. He was concerned about money, especially for his future, but at the same time he was unselfish about it. "He just wanted to improve the whole world, and everything in it."[52]

Sometimes his proposals stunned his audience and it was only later, sometimes much later, that it was realized that they made very good sense. It was not
rare that he would make a suggestion in a much twisted way to bring his message
home. In a nationally broadcast radio discussion about new weapons with Hans
Bethe, Frederick Seitz, and Harrison Brown, he proposed that the hydrogen bomb
should be made so dreadful that no nation would dare to use it. He suggested
that adding cobalt to the hydrogen bomb would cause it to generate radioactivity strong enough to annihilate the whole human race.[53] His partners were upset
by this suggestion because they saw in it a belittling of the monstrosity of the already existing weapons. Yet Szilard's approach found expression in the policy of
mutually assured destruction (MAD). Of course, Szilard did not work for accomplishing MAD, as Teller did, but it is noteworthy that the idea came to Szilard's
mind as well.

He would shock his lecture audiences by declaring that "Mass murderers have
always commended the attention of the public, and atomic scientists are no exception to this rule."[54] Szilard made forays into the economic sciences impressive enough to be noted by the Nobel laureate economist Milton Friedman.[55] He
also engaged in extensive writings, although these were shorter pieces rather than
longer works. They included "My Trial as a War Criminal," "The Mark Gabel
Foundation," "Science Is My Racket," "Report on 'Grand Central Terminal',"
"Calling All Stars," and "Nicolai Machiavellnikow."

Occasionally Szilard was called the "father of the atom bomb."[56] This may
have prompted Szilard to imagine himself as a condemned "war criminal" in the
work "My Trial as a War Criminal." In the story, Szilard stands trial before the
Soviets following a Soviet invasion of the United States. The Soviets have used a
deadly virus in their attack but eventually need American help in combating an
epidemic in the Soviet Union that is a consequence of their mishandling of their
own viruses. The final outcome is favorable to the Americans, and the war crime
trials are stopped. This story seems remarkable when viewed from the perspective of the twenty-first century and its fear of biological weapons.

Szilard drew knowledge and analogies from ancient history and in particular
from the war between Athens and Sparta, which started with a war between an
ally of Athens and an ally of Sparta. He imagined a war similarly starting between
a NATO country and a Warsaw Pact country. The Korean conflict might also have
developed into a world war without the superpowers necessarily willing to fight
each other. At times Szilard carried Thucydides's *History of the Peloponnesian War*
in his pocket.[57]

Szilard's most important activities during the Cold War period were aimed
at arms control. He was conspicuous among the arms control activists in that he
had been instrumental in creating the very weapons that he was now trying to
curb. He was not considered to be as successful as some others, for example Linus
Pauling, who won the Nobel Peace Prize in 1963. Lanouette considers the reasons
why Szilard failed: "he was too visionary, too rational, too clever, and too impa-

tient."[58] While Pauling concentrated on fighting for the ban on nuclear testing, Szilard viewed the concerns for the dangers of such testing as exaggerated.[59] In fact, Szilard thought that research and testing should continue, with the purpose of creating a "cleaner" hydrogen bomb, and that the results should then be shared with the Soviets.[60] He was interested in accepting the reality of nuclear weapons and finding ways to coexist with them.

It was characteristic of Szilard that he always went to the top, whether it was a political issue or a scientific one. He was catapulted into this attitude during the Berlin colloquia. When he wanted political contact, he wrote letters to the American presidents, first using Einstein, later in his own name. When he wanted attention from the Soviets, he turned to the top, first to Stalin, later to Khrushchev. He never received a response from Stalin, but Stalin did not engage much in communication: Peter Kapitsa was known to have written many letters to Stalin and received a grand total of two responses, both very short.[61] Szilard suggested to Stalin in 1947 that he should talk to the American people by radio and that President Truman should address the Soviets. Nothing happened then, but eventually Reagan and Gorbachev did what Szilard had originally proposed, except that they used television rather than radio.

Szilard had better luck with Khrushchev than with Stalin.[62] For those who did not live through the Stalin period, it is difficult to appreciate the change that Khrushchev's emergence in the Soviet leadership signified. He brought a fresh atmosphere with him, he was less secretive, and he advocated peaceful coexistence in 1959, during his visit to the United States. Alas, in 1960, he cancelled his meeting with Eisenhower in Paris because of the U-2 scandal. Even though there were negotiations between the United States and the Soviet Union, the Americans continued the flights of the U-2 spy planes over the USSR. The Soviets downed one of these planes and angrily protested. Only some days after the Americans had denied the existence of the flights did the Soviets produce the downed pilot alive. It was humiliating for the American president and the relationship between the superpowers reached a new low. Szilard protested the American handling of the U-2 affair in strong terms.[63]

Szilard wrote to Khrushchev in June 1960, received no response, and wrote again in August 1960, this time receiving a response to his first letter. Khrushchev came to New York on United Nations business, and Szilard met him on two social occasions, but these were meetings with many people present. Then, on October 5, Szilard received word that Khrushchev would see him at 11 A.M. for fifteen minutes. Their meeting lasted fully two hours, although Szilard several times offered to leave. He brought Khrushchev a gift, a disposable shaving kit, and showed the Soviet premier how to use it, promising to supply him with new blades from time to time if war did not prevent their communications. Khrushchev told Szilard that if war broke out, he would stop shaving.

It is of interest to report a few characteristic tidbits from their conversation.[64] At places Szilard appeared as if he were trying to coach the Soviet premier. He suggested to Khrushchev that he talk not only about his disagreements with the United States, but also about the points on which he agreed with American politicians. The American presidential campaign between Kennedy and Nixon was underway, and the idea was that Khrushchev could express whatever he wanted to say about the American candidates, however negative, just by repeating what Kennedy said about Nixon and Nixon about Kennedy. Szilard handed Khrushchev a seven-page memorandum in Russian. He was well prepared for the meeting: this was not the impatient Szilard who would hurry from topic to topic, but a meticulous Szilard, who was leaving nothing to chance.

Szilard found it important for the two superpowers to establish consensus about encouraging citizens in the other country to report violations of arms reduction agreements. This was a recurring topic for him. The informants should receive financial rewards and they should be able to get asylum in the other country if they so desired. Szilard further suggested the establishment of an international arms control authority, above national sovereignty. With this, Khrushchev seemed to be in agreement. Szilard advocated a stop to nuclear weapons testing. Khrushchev liked this because the Soviet Union at that moment was not much interested in further testing. The Americans, however, were working on further development of their nuclear weaponry.

In their discussion there was an interesting revelation about Szilard's insight into the dealings with the Soviet Union. He understood that the American citizens who dealt with questions of disarmament in non-governmental organizations did not necessarily represent their government, whereas any Soviet negotiator automatically reflected Kremlin policies—as people in a dictatorship were supposed to.

An important issue in the conversation was the telephone hotline between the two governments, to be used in case of emergency. Szilard made this suggestion and Khrushchev found it a useful proposal. At the end of August 1963, the Moscow–Washington hotline (telex rather than telephone) went into service. When Khrushchev encouraged Szilard to discuss other issues, Szilard offered a solution to the Berlin problem. The meeting was a success, even though there were hardly any immediate results and, of course, Szilard did not represent the American government. It is remarkable that Khrushchev accepted Szilard as partner in negotiation, even if only for two hours, when Szilard did not represent anybody except himself, but Khrushchev was rather isolated diplomatically at that time. There were similarities between the two men, even physically, but beyond that as well. Both were establishment outsiders in their own countries and both were committed to arms reduction. Khrushchev at that time wanted material resources to be turned away from weapons and toward strengthening the Soviet economy.

The Moscow Pugwash meeting in November 1960 followed soon after, and it was not a great success. Szilard asked for a meeting with Khrushchev, but the Soviet leader did not receive him and cancelled even the promised reception for the Pugwash delegates. Szilard lingered in Moscow for weeks hoping for a meeting, but it did not materialize. It must have been humiliating, let alone boring, for

Szilard to spend weeks in Moscow. He was practically confined to his hotel in a strange city without friends, or interactions with anybody except his wife, who accompanied him. One wonders why Khrushchev did not even let Szilard know that he would not be available. Szilard was never given to complaint, and he came away with some humorous tidbits about life in the Soviet Union. He understood the Soviet system. He valued American democracy and only wanted improved relations between the two superpowers, but he was realistic about what the Soviets stood for. "He was no *peacenik*," stressed Matthew Meselson, who knew Szilard and who has long been involved with disarmament.[65]

On their way home, the Szilards stopped in Vienna, and Szilard telephoned an old friend in Budapest, suggesting that he come to Vienna to meet them. The friend urged Szilard to visit Budapest, but he refused because "he feared the Fascists."[66] This was in the fall of 1960, when the bloody communist reprisals over the 1956 revolutions were finally quieting down in Hungary. It is unlikely that Szilard would have been in any danger in Budapest, so his expression of protest was symbolic. Szilard did not forget, nor did he forgive, what he had experienced in Hungary in 1919 and what he had learned about Hungarian collaboration with the Nazis during World War II. Nonetheless, a few years later Szilard indicated in a letter to Wigner that he had a standing invitation from the Hungarian Academy of Sciences and that he might visit Hungary.[67] However, he had a condition, which he explained to the Hungarian Ambassador in Washington in spring 1963, namely, that there should first be a general political amnesty. Szilard never went back to Hungary. Von Kármán and Wigner took a milder attitude toward communist Hungary: von Kármán would soon be going to Budapest to receive an honorary doctorate from his Alma Mater, and Wigner would also visit Budapest long before the fall of communism. Teller, however, would wait until the political changes of 1989–1990.

There is much information available about Szilard's activities in trying to stop the arms race. When the United States exploded its first hydrogen bomb, Szilard took a three-month leave without pay from the University of Chicago to devote himself fully to working for arms control. By then he thought that the hydrogen bomb made the world less stable, and feared a war in which it would be used. He proposed to set up a private school in Mexico and suggested to his colleagues that they send their children away from the United States to protect them from such a war. At the same time he was against judging anybody's loyalty to the United States on the basis of that person's opinion about whether the hydrogen bomb should be developed or not.[68]

Surprisingly little is known about Szilard's stand on the initial debate about the development of the hydrogen bomb; it is generally assumed that he was against it. However, a caveat should be issued: there is a difference between developing the hydrogen bomb in general and developing it in a certain world situation. If the question was whether there should be a hydrogen bomb in the arsenal of armaments that humankind possesses, it is a safe assumption that Szilard opposed it. However, if the question was whether the hydrogen bomb should be available for the defense of the United States in case the Soviet Union had the hydrogen bomb, then Szilard must have favored its development by the United States.

Szilard discussed this issue at a dinner lecture he gave in Los Angeles on December 8, 1954. The title of his talk was "The Sensitive Minority among Men of Science," and he added two subtitles: "Why did the Germans miss out on the atomic bomb," and "Why did America come so close to missing out on the hydrogen bomb?" Szilard summarized the pre–World War II situation leading to the development of the atomic bomb in the United States. The principal reason was the fear of the German atomic bomb. It had been thought, up to the end of 1943, that the Germans and Allies were in a race to develop the atomic bomb. The scientists considered the American atomic bomb as a safety device that would restrain the Germans from using theirs against American cities. Szilard also talked about the disappointment of many American scientists when the Allies mass-bombed German cities with jellied gasoline bombs and when the atomic bombs were dropped over Hiroshima and Nagasaki. Szilard argued that these actions made the American scientists doubt the sincerity of their government. Although they were "just as apprehensive of Russia as a potential enemy as they had felt before the war about Germany," they became less trustful of their own government. This is why, Szilard continues, the United States "would have missed out on the hydrogen bomb altogether had it not been for the accident that there was still one man left who—for a variety of reasons—still liked to think about the problems of the bomb."[69] That man was Edward Teller, and Szilard called this an accident, because if there is only one man left, it might just as easily happened that there was no-one left.

Even after fifty years, Matthew Meselson clearly remembers this Szilard speech, which was given at the Ambassador Hotel.[70] Meselson was Linus Pauling's graduate student at Caltech at the time and served as Szilard's chauffeur during the visit. Meselson was also Szilard's proxy audience when he rehearsed the "Sensitive Minority" speech.

Szilard does not discuss the desirability of developing the hydrogen bomb in general, but refers specifically to the development of the American hydrogen bomb in response to the Soviet threat. He then adds that when the Soviets exploded their first atomic bomb in 1949, he felt a responsibility to call the attention of the White House to the dangers of the situation, and talked to an official about it. At this point a Szilard-like twist appears in the story. As Szilard was telling the White House official, who understood the gravity of the situation, about his worry, the man came out with a warning that shocked Szilard. He told him that he should keep Teller's name a secret because if the Soviets found out about his identity, they could blacken his name and thus make it impossible for him to continue his work. This was a clear reference by Szilard to the impossible situation that the United States, including its State Department and defense establishment, had put itself in with McCarthyism. As is well known, Senator McCarthy launched his anti-communist crusade in February 1950—soon after both the first Soviet atomic bomb explosion and President Truman's decision to go ahead with the development of the American hydrogen bomb. By the time of Szilard's talk McCarthy had already been censured by his colleagues in the Senate; but there was always the possibility that a new McCarthy might emerge.

Szilard's description of the events could be interpreted as only his expression of having been deeply worried that the United States might have been left defenseless in a world in which only the Soviet Union had possessed the hydrogen bomb. Szilard's story, however, continues. As a consequence of the Oppenheimer loyalty case in 1954 (see chapter 6), the public became interested in the question of whether there was any delay in developing the hydrogen bomb after President Truman had given the directive to construct it in January 1950. Szilard assures the public that this was not the case. The physicists held a meeting soon after Truman's decision and issued the following statement:

> A few days ago, President Truman decided that this country should go ahead with the construction of a Hydrogen Bomb. We believe that no nation has the right to use such a bomb, no matter how righteous its cause. This bomb is no longer a weapon of war but a means of extermination of whole populations. Its use would be a betrayal of all standards of morality and of Christian civilization itself. . . . We urge that the United States, through its elected government, make a solemn declaration that we shall never use this bomb first. The circumstance which might force us to use it would be if we or our allies were attacked by THIS bomb. *There can be only one justification for our development of the hydrogen bomb, and that is to prevent its use* (italics added).[71]

Although Szilard was not among the signatories to the statement, many distinguished physicists and representatives of all major research centers were. The statement made it clear that it was regrettable to develop the hydrogen bomb, but it also made clear that only by developing the American hydrogen bomb would it be possible to prevent others from using one. In the period between 1945 and 1950, Szilard was sure that the statement did not slow the development of the American hydrogen bomb but that the doubts he referred to above did. In an interview in 1960, Szilard reiterated his notion that Hiroshima's example hindered many scientists from coming out for the development of the hydrogen bomb in the period between 1945 and 1950. Without Hiroshima, "many physicists would have continued to work on atomic energy after the war who did not,"[72] he said.

Szilard found it important to give assurances about the scientists' dedication to defense "to those who are concerned about our national security." Finally, Szilard adds that "the salvation of the United States cannot come from any further advances in the science of warfare," it "can come only from political sagacity." Szilard, who was often so prescient, expressed his regret that in this case he was in no position to predict whether such political sagacity was forthcoming or not. Szilard's speech in 1954 and his 1960 interview notwithstanding, he was critical of Teller when Teller compared his crusade for the development of the American hydrogen bomb to Szilard's struggle to initiate the American atomic bomb project against Germany in 1939.[73]

There were further events that contributed to the intensification of the arms race in the 1950s. Julius and Ethel Rosenberg were arrested in June 1950 for spying for the Soviet Union and giving out atomic secrets. They were tried, sentenced to death, and executed. In June 1950, North Korea invaded South Korea, ultimately bringing China, through "volunteers", and the United States, as part of the United Nations, into this conflict. The possibility of using the atomic bomb loomed on the horizon. In August 1953, the Soviet Union tested its first hydrogen device. As the development of the American hydrogen bomb to a large extent was in response to the Soviet military preparations, it is of interest to see the issue from the point of view of Soviet scientists. This is what Vitaly L. Ginzburg, a Nobel laureate physicist, had to say on this matter in 2004:

> Those Soviet physicists, whom I knew, including [Andrei] Sakharov and [Igor] Tamm, justified their participation in the nuclear project by the necessity of counterweighing the American monopoly in this respect. We can accept it that having more than one power in possession of this terrible weapon—representing mutually assured destruction—has to a certain extent stabilized the situation by serving as a deterrent. I participated within some limits in the creation of the Soviet hydrogen bomb in the period of 1948–1953. At that time it never occurred to me that the Soviet Union might use such a weapon as a means of aggression. I am sure of the same for Tamm and others with whom I had occasions to discuss this question candidly. I must admit that we did not understand Stalin's real aspirations. It was only recently that I learned about a Soviet physicist who worked on the bomb while he understood Stalin's aims, and this physicist was acting out of fear. He kept silent about it at that time and I cannot condemn him now, and would not identify him either. At this time I fully understand that Stalin was an arch bandit who would have employed even the most terrible weapons without hesitation if he had thought he would need them in accomplishing his goals, and could get away with such an action. It is the luck of humankind that Stalin and Hitler did not possess atomic bombs first.[74]

For the American scientists, the desirability of talking directly with Soviet scientists about the arms race and its control were first brought up in September 1951 during a nuclear physics conference in Chicago. Szilard and a few other participants made such a suggestion and this topic played heavily in subsequent years in Szilard's actions. Ultimately they bore fruit.[75] The first Pugwash conference, bringing together American and Soviet scientists and some from other nations as well, opened in July 1957 to discuss arms control possibilities. Szilard advanced his "crazy" idea of offering cities for retaliation and compiling a list of such cities. The idea was crazy, but it was also a rational solution to the most irrational problems. Szilard wanted to offer adequate periods of warning during which the cities could be evacuated in an orderly manner. This was also a kind of deterrence policy: at least it would not lead to the annihilation of the whole human race, only to a well-defined minimum. The atomic powers would be allowed sufficient amounts of weaponry, but not more, for these retaliations.

Szilard was not only one of the initiators of the Pugwash movement, he also helped to save it from becoming a large popular organization. He preferred to have a small, private group of influential scientists gathering for relatively long periods of time for detailed discussions.[76] The Pugwash meetings proved to be helpful in preparing United States–Soviet treaties, including the 1972 ABM (antiballistic missile) Treaty.

Szilard did not advocate the complete elimination of nuclear weapons; he advocated only a drastic reduction and he called for political agreements to exclude their use.[77] Because the two superpowers could mutually destroy each other, they were interested in the stability of the stalemate, so they had coinciding interests. He was very much against testing fresh nuclear weapons with the purpose of creating new and more specialized weapons that could be used, for example, on battlefields or for antiballistic missile defense. This is a point on which Szilard and Teller strongly disagreed. In his writings, Szilard foresaw the stalemate that eventually led to arms reduction efforts in the late 1970s and 1980s.[78]

A noteworthy event took place in 1957 under Eisenhower: the formation of the President's Science Advisory Committee (PSAC). This was also an old Szilard idea that had been exposed in Einstein's original letter to Franklin D. Roosevelt in August 1939. Presidential scientific advising has since become an important issue, gaining sometimes more and sometimes less importance under different presidents.[79] John F. Kennedy was president for less than three full years before he was assassinated in 1963. The Kennedy administration was more open to scientific advising than the subsequent Johnson and Nixon administrations. During the Kennedy era, the Szilards lived in Washington, and Szilard's main occupation was lobbying for arms control. His motto was that he was "dispensing wisdom," and it was up to the administration how much of his offering they would take. Apparently, they did not take as much as he would have liked to provide, but he had more interactions with the officials of this administration than those under other presidents. He was never received by President Kennedy, but he had contacts with Jerome Wiesner, Kennedy's science advisor, McGeorge Bundy, Kennedy's national security advisor, Chester Bowles, undersecretary at the State Department, and Glenn T. Seaborg, the AEC chairman.[80] Senator John F. Kennedy (as he was then) recognized Szilard's services to the United States when he wrote to Szilard on May 27, 1960: "This country owes many debts to you, not only for your scientific achievements but for the great responsibility and imagination you have brought to the problem of securing peace."[81] At the time Kennedy wrote this, he was already actively campaigning for the presidency.

It was still during the election campaign in the fall of 1960 that Szilard offered to both candidates to share with them his experience with Khrushchev, but neither took him up on his offer. It might have been useful for Kennedy, who had a bumpy encounter with Khrushchev in Vienna soon after having taken office. Not everybody was happy, though, with Szilard's overtures. Some considered them a trespass on the prerogatives of the State Department amounting to a violation of the law (Logan Act of 1799) which prohibited private diplomacy. Nonetheless, from time to time there are people who conduct such missions, sometimes against the expressed view of the administration; and when it bears fruit, it may be appreciated.[82] The fact is that nobody tried seriously to curb Szilard's activities. He considered his overtures to the Soviets important not only because of the gravity of the issues involved but also because he considered Kennedy an amateur and his people no match for the Soviets intellectually or by training.[83] No wonder that Szilard regarded himself as a shadow State Department.[84]

In the fall of 1962 the Cuban missile crisis developed. The Soviets placed missiles in Cuba and the Americans reacted by blockading the island state, but fortunately they did not fully enforce the blockade and the Soviets did not retaliate as they might have. Szilard made a blunder by fleeing from the United States to Geneva. There were signs of a forthcoming calamity, but this was a rare occasion where he misjudged the situation. In this case he was not ahead of anything but managed to disappoint some of his friends by giving them a feeling that he was abandoning them.[85] We have already seen, above, that the creation of European molecular biology projects was an important by-product of his fleeing to Europe.

It was even earlier—soon after Kennedy assumed the presidency—that the Bay of Pigs invasion against Cuba happened. Szilard was greatly distressed. The event occurred at about the time when he was elected to the National Academy of Sciences (NAS). He wanted to make use of his new membership at once, and compiled a petition to the president protesting the invasion. The number of signatures was not very impressive, but Szilard noted that academicians usually refrain from signing petitions. Most of Szilard's friends signed, but notably James Franck, his old and trusted friend, did not. Instead, he wrote a letter explaining his abstention, and his reasoning was profound. Franck was "against it that scientists as a class believe that their scientific reputation is a proof that they are also experts in political reasoning." Further, "We endanger our influence in these particular questions if we speak up as a group in matters not directly connected with our profession." [86] Szilard took it to heart and never again used the technique of petition to further his political aims.

He continued to have ideas, realistic and not so realistic. He was remarkable in considering not only "recognized problems" but also unrecognized ones, such as the question of new forms of democracy suitable for developing countries. It sounds as timely as ever, with the American–British coalition having won the war in Iraq in 2004, but not yet the peace. Szilard was also looking for novel ways to arbitrate international conflicts. He recognized the problem of fertility and population control, the challenge of having expanded leisure time in modern society, and took up the idea of finding biological means to eliminate the need for sleep.

The question of divided Berlin was on Szilard's mind when the Berlin Wall went up in April 1961, first as a barbed wire and eventually as concrete blocks and mortar. It was meant to keep much needed professionals inside East Germany, but was a moral defeat for the Soviet system. What could be said about a regime that builds a wall around itself, not to keep unwanted people out, but to prevent its own people from leaving?

In September 1961, the Soviets broke the nuclear-testing moratorium they had honored for nearly three years. In April 1962, the United States also resumed nuclear weapons tests. There was a lot of activity directed toward a ban on atmospheric testing. The 1961 Pugwash meeting discussed it and, finally, in August 1963, the two superpowers concluded a ban on nuclear tests in the atmosphere, in space, and under the sea. A little later that year, Linus Pauling's Nobel Peace Prize for 1962 was announced. One might wonder whether Szilard could have been included in the award. However, Pauling fought for the nuclear test ban not only relentlessly but also single-mindedly, whereas Szilard had many different schemes.

Another one of Szilard's plans was to set up a political action committee for arms control, called the Council for a Livable World. This scheme survived Szilard and has been most successful.[87] It has collected and used money to advance the election or re-election of senators who would support arms control. Szilard considered it an efficient investment with good returns to spend the money on senators, especially in less populous western states. Senators are elected for six years, and in the fortunate cases where there is a close race, a small margin can decide the outcome. He determined that an informed minority could use its unity and its money very effectively. The 1962 congressional election was the first time the Council for a Livable World participated in the process, and very successfully too.

Szilard's "Angels Project" was a scheme for working out policy alternatives by experts, which the governments could then consider adopting in American–Soviet dialogs.[88] He involved such people as Freeman Dyson and Jerome Wiesner. Some others declined, like Hans Bethe, saying that there were enough channels for superpower interaction. Szilard coined imaginative names: "saturation parity" denoted the minimal deterrence that might stabilize the United States–Soviet nuclear arms race, and "the sting of the bee" meant the minimal deterrence a country might need and how it might use it, having in mind that the bee dies after it attacks with its sting.

With President Kennedy's assassination in 1963, Szilard's access to the Washington policy-makers dried up, and he withdrew from trying to take an active hand in world politics. His retreat to La Jolla might have been temporary, though, and we can only speculate about how he would have handled the arrival of the new world leaders and the ever-escalating war in Vietnam. Szilard died in his sleep on May 30, 1964. Soon after, Communist Party General Secretary Khrushchev was removed from power in Moscow. An era came to end.

Eugene P. Wigner

Wigner had abandoned the ivory tower of physics for the sake of defending the United States and the Free World, but he was determined to return to pure physics after the war. However, the war introduced some irreversible changes in his life. He could never again live in a "splendid isolation" from politics, although he would never become as deeply involved in it as Szilard and Teller. Although Wigner has remained one of the lesser known leading physicists of the Manhattan Project, he also gained some notoriety, which perhaps helped him in his position at Princeton. He was dismayed by the United States not standing up for Eastern Europe and letting the Soviet Union dominate and brutalize it. The postwar history of Hungary was a case in point, the ruthless communist takeover of power in 1949 following a brief spell of democracy between 1945 and 1948. It pained Wigner that his colleagues ignored this, just as they had ignored the Nazi buildup in Europe in the 1930s.

After the war, Wigner was made director of research and development at the Clinton Laboratory in Oak Ridge, Tennessee, which is today the Oak Ridge National Laboratory.[89] His close associates, Alvin Weinberg and Gale Young, went with him to Clinton. It was a laboratory with 400 people building nuclear reactors, not bombs, and Wigner enjoyed practical engineering where he could use his physics, too. Although Szilard is better known for patenting, Wigner filed scores of patents connected with the design and operation of nuclear power plants. One of the problems in nuclear reactors is called *Wigneritis* after him.[90] This occurs when graphite accumulates energy as a consequence of its being used to slow neutrons in a reactor operating at lower temperatures. The energetic neutrons displace carbon atoms from the graphite sheets of hexagonal structure into the space between the sheets, and there they possess a great amount of potential energy. At higher temperatures the displaced atoms find their way back to regular positions, but at low temperatures they cannot, and the energy keeps building up. It could be dangerous in case of overheating because this would add to the energy being released.

Wigner enjoyed innovation and patenting, but he did not like being a director and administrator. Nevertheless, he may have been a good director who earned the admiration of his associates. He "not only tolerated but sought employees who had the guts to disagree" with him.[91] However, Wigner preferred teaching and independent research. At Oak Ridge, he felt "almost like a janitor, quite a prestigious janitor, of course, with a spacious office, a range of privileges, and a staff who consulted my opinions assiduously."[92] When he left, Alvin Weinberg took over his job, and Wigner remained a frequent visitor and advisor.

He returned to Princeton University, and there were many reasons why he felt more comfortable there than being the director of a big plant.[93] He found the university more challenging than a big laboratory or research institute. There are always new people, young, bright students to whom the professor has to prove himself and his research, time and again. Due to his prominence, Wigner was asked to join various committees and panels of influence, at the National Research Council and National Science Foundation, for instance, and he was a member of the General Advisory Committee of the Atomic Energy Commission (AEC) for ten years. Wigner's main advice was to relax the security rules of the AEC laboratories. He thought that the basic reactor designs should be widely known, but most of those in the AEC disagreed.

Gradually, he was dropping out of frontier developments in physics and this made him rather isolated. He was criticized for having attended the conferences of the Unification Church of the Reverend Sun Myung Moon. His involvement may have happened because, as the years went by, he was becoming increasingly lonely, and it was an opportunity for him to go somewhere where he had a voice —a political voice, that is. He said, "The atomic bomb made us all little politicians."[94] However, his politics were rather rigidly on the conservative side, and this added to his isolation from his colleagues. A case in point was when his fellow professors supported David Bohm and he did not. In the end Princeton University did not protect Bohm, who was let go for political reasons, to the long-term embarrassment of his colleagues.[95]

Wigner's pet project became civil defense, and he grabbed every opportunity to advocate its needs.[96] He studied the civil defense of other countries on both sides of the Iron Curtain. He knew about the efficient use of the subway installations in both London and Moscow during World War II, and he knew that the tunnels of the Budapest subway were located deep underground for civil defense purposes.[97] At one point he wanted everybody to build a shelter, and some colleagues found his approach childish.[98] He examined civil defense from a historical point of view and found that the United States spent incredibly little on civil defense as compared with the huge military expenditures, of which, however, he did not disapprove. He regarded the concept of "mutually assured destruction" as flawed, leading as it did to the neglect of civil defense. He discussed the danger of nuclear terrorism, meaning state terrorism. He was strongly opposed to succumbing to blackmail, suggesting instead that the country should be prepared to fight limited nuclear wars. Wigner genuinely believed that civil defense would be "a crucial element in staving off thermonuclear war."[99]

Wigner opposed those who discarded civil defense, including shelters, people who wanted to "die on our feet" rather than "live on our knees" in an underground bomb shelter. He advocated making careful plans for every eventuality. He ascribed the unwillingness of the general population to build a strong civil defense to its apprehension about bringing the thought of actual war to its door-step. Paying dearly for a strong army was a more abstract approach to the possi-bility of war than building shelters in their homes. Wigner remembered that he learned from his father that people do not build their beliefs on a foundation of reason; rather, they find reasons to justify their beliefs. Nonetheless, he did not give up and continued relentlessly to popularize the idea of civil defense. He was proud that he could talk about it to President Kennedy and his aides in the White House, even if only for a few minutes. But he was discouraged by his colleagues, whose typical response, when he tried to talk to them about civil defense, for example, was "Oh, Eugene, not again, I am a scientist, not a politician. Please leave me alone."

John von Neumann

As World War II was ending, von Neumann became pessimistic about a future war with the Soviet Union and he wanted the United States to be prepared for it. He remembered the failure of the policy of appeasement with the Nazis in the 1930s and this made him feel that Stalin should be dealt with, with a heavy hand. He did not support the suggestion popular among many, including Einstein at that time, that the nuclear secret should be shared internationally. This was fi-nally removed from the agenda when Stalin rudely rejected America's proposal for the internationalization of nuclear projects. Until 1941 some Soviet scientists were engaged in nuclear research, but after the German attack in June 1941 they were directed to more pressing tasks. From mid-1945 they went back to the nuclear program, and they were outstanding scientists. Von Neumann expected the Soviet Union to have nuclear weapons within five years, and to help American readi-ness, he spent two months per year at Los Alamos after 1945. He considered it dangerous to have left the installation almost empty when the war ended, and his visits were much appreciated by the remaining staff because he was a problem solver. He was able "to take the most difficult problem, separate it into its com-ponents, whereupon everything looked brilliantly simple."[100] He was a master at working out approximate solutions on the basis of a small sample of data, and he could assign error limits and probabilities to his approximate solutions. He wanted to make nuclear weapons much more powerful than the Hiroshima and Nagasaki bombs to develop them as a deterrent. He expected, though, to use nuclear sci-ence not only for creating weapons but also for peaceful energy. He wanted to utilize both fission and fusion.

Von Neumann would have preferred to risk war with the Soviet Union right after World War II rather than later, and some even thought that he wanted a first nuclear strike on Moscow. He would have liked to see a tougher U.S. policy in defending Poland, Czechoslovakia, Hungary, and the rest. He was committed to the arms race and deployment. He declared in 1950, "If you say why not bomb them tomorrow, I say why not today? If you say today at five o'clock, I say why not one o'clock?" He moved swiftly from working on the fission bomb to the hydrogen bomb, and then to the means of delivery, that is, to the bomb-carrying intercontinental missiles. Nonetheless, he did not develop a hawkish image because he shunned publicity, preferred to remain in the background, and was not given to making public statements and granting interviews.[101] The progress he engineered in modern computing was crucial, not only in creating new weapons, but also in simulating war actions on the electronic battlefields that were being increasingly utilized in the Pentagon. Gradually he became a most trusted and influential personality for the military.

Von Neumann could have earned considerable royalties had he patented his inventions in connection with the development of the modern computer of that time. He fell into disputes with some colleagues about questions of priority, and rather than letting the situation worsen he opted for placing all his innovations into the public domain. According to his closest associate in computer science, Herman Goldstine, had they patented, their fame might have been even greater than it has been.[102]

From 1945 to 1948, von Neumann had no real influence in Washington. Although he was closer to the Republicans than to the Democrats, in 1948 he supported Truman because he was a known quantity to him, whereas he did not know the Republican Dewey.[103] From 1948, von Neumann held several consultancy posts with both the navy and the army, and a number of others with private companies. In addition, he was working on the computer and had his job as professor at the Institute for Advanced Study (IAS). However, he hardly had any contacts with major politicians until 1952.

Von Neumann and Teller both happened to be at Los Alamos when the Soviet nuclear explosion story broke in 1949. Their reaction was uniformly that the United States should develop the hydrogen bomb. They held that "if the Super can be made, it should be made in America." Von Neumann was sure that the Soviets would not delay in starting work on the hydrogen bomb. He assessed correctly that no debate among the physicists or others would hinder such work in the Soviet Union. Today we know that von Neumann and Teller were right in guessing Soviet intentions (see Ginzburg's statement in the section on Szilard) and that the Soviet scientists were well into researching the thermonuclear reactions as early as 1948. Von Neumann tried, but failed to convince Oppenheimer and others that the American hydrogen bomb was necessary. They "somehow assumed that if America did not research into how to produce the next evil, then nobody else would."[104]

In 1950, Truman directed the AEC to continue its work on all forms of atomic weapons, including "the so-called hydrogen or super bomb." The scientists returned to Los Alamos, among them such opponents of the hydrogen bomb as Fermi and Bethe. Bethe hoped that it could not be made, while Fermi accepted the call by the president to do the job. During 1950, it became clear that Teller's original design would not work. Stanislaw Ulam worked fervently on finding a solution after he had joined the project at von Neumann's initiative. Whereas some enjoyed the situation that Teller's design did not seem to fulfill his expectations, Ulam and von Neumann did not. What later became the Teller–Ulam invention happened in January–March 1951. Some of it is still classified. Once the Teller–Ulam solution was proposed, everybody agreed that they should proceed with it at Los Alamos.

In November 1952, Eisenhower was elected president; Lewis Strauss became his aid in nuclear matters and then chairman of the AEC. He and other big players regarded von Neumann "as America's quickest-thinking scientific genius." As von Neumann became increasingly involved in defense discussions at higher levels, he found the military ineffective. He wanted to introduce scientific methods into the military bureaucracy. This was similar to von Kármán's efforts to introduce scientific methods into building up the U.S. Air Force. Von Neumann had plenty of appointments in important committees to have an impact.[105] In 1950, he was involved with the Weapons Systems Evaluation Group and the Armed Forces Special Weapons Project; then, in 1951–1952 there were additional appointments: he became consultant to the CIA, a member of the General Advisory Committee (GAC) to the AEC, consultant to the Livermore Weapons Laboratory (in close cooperation with Ernest Lawrence and Teller), and a member of the Scientific Advisory Board of the U.S. Air Force (in close cooperation with von Kármán).

Von Neumann joined the AEC General Advisory Committee just as Oppenheimer was leaving it, and was involved in the security hearing about Oppenheimer. He disagreed with Oppenheimer about the hydrogen bomb, but he did not consider Oppenheimer a security risk. Strauss was "hopping mad" with Oppenheimer, whereas most at the IAS in Princeton supported him. In contrast, von Neumann advocated neutrality and considered a "scholar to be a person who did not sign manifestos that tabled joint emotions." He played no part in McCarthy's dealings and reacted to them with his usual humor. He wrote letters urging that "the best men should always be chosen for any scientific post or grant, irrespective of past or even present communist leanings."[106] He also urged people whom he thought might be at risk of being considered communists or sympathizers not to apply for jobs where this might be an issue.

Ernest Lawrence was considered to be right wing, not of the von Neumann kind but politically radical and reckless. Von Neumann, along with Fermi, warned Teller "against joining with Lawrence."[107] Even though von Neumann advocated preventive war against the Soviet Union, he was considered a dove compared with the hawkish Lawrence. In view of the animosity that existed between Los Alamos and the Livermore Laboratory during the initial period of Livermore's existence, it is remarkable that von Neumann was a consultant at both from the start. He was always for competition. This is how Herbert York, Lawrence's hand-picked first director of the Livermore Laboratory, characterized von Neumann: "He was very powerful and productive in pure science and mathematics and at the same time had a remarkably strong streak of practicality."[108] Further, "This combination of scientific ability and practicality gave him a credibility with military officers, engineers, industrialists, and scientists that nobody else could match." This latter statement could not be applied to all the other Martians: definitely not to Szilard, not so much to Wigner, and not always to Teller, but perhaps it did apply equally to von Kármán. Elsewhere, York noted that von Neumann, "whose opinions always carried very great weight, favored a high-priority program for the development of the super."[109]

In his position as chairman of the nuclear weapons panel of the Scientific Advisory Board to the air force, von Neumann helped to turn around American defense policy and with it its foreign policy. The panel observed in 1954 that it was possible to build rocket-powered ballistic missiles that could carry a nuclear warhead across a quarter of the world and deliver it with accuracy; that the Soviets might be some years ahead of America in this field; and that in the United States, new management techniques would be needed for catching up. The results of their activities began emerging in the years to come; they included intercontinental missiles, viz., the Atlas, Titan, and Minuteman; intermediate range missiles, the Thor and Jupiter; and the submarine-launched Polaris.[110] Although many participated in the various decision-making processes, von Neumann's impact could always be singled out. For example, the fact that there were so many different kinds of missiles corresponded to his emphasis on both competition and collaboration.

As von Neumann held numerous committee positions, he had to commute between many locations, such as Princeton, Washington, New York City, and Berkeley. Strauss wanted to ease the situation by making him an AEC commissioner, which was nominally a full-time job. Von Neumann accepted and, from March 1955, became the highest-ranking Martian. The prestige of the position probably played a role in von Neumann's decision. Although it was a full-time job, for von Neumann it did not consume his full time, but the position gave him a feeling of being able to contribute to the defense matters of the United States at the highest level. Macrae suggests that von Neumann envisioned himself as the brain behind the negotiations with Stalin's successors, who might be more reasonable than Stalin.[111] He wanted to be near the decision-making power, and for the short time he was able to function before his devastating illness, he became a decisive voice in the AEC.

The general consensus was that America caught up with the Soviet Union in missile matters within a few years, by which time von Neumann was dead. He was no longer around, either, when the Soviets sent their first Sputnik up, which had an awakening effect on American scientific research, technological development, and science education. And of course he was not around to see the United States catch up with the Soviet Union in space exploration, including sending a man to the Moon and bringing him back, but all agreed that he had contributed much to laying the foundations to these successes.

In January 1956, President Eisenhower awarded the Medal of Freedom to John von Neumann. By then von Neumann was so ill that he was confined to a wheel-chair. In his hospital room there was a guard twenty-four hours a day lest he give away military secrets. Eventually he started talking in Hungarian, which the guards did not understand.

Edward Teller

When World War II ended, Teller did not return to George Washington University; rather, he accepted a better offer from the University of Chicago, which organized a new institute under Fermi to continue nuclear research. Those who came included Harold Urey, James Franck, Cyril Smith, Joe and Maria Mayer—though, conspicuously, not Leo Szilard—and Teller was also invited. Teller hesitated to leave Los Alamos, where Norris Bradbury wanted him to take over the theoretical division from Bethe. Teller set two conditions, and he would have been satisfied if either of them had been fulfilled. One was that there should be a serious further development of the fission bomb, with a dozen annual tests, the other that there should be serious work on the hydrogen bomb. When he received no assurance for either, he signed up with Chicago.[112]

When the question of civilian versus military control of nuclear energy and weapons came up in Congress, at Stephen Brunauer's suggestion Teller was invited to testify in February 1946. For Teller, it was a moving moment; he did not take for granted, as Szilard did, that the United States Congress should listen to his advice: "I, a citizen for less than five years, was invited to make suggestions to members of Congress on a most important matter." Teller carefully assessed the

Edward Teller
(drawing by István
Orosz).

need for defense and found, similarly to von Kármán, that complete security and satisfactory defense was impossible but that there was a difference between unsatisfactory defense and no defense at all. He also discussed various peaceful utilizations of nuclear power and products. Even at that early stage he advocated the need for weapons tests. He also stressed the need for public education on the topic of atomic science and warned of the harmful effects of secrecy.[113]

Teller's changing from the almost playful occupation of a physics professor to advising Congress symbolizes the changes that physics and physicists had undergone in just a few years. Teller's main topics became defense, nuclear energy, medical and biological applications of isotopes, the importance of testing, education, and secrecy. Teller was still a popular member of the physics community; their big Chicago home saw many guests, some of whom would stay for extended periods. The beginning of their life in Chicago resembled their happy years in Washington, but 1946 was not the mid-1930s. Rifts within the physics community started to show up. For example, Niels Bohr thought that nuclear weapons were so destructive that scientists should no longer work on weapons. At the conclusion of the war, Teller helped to found *The Bulletin of the Atomic Scientists of Chicago*, but eventually found it too liberal for his taste.[114]

The results of new calculations for the hydrogen bomb again pointed to its feasibility, and toward the end of 1945 this optimism prevailed.[115] It soon emerged, however, that the calculations were flawed. Fermi and Ulam raised doubts about them but there was not much interest in checking the calculations because work on the thermonuclear bomb had been halted. Teller was still optimistic, but Bradbury held that such bombs would not be built within the foreseeable future. It was not only those people who did not find it feasible that opposed the work on the hydrogen bomb. Others thought that it should not be built because it was so dangerous. There was no defense against it therefore it should not be developed. In hindsight, this appears to be a naïve approach: the Soviet Union would have built it anyway. This naïve approach stemmed from blind arrogance: if the United States would not build it, nobody would, because—presumably—they could not. According to this arrogance, only espionage could make the Soviet Union capable of building such a device. There was a great contrast between the pre-atomic bomb time and the pre-hydrogen bomb time. The American physicists were committed to an all-out effort to build the atomic bomb lest Nazi Germany build it first—they had no doubt about the Germans' scientific and technological capabilities. They did not entertain such fears about Stalin's Soviet Union, however, because they did not place its capabilities very high.

It was a farsighted idea that the general public should be educated about physics; Teller started offering such a physics course at Chicago and kept giving it for the next forty years.[116] He continued teaching and directing research. Some of his students became famous: Murph Goldberger served as president of Caltech and C. N. (Frank) Yang earned the Nobel Prize in 1957 with T.-D. Lee for the discovery of parity violation in the weak interactions of elementary particles.[117]

Teller's parents were still alive after the war. He wanted them to get out and he sent affidavits for them to Hungary in 1947, as he also did for his widowed sister (her husband had been killed in the Holocaust) and her son. Nothing came of it. It is not clear why Teller's family did not leave during the three years of democracy that Hungary enjoyed immediately after the war—maybe his parents were unwilling to at that time. It is also curious that he did not visit them when he was visiting Germany after the war. Teller writes that he "became for the first time actively (though slightly) involved in politics" in the fall of 1948.[118] So an apprehension of what he later feared in going behind the Iron Curtain, which was only just beginning to descend, anyway, could not have been the reason between 1945 and 1948.

The Tellers went back to Los Alamos in the summers, and so did the Fermis and others. Teller visited Wernher von Braun in El Paso to find out how much weight his rockets could carry. He found von Braun indiscreet: he made disparaging comments about the Americans and their ability to build rockets in front of Teller in German, supposing that Teller did not understand German, a sign of ignorance on von Braun's part. Teller most enjoyed working with von Neumann, whom he found "the most versatile and brilliant scientist I have ever known. His mind operated at speeds that suggested neural superconductivity."[119] They saw politics in an identical way and they were both interested in the hydrogen bomb. Von Neumann's computers were becoming increasingly instrumental in the development of nuclear weapons.

In a way, Mici Teller had become active in hands-on politics before her husband. She went out canvassing votes for a congressional candidate who opposed a member of the House Un-American Activities Committee. While she was engaged as an activist, Teller was home baby-sitting. The man whom the Tellers supported won. Teller, who was a Democrat for quite a while after he immigrated, also wanted to see Truman elected. It was only later that he became a Republican.

Teller, like Wigner, had a different perspective from his American colleagues on the political situation developing in the immediate postwar years, especially concerning affairs in Europe. This difference contributed to stresses now and again. When in 1948 he was considering leaving his professorship and returning to working on weapons, he suffered from indecision to the extent that he consulted a doctor, who told him that his health would not improve until he made his decision.[120] Teller thought that at Los Alamos he could make a real contribution, whereas at the University of Chicago he was dealing with particle physics, which discouraged rather than challenged him. Even though there was practically no work on the hydrogen bomb going on at Los Alamos, he decided that they should go back there for one year.

The Atomic Energy Commission had been established in 1946, but there was only one physicist among the commissioners, although, as mentioned earlier, a

General Advisory Committee (GAC) had also been formed, with a membership that boasted a number of high-ranking scientists. In 1947, a subcommittee on the safety of nuclear reactors was set up, which included the physicists Wheeler, Feynman, and Teller, and the chemist Joseph Kennedy. The members elected Teller chairman of the Reactor Safeguard Committee (RSC). Feynman dropped out after the first meeting, but others were invited to join.

Teller took the risk of nuclear reactors very seriously, and at one point his subcommittee was criticized for being overcautious.[121] Teller and his colleagues worked out stringent safety requirements for nuclear reactors. The RSC turned down the AEC when it wanted to increase power production at the Hanford reactors while simultaneously reducing the area of buffer land around them.[122] The RSC was not directly overruled by the AEC, but another committee was established and the jurisdiction of the Teller committee was reduced. Later the two committees merged and Teller continued as a member for some time. He was a zealous advocate and promoter of nuclear power to the end, and he brought the same intensity to his concern with nuclear safety. For him, "the two issues were synergistic."[123] He realized that nuclear energy would be acceptable only if its production was safe and secure.

When Klaus Fuchs's betrayal of atomic secrets to the Soviets was unmasked, it helped Teller to make the acceleration of weapons research an issue.[124] Another factor was the news that the Soviets had exploded an atomic bomb. The wishful thinking that the Soviet Union would need a long time to build an atomic bomb was shattered. Teller never subscribed to such thinking because he was familiar with the workings of totalitarian states and with brilliant Soviet scientists like Lev Landau. Lewis Strauss also took the Soviet threat seriously, and it was he who had suggested air sampling to monitor nuclear explosions around the world. Monitoring started in 1947, and in 1949 it justified itself spectacularly by detecting the Soviets' first nuclear explosion, which also meant that they were catching up with the United States in nuclear matters. Then, in 1953, the monitoring system discovered the first Soviet thermonuclear explosion. Had the Americans not learned of the 1949 Soviet nuclear explosion, the American thermonuclear bomb might not have been developed and the Soviet Union could have become the first power to possess the hydrogen bomb.

When Teller heard about the Soviet bomb in 1949, he called Oppenheimer with the question, "What do we do now?" At this point Oppenheimer still represented authority for Teller. Oppenheimer had already demonstrated to him that he did not favor going ahead vigorously with either the fission bombs or with developing the fusion bomb. Oppenheimer brushed him off by responding, "Keep your shirt on." At this juncture Teller had little doubt that the hydrogen bomb should be developed and had no doubt, either, that the Soviets would be busy developing their own. Oppenheimer's opinion, however, still counted and he had authority by being the head of the General Advisory Committee. Teller also knew

that the leadership of Los Alamos would not be enthusiastic about the thermonuclear weapon either, as it never was.[125] Only an initiative from higher up in
Washington could change the situation.

At this crucial moment, it was a great compliment to Teller that Ernest
Lawrence and his subordinate Luis Alvarez visited him. Lawrence was the inventor of the cyclotron, a Nobel laureate, and a great organizer. Alvarez was a versatile physicist and a future Nobel laureate. Teller informed his visitors of the status
of the hydrogen bomb and Lawrence thought that they should go ahead with the
project. Teller was no longer alone. Lawrence gave him a demonstration of how
simply drip-dry shirts could be washed. Such shirts were a novelty and they made
a traveler's life easier. This was Lawrence's way of telling Teller that he should do
a lot of traveling if he wanted to gather support for his far-reaching plans.[126]

Teller started visiting influential people to win them over. He went to see
Senator McMahon, who was a supporter of strong defense and chaired the congressional Joint Committee on Atomic Energy (JCAE). The question whether the
United States should be developing the hydrogen bomb was becoming a much
debated issue in scientific circles. Great authorities of the scientific establishment
expressed their views against it. James B. Conant, who technically had been
Oppenheimer's superior during the Manhattan Project, declared that the hydrogen bomb project would go ahead "over my dead body."[127] The General Advisory Committee of the Atomic Energy Commission examined the question and
made its recommendation at the end of October 1949. There was a majority report and a minority report. Both opposed the hydrogen bomb project. They are
of interest because they help us to understand the atmosphere in which Teller
had to continue his struggle for developing the American hydrogen bomb.

The GAC consisted of truly prominent scientists: Robert Oppenheimer was
the chairman and its members included James B. Conant, Enrico Fermi, Isidor I.
Rabi, Glenn T. Seaborg, Cyril Stanley Smith, and Lee A. DuBridge, who had been
director of the radiation laboratory at MIT.[128] Teller, however, was conspicuously
missing. Von Neumann had not yet achieved national prominence, so his absence
was less noticeable.

Significantly, Seaborg, one of the pioneers of nuclear chemistry, was absent
from the crucial meeting of the GAC: he was on a trip in Sweden which had been
long in the planning. Seaborg was of Swedish extraction, but his Swedish connections were important for him beyond that: he knew that he had been nomi-
nated for the Nobel Prize that he would share with Edwin McMillan in 1951 for
their discoveries in the chemistry of the transuranium elements. Seaborg expressed
his views in a letter to Oppenheimer just before his departure for Sweden. In this
letter, as he commented later, he "had reluctantly come to the conclusion that
the United States should proceed with such a program because it was certain that
the Soviet Union would do so."[129] In the letter itself, concerning the development
of the hydrogen bomb, Seaborg stated: "Although I deplore the prospects of our
country putting a tremendous effort into this, I must confess that I have been

unable to come to the conclusion that we should not."[130] Seaborg's would have been the only dissenting opinion from both the majority and minority opinions, but unfortunately Oppenheimer chose not to present the letter for discussion at the GAC meeting.[131] This became a damaging oversight which figured heavily during Oppenheimer's security hearing in 1954.

However, the opinion expressed in Seaborg's letter to Oppenheimer could have been aired at a subsequent meeting of the GAC in early December 1949 where Seaborg was present. The topic of the development of the hydrogen bomb came up again, and Seaborg could have voiced his opposition but did not. He later explained that he had felt diffident about speaking up, being the youngest member of the GAC, after the other members, all senior to him, had expressed their views opposing the hydrogen bomb.

The majority opinion of the GAC recommended strongly against initiating an "all-out" effort to develop the hydrogen bomb and condemned it as a tool of genocide, which, of course, it could be. It stated, among other things, that:

> The existence of such a weapon in our armory would have far-reaching effects on world opinion: reasonable people the world over would realize that the existence of a weapon of this type whose power of destruction is essentially unlimited represents a threat to the future of the human race which is intolerable. Thus we believe that the psychological effect of the weapon in our hands would be adverse to our interest.
>
> We believe a super bomb should never be produced. Mankind would be far better off not to have a demonstration of the feasibility of such a weapon until the present climate of world opinion changes.
>
> It is by no means certain that the weapon can be developed at all and by no means certain that the Russians will produce one within a decade. To the argument that the Russians may succeed in developing this weapon, we would reply that our undertaking it will not prove a deterrent to them. Should they use the weapon against us, reprisals by our large stock of atomic bombs would be comparably effective to the use of a super.
>
> *In determining not to proceed to develop the super bomb, we see a unique opportunity of providing by example some limitations on the totality of war* and thus of limiting the fear and arousing the hope of mankind (italics added).[132]

The minority report by Fermi and Rabi was even more strongly worded, although it was not necessarily more negative. It stated, in part, that:

> [T]he use of such a weapon cannot be justified on any ethical ground which gives a human being a certain individuality and dignity even if

he happens to be a resident of any enemy country. It is evident to us that this would be the view of peoples in other countries. Its use would put the United States in a bad moral position relative to the peoples of the world. Any postwar situation resulting from such a weapon would leave unresolvable enmities for generations. A desirable peace cannot come from such an inhuman application of force. The postwar problems would dwarf the problems which confront us at present. The application of this weapon with the consequent great release of radioactivity would have results unforeseeable at present, but would certainly render large areas unfit for habitation for long periods of time.

The fact that no limits exist to the destructiveness of this weapon makes its very existence and the knowledge of its construction a danger to humanity as a whole. It is necessarily an evil thing considered in any light.

For these reasons we believe it important for the President of the United States to tell the American public, and the world, that *we think it wrong on fundamental ethical principles to initiate a program* of development of such a weapon. At the same time *it would be appropriate to invite the nations of the world to join us in a solemn pledge not to proceed in the development or construction of weapons of this category.* If such a pledge were accepted even without control machinery, it appears highly probable that an advanced stage of development leading to a test by another power could be detected by available physical means. Furthermore, we have in our possession, in our stockpile of atomic bombs, the means for adequate "military" retaliation for the production or use of a "Super" (italics added).[133]

Looking back, it is easy to see how wrong the majority opinion was with respect to its estimate of the Soviets' nuclear bomb project. The minority opinion did not make such a misjudgment, but it found the American stockpile of atomic bombs to be sufficient for responding to any Soviet thermonuclear danger. In this it concurred with the majority opinion. Both opinions pointed in the same direction of rejecting the need for the fusion bomb, with Fermi and Rabi expressing stronger revulsion against creating it. They also suggested "to invite the nations of the world" for a joint pledge not to produce the Super. Fermi and Rabi's opinion thus could be interpreted in a more flexible way than the majority opinion and it could also be understood that they did not want the United States to initiate such a project.[134] Herbert York in his 1976 book reported a recent conversation in which "Rabi stated it was his firm recollection that he and Fermi definitely intended *to couple American forbearance with a Soviet pledge to do the same*" (italics added).[135]

Some of those in the GAC may have assumed that if the United States chose not to make a hydrogen bomb, the Soviet Union would not either. By then an accelerated Soviet program was underway, using outstanding physicists and slave labor. How different this was from the American democracy and from James Conant's "over my dead body" statement. The work in the Soviet Union would have continued literally over anyone's dead body, had anyone dared to oppose the development of the hydrogen bomb, and in fact it did continue over the dead bodies of many slave workers, who toiled under inhuman and unsafe conditions.

Lewis Strauss noted that the Americans tended to consider the question whether to develop the hydrogen bomb or not as an internal problem of the United States or at best as an internal problem of the Free World. In his words, "To a surprising degree the world has maintained its wide-eyed and childlike credulity about Soviet pronouncements. It is a state of mind that, astonishingly, survives periods of disillusionment when the actions of the Soviets expose their insincerity and untruthfulness. The phenomenon is unexplained." At the same time he noticed the general tendency to underestimate what the Soviets/Russians are capable of achieving. Estimates varied of when the Soviets would be capable of producing their first atomic bombs, but "in general none expected the Soviets to detonate any atomic device before 1952. The majority opinion set the time substantially further in the future, while not a few believed it beyond Soviet capacity in *any* time scale likely to be of much concern to us" (italics in original).[136]

There was no debate about the hydrogen bomb in the Soviet Union. The Soviet scientists were not aware of any of the discussions going on in America at that time: their isolation from the rest of the world was complete. They could not even have communications with their Western colleagues about purely scientific matters. They did not think about the dangers of the hydrogen bomb in broader terms, regardless of whether it was in the hands of a democracy or a dictator. According to Ginzburg, "Even asking such a question would have been a stupid act. We have to be realistic about life."[137]

Ginzburg's testimony is important because it provides a rare glimpse into the dealings of the Soviet projects from a personal point of view, by a leading scientist who received the Nobel Prize in 2003 for works that he carried out at the time when development of the hydrogen bomb was underway in both superpowers. Ginzburg's ideas contributed to the success of the Soviet hydrogen bomb although he was excluded from direct access to the works due to his lack of security clearance. The reason was that his wife was in exile, ostensibly for anti-Soviet activities. Ginzburg's experience, along with other evidence, makes it clear that it was ridiculous to maintain that the United States could have stopped the development of the hydrogen bomb by its own example of refraining from it. Kenneth Pitzer, who was the research chief of the Atomic Energy Commission at the time, took satisfaction when the Cold War was over and information from the former Soviet Union was made available: "They were going to go right ahead with that [the hydrogen bomb]. We got there first but not by much. It would have been quite a situation in this country if they had gotten there first and it would have been known that we had been intentionally slow about it."[138]

The Soviets would have not been influenced "by example," except for probably considering it as a sign of weakness. Andrei Sakharov noted that the Soviet leadership was set on developing thermonuclear weapons regardless of American actions. American restraint in developing the Super, in Sakharov's words, "would have been perceived either as a cunning and deceitful maneuver, or as evidence of stupidity or weakness."[139] It would have not stopped the development of the Soviet super bomb.

Of course the GAC did not make policy, only recommendations for the Atomic Energy Commission. It was not within the jurisdiction of the AEC, either, to decide about the Super; it made its recommendation to the president. The majority opinion of the GAC indicated that the Americans tended to underestimate the Soviet potential for such highly sophisticated projects as the super bomb. In this, they were not alone. President Truman "simply could not bring himself to believe that 'those Asiatics' could build something as complicated as an atomic bomb."[140] When the report on the first Soviet nuclear explosion arrived, Truman made some members of the AEC sign a statement, after having studied the evidence, that they really believed the Soviets had done it. Teller, on the other hand, tended to overestimate, according to some, the scientific and technological capabilities of the Soviets, perhaps to compensate for the Americans' tendency to belittle them. In general, the Soviet Union *was* a technologically backward country compared with the Unites States, Japan, and Western Europe, but it had the outstanding ability to focus its resources and efforts to key areas; besides, it had excellent traditions and manpower in theoretical physics.[141]

Teller was not alone in advocating the development of the Super as the right response to Soviet nuclear advances. Apart from Lawrence and Alvarez, the noted Berkeley chemist Wendell Latimer, the chairman of the JCAE Senator McMahon and his chief of staff William L. Borden, and AEC commissioner Lewis L. Strauss, sided with him. Lawrence continued to be an important ally; like Teller, he did not have any formal involvement, but he had plenty of informal channels and he used his influence at the JCAE, the Pentagon, and the AEC in the debate about the Super.[142] Although Alvarez was Lawrence's protégé, he was becoming a force in his own right. Alvarez's influence was strengthened by his recent great services to the military, for example, his Ground Controlled Approach (GCA), which made it possible for United States' planes to land safely in Berlin and thus to break the Soviet blockade in 1948.[143] Many at Los Alamos also favored an intensified program for the super bomb and resented the GAC belittling its significance in their reports.[144]

Admiral Strauss stated in his letter of November 25, 1949, to President Truman "that the United States must be as completely armed as any possible enemy." He had every reason to distrust that the Soviet government would make its decision on "moral" grounds. However, Strauss used an argument that was, to say the least, out of place, when he wrote: "[145] A government of atheists is not likely to be dissuaded from producing the weapon on 'moral' grounds." There were many atheists among the leading scientists who opposed the development of thermonuclear weapons in the United States, and many who then engaged themselves in building them.

Truman's National Security Council, consisting of Defense Secretary Louis Johnson, State Secretary Dean Acheson, and AEC Chairman David Lilienthal, voted two to one to support the development of the super bomb. Acheson "was deeply pessimistic about the possibility of achieving any useful agreement with Stalin and the Soviets in the matter of the Super."[146] At the end of the October meeting of the General Advisory Committee, Oppenheimer had told Acheson that the United States would, by restraining itself in the matter of the hydrogen bomb, provide an example for the Soviet Union to follow. But Acheson doubted that: "How can you really persuade a hostile adversary to disarm 'by example'?"[147] Some at the State Department, though, argued for showing "confidence in others, and to accept a certain risk . . . in order to achieve international agreement."[148] In spite of Acheson's stand, he was bitterly attacked by Joseph McCarthy as being soft on communism and the senator accused the State Department of sheltering communists.[149]

It was a great victory for Teller when President Truman announced his decision on January 31, 1950, giving directions to continue research on all atomic weapons, including the hydrogen bomb. Teller compared the situations in 1939 and 1950.[150] In 1939, in their first meeting with the representatives of the military, Colonel Adamson had argued that new weapons do not win wars and the scientists argued for the atomic weapons. In 1950, the military wanted the new weapons and most of the scientists were against them. There was another contrast with 1950: in 1945, Oppenheimer had explained to Teller that the scientists do science and the politicians decide what to do with their products. Now Teller wrote, "it is not the scientist's job to determine whether a hydrogen bomb should be constructed, whether it should be used, or how it should be used."[151] Of course, the hydrogen bomb was deplorable in every respect, and mankind would have been better off without it. On the other hand, Stalin, as the sole possessor of the hydrogen bomb, might have tried to enslave the whole world. This is why Harold Urey warned that America should not "intentionally lose the armaments race; to do this would be to lose our liberties, and, with Patrick Henry, I value my liberties more than I do my life."[152] The same sentiment is expressed on every New Hampshire license plate: "Live Free or Die."

After President Truman had announced his decision to go ahead with the hydrogen bomb, Hans Bethe insisted that the most important question was a moral one. He stated, "It is argued that it would be better for us to lose our lives than our liberty, and with this view I personally agree. But I believe this is not the choice facing us here; . . . in a war fought with hydrogen bombs we would lose not only many lives, but all our liberties and human values as well." Bethe argued that even if the United States did not have the hydrogen bomb and the Soviet Union did, and used it, "Though it might devastate our cities and cripple our ability to conduct a long war with all modern weapons, it would not seriously affect our power for immediate retaliation."[153] Such a statement makes one wonder whether Bethe might have seriously thought that responsible political leaders in the United States would take upon themselves the responsibility of allowing their country to face such an eventuality. Many years later, Bethe admitted that "Truman had no choice in the political atmosphere of the time. Had Russia developed the H-bomb and the US not, he and the scientific community that opposed it would have been considered traitors."[154]

In 1950, the inception of the Korean War gave further timeliness to the weapons work. The Martians were strongly supportive of the development of the hydrogen bomb. As we have seen above, Szilard was even frightened that for some time Teller was alone in trying to ensure that the United States would not remain defenseless in view of the probable Soviet construction of the hydrogen bomb. Later Szilard did much to curb the dangers of nuclear weapons.

During all the discussions about whether or not to develop the Super, however, nobody really knew how to do it. It was taken for granted that once the go-ahead was given a highly focused and all-out program would yield the knowledge. This did prove to be the case eventually, but it was far from being a formality. According to some accounts, work on the Super was going on at Los Alamos even before Truman's decision.[155] Stanislaw Ulam alleged that Teller tried to downplay the significance of such work because he wanted to minimize the credit for Los Alamos and its director. In any case, as soon as the president declared his decision, people were needed for Los Alamos.

John A. Wheeler faced the dilemma whether to join the hydrogen bomb project or not. At the time he was working in Paris and he struggled to choose between what he perceived as his patriotic duty and his love for physics. The next time he met Niels Bohr, Wheeler presented his dilemma to his old mentor. Bohr was known to be hesitant and not given to coming out with unambiguous answers even to less controversial questions. However, this time Bohr asked him, "Do you think that Europe would be free of Soviet control today had it not been for the atomic bomb of the West?"[156] Wheeler soon joined the hydrogen bomb project.

Of course, not everybody thought like Bohr and Wheeler. The Wheelers' next door neighbors in Princeton were the liberal Panofsky family. Erwin Panofsky was a famous art historian and his two sons were physicists, known by their nicknames of the bright Panofsky, who had been the top student in his class, and the dumb Panofsky, who had been the next to top. Wheeler knew that Erwin Panofsky did not approve of the development of the hydrogen bomb. When FBI agents came to the neighborhood to check upon Wheeler's reliability, they asked the Panofskys whether they knew of any subversive activities of the Wheelers? Panofsky's response was, "They are not subversives, they are mass murderers! We are the subversives." [157]

John von Neumann interrupted his vacationing in France to return to work on the hydrogen bomb and continued his calculations at Princeton. Fermi returned to Los Alamos.[158] Teller enlisted Frederic de Hoffmann, a native of Vienna, to whom Teller would later assign much credit for the success with the hydrogen bomb, ostensibly because doing so would detract from Ulam's credit but not from Teller's.[159]

Teller and Ulam now questioned earlier calculations and estimates. Teller "had developed an allergy" to Ulam and thought that their antipathy was mutual. They had to work together, but were increasingly at odds with each other. According to Ulam's calculations, the hydrogen bomb would not work using the design they were working on at the time. Teller was skeptical, but Ulam proved to be correct. As doubts about the feasibility of the original design strengthened, an idea started to come up about a second weapons laboratory.[160] Its backers did not leave anything to chance by arguing that a second laboratory might be desirable even if the first tests were successful, as in that case many new projects would need to be initiated.

In the meantime, von Neumann continued his support of the development of the H-bomb by carrying out a huge number of calculations on his ever-improving computers, the ENIAC and the MANIAC. His wife, Klári, was also involved. Von Neumann estimated that just one of their calculations required more multiplications than the total number of multiplications performed by humankind up to that point.[161] The calculations reinforced the doubts about the original design.

It was a frustrating period for Teller. Had he been sure that the hydrogen bomb would be impossible to build, it would have meant that nobody could have it, but he was tormented by the thought that, while the Americans might not be able to produce it, the Soviets might succeed. It is to his credit that under such an impossible tension he was still capable of thinking about new solutions.

It was increasingly clear that Teller and Ulam were the two main players, and both wanted the project to succeed even though their personal animosity hindered their interactions. Teller appeared very possessive of the project, but Ulam was to play a key role in finding the solution. Ulam and his co-workers made one more run in their calculations at Teller's scheme. They calculated the progress of a thermonuclear reaction, that is, how the burning would proceed in a mass of deuterium or a deuterium–tritium mixture. The results showed that the progress of the reaction would be too slow to achieve their goal. Teller was frustrated by their results, but von Neumann's calculations supported Ulam's findings. Again, it would have made everybody happy had it been proven conclusively that the hydrogen bomb was an impossible device. But it was a devastating thought that while they might have been unable to find the solution to the problem, others might be more successful.

The problem was that a lot of energy would be dissipated during the fission explosion by radiation. The higher the temperature, the more probable fusion becomes, but at the same time more of the energy leaves the system. However, as Teller suddenly realized, while the particles carry energy in proportion to their number, radiation carries energy in proportion to volume. If the number of particles could be increased with a simultaneous decrease of the volume, more energy would stay with the particles. So the question was whether it would be possible to compress the mass of deuterium that they planned to use. If even heavy metals could be compressed in the implosion process, then surely it should be possible to compress liquid deuterium. If the deuterium mass is strongly compressed, thermonuclear reaction would be possible. This is how Teller remembered the events.[162] According to others, though, whenever the question of compression came up in the discussions, Teller always rejected it.

One day, Ulam suggested a practical and feasible solution to the problem.[163] Instead of using the heat produced by the primary fission bomb, they should use the enormous flux of neutrons emitted during its explosion to compress, mechanically, the secondary fusion bomb by implosion. In Ulam's words, "perhaps the change came with a proposal I contributed. I thought of a way to modify the whole approach by injecting a repetition of certain arrangements."[164] Much of the technology involved is still classified. Teller then told Ulam that he had thought of something that would work even better: they should use the X-rays emitted by the primary fission bomb to compress the deuterium; that is, the compression should happen through radiation. Teller had the impression that Ulam refused to listen to him. Everybody agrees that compressing the deuterium by radiation was better because the compression had to be symmetrical, and continued symmetrical compression could be better achieved with radiation. In any case, the impasse was resolved by Ulam, even though Teller did not seem to welcome it with sufficient enthusiasm, considering that Ulam saved the American hydrogen bomb project. In fact, Teller remembered years later that he had also thought about the possibility of compression shortly before Ulam came to him with his ideas.[165]

When Ulam hit upon his innovative ideas, he did not talk about them right away with Teller.[166] First he discussed them with the head of the theoretical division, then with the director, Bradbury, and then he turned to Teller. Again, in Ulam's words, "At once Edward took up my suggestions, hesitantly at first, but enthusiastically after a few hours. He had seen not only the novel elements, but had found a parallel version, an alternative to what I had said, perhaps more convenient and generalized."[167]

Teller must have been bothered by his errors and he must have offended various people by his blind and passionate interest in making the hydrogen bomb a success. At least this is how he himself thought about his behavior in retrospect. He referred to Niels Bohr's definition of an expert to characterize his own fallibility that an expert from his own experiences discovers all the mistakes one can commit in a very narrow field.[168] Teller and Ulam wrote a first sketch of the proposal and after some further changes, they wrote a joint report, dated March 9, 1951.[169] They call it the "Teller–Ulam design" and it became the fundamental basis for the design of the first successful thermonuclear weapon test, called "Mike," in the Pacific at the Eniwetok Atoll (Marshall Islands) on November 1, 1952. Their joint report signified a turning point in making the hydrogen bomb. About a month later, Teller and de Hoffmann wrote another report, in which they placed a second fission component, a subcritical amount of uranium-235, at the core of the thermonuclear material. Long before "Mike," the first thermonuclear device, named "George," was tested on May 9, 1950, at the Eniwetok Atoll. It used a quantity of tritium that would not be realistic to use for a weapon, but it was important to see whether the calculations would be confirmed.[170] At the GAC meeting in Princeton that evaluated the experiment, in June 1951, Teller talked about his new suggestion (the Teller–Ulam proposal) and approval was given to work it out. At Los Alamos, one of the positive developments was the arrival of a bright young physicist named Richard Garwin, who designed the hydrogen bomb according to the new proposal.[171] Even Bethe approved the design.

It occurred to Teller that lithium-6 might also be used in the form of ^{6}LiD as fusion material.[172] We now know that lithium deuteride also figured in the Soviet hydrogen bomb designs due to Vitaly Ginzburg's suggestion.[173] It was a convenient fusion material because it is a solid and easy to store, whereas deuterium is a gas and could be stored as a liquid only under high pressure or at very low temperature. Besides, lithium itself can participate in fusion reactions.

The friction that existed between Teller and Ulam has spoiled all attempts to unambiguously assess the events around the development of the American hydrogen bomb, although both seemed to have tried to objectively evaluate their respective roles. Reading their accounts, however, the impression is that Teller could have been more magnanimous in appreciating Ulam's role. The fact remains that Teller refused to develop their joint work into a co-authored paper or patent. According to Ulam's wife, Françoise, it seemed that when it became clear that Ulam had saved the project, "from then on Teller pushed Stan aside and refused to deal with him any longer. He never met or talked with Stan meaningfully again."[174]

When the blast effect of the hydrogen bomb was investigated, it turned out to be far from unlimited; the conclusion was that the equivalent of 10 million tons of TNT would be typical.[175] But even a bomb of this size would destroy everything for several miles in every direction. There was also a chance that it would blow away a huge chunk of the atmosphere because the incredibly high temperature would provide the air molecules with sufficient kinetic energy, that is, velocity, to leave the earth's gravitational attraction. The radioactivity would be blown more into space than over the earth. There was scope for further increasing the size of the bomb, and the Soviets had the dubious honor of holding the record in this respect, with an explosion of the equivalent of one hundred million tons of TNT. However, the most cost-effective size would come to be established at the equivalent of one million tons of TNT. It was especially frightening that the hydrogen bomb proved to be relatively inexpensive to produce, and it prompted those who could to produce them in large numbers.

There were similarities between Teller's struggles for the second laboratory and the hydrogen bomb. The GAC did not support the establishment of the second laboratory, with the exception of Willard Libby.[176] As was the case with the H-bomb, the initial failure did not stop Teller; rather, it hardened his determination.[177] He argued that the second laboratory would provide competition to Los Alamos, and it would be very open to innovation. Teller accused Los Alamos of not being vigorously enough concerned with the nation's defense, but of being very much concerned with public relations. Teller again became active, seeing every politician who would see him. He found a great partner in Lewis Strauss, who understood that peace had been lost in the 1930s when the democracies disarmed themselves through neglect and negotiations. They both advocated that peace could be saved only by a strong United States.

Teller discussed his ideas with the secretary of the Air Force, and then with Secretary of Defense Robert A. Lovett, and made a presentation to Secretary of State Dean Acheson and other high administration officials. He turned to the air force for support and the air force enthusiastically backed his proposal.[178] There were other important supporters that the GAC could not ignore, including the Joint Committee on Atomic Energy (although McMahon was by then terminally ill), and some at the AEC. Finally, the GAC and the AEC gave their formal approvals to the project in June 1952. While the director of the new lab was Lawrence's man, Herbert York, Teller had power of veto over the decisions of the scientific steering committee. The establishment of the Livermore Laboratory further strained Teller's relationship with the leadership of Los Alamos. This changed only in 1970 when Harold Agnew became the third director of Los Alamos and began to regularly invite Teller for visits.[179] York left Livermore in late 1957 for a higher position in Washington, and Teller became director of Livermore for two years. In time, Teller would consider the establishment of the second weapons laboratory to be one of the most important contributions, if not the most important, of his entire oeuvre.[180]

The struggle for the second laboratory made Teller and Lawrence especially strong allies. Lawrence suggested a site in northern California near Livermore, some thirty miles east of Oakland. He was an influential and shrewd player both at the University of California and in Washington. He practically named the first director and stipulated that he should report to him. Teller badly needed an ally as strong as Lawrence, although he was aware of Lawrence's unpopularity because of his strong conservative politics. Many considered him, in Teller's words, a "right-wing extremist."[181] Furthermore both Fermi and von Neumann, independently of each other, warned Teller in 1952 not to move from Chicago to California. They thought that Teller's move would exclude him from the community of physicists. The fact that he received such a warning is of interest in itself. His two friends did not represent a unified view with respect to the hydrogen bomb, as Fermi opposed it while von Neumann was greatly in favor. They both genuinely cared for Teller. The warning is also of interest because it shows that it was not only the Oppenheimer case (in 1954) that alienated Teller from the community of physicists (as will be seen later). Teller was overzealous, and simply could not stop himself moving in the direction that he considered to be ahead.

In the summer of 1952, the Teller family moved to California and Teller started to work for Livermore, first on a temporary basis, then, after a year, permanently. He also became a professor of the University of California. He had to take part in the planning of the work at Livermore to make sure that new weapons would be among its priorities. He enjoyed the pioneering spirit that existed at Livermore in 1952, just as he had enjoyed it at Los Alamos in 1943, and now he was playing a leading role. Their goals included the development of versatile hydrogen bombs, not so much ever larger bombs but flexible ones. They even wanted to have smaller hydrogen bombs that could be deployed against a tank attack. The first tests from Livermore were failures.[182] It took quite some time for the new institution to establish itself as a successful weapons laboratory, which it eventually did.

Teller's overzealous attitude, which caused him self-inflicted wounds, came to the fore in a most hurtful way in the Oppenheimer security hearings. This story is discussed in a separate section in the next chapter, to give it more exposure and to augment it with some aspects of Oppenheimer's background. When the minutes of the Oppenheimer hearings became public, Teller found himself in an internal exile. He considered it his third exile (following those from Hungary and Germany), and it was the more painful because it ostracized him from the community of his fellow physicists. His two previous exiles had brought him to broader horizons, but this one closed in on him. From here, there was no place to go. Many considered Teller's testimony against Oppenheimer as his revenge for Oppenheimer's having opposed the development of the hydrogen bomb. Teller states in his *Memoirs* that he "never wanted Oppenheimer's opinion on the hydrogen bomb to count in the decision on his security clearance," and that revoking Oppenheimer's clearance was not justified. If everything that Teller said in his *Memoirs* is true, then at the very least he was a poor politician. Teller wrote to Maria Goeppert-Mayer in 1954, with almost masochistic frankness, remembering a conversation a long time before about backbone: "I seemed to get along fine without one. Now there seems be some growing pains. I also wonder whether it is growing in the right direction."[183]

To make matters worse concerning Teller's position among his colleagues, two journalists, Shepley and Blair, published a book about the hydrogen bomb in which they exaggerated Teller's role at the expense of others.[184] In addition, the book portrayed Oppenheimer as a spy. Teller wrote a rebuff under the title "The Work of Many People."[185] His aim was to give credit to others for creating the hydrogen bomb. In a footnote he says that he went so far as to give Stan Ulam credit for a suggestion that had been Teller's. This he calls a white lie, but it confuses matters. Later, when Teller was asked to sign a patent application that named him and Ulam as co-discoverers, he refused, claiming that Ulam did not understand Teller's design and had declared that it would never work. Where was the generous Teller at this moment, the Teller who even told white lies to exaggerate Ulam's contribution to the hydrogen bomb?

The Shepley–Blair book haunted Teller in unexpected ways. Upon being introduced to John F. Kennedy, Teller took it as an insult when the sophisticated senator (as he was then) praised him for what he had read about him in the Shepley–Blair book. Later, under the Kennedy administration, Teller was among the president's scientific advisors, but hardly any of his advice was taken. Teller managed to be disrespectful to Kennedy during his presidency. Teller at the time was advocating peaceful uses of nuclear energy, and he called his scheme the Plowshare Program. When Kennedy asked him about the proposed new canal on the Panama isthmus in the framework of this program, inquiring about how long it would take to build, Teller's response was: "It will take less time to complete the canal than for you to make up your mind to build it."[186]

It was in 1955 that Teller first suggested that nuclear warheads small enough to be carried on, and launched from, submarines be developed.[187] This eventually proved crucial, because the air bases used by strategic bombers and the silos with land-based missiles could be destroyed by a Soviet surprise attack, but hardly the nuclear-powered submarines. Even in Teller's supposedly biased description of the navy meeting it sounded like a bidding war between Los Alamos and Livermore, with Teller raising the stakes; it was his usual approach, for which he was repeatedly and bitterly criticized.

In 1957, the Soviet Sputnik gave a push to the American rocket and missile program. It also brought home the message that the United States should improve its science education. In this the Soviet advances were unambiguously beneficial for America. Teller noted that "suddenly, the concerns that we Martians had been describing were realities." *Time* magazine ran a major story about the American physicists in one of its November 1957 issues, with Teller on the cover. In 1958, Teller gave a series of twelve programs on physics on public television in California.[188]

There were changes in Teller's life in the mid-1950s, apart from the Oppenheimer case. In quick succession he lost three of his few friends, Fermi in 1954, von Neumann in 1957, and Lawrence in 1958. In 1958–1960, as director of the Livermore Laboratory, he fiercely fought against all attempts for a test ban. He stressed that the tests increased knowledge and that the Soviets would be cheating anyway. Teller and Szilard could not have been farther from each other in these matters, and at one of their public debates, the discussion became so heated that they felt compelled to shake hands to ease the tension. Linus Pauling was Teller's most conspicuous opponent in the public debates.[189] Pauling considered fallout to be dangerous, but Teller wanted more knowledge on nuclear explosions and considered low-level fallout even advantageous. His considerations of fallout effects resulted in a book.[190] The Soviet leader, Khrushchev, advocated an informal test ban on nuclear weapons while the negotiations that led to the August 1963 treaty were going on. This was a public relations coup because people were afraid of the fallout from testing.

After the test ban treaty with the Soviet Union, only underground testing remained, but Teller found even that to be a good opportunity for learning about explosions, and it worried him that the Soviet Union might use such tests without reporting them.[191] He was also concerned that the test ban could be circumvented by using outer space.[192] He imagined a scenario in which one rocket would carry the nuclear bomb and another would carry the instruments to measure the radiation from the blast. The explosion would take place between ten thousand and a hundred thousand miles out in space and nobody would know. There is no indication that any country ever attempted such a mission to cheat on the test ban.

Teller also paid a lot of attention to the possibilities of his Plowshare Program, but the public was so afraid of the resulting radiation that it was aborted. Teller was disappointed in these failures and envied the Soviet Union, where similar projects had been completed.[193] There, of course, the people did not have a say about which projects to implement and which not to. Teller apparently would, on occasion, have preferred to benefit from the mechanisms of a totalitarian society, and in this he was not alone. We have seen that General Groves, too, would have relished some of the possibilities, unavailable to him in a democracy, that a totalitarian society could provide. Henry Kissinger, Richard Nixon's national security advisor and later secretary of state, was another who lamented about how much easier his task would have been in a nondemocratic state.

Teller was consulting for Nelson Rockefeller and the Rockefeller family. Rockefeller built up an efficient and comprehensive advising system in preparation for his repeated bids for the presidency, unsuccessful as they were. In 1959, Teller changed his party preference from Democrat to Republican to vote for Nelson Rockefeller.[194] In 1964, he supported Rockefeller against Barry Goldwater in the quest for the Republican nomination for president, but Rockefeller lost to Goldwater (and then Goldwater lost to Lyndon Johnson). Later, during the Nixon presidency, when Rockefeller was governor of the state of New York, he organized a commission to consider the policies of his state for the future. President Nixon asked him to extend these considerations to the whole nation. Rockefeller resigned the governorship to fulfill Nixon's request, and the result was the Commission on the Critical Choices for Americans, in which Teller participated.[195] This was just one of several indications that Teller had become a member of the Establishment. Rockefeller's highest office was vice president, and this was achieved by appointment, not election, when Nixon resigned in 1974 and Gerald Ford became president. Rockefeller died in 1979.

While the Kennedy administration lived through several crises, such as the Bay of Pigs and the Cuban missile crisis, the Soviet Union demonstrated superiority in missiles (ICBMs). Following the 1957 Sputnik, they launched Yuri Gagarin, and soon after German Titov, into orbit around the Earth. The Americans could only shoot up astronauts who then came straight back. In August 1961, Khrushchev withdrew from the interim test ban and the Soviet Union started mass testing of huge nuclear weapons. Also in 1961, Andrei Sakharov started his protests in the

Soviet Union, and about three years later he was removed from the Soviet weapons program. Khrushchev dismissed Sakharov's protests against the testing, as Oppenheimer had dismissed Szilard's petition in 1945.[196] Khrushchev declared that the scientists did not have the overview needed to make foreign policy and that they should remain scientists and leave politics to the politicians.

To underscore the importance of defense preparations, Kennedy visited Berkeley and met with Livermore scientists. The visit brought about another negative incident for Teller: Kennedy cut him off while he was explaining the possible beneficial effects from low-level radiation. The basis for his claim was that certain flies lived longer when they were exposed to a low level of radiation, but it was known that the flies harbored a parasite, or bacteria or fungus, that was sensitive to radiation, hence the flies benefited from it. Szilard accused Teller of knowing the real reason why the flies lived longer, yet Teller continued using the argument.[197]

In 1962, Kennedy awarded Teller the Fermi Prize, which included $50,000, for his "contributions to chemical and nuclear physics, for leadership in thermonuclear research, and for efforts to strengthen national security." The next year Teller nominated Oppenheimer and Kennedy confirmed the award. Oppenheimer received the 1963 Fermi Prize from President Johnson, a little over a week after Kennedy's assassination. Teller had hoped that the division between him and the rest of the physics community would be narrowed by Oppenheimer's award, but this did not happen.[198]

Teller continued to be interested in missile defense.[199] The Soviet tests in 1961–1962 were in part directed at such defense, indicating that the Soviet Union was also interested in working out a missile-defense system. As early as 1950, Petr Kapitsa wrote a letter to one of the party leaders, Georgii M. Malenkov, proposing work on high energy radiation that would be able to destroy incoming missiles. Here is a paragraph from the letter:

> During the war I was already thinking a lot about methods of defense
> against bombing raids behind the lines more effective than anti-aircraft
> fire or just crawling into bolt holes. Now that atomic bombs, jet aircraft
> and missiles have got into the arsenals, the question has assumed vastly
> greater importance. During the last four years I have devoted all my
> basic skills to the solution of this problem and I think I have now
> solved that part of the problem to which a scientist can contribute. The
> idea for the best possible method of protection is not new. It consists in
> creating a well-directed high-energy beam of such intensity that it
> would destroy practically instantaneously any object it struck. After
> two years' work I have found a novel solution to this problem and,
> moreover, I have found that there are no fundamental obstacles in the
> way of realizing beams of the required intensity.[200]

Teller was mindful that the Americans would have just twenty minutes between detecting an approaching Soviet missile and it hitting them. Teller wanted active defense: he wanted to detonate a nuclear bomb near the incoming missile to explode it.[201] He estimated that if done at sufficient altitude, say five miles, this would be safe even if it happened over the United States. In the 1960s, efforts started to develop an antimissile defense system in the United States, but they were stopped in 1972.

When the test ban treaty was being discussed in the U.S. Senate in 1963, Teller testified against it, in vain; Kennedy was strongly for it and the Senate would finally ratify it.[202] Kennedy realized Teller's powers and prevented him from talking to the meeting of the southern governors, which he had been invited to address. Teller felt flattered. The Limited Test Ban Treaty was ratified and went into effect in late 1963.

Teller placed great emphasis on his lecturing to students and he established university level education at Livermore. A graduate Department of Applied Science was created at the University of California, which had both full-time students and part-time students from Livermore. Teller was its first chairman. Based on his teaching, Teller and his associates wrote two books.[203] When Teller stepped down as director of Livermore, the University of California named him Professor of Physics at Large. He could teach physics at any campus—it was close to the ideal position that Szilard might have liked in research.

Teller had by now acquired a very high position in American society, with various prestigious committee memberships and other assignments. He was asked to serve on the President's Foreign Intelligence Advisory Board in 1969.[204] He claimed, however, to have never had any connection with policy-making regarding the Vietnam War. Fear of the so-called domino effect played a great role in convincing the United States to become involved in Vietnam: it was supposed that countries would fall under communism one after another unless the succession could be stopped. The validity of the domino effect was never proved, whereas it was a mistaken assumption to consider the whole communist world to be monolithic.

There was increasing protest, especially student protest on the campuses, against the Vietnam War and Berkeley was most active in these protests. The protesters made it increasingly difficult for Teller to give his lectures, and finally they made it impossible. The students and other radical organizations initiated "war crime trials" and their number one target was Edward Teller. Again, a parallel with Szilard comes to mind: he envisaged the possibility of a war criminal trial against himself, as we saw earlier, but others never played with such an idea. Teller was even threatened physically. The protesters used what they claimed was a Teller statement advocating limited nuclear war—it may have indeed been Teller's, but it was related to an earlier European situation rather than to Vietnam.[205] This was a different kind of opposition to that of his colleagues in the physics community, and it was also painful, because Teller had found much solace in teaching students. The Tellers barely escaped harm.

Teller took great satisfaction in the establishment of the Livermore laboratory. By 1967, Livermore was working on developing a ballistic missile defense system. The Spartan warhead developed at Livermore was intended to destroy incoming thermonuclear missiles at high altitude, outside the Earth's atmosphere, mostly with X-rays. Los Alamos was developing another defensive missile using high-energy neutrons to destroy incoming missiles at low altitude, just before they were to detonate over their targets.[206]

In 1966, Teller was introduced to Ronald Reagan, the former movie star and labor leader who later that year was elected governor of California. Teller invited him to visit Livermore, and Reagan went in 1967. Sixteen years later it would become clear that the visit had been important.

Defense-related issues in which Teller was involved could be very divisive and controversial.[207] Thus, for example, the U.S. Senate approved the deployment of the defense system of antiballistic missiles by a margin of one vote. However, in 1972, more extensive work was stopped by the provisions of the American–Soviet Antiballistic Missile (ABM) Treaty. It limited the number of sites that could be protected by antiballistic missiles to two. Then, in 1974, that number was reduced to one. For the Soviet Union, the choice was Moscow, whereas the United States chose a site in North Dakota where they stored their retaliatory missiles. Even that was eventually abandoned for lack of money. Teller criticized the policy of abandoning the defense systems against incoming missiles. According to him it left the population of the United States defenseless and for the Soviet Union it made a first strike more attractive than before. The territory of the Soviet Union was more extensive; its population was more dispersed; and it had a well-developed civil defense system. The arrangement with the Soviet Union was part of MAD, mutually assured destruction, but the United States remained more vulnerable to a first strike than the Soviet Union.

When Teller reached the compulsory retirement age in 1975, he retired from Livermore, but continued to serve on a one-third basis as consultant. He remained as professor emeritus at the University of California System, and the Hoover Institution at Stanford University asked him to be a senior research fellow, also on a third-time basis. Teller spent the remaining third of his time consulting and giving speeches. In 1979 he suffered a heart attack, which coincided with the accident at the Three Mile Island Nuclear Power Plant in Pennsylvania. He liked to joke about it, saying that he was the only victim of the accident.[208] In the meantime, the Tellers moved to Stanford to be near the Hoover Institution. An editorial assistant, Judy Shoolery, was hired to help him work with his writing assignments, and their products included two books.[209] Shoolery then became the co-author of his *Memoirs*, and she more or less had to put together the second half of it because of Teller's deteriorating health.[210]

Teller's last big project was the Strategic Defense Initiative (SDI), also known by its popular name of Star Wars, although Teller did not like this epithet.[211] As early as 1945 he had raised the question of defense against nuclear weapons in his report to the navy. He determined that perfect defense did not exist; that defense always lagged behind offense; and that defense was always at the mercy of offense, which had more flexibility and unpredictability than defense. However, at that time only the United States had nuclear weapons.

In 1980 Teller campaigned for Reagan, as chairman of the movement of Hungarian-Americans for Reagan. Reagan was elected in November 1980 and took office in January 1981. The two did not meet until the fall of 1982. That is not to say that Teller did not have influence on the Reagan White House, because George A. (Jay) Keyworth became the White House science advisor upon his recommendation. Teller was named a member of the White House Science Council, where he suggested establishing a group to review the technical basis for strategic defense; in turn he became a member of this group. Teller also had consultations with such high officials as the secretary of energy and others.

Teller's active participation in SDI made him even more unpopular among his colleagues, even though SDI was an attractive slogan of a very popular president . President Reagan declared that rather than avenge the American people in retaliation for a nuclear attack by the Soviet Union, he would prefer to protect them. Teller had briefed Admiral James D. Watkins, chief of naval operations, on January 20, 1983. Watkins used this sentence after his meeting with Teller, and the expression found its way into President Reagan's vocabulary.[212] Rather than subscribing to the policy of "mutually assured destruction," it would be a policy of "assured survival."

President Reagan launched SDI on March 23, 1983, in a televised speech from the White House, in front of a group of top scientists. Teller was present and so was the Nobel laureate physicist Charles Townes, the principal inventor of the laser.[213] Townes's presence was significant because the main tool for knocking out enemy ballistic missiles would be powerful laser beams. The president directed the American scientists to develop a defense system that "could intercept and destroy ballistic missiles before they reached our own soil or that of our allies." By so doing his declared aim was to render "nuclear weapons impotent and obsolete."[214]

The policy of MAD put emphasis on offensive rather than defensive weapons, and a balance between the two superpowers had been reached. There were dangers in developing a new class of defensive weapons in that they might tip such a balance and facilitate the triggering of a war. It seems paradoxical, but apparently this was the situation when the United States embarked on its ambitious new strategic defense initiative in 1983.

Superficially, Reagan's 1983 speech resembled Roosevelt's 1940 speech calling for scientists to take part in the defense of the nation, democracy, and freedom. It also resembled Truman's publicly announced decision in 1950 to go ahead with developing the hydrogen bomb. There were differences, though. In 1940, war was inevitable and a few scientists were contemplating the possibility of an atomic bomb. This became a near certainty following the experiments that showed that a nuclear chain reaction was feasible. The scientists, especially those with experience in Germany, feared that Hitler's Germany might develop the bomb first. In 1950, it was again a high-tension situation, where the Soviet Union was expected to develop a hydrogen bomb regardless of whether the United States chose to or not. The circumstances in 1983 were different, as there was no indication that the Soviets would be seeking to develop anything similar to SDI.

The SDI program poured billions of U.S. dollars into high-tech research and development in the United States and allied countries, and it was possible to view this as a positive development. Another positive development was that the Soviet Union sooner or later would have to match these expenditures and it was hardly in the position to do so. Andrei Sakharov considered this question and observed (in 1988) that "the Soviet Union's leaders greatly feared the implementation of SDI, but felt unable to create a comparable system of their own."[215] The Soviet Union had evolved, from a tight and rigid dictatorship into a softer one. Dissidence was still not tolerated, but it was not liquidated as under Stalin; rather, it was fought with other means, and became a fact of Soviet life. Also, an increasing number of Soviet citizens declared that they would like to leave the Soviet Union, and they became an embarrassment to the Soviet leadership. The standard of living was already very low, with constant shortages of all kinds. Even if Soviet society could have tolerated further lowering of the standard of living, such a gain would have been very difficult to convert into advancement in military technology.

In fact, the Soviet Union was lagging fatally behind the West in technology and, in particular, in electronics, computerization, and miniaturization. Star Wars challenged exactly that sphere of the USSR's enterprise that was most vulnerable to such a challenge, although it was not the Soviet scientists who lagged so far behind their Western counterparts. On the contrary, even though conditions were more difficult, Soviet physics thrived in selected branches, as demonstrated by Nobel Prizes not only for discoveries in pure science but also in areas that were not unrelated to technological applications. Suffice it to mention Nikolai G. Basov and Aleksandr M. Prokhorov, who shared the Nobel Prize for the laser with Charles H. Townes in 1964, and Zhores I. Alferov, who shared the Nobel Prize with two Americans in 2000 for the development of semiconductors for high-speed and opto-electronics, which had been underway since the late 1950s. But there was no mechanism in the Soviet Union for translating scientific advances into technologies that could have a broad impact on Soviet life and industry.

No wonder that the Soviet leadership under Mikhail S. Gorbachev was apprehensive of SDI. Gorbachev offered Reagan a compromise in October 1986 at the Reykjavik summit. He suggested that the two superpowers eliminate all offensive strategic arms (ballistic missiles, bombers, and cruise missiles) and limit SDI to the laboratory. Even today, this offer sounds incredibly attractive. Had SDI achieved such an agreement, it would have become a worthy investment. However, the American president was so enamored with SDI that he refused the offer. This failed attempt will have to be further investigated to fully make clear the motivations for the offer and its rejection. Reagan's gamble paid off because, at the end, the Soviet Union collapsed, but it is a frightful thought that it was a gamble with unbelievable stakes.

The Soviets vigorously protested the SDI. A case in point was the episode that happened during Gorbachev's visit to Washington in December 1987. The Reagans gave a reception at the White House, and Teller was among the invitees. When he reached the receiving line, he had a pleasant exchange with Raisa Gorbachev, and then his turn came to meet Mikhail Gorbachev. Teller put his hand out to shake hands as President Reagan was introducing him to the Soviet president. It went like this,

> Reagan: "This is Dr. Teller." Teller put his hand out for a handshake, but Gorbachev stood unmoving and silent. Reagan then repeated the introduction, "This is the famous Dr. Teller." Gorbachev then said, with his hands at his sides: "There are many Tellers." To which Teller said: "There are, indeed, many Tellers," and he left the receiving line.[216]

Teller wrote that he felt greatly complimented by the leader of the Soviet Union.[217] According to a less elegant variant, Teller did not put out his hand to shake hands; rather, he stated that Gorbachev's behavior gave him "an excuse not to shake his hand."[218] Teller had been repeatedly attacked in the Soviet media; for example, the Soviet news agency, TASS, had fiercely criticized Teller on the occasion of his being awarded the National Medal of Science by Reagan in May 1983. TASS characterized him as "one of the most rabid nuclear maniacs . . . blinded by militarism and rabid anti-Sovietism, [who] has always placed the results of his work at the Pentagon's service."[219] What would TASS have expected Teller to do? On the last day of his presidency, Reagan received Teller in the Oval Office and presented him (and a few others) with the Citizen's Medal.

A number of technological accomplishments were expected of SDI, the most noteworthy initially being the ability to destroy enemy missiles with X-ray lasers of unprecedented power. Eventually, when the X-ray lasers were found to be unable to deliver what they were supposed to, another concept took its place. That was the so-called Brilliant Pebbles: there never was a shortage of buzzwords and catchphrases. These would be small interceptor rockets wrapped in electronics that were going to destroy enemy missiles by their sheer kinetic energy. Teller was a loud advocate of the new technologies, which were being developed at the Lawrence Livermore National Laboratory, as it was called by then. However, in this case, he was more the spokesperson in front of the project than the scientist behind it. This also explains why he was running ahead of the actual program with claims and promises that others, more intimately involved with it, found at times exaggerated and irresponsible. By the time of SDI, he had completed the process that had made him "less of a scientist who asked questions and more of a politician who gave advice."[220] Teller must have felt desperate in his actions, knowing that it would be his last struggle, not only because of his age but also because the Reagan administration provided a dreamlike medium for him to operate in.

William J. Broad describes a scene in his book *Teller's War* that should serve as illustration of the foregoing. On September 6, 1985, there was a meeting in the Pentagon presided by the director of the Pentagon office of SDI, General Abrahamson. The topic was the distribution of one hundred million dollars of additional funding for X-ray laser research and related topics. The money was to be divided among Livermore, Los Alamos, and the Sandia National Laboratory in Albuquerque, New Mexico. There was a preliminary understanding among the three laboratories that they would be receiving sixty, thirty, and ten millions, respectively. The discussion was in progress; General Abrahamson had listed the three laboratories on the display board and was about to add the corresponding amounts, when in walked Edward Teller and took the floor immediately. He wanted to have the entire amount for Livermore and he said he would give two reasons. One was a longer justification involving various factors that sounded reasonable and could be subject of discussion. Then he continued: "'The second reason was more important.' He paused. 'President Reagan told me I could have it.' No one in the room stirred."[221]

Charles Townes carefully characterized the president's 1983 speech as technically correct, but idealistic and as drawing up a plan "that would keep the technical community busy."[222] It was an ambitious plan to destroy hundreds of incoming missiles in fifteen minutes or so amid decoys and electronic jamming. Townes sensed from the beginning that SDI had doubters not only in the scientific community but in the administration as well, but the president was all for it and gave his directions, so the project went ahead. The development of the hydrogen bomb and the Apollo space program, triumphantly putting a man on the Moon and bringing him back safely, must have been on his mind as successful examples of how money, hard work, and knowledge make miracles. However, SDI proved to be different, not because money, hard work, or knowledge were missing, but because the objectives were ill-defined and there was no consensus about the feasibility, or even about the reasonableness of the program.

As time went by, the program was unable to deliver what it had promised, although some aspects had already been reported as accomplished. Even some of those who were to gain from Teller's reckless promises and boasts of results began to feel embarrassed by the increasing gap between them and reality. In this, Teller was indeed not alone: unlike the case with the hydrogen bomb, he could not have been called the father of SDI, and it is not clear who could be given that title, possibly President Reagan. This in itself is paradoxical considering Reagan's background in science and technology. But there grew up a generation of young, ambitious, and gifted scientists who seemed to have developed methods of deceit in communicating with administration officials as well as with the public.

Browsing over the SDI literature of the 1980s, an impression forms that Teller was not the conductor of the events, rather that he was their prisoner. It was as if he was playing a role that the casting assigned to him, and he played it to the best of his extraordinary abilities. In spite of his age Teller remained visible, and the

80-year-old scientist briefed President Reagan, the vice president, and others on July 26, 1988, on various questions of the SDI program. Then came the political changes in Europe: the Berlin Wall fell, the Soviet Union disintegrated, the Cold War was won by the United States and its allies, and a new world situation arose, with its new dangers. George Bush was elected president in 1988 and assumed office in January 1989. He visited Livermore in 1990 and reviewed some aspects of the SDI. But Bush was not reelected, and the program was discontinued under President Clinton.

There was justified criticism of SDI in that the program wasted billions of dollars and raised false hopes. Internationally, though, and however indirectly, it performed a positive service in that it scared the Soviet Union and forced it into expenditures that it could afford far less than the United States. Eventually, SDI was, in Townes's words in 1999, "to decay into a more modest effort, with much more limited goals."[223] When asked five years later, Townes had nothing to add to this evaluation.[224]

Teller summarized his activities in which he differed from the majority of politically active scientists, focusing on three questions: whether to develop the hydrogen bomb, which he won; whether to open a second weapons laboratory, which, again, he won; and whether to implement SDI, on which the last word had not yet been spoken, according to his *Memoirs*.[225] A more important judgment, a judgment of history on his activities, will take longer to form.

CHAPTER SIX

Being Martian

. . . I have not been able to grasp the personalities not only of
Wigner but also of Szilard and Teller.

Abraham Pais

After 60 years in the United States, I am still more Hungarian
than American.

Eugene P. Wigner

To advance understanding of the Martians, in this chapter I review their characteristic traits, starting with a couple of comparisons with other scientists.

Comparisons

The first comparison is between Enrico Fermi and Leo Szilard. Fermi had an
impeccable reputation both as a physicist and a human being, and he was among
the greatest physicists of the twentieth century. This comparison is not concerned
with their places in the history of physics but rather with the differences in how
they reacted to the challenges of the outside world. In the other comparison,

between Oppenheimer and Teller, the two were more commensurable as scientists. Both were outstanding physicists and both made great contributions to the defense of the United States. Also, both were controversial human beings. They had irreconcilable differences, although there were more similarities than differences in their backgrounds.

Szilard and Fermi

Fermi was a scientist from beginning to end, whereas for Szilard science was only a means to do something for mankind.[1] Perhaps this was their most important difference. Their names are linked in the experiments that Einstein mentioned in his historic letter to Roosevelt. They determined that nuclear fission of uranium produces sufficient numbers of neutrons to maintain a nuclear chain reaction, they co-designed the world's first nuclear reactor, and they had a joint U.S. patent issued publicly in 1955 (sadly, by then Fermi had died).

Each grew up in a loving family. Fermi experienced early personal tragedy when he lost his brother, who was one year older. Neither Fermi nor Szilard had any special mentor in physics. Fermi, though, had a patron, the physicist–politician Orso Mario Corbino. Fermi learned physics from books, became an important physicist on his own, and collected a group of talented young colleagues around him at the University of Rome. He did not meet people from whom to learn until he visited the laboratories of famous physicists in Europe. Even then it was a limited exercise because his timidity did not let him quite open up. Szilard made contact with the greats of physics while still a student in Berlin; he did not feel intimidated and made the most of the opportunity.

From the time of his early schooling Fermi constructed everything with his own hands, whereas Szilard let others do manual work, whether they were his drawings at the university or experiments in his collaboration with Fermi. It was

(Left) Enrico Fermi,
American stamp;
(right) Leo Szilard,
Hungarian stamp.

natural for Szilard, and alien to Fermi, to hire someone to substitute for him in actual experimental work. A caveat must be issued, however: Szilard did do experiments with his own hands when he regarded them as inevitably important and could find no substitute for himself. Examples were his work with Chalmers in nuclear physics in London, and his later work with Novick in biology in Chicago. Fermi's personal involvement, even in the literally dirtiest experiments, won the admiration of young colleagues and enhanced his ability to attract them to work with him. Szilard did not have students and rarely had younger associates. In this, he could easily have fared better. When he asked Aaron Novick whether he would like to work with him on some biological experiments, Novick immediately accepted the invitation, although Szilard would have let him think it over. The chance to be privy to Szilard's intellect must have been a great attraction to younger colleagues like Novick; alas, few had similar opportunities to experience it. Szilard was more prone to hold court than to have pupils; nevertheless, he influenced some young scientists' "developing social conscience."[2]

Fermi was more modest in his goals than Szilard. Simply stated, Szilard wanted to save mankind. Fermi wanted to make discoveries, but he was not aiming at a major synthesis in physics, like Einstein or Bohr. Fermi felt more comfortable with analyzing definite phenomena whose explanation required a recondite use of known principles. Nor did he have a philosophical bent. Perhaps it was his forte to measure his abilities and be realistic about them. It is an interesting notion that some truly great scientists can assess their abilities and shape their goals accordingly. Lest the reader find this in any way belittling, we can invoke other great physicists of the twentieth century: Rutherford, for example, expressed this succinctly by saying that one should never attempt a difficult problem. Of course, something that was not a barrier to Rutherford might still have been forbiddingly difficult for others.

To emphasize that Fermi was a giant in twentieth-century physics, we list here a few of his discoveries: the Fermi statistics, the Fermi–Thomas atomic model, the theory of beta-decay, the discovery of slow neutrons, and the establishment of the first nuclear chain reaction. He coined the term "weak interaction" for a newly discovered type of force. Eugene Wigner admired Fermi, but found his style simplistic. This is how he wrote about Fermi's seminal paper on beta-decay: "The paper is pervaded with an apparent naïveté which invites criticism and generalizations and a more learned presentation. In this writer's opinion this apparent naïveté is characteristic of Fermi's taste and did not represent his state of knowledge when he wrote the beta decay article." Wigner generalized his observation, and pointed out that simplicity and realism and "his willingness to accept facts and men as they were" was Fermi's most striking trait.[3]

Fermi discovered slow neutrons in the fall of 1934, and the discovery had an important bearing on the development of nuclear physics. He and his colleagues bombarded various targets with fast neutrons and detected the consequences, the neutron-induced radioactivity. Then Fermi decided to put something like a filter between the neutron source and the target. Originally he thought of a piece of lead and he meticulously worked on the shape of the lead piece for some time. Then suddenly, on impulse, on October 22, 1934, he put there a piece of paraffin, a hydrocarbon, which was just laying around, and a multiple of the amount of radioactivity was detected as compared with the experiments without the "filter." Everybody was puzzled, because the expected effect would have been a decrease rather than an increase in the resulting radioactivity. They went home for lunch and took their siestas.

On their return, Fermi had the explanation. The collisions of neutrons in paraffin slowed down the neutrons and thereby they became more—rather than less—effective. That evening Fermi dictated a brief communication about their discovery, which was submitted the next morning to *Ricerca Scientifica*.[4] Fermi and co-workers patented the discovery and wrote an English-language paper on it as well.[5] The patenting of the slow-neutron discovery was similar to Szilard's habit of patenting everything that came his way, but Fermi did it to a far lesser extent than Szilard. Patenting was not as common in the 1930s, either, as it became later. That he did patent this discovery meant that Fermi recognized its far-reaching consequences. Fermi could be a little secretive as he wanted to be absolutely sure that he was right when he came up with an explanation or new suggestion. When they discovered the slow neutrons, Fermi did some calculations before telling his associates about his explanation, but he never mentioned them to anybody until years later.[6]

Fermi had a definite publication strategy, while Szilard had none.[7] During his Italian years, Fermi tried to publish as many papers as possible because he expected that such activity would secure his promotion. But he published many papers in Italian and only the best ones in German. Szilard rarely published. Once he had patented, let alone published a new result, he moved on without trying to exploit the fruits of his innovation or discovery with follow-up publications.

Fermi's career in Italy reached a height that was unprecedented for one of his age when he received a chair in physics at the University of Rome at twenty-six. He wrote an introductory physics text and reached out to a wide audience with his popular lectures. Szilard could lose his patience in explaining concepts and phenomena to a lay audience, even when he was desperately trying to convince them about something. Nobel laureate Donald Glaser was spending a summer at Woods Hole, Massachusetts, and Szilard was there to promote his movement for a livable world. At a meeting Szilard was describing his ideas to an audience of scientists and local citizens. People were asking questions and Szilard was answering them, but he was gradually losing his patience, and at one point replied to a questioner with something like: "You idiot, you don't understand anything."[8] According to Glaser, Szilard insulted one person after another, until it became so bad that he had to ask Glaser to take over and run the meeting.

Szilard was famous for dispersing his ideas without taking credit for them, whereas Fermi did not like to assign subjects for investigation to his students and associates.[9] Fermi's approach helped them to become independent, but he confided in Emilio Segrè that he did not easily find subjects to suggest. Fermi treated his students and associates in a friendly manner; he was never unkind and never overconsiderate, either.

Fermi was meticulous and systematic in his research, far from Szilard's boldness. This was his approach to research: "one must take experimental data, collect experimental data, organize experimental data, begin to make a working hypothesis, try to correlate and so on, until eventually a pattern springs to life and one has only to pick out the results."[10] Fermi often preferred to test his working hypothesis himself before telling others about it. He was overly careful lest his working hypothesis influence his final conclusions. In contrast, he was aware of the fact that such carefulness might lead to missing some fundamental discoveries. Fermi recognized the great dilemma involved in trying to reconcile boldness with conservatism, and, to his credit, he did not transfer his hesitations to others.

When Fermi and his co-workers irradiated uranium with neutrons, they thought that the result was new transuranic elements, an error that was corrected only years later by independent studies. Fermi and his associates expected (as was natural for most nuclear physicists at that time) that the transuranic elements would behave similarly to rhenium, osmium, iridium, and platinum. Later it was shown that the transuranic elements formed a second family of rare earth elements.

Fermi could have discovered nuclear fission in these experiments in 1934, but he did not think about that. This is the more surprising because he even received a warning by a German scientist, Ida Noddack, who had considered the possibility of splitting a heavy atom. Noddack sent Fermi a letter, but to no avail. It was, of course, a double miss: he thought, mistakenly, that he had discovered new elements, while he did not discover nuclear fission, which he could have done. Scientists who are active in research are prone to make errors, but it is an ironic twist of fate that such a careful scientist as Fermi could have made such a monumental error. The error was easy to commit and it might seem overkill to call it monumental. However, it is magnified in hindsight because the proper interpretation of these experiments would have meant the pivotal discovery of nuclear fission a good four years before Hahn and Strassmann and Meitner and Frisch came to it.

Fermi was as careful as ever in drawing conclusions from his experiments, but Corbino boldly announced the discovery of the new transuranic elements in Italy. The Fascist press and the international press gave these (erroneous) discoveries ample exposure. Fermi was glorified in Italy and his scientific results were considered a great success of Mussolini's reign. Ancient names of Italy were suggested for the new elements: "Ausonium" and "Hesperium." At the Nobel Prize award ceremonies in December, 1938, both the presentation speech and Fermi's lecture mention the discovery of these two new elements, with their names. However, in the printed version of Fermi's Nobel lecture, soon after the discovery of nuclear fission, Fermi inserted a footnote to the effect that the new discovery called for reexamination of "all the problems of the transuranic elements."[11]

Although Fermi was not elected to the *Accademia dei Lincei*, the Italian science academy, in spite of Corbino's lobbying, he received another exceptional distinction. Mussolini was dissatisfied with the *Accademia dei Lincei* for other reasons, and the dictator created a new one (without touching the old one), the *Accademia d'Italia*. He gave its members extra salary, titles, fancy uniforms, and other privileges, and Fermi was appointed to it (rather than elected) by Mussolini. Fermi was very pleased, although in later years he showed little interest in memberships of learned societies and other distinctions.[12] It is superfluous to mention that Szilard never received similar recognition in Germany, let alone in Hungary.

Whereas Szilard moved on from a place when he sensed danger and usually did so before others might have realized it, Fermi tried to bury himself in work in the 1930s as the international and Italian situations kept worsening. Fermi was not Jewish, and had he not been married to a Jewish woman he might have stayed in Italy. Segrè is a little defensive when describing Fermi's attitude toward the political situation in Italy.[13] It is clear that Fermi never became a fascist, but also that he never took a discernible anti-fascist stand in Italy. He came from a middle-class family of civil servants and this was the class that especially fell for Mussolini and fascism, for the false glorification of Italy. Fermi did not believe in this because he had a critical mind, but, apart from Corbino's advice, he had no guidelines. Corbino was not a fascist, but he participated in Mussolini's early coalition governments. Fermi tried to ignore what was going on around him until he was affected personally. When the Fermis finally left, he had the 1938 Nobel Prize in Physics in his pocket and a secure job at one of America's leading universities. This was very different from Szilard's departures, first from Germany for England and then from England for America. He did not have financial security or the prestige of the Nobel Prize, nor did he have an appropriate job waiting for him.

Fermi was not prone to wage big battles and he tried to avoid lost causes. This was in marked contrast to Szilard. Fermi withdrew when he faced superior forces, whereas Szilard seemed to welcome them and he thrived on such challenges. Fermi did not have much interest outside physics. Politically, he was hardly a partisan in the United States; he considered himself Republican as far as American political parties go, but he voted for individual candidates rather than for party tickets.[14]

More important than Fermi's conservatism in politics was his conservatism in science.[15] His having been in error about the transuranic elements haunted him. However, the story most characteristic of Fermi's conservatism is one that puts it in direct contrast with Szilard's conservatism. Szilard describes a meeting in which he and Isidor Rabi talked with Fermi about the possibility of the atomic bomb coming out of a nuclear chain reaction.[16] The issue revolved around what Fermi characterized as a "remote possibility" for a chain reaction with uranium. By remote possibility he meant a ten percent probability. Something that has a ten percent probability of happening can be considered to be "remote," and this is how Fermi viewed it.

For Szilard and Rabi ten percent was a lot if, in Rabi's words, "we may die" as a consequence of the event occurring. In this case Fermi's conservatism was a purely formal one, whereas Szilard and Rabi considered the implications. In that case a ten percent probability was something to take seriously. In terms of the implications, conservatism meant, at least for Szilard and Rabi, the necessity to be prepared for it. For Fermi, the ten percent probability was something to play down whereas for Szilard (and in this instance, Rabi), it represented a real danger.

For most of Fermi's adult life Mussolini's Fascism was somewhat benevolent, whereas Szilard had by then experienced totalitarianism in Hungary and the rise of the Nazis in Germany. The latter was especially instructive in that Hitler and his bands had not been taken seriously for many years. Even many clever people would not have regarded it as more than a "remote possibility" that Hitler might take over Germany, let alone that it would be via parliamentary elections. Szilard had learned that remote possibilities should be taken seriously. This was *his* conservatism. In his words, "We both wanted to be conservatives, but Fermi thought that the conservative thing was to play down the possibility that this may happen, and I thought the conservative thing was to assume that it would happen and take all the necessary precautions."[17]

We can see everything through the eyes of Szilard with the benefit of hindsight. But in 1939, Szilard was the odd man out, and Fermi's approach was more mainstream. And if the remote possibility of a nuclear chain reaction caused Fermi, a refugee from fascist Italy, such little fear, we can imagine how the American physicists might have found it even less frightening. It is also true that the conflicts of World War II were already looming over the then neutral America, but most of the American physicists engaged in war-related research were involved with radar.

Lanouette ascribes the difference between Szilard and Fermi in their approaches to such "remote possibilities" to their different views about the connections between life and science. Science was Fermi's life, whereas for Szilard science was for the sake of life and he felt keen sensitivities for the political and personal implications. Fermi was not convinced that fission would lead to chain reactions and the chain reactions to a bomb, and he found it difficult to move without conviction. To Szilard, even a remote possibility made it mandatory to find out whether it would work.[18] Segrè writes, "Szilard and Fermi were extremely different in personality, habits of work, outlook on life, and almost everything else; they had high regard for each other, but could scarcely work together on the same experiment."[19] Whereas, on someone else's initiative, Fermi agreed to lecture to naval representatives about the possibility of nuclear explosives (with little consequence), for Szilard, it was the president of the United States that he would alert.

There was another crucial moment when Fermi's behavior could be scrutinized in comparison with Szilard's, which was in connection with the deployment of the first atomic bombs against Japan. Fermi and Szilard were in different
positions to voice their views. Szilard by then was more or less out of the Manhattan Project. He was very active, along with some others, in voicing his opposition, helping to construct a petition against using the atomic bomb without prior
demonstration, and working to collect signatures for it. Fermi was a member of
the small advisory board to the interim committee, which then made the final
recommendation for President Truman. It must have been a formidable task for
Fermi to be a member, the only immigrant, of the panel of scientists, giving advice on a matter of truly enormous consequence. The committee voiced no opposition to deploying the bombs and specifically advocated their use. After the
war, when the question arose whether there should be military or civilian control of atomic energy matters, Fermi sided with Oppenheimer and Lawrence, who
were for military control. This surprised some who knew Fermi.[20] Szilard was for
civilian control and actively lobbied for it. He was convinced that nuclear matters were too important to leave in the hands of the military.

Their personal traits were also different.[21] Szilard was a visionary; Fermi was
not. Szilard foresaw the prospect of atomic weapons and predicted that it would
be possible to create them within a few years; Fermi's first estimates were much
longer times. Szilard very early on recognized the importance of secrecy in working on nuclear physics that might lead to the bomb; Fermi initially was annoyed
by Szilard's calls for secrecy. When the armed forces had promised financial support, but the money had not been delivered (this was before the Manhattan Project
had begun), Fermi did not suggest doing anything: he accepted the situation as it
came; not so Szilard. He was not content with being a passive spectator of events:
he wanted to make events happen. Once the money arrived, though, Fermi resumed his experiments in earnest. Szilard had an exuberant personality; Fermi
was a practical man. He wanted to complete an experiment before contemplating its implications; for Szilard, the implications occupied him at every step.

Lanouette finds further important differences between the two.[22] Szilard challenged conventions, and every authority and every hierarchy, and did not mind
waging any battle alone; Fermi was a team player. Szilard was impulsive and bold,
and did not refrain from making intuitive leaps; he could then arrive at prescient
results, often highly original. Fermi was systematic; he enjoyed collaboration; he
rigorously focused on his tasks.

Had it been up to Fermi, the American atomic bomb might have not happened, the Manhattan Project might have not been initiated, and Germany might
have built the bomb for all the Americans knew at that time. The same could be
said about the American hydrogen bomb. However, these remarks concern the
initiation of the projects. Once they had begun, Fermi's participation was total.
Although Fermi strongly opposed a crash program for the hydrogen bomb in 1949,
once President Truman had made his decision in 1950 to go ahead with the

H-bomb's development, Fermi immediately signed up to work on it and returned to Los Alamos to do so.

Szilard himself mused about their differences and concluded that "Fermi is a scientist pure and simple." Whereas he lived in one world, Szilard lived in two. In one world he tried to predict what would happen and science was part of this. In the second world he fought, disregarding the predictions, for what he wanted to see happen. Obviously, for Szilard this second world was of utmost importance, whereas for Fermi it did not exist. Szilard thought that he had become aware of this second world because of "certain accidents of my education." From the start, Fermi and Szilard disagreed about every issue that involved principles of action in the face of the approaching war. But then Szilard magnificently states: "If the nation owes us gratitude—and it may not—it does so for having stuck it out together as long as it was necessary."[23] With this, Szilard acknowledged that, for a person who did not recognize his second world, cooperating with Szilard on his terms, as Fermi did, was a most extraordinary accomplishment.

I conclude this brief comparison by mentioning something about which Fermi and Szilard felt the same way. Concerning the Oppenheimer hearing (see next section), Fermi remarked, "What a pity that they attacked him and not some nice guy like Bethe. Now we have all to be on Oppenheimer's side!"[24] Fermi testified in the hearing, expressing full trust in Oppenheimer, and Szilard also felt that he would have to defend Oppenheimer if Teller attacked him.[25] It was a complex situation. Szilard opposed Teller, whom he liked but disagreed with, while he supported Oppenheimer, whom he agreed with but disliked. Both Fermi and Szilard felt that Teller should have been protected from Teller.

Teller and Oppenheimer

Teller's and Oppenheimer's lives intersected in a major way. Teller's testimony at the Oppenheimer security hearing in 1954 was an important event that would haunt and taint Teller's life thereafter. It was less important for Oppenheimer, because in all probability his security clearance would not have been extended even without Teller's damaging testimony. Teller's testimony resulted in his third exile, from the larger community of American physicists, and this time it was self-inflicted. Whereas his first two exiles did not have adverse effects on his scientific career, the third did because his room for interacting with other physicists—his major means of doing research—considerably narrowed after 1954. Our discussion will be cursory. There are excellent references treating Oppenheimer and the Oppenheimer hearing in great detail.[26] I focus here on aspects of Oppenheimer's life and activities that are most relevant for the comparison with Teller and that are helpful in assessing the importance of Teller's clashes with Oppenheimer.

J. (Julius) Robert Oppenheimer was born in New York City in 1904 into a nonreligious Jewish family. His father was an immigrant from Germany; his mother had been born in Baltimore. They lived in a good neighborhood, in the upper west side of the city. They did not speak Yiddish, considered themselves American Hebrews, and were eager to assimilate, but they wanted to keep their Jewishness. The anti-Semitism in American society toward the end of the nineteenth century and in the first half of the twentieth century was expressed primarily in discrimination.[27] That was felt more by the aspiring Jewish upper classes than by the masses struggling for economic survival. Although in the Hungary of that same period anti-Semitism flared up from time to time in cruel forms, Jewish pupils could attend the best secondary schools regardless of whether they were state-run or denominational. In the United States, anti-Semitic discrimination was common in hotels and resorts, and, yes, in schools. Such discrimination continued through the 1940s, not only for Jewish pupils but also for Jewish professors. Isidor I. Rabi was, for example, the first Jewish professor at Columbia University.

Discrimination stimulated the Jewish community to search for solutions, and the outstanding school of the Ethical Culture Society, where Oppenheimer would eventually go, was among the answers. The Ethical Culture Society was a religion to some who did not care for Judaism, who did not want to become atheist, and who wanted to feel comfortable in following high-minded moral principles. The Ethical Culture School in New York City was "an ideal place for the precocious, dazzling, but insecure young Robert."[28] He had few if any friends in childhood and found it difficult to relate to others. There is similarity with Teller, who did not have friends in early childhood and did not spend much time among children because his mother was very protective. When Teller started attending school the other children teased him, and it took large efforts on his part to get rid of the teasing and develop friendships. This is probably why he cherished friendships and suffered so much when he lost them later in his life. Both Teller and Oppenheimer liked to write poetry, both eventually became more popular among their peers, and both cultivated such popularity.

Both Teller and Oppenheimer went to study in Germany, and they both gained their doctorates there. There was a difference, though. For Oppenheimer it was more of a trendy choice, whereas for Teller it was a necessary step. Oppenheimer spent years in Germany and elsewhere in Europe, while having a secure American background to which he could return. Teller thought that he would have to establish himself in Germany for good. Oppenheimer did not have to dedicate all his time and energy to physics, and so engaged in activities like studying the Sanskrit language, and pursuing other humanistic interests. Teller's dedication to physics was total, except for light diversions such as playing the piano and table tennis with his colleagues.

There is no indication of Teller feeling uncomfortable about his Jewishness even in his Hungarian period. He did not go to a primarily Jewish school, but his circle of friends was Jewish. Oppenheimer, in contrast, never felt comfortable with his Jewishness. According to Isidor Rabi, "Oppenheimer was Jewish, but he wished he weren't and tried to pretend that he wasn't."[29] Although institutions of higher learning, such as Harvard University, imposed restrictions, academically outstanding and financially well off Oppenheimer's road to Harvard was straightforward, but he felt isolated there because of the quota system.

Both Oppenheimer and Teller were relative latecomers as far as political interests are concerned. Oppenheimer developed a strong left-leaning interest in politics from the mid-1930s, focusing on issues like the plight of Jews in Germany and support of Republican Spain. He was disappointed in the economic situation in America, although for years he had not noticed the Great Depression. He later characterized the arousal of his political attention in the following way, "I had had a continuing, smoldering fury about the treatment of Jews in Germany. I had relatives there. . . . I saw what the depression was doing to my students . . . and through them, I began to understand how deeply political and economic events could affect man's lives."[30] Through friendships and personal interest, Oppenheimer became active in communist front organizations, but there is no evidence that he ever became a member of the party.

Teller was exposed to communist and Nazi ideologies early on. From the short-lived Hungarian "Soviet" Republic of 1919, when he was eleven years old, he retained only a feeling of discomfort. The Nazism in Germany was unacceptable to him. Personal friendship with Laszlo Tisza made him witness the dedication of a communist sympathizer and his later disillusionment with the Soviet Union. Teller became an anti-communist as a result of a long process and his political education was completed by Arthur Koestler's *Darkness at Noon.* Oppenheimer had had similarly disappointing impressions of the Soviet Union when two of his physicist friends visited him in the summer of 1938.[31] Victor Weisskopf and George Placzek had spent some time there and told him about Stalin's tyranny, the staged trials, the concentration camps, and the poverty of the masses. However, Oppenheimer could not quite identify himself with Weisskopf and Placzek to the extent Teller could with Tisza. At that point, Oppenheimer's view of the great socialist experiment had not quite been crushed.

In view of Oppenheimer's later troubles because of the leftist interest and affiliations of his youth, and because of decades of blind anti-communism in American society, it is important to point out that communist ideology has been more acceptable in Europe than in the United States. It is also important to distinguish between the original communist ideology and Soviet communism, which distorted the original communist ideals like the Inquisition distorted original Christianity. The distortion of communism reached such a degree that Soviet communism could be paired with Nazism with good reason. However, there are important differences. The great Italian author and Holocaust survivor Primo Levi invoked a passage from Alexander Solzhenitsyn's writings to characterize the Soviet concentration camp. There, the prisoners protest against the authorities, saying "You're not Soviets! You're not Communists!" In the German concentration camp where Levi was an inmate, the prisoners said to their captors: "You're perfect Nazis; you're the embodiment of your ideal."[32] The distinction was that the Soviets broke faith with the original, and obviously utopist communist ideal, whereas the Germans carried out to perfection what Hitler had advocated all along.

In the 1930s, many intellectuals in the West had an open mind about communism and a number became party members. It was considered a possible approach to righting the economic wrongs of capitalism at the time of the Great Depression. In addition, the communists were consistently against the Nazis from the beginning up until the German–Soviet Non-Aggression Pact in 1939. Then, after the German attack on the Soviet Union in 1941, it was the Soviet Union that sacrificed the most in its struggle against Germany. There was also a blind devotion to communism and the Soviet Union for many who had been indoctrinated. In view of this, there was a basis for fears that dedicated communists might be dedicated to Moscow as well. There is a puzzle here in that many liberals in the West viewed the Soviet Union, a country where liberals were persecuted and liberal ideals ruthlessly suppressed, with sympathy. However, Western liberals who viewed the Soviet system and practice with an open eye and cared for authentic information from the Soviet Union were not misled. While Szilard advocated overtures to the Soviet Union, he knew perfectly well that he could not have survived in such a system. Incidentally, the label "liberal" does not have the sinister connotation for most in Europe that it has for some in the United States.

Oppenheimer graduated from Harvard in 1925 and in the same year he started his graduate studies in Cambridge, England. There, again, he found it hard fitting in.[33] Cambridge was for Oppenheimer what Berlin was for Wigner and Szilard and Leipzig for Teller; the change after Harvard, however, was less drastic than that experienced by the Hungarian physicists after Budapest. At Cambridge Oppenheimer encountered Ernest Rutherford, J. J. Thomson, Niels Bohr, Paul Ehrenfest, Patrick M. S. Blackett, and others. Meeting famous physicists helped him in setting his standards high, although it may also have been intimidating for someone of his lofty aspirations. In the year he arrived at Cambridge and started his studies, with often boring course work and laboratory exercises, quantum mechanics was born, and it was a revolution begun by people who were, in most cases, only slightly older than him.

As in Teller's research, Oppenheimer's first projects were in molecular physics, and he made contributions of lasting impact in this field. At Cambridge he met Max Born, who invited him to Göttingen where their collaboration resulted in, amongst other things, the famous Born–Oppenheimer approximation.[34] Every student of chemical physics and physical chemistry today learns about it. Nonetheless, for Oppenheimer it must have been painful that he arrived in the second wave, after the true creators of quantum mechanics. He, and others, like Teller, had to be content with picking up the pieces left by the likes of Heisenberg, Born, Dirac, and Schrödinger.

Oppenheimer received his doctorate from the University of Göttingen in 1927. He was twenty-three years old. Teller completed his doctorate in Leipzig in January

1930, when he was not yet twenty-two. Their careers were advancing more or less in parallel. It must be noted, though, that whereas in the United States the PhD was the "terminal degree," in Germany a second doctorate, the habilitation, was (and is) needed to gain tenure and to become a full professor.

Oppenheimer split his time between Caltech and Harvard in 1927–1928. Then he toured the European centers of physics in 1928–1929. His stay with Wolfgang Pauli in Zurich was especially influential for him. In 1929, he went to California and split his time between Berkeley and Caltech. That he moved to California is of interest in itself: he was a true intellectual Easterner and would eventually return to Princeton, but by then he was past his creative prime. In contrast, Teller simply went where he felt he was needed.

Oppenheimer's arrogance may have been an overcompensation for his insecurity. Even the mild-mannered Max Born had to take measures to curb Oppenheimer's aggressive interruptions of seminar speakers. To Born, Oppenheimer "was a man of great talent, and he was conscious of his superiority in a way which was embarrassing and led to trouble." A much later characterization of Oppenheimer referred to negative traits which he retained even at the peak of his career: "vast insecurities lay forever barely hidden behind his charismatic exterior, whence an arrogance and occasional cruelty befitting neither his age nor his stature."[35]

From the mid-1930s, there was a drastic change in the relationship between the sciences of the United States and Germany. The center of gravity of scientific progress, and in particular of physics, shifted to America. The change had two principal components. One was the American aspiration, and in a country where national efforts are seldom in place, the strengthening of physics took on the likeness of a national emergency program. This was most all of a change in the status of theoretical physics, which up to that point had enjoyed less interest and respect than experimental physics. Likewise, applied engineering was higher in status than the cultivation of its mathematical foundations, a situation which was then changed, in no small degree, by von Kármán's activities. The other principal component was the sudden influx of European, and almost exclusively Jewish, talent onto the American campuses.

Oppenheimer became a popular teacher in California for sophisticated and aspiring students, but he was not above being sarcastic at his students' expense. He could be charming and arrogant, despising and endearing. He was not very good with those who were intellectually inferior to him and had no patience for undergraduate teaching. Oppenheimer had the ability and the opportunity at Berkeley to work concurrently with as many as twenty students and postdoctoral fellows, and suggested interesting and challenging topics to them.

Oppenheimer greatly contributed to bringing up the level of theoretical physics in the United States. In Hans Bethe's words, "More than any other man, he was responsible for raising American theoretical physics from a provincial adjunct of Europe to world leadership."[36] Among Oppenheimer's students and associates were at least three future American Nobel laureates, Julian Schwinger,

Willis Lamb, and Carl Anderson. Of course, to build up a great school takes more than an outstanding scientist, however charismatic he may be. Oppenheimer also represented taste in science and style, and he attracted streams of important visitors and carried out a stimulating seminar program. One of the invitees was Edward Teller.

In contrast to Oppenheimer, Teller was an excellent lecturer at the popular level. However, he did not build up a school when he was professor of physics at George Washington University, whereas Oppenheimer did in California. Teller preferred working with people one on one. After World War II, he continued a university career at the University of Chicago for some years, but did not build up a school there, either. Oppenheimer did not even make an attempt to return to academia after the war.

Classifying scientists as drillers and diggers helps assess both Oppenheimer and Teller as researchers.[37] A driller spends a very long time, sometimes his entire career, on one topic, boring deeper and deeper. The digger, on the other hand, goes from topic to topic and contributes to many areas of his science. Both Oppenheimer and Teller were diggers. For each, there were several topics that could have become bases for longer-range projects, but neither stayed long with any particular area of research. Nonetheless, what they achieved would have sufficed for several bright careers in physics.

Oppenheimer made important contributions to physics, including astrophysics. According to some evaluations, had he lived longer he might have been considered for the Nobel Prize for his work on neutron stars and black holes. John A. Wheeler's coining of the name black hole came much later. Oppenheimer and others might have also been considered for the Nobel Prize for inventing so-called renormalization: this introduced consistency, replacing the earlier contradiction, between the theoretical infinite quantities and the experimental finite values of masses and charges of elementary particles.[38]

Oppenheimer gradually decreased his political involvement from the late 1930s, but he did not break with his Communist friends even after the detestable Soviet–Nazi pact in 1939. There was, though, a difference: after the German–Soviet pact had been signed, but before the Nazi attack on the Soviet Union, the Communist Party favored American non-intervention whereas Oppenheimer was for intervention. After the Soviet Union had become a belligerent of Germany, the Communist Party was also for all-out support of the new victim of German aggression.

Oppenheimer's sensitivity toward the plight of Jewish refugees was easy to understand because of his own background. But he had also been sensitive to the Spanish cause. His biographers have noted his adaptability. Oppenheimer found it easy to transform from being an ivory tower professor into a leftist activist in the mid-1930s. Then the second transformation came, when he joined the Manhattan Project and abandoned his leftist associations. This second transformation happened at about the time when Teller was reading *Darkness at Noon*, which completed his political transformation, but for Teller it was a less drastic one. Also, Oppenheimer was a less robust personality, which may explain why he wanted to overcompensate for his prior involvements in causes that the authorities were frowning upon. He was eager to prove himself, and this may be why he occasionally behaved (in his later words) as an "idiot." General Groves and others told him that if he had to choose between his friends and his country, he should side with his country. His tragedy was that, although he did not have to make such a choice, he did it artificially, as future events would prove.

Groves met Oppenheimer in the fall of 1942. They discussed the desirability of bringing together the last phase of the atomic bomb project in a single location, which would soon be Los Alamos. Groves was so impressed by Oppenheimer that he wanted him to be the scientific director of the new laboratory. It was his opportunity to make a personnel decision: the other laboratories had been organized before his joining the project and their heads had been selected by others.

Groves had a feel for Oppenheimer, but the new laboratory was to create a bomb, which necessitated solving numerous practical problems. And not only was Oppenheimer no expert (as nobody else was yet) but he had also not been an experimental physicist. At that time nobody with whom Groves talked "showed any enthusiasm about Oppenheimer as a possible director of the project." Oppenheimer did not even have administrative experience. On top of everything, he was considered to be a security risk because of his past left-leaning associations. Nonetheless, Groves decided to overrule all the doubts of others, and named Oppenheimer the director of Los Alamos. "I have never felt that it was a mistake to have selected and cleared Oppenheimer for his wartime post," Groves wrote in 1962, well after Oppenheimer's security clearance had been withdrawn.[39] However, when Groves was asked during the security hearing in 1954 whether he would grant Oppenheimer security clearance under the current rules, he felt obliged to say that he would not.[40] There is an opinion that one of Groves's motives in choosing Oppenheimer was his hold over him because of Oppenheimer's political past, which could always be used to keep him under Groves's thumb.[41] It is a humiliating consideration for such an important person in such an important job, but Groves was a practical man for whom only accomplishing his task mattered.

Theoretically, Oppenheimer's past leftist associations should not have been a consideration in gaining security clearance in 1942–1943. The Soviet Union was an ally of the United States and was making tremendous sacrifices in fighting its life-or-death struggle against Nazi Germany. However, there were already forces within the United States (John von Neumann was a good example) that believed the Soviet Union would be an enemy in the long run more dangerous than Nazi Germany. Of course, assuming that left-leaning scientists were a threat to the security of the United States was a simplistic approach in any case. It was also an exaggeration that communists invariably were more loyal to the Soviet Union than to their own country. The atomic project was a latecomer as far as war-related scientific activities were concerned. This is also why the staff at Los Alamos included a number of leftist scientists and even former Communist Party members who had not been tapped for other war projects.

Teller and Oppenheimer initially developed a cordial relationship based on respecting each other's intellects. Then, in the fall of 1942, they traveled together to New York and an incident occurred. By then the army had taken over the Manhattan Project, and General Leslie Groves had been appointed its commander. Oppenheimer complained to Teller about working with Groves. He said something that disturbed Teller greatly: "No matter what Groves demands now, we have to cooperate. But the time is coming when we will have to do things differently and resist the military."[42] It sounded wrong to Teller to resist the military authorities, and he expressed this to Oppenheimer. The warmth in their relationship was gone from that moment. This early encounter with Teller was rather characteristic of Oppenheimer's ambivalent behavior.

In January or February 1943, while they were still in Berkeley, the Oppenheimers entertained their friends Haakon and Barbara Chevalier at home. They were a leftist couple, and a brief exchange between Oppenheimer and Chevalier took place which was to have repercussions on their lives. According to one version, Chevalier told Oppenheimer that a British chemical engineer by the name of Eltenton would be willing to transmit technical information from American scientists working on war-related projects to the Soviets. Oppenheimer made it clear immediately that he would not be party to such a transaction. The situation was ambiguous, and Oppenheimer described it in different versions in subsequent years. The exchange could be interpreted as Chevalier warning his friend about the dangers of such approaches. Alternatively, it could be interpreted as Chevalier trying to see whether Oppenheimer might be willing to participate in such transactions. Chevalier's motivations are not of importance here, but Oppenheimer's reaction is. There seems to be no doubt that Oppenheimer rejected the idea, and he was never even seriously accused of having participated in such activities.[43]

By March 1943, when he went to Los Alamos and began directing this unprecedented operation, Oppenheimer was fully dedicated to its cause. He would have agreed to have the whole project set up as a military rather than civilian establishment, with all the scientists having military ranks. However, the other scientists did not like the arrangement, so a compromise was reached: there would be no military rule at Los Alamos for the scientists, but stringent security measures were taken, and Oppenheimer was "extremely cooperative" in them.[44]

Although Oppenheimer had Groves's vote of confidence, he did not have that of the security people. He was watched and followed everywhere he went, his telephone was tapped, and his every move was recorded and analyzed. The security people supposed all along that Oppenheimer might be revealing secret atomic information to the Soviets. Even while the work at Los Alamos was going on, there were recommendations to remove him from his position and dismiss him from government employment.[45] However, Oppenheimer continued his dedicated work and, whenever the opportunity arose, gave additional evidence of his loyalty.

Eight months after the brief conversation with Chevalier, Oppenheimer told the security people about Eltenton, though not about Chevalier. He also appeared to embroider what had really happened by telling the security officers (his interrogators) that a total of three people had been approached about gaining information for the Soviets, but he insistently refused to name the person who had approached them. He never revealed the other names, and such approaches may never have taken place. When this topic came up in the hearing in 1954 and Oppenheimer was asked why he had exaggerated what Chevalier was doing, his shocking response was that he was an idiot. Alternatively, he may have later changed his testimony with the intent of protecting other people, including his brother Frank. This will never be known. While Oppenheimer refused to reveal Chevalier's identity freely, he told Groves that if the general ordered him to do so, he would. Groves did not.

However, the intelligence people continued pressing Oppenheimer to reveal the name. Lengthy interviews ensued in the midst of the atomic bomb project when Oppenheimer's time was most precious, and there is no trace of any protest on his part against such interviews. Oppenheimer was being humiliated, especially when being asked about possible party affiliations of his associates at Los Alamos, and he did not refuse the suggestion by the intelligence people that he gather information about his colleagues.[46] A sad picture emerges both for Oppenheimer and for the security services; for the latter especially, because, with the benefit of hindsight, they were actually hindering the success of the project. At the same time, they never detected the ongoing espionage by Klaus Fuchs, a member of the British delegation of physicists, whose espionage was uncovered after the war. Back in Britain, the German refugee Fuchs "never concealed the fact that he was a Communist."[47]

The security people persisted in investigating Oppenheimer and in December 1943, General Groves felt it incumbent on him to "order" Oppenheimer to reveal Chevalier's name. It was only in 1954 that Chevalier understood why he had been blacklisted and why he had lost his job and even his citizenship, while Oppenheimer continued his friendship with him. Later Oppenheimer called his own fabrication a "cock and bull" story. Alas, the Chevalier story was not the only case of such disloyalty to friends by Oppenheimer.

The most conspicuous case was that of Bernard Peters. He was a German Jew, a former communist or communist sympathizer, who early on fought the Nazis and was incarcerated in the first German concentration camp, Dachau. His mother bribed some officials and was able to have her son transferred to a city jail. Eventually he was released and escaped to the United States. Peters did his doctoral work under Oppenheimer in Pasadena. Lacking security clearance, he could not participate in the work at Los Alamos, but worked at Berkeley during the war. In his wartime interviews with the security people, Oppenheimer gave damaging testimony about Peters. He even held it against him that he had fought physically against the Nazis, taking this as a sign of a violent temper, and regarded it as a flaw in his character that he had been freed from Dachau "by guile."[48]

Oppenheimer's encounters with the security investigations were the dark side of his life during the Manhattan Project. The bright side was his being the scientific head of Los Alamos, and friend and foe alike praised his performance without reservation. He kept a watch on the larger picture and he was at home with the details. He provided encouragement and his associates worked not only for the larger goal but also for his personal recognition. Philip M. Stern in his *The Oppenheimer Case* contrasted Oppenheimer with Teller. Whereas Teller was "voluble and gregarious," Oppenheimer was "quiet and private." Whereas Teller was "extravagant in speech and in thought," Oppenheimer was "more precise in both."[49]

Their personal lives were also very different. For Teller, his wife, Mici, was the only woman in his life from the time he was a teenager. He conducted at times painfully frank correspondence with a colleague, Maria Goeppert-Mayer, but she was only a soul mate.[50] Oppenheimer was a tormented personality in his youth where women were concerned. His relationships were sometimes unstable: he started the affair with his future wife while she was still married, and during their own marriage he felt obliged to comfort a woman he had known earlier.

When Harry Truman became president on April 12, 1945, he was informed about the atomic bomb project and was immediately confronted with the question of deployment. He created an interim committee and augmented it with a four-member Scientific Advisory Panel consisting of three Nobel laureates and Oppenheimer. The main question was whether the first bombs should be dropped on Japan with or without prior demonstration. Oppenheimer's followers might have expected him to oppose deployment without warning, but in the final account he did not. He talked Teller out of signing the petition that Szilard had sent to Teller and asked him not to circulate it among the Los Alamos scientists. Oppenheimer did not let Teller know that he had been more knowledgeable about the events than Teller might have supposed.

In the immediate aftermath of the bombs over Japan and the end of World War II, the Association of Los Alamos Scientists was set up and its elected committee issued a statement expressing concern over the fate of nuclear weapons. The committee consisted of four scientists, Hans Bethe, Jerrold Zacharias, Frank Oppenheimer, and Edward Teller. The fact that Teller and Frank Oppenheimer were on the same committee is surprising in hindsight; Teller makes no mention of this association and its activities in his *Memoirs*.

The Los Alamos scientists considered Robert Oppenheimer to be their representative to the outside world, in particular to the officials in Washington. At this time, however, he sided more with the administration than with the scientists, and in November 1945 Oppenheimer departed from Los Alamos. As this happened after he had pleaded with the scientists to stay on in the laboratory, Teller felt betrayed by him.

When Oppenheimer resigned from the directorship of Los Alamos, he was considered to be a great national hero, in addition to being a great expert. He was also called to testify before Congress in the debate about military versus civilian control over nuclear matters. It was a typical Oppenheimer performance: "He talked in such a manner that the congressmen present thought he was for the bill but the physicists present all thought that he was against the bill."[51]

The new civilian authority of atomic energy was organized in 1946 and started its activities in 1947. The five-member Atomic Energy Commission (AEC) was augmented by a nine-member General Advisory Committee consisting of scientists and chaired by Oppenheimer. He served as chair of a total of seven government committees in the postwar era. His politics and his attitude towards the Soviet Union had changed. He urged the U.S. representative in the United Nations Atomic Energy Commission to discontinue negotiations with the Soviets about world control of atomic energy. He was convinced that the Soviet Union did not want an agreement but would use the negotiations for propaganda purposes. This was in 1947, when the extended security investigations of Oppenheimer were intensifying. His FBI files were scrutinized by each member of the AEC; they were appalled by the damaging information about his past associations and politics and in particular about the Chevalier incident, but did not find the documents injurious enough to remove him from his position.[52]

His leftist past, and especially his disloyal declarations about his friends to the security organizations, started to catch up with Oppenheimer in various hearings, investigations, and press releases of his previous testimonies. This was at a time when his popularity and fame extended far beyond the scientific community, when he was becoming known as the father of the atomic bomb. Initially the hearings were sympathetic to Oppenheimer, but his physicist colleagues condemned him for his role in the Peters case. He was compared to a magnet, which has two poles. The positive is "the charmer, the persuader, at times almost the hypnotizer." The negative is "the humiliator, the witherer, the arrogant, impatient condescender of intellects lesser than his own."[53] One of the considerable number of persons Oppenheimer had managed to ridicule was Admiral Lewis Strauss. Strauss was a persistent person who would play an important role in bringing him down.

Another tenacious opponent of Oppenheimer's was Edward Teller. When Oppenheimer was in charge of Los Alamos he made decisions that were not always to Teller's liking, one of which was appointing Hans Bethe to head the Theoretical Division. Teller was unable to subordinate himself to Bethe's superiority and when Oppenheimer recognized this he did his best to pacify Teller: he made it a point to meet and discuss matters with him weekly. In his turn, Teller turned to Oppenheimer for advice at crucial moments, and continued this practice after they had both departed from Los Alamos. Oppenheimer had superior positions, and in being the chairman of the General Advisory Committee of the AEC he continued to represent authority for Teller. It was characteristic that, when the first Soviet atomic explosion was detected, Teller turned to Oppenheimer for direction, and Oppenheimer responded in a dismissive way. This moved Teller to look for others with whom he could ally himself in charting further activities to build new weapons and in particular the hydrogen bomb. He found them in the persons of Ernest Lawrence and Luis Alvarez.

Both Oppenheimer and Teller possessed a considerable amount of vanity: they liked to be associated with high officials and both liked to let such associations be known of by their peers. Oppenheimer was at the top of his public standing after World War II: he had access to high government officials, and he liked to refer to them by their first names. He continued rising in fame and appointments, and, until the devastating hearings in 1954, was a highly positioned and influential statesman in nuclear and other defense matters. He appeared to be ubiquitous in decision-making positions, which might have represented a conflict of interest. Thus, for example, he advised the Pentagon that the hydrogen bomb was not feasible technically and hence the Pentagon did not claim that there was a military need for it. Then he told the AEC that there was no request from the Pentagon for the hydrogen bomb.[54]

Teller was apparently immune from being in any way associated with leftist causes. His anti-communism was more ideological than practical at the time when his political views were being formed. Later, his ideological views became subordinated to his dedication to the defense of the United States. His persevering commitment to the hydrogen bomb was in contrast to his scattered approach to physics.

Both men could be charmers and excellent debaters. Once Oppenheimer faced a not-very-friendly congressional committee, the House Un-American Activities Committee (HUAC), which included the then California Congressman Richard M. Nixon. At the end of the hearings, however, all congratulated him and thanked him for his performance. Later it was Vice President Nixon who saved Oppenheimer from a McCarthy investigation.[55] Edward Teller took part in debates in the media; his partners not only admitted defeat but declared that it was impossible to argue with him successfully.[56] In a debate about SDI in Washington, DC, the Nobel laureate physicist Philip Anderson was pitted against Teller, in the presence of a large gathering of public figures, celebrities, scientists, and hundreds of high school seniors.[57] Anderson presented his technical arguments but Teller brushed them aside, saying that science would find a way out of the threat of nuclear destruction. He won a standing ovation from the students.

Both Teller and Oppenheimer let themselves be victims of inter-service competitions, squabbles, and rivalries.[58] Early on Oppenheimer angered the air force, whereas Teller found in it an early ally in his advocacy of the development of the hydrogen bomb, and especially in his struggle for the second weapons laboratory.

Oppenheimer often lacked consistency in his behavior. A case in point was his change of attitude towards the development of the hydrogen bomb. Initially he was interested, and after the Trinity test of the plutonium fission bomb he wanted to accelerate the work on it. Immediately after the Japanese surrender, however, he stopped the work on the Super and became a vocal opponent of its development. He was in a key position to oppose the hydrogen bomb; in fact, he was in several key positions to put up a barrier against it. However, when after many months of aborted attempts the Ulam–Teller approach provided the technical solution to making the hydrogen bomb, Oppenheimer declared in an oft-quoted statement that the program had become too technically sweet to argue about. So it seemed as if his previous reservations had been of a technical kind; but where were his often-proclaimed moral scruples?

In 1952, Oppenheimer was not reappointed to his position in the GAC, although he continued as a consultant to the AEC. He still had other positions, but his great authority started diminishing. The Department of Defense, for example, abolished its entire Research and Development Board in 1953 and thus got rid of Oppenheimer as their consultant.[59] Soon, Oppenheimer's term as consultant to the AEC would expire. Had it not been extended, he and Teller's lives would have been simpler.

In November 1953, William Borden, who had been involved in a variety of jobs related to nuclear matters and national security, sent a letter to the director of the FBI, J. Edgar Hoover. Borden accused Oppenheimer of having been a communist, of continuing his association with the Communist Party, and of opposing the hydrogen bomb because of his being an agent of the Soviet Union. The letter contained hardly any new facts. However, towards the end of 1953 the accusations took on a new life, because the atmosphere in the United States at this time was such that they could not be ignored. Besides, there was no national project with a General Groves as its head that would brush off such accusations.[60]

The first consequence of the Borden letter was that President Eisenhower ordered that a "blank wall" be put between Oppenheimer and any classified information.[61] At this point, the AEC could have just let Oppenheimer's consultancy lapse when it expired in the summer of 1954, and in fact they offered him the possibility of withdrawing quietly, but he wanted to clear his name. Thus the AEC set up a three-man board to conduct a hearing, and heavy charges, by the standards of the day, were leveled against Oppenheimer. Twenty-three of them dealt with his past associations with communists and communist causes, all prior to 1947. The twenty-fourth related to his opposition to the development of the hydrogen bomb, and it differed from the other charges in that it concerned Oppenheimer's *opinion* rather than his actions.

It was stressed throughout that his hearing was just that and not a trial, but this turned out to be disadvantageous to him in a number of respects. His counsel, lacking the appropriate security clearance, could not be present at certain portions of the procedure. The Gray Board, playing the role of judge, was taking account of additional material in its judgment, not only what was aired during the hearing, whereas at a trial all evidence would have had to be presented as part of the process. In a real trial the defendant has the right to face his or her accusers, whereas at the hearing accusations could be introduced from sources that were not present, and sometimes not even properly identified. There was no impartial jury. The government representative, essentially the prosecutor, had much broader latitude for action than Oppenheimer's counsel.

There were plenty of testimonies during his hearing that were damaging for Oppenheimer, but most of the scientists came out in his favor. Nobel laureates Enrico Fermi and Isidor Rabi, and future Nobel laureate Hans Bethe spoke for him, as did his wartime superiors in scientific administration, Vannevar Bush and James B. Conant. In addition, two former AEC chairmen and three former AEC commissioners testified on his behalf. One of the former AEC chairmen, David Lilienthal, compared the proceedings to the Spanish Inquisition, and Vannevar Bush noted that Oppenheimer was being tried among others for his opinions. Bush likened the procedure to the "Russian system." In contrast, Kenneth Pitzer accused Oppenheimer, not because he opposed the development of the hydrogen bomb, but because he failed to "enthuse," because he did not "enthusiastically urge individuals to participate in the program."[62]

Teller's testimony was of the greatest interest, although there is general agreement that the board's decision would have been the same without his taking the stand. Some verbatim excerpts from the testimony are quoted here.

> Question [by the government representative, Mr. Robb, in the direct examination]: Dr. Teller, may I ask you, sir, at the outset, are you appearing here today because you want to be here?
>
> Teller: I appear because I have been asked to and because I consider it my duty on request to say what I think in the matter. I would have preferred not to appear.
>
> Question: Is it your intention in anything that you are about to testify to, to suggest that Dr. Oppenheimer is disloyal to the United States?
>
> Teller: I do not want to suggest anything of the kind. I know Oppenheimer is an intellectually most alert and a very complicated person, and I think it would be presumptuous and wrong on my part if I would try in any way to analyze his motives. But I have always assumed, and I now assume that he is loyal to the United States. I believe this, and I shall believe it until I see very conclusive proof to the opposite.
>
> Question: Do you or do you not believe that Dr. Oppenheimer is a security risk?
>
> Teller: In a great number of cases I have seen Dr. Oppenheimer act— I understood that Dr. Oppenheimer acted—in a way which for me was exceedingly hard to understand. I thoroughly disagreed with him in numerous issues and his actions frankly appeared to me confused and complicated. To this extent I feel that I would like to see the vital interests of this country in hands which I understand better, and therefore trust more.

In this very limited sense I would like to express a feeling that I
would feel personally more secure if public matters would rest in other
hands.[63]

This statement by Teller has been much quoted. He lamented in his *Memoirs* that
this exchange had come much too soon in the testimony.[64] Prior to giving his
testimony, Teller had been shown excerpts of Oppenheimer's, in particular those
referring to the Chevalier incident in which Oppenheimer admitted that he had
years ago concocted a story. According to Teller, his having seen this senseless
testimony made him say things that sounded more general than they should have.
However, the FBI had interrogated Teller before, in 1952, and he was not a sympathetic witness for Oppenheimer then, either. Teller declared to the FBI that "He
would do most anything to see [Oppenheimer] separated from the General Advisory Committee because of his poor advice and policies regarding national
preparedness and because of his delaying of the development of H-bomb."[65] This
also means that Teller's damaging testimony at the Oppenheimer hearing in 1954
was not given on the spur of the moment; rather, he was expressing his long-held
views concerning Oppenheimer's activities.

Many questions were asked about Oppenheimer's attitude toward the hydrogen bomb project and toward the opening of a second weapons laboratory. The
quality of his advice also came under scrutiny, although this should not have been
relevant for Oppenheimer's security clearance. Teller gave examples of cases in
which he found Oppenheimer's advice damaging, but he also mentioned examples
when it was helpful. Finally, to the closing questions, Teller again produced some
widely quoted responses:

> *Question [by Mr. Gordon Gray, the chairman of the three-man board]*:
> Do you feel that it would endanger the common defense and security
> to grant clearance to Dr. Oppenheimer?
> *Teller*: I believe, and that is merely a question of belief and there is no
> expertness, no real information behind it, that Dr. Oppenheimer's
> character is such that he would not knowingly and willingly do
> anything that is designed to endanger the safety of this country. To the
> extent, therefore, that your question is directed toward intent, I would
> say I do not see any reason to deny clearance.
> If it is a question of wisdom and judgment, as demonstrated by
> actions since 1945, then I would say one would be wiser not to grant
> clearance.[66]

Teller notes in his *Memoirs* that he had a second chance here and in retrospect he wished that at this late stage of his testimony he had clarified his initial
"ambiguous" remarks.[67] Instead, he amplified what he had said, and he went farther. The question was security clearance and the first part of Teller's response

referred to it. The second part referred to Oppenheimer's wisdom and judgment, which should not have come into consideration. Teller acted as if to make sure that his words carried sufficient weight and in this light his preceding positive comment could serve only to enhance the negative effect of his conclusion.

As Teller was leaving the witness chair, he went to shake Oppenheimer's hand and told him, ""I'm sorry." Oppenheimer's answer was "After what you've just said, I don't know what you mean."[68] There may have been only one person in the room who correctly guessed the significance of Teller's testimony: Ward V. Evans, a chemist, judged by some to be the least significant of the three men who composed the board. He had put this question to Teller: "Do you think the action of a committee like this, no matter what it may be, will be the source of great discussion in the National Academy and among scientific men in general?"[69] Evans did not ask Teller this question by accident: he noted that the "scientific backbone of our nation" came out in the defense of Oppenheimer.[70] The board, with Evans dissenting, recommended that Oppenheimer's security clearance be withdrawn, and the AEC's general manager followed suit. Finally, the AEC came to the same decision, with the sole dissenting voice cast by its sole scientist member. When the decision became public, Albert Einstein expressed his respect and admiration for Oppenheimer in a statement.[71]

The decision of the AEC was made just a few hours before Oppenheimer's security clearance would have expired anyway. Over the course of the hearing he was judged by friend and foe alike to be his own worst enemy. Gone was the brilliance of the articulation that had won over the hostile members of the House Un-American Activities Committee five years earlier.

There have been a lot of speculations about Teller's motivations. That he testified must have come from his feeling of duty, and that he testified against Oppenheimer must have come from his conscience. Yet one cannot avoid the impression that it was partly revenge and partly to please people that were in some sense Teller's superiors. These included the air force, which was an enthusiastic supporter of his initiatives, and Lewis Strauss, the powerful chairman of the AEC, who had suffered from Oppenheimer.

For Teller, the consequences of his testimony were immediate as soon as the transcripts were made public. It is hard to imagine that he did not anticipate the condemnation of his behavior by his colleagues. Even the super-conservative Ernest Lawrence had withdrawn from testifying at the last moment, quoting, genuinely, severe illness. However, he had also urged his associate Luis Alvarez to withdraw. Lawrence explained to Alvarez that their Berkeley laboratory might suffer if they testified against Oppenheimer, but after some hesitation Alvarez testified anyway; however, he did so cautiously.

John von Neumann also testified before the hearing. He was not a great friend of Oppenheimer's, and especially not of his anti-hydrogen bomb politics, but he never questioned Oppenheimer's integrity and loyalty, he hinted that he had no doubts about his handling classified information, and he expressed "every confidence in him."[72]

It was recklessness on Teller's part to ignore the dangers in his behavior. Szilard, on the other hand, realized the risks Teller might be taking by such a testimony. He tried to reach his friend on the eve of his appearance at the hearing, but did not find him.[73] Teller did not expect the transcripts to become public (he had been promised this would not happen), but then, due to some administrative mix-up, the AEC decided that it needed to do just that. It was before they became public that John Wheeler wrote to Teller: "I am so glad not to have had to testify in the Oppie [Oppenheimer] matter, and just want to say how much I admire your courage and honesty and clarity in speaking as you did. I have yet to see the complete testimony."[74] It was perhaps more the way Teller gave his testimony than its actual content that invited the wrath of his fellow physicists. A few weeks later he was in Los Alamos, and there Isidor Rabi, one of the doyens of American physics, ignored Teller's proffered hand in the presence of many. To make sure he understood the reason, Rabi congratulated Teller on the "brilliance" of his testimony and the "extremely clever way" in which he had expressed his opinion that Oppenheimer was a security risk.[75] For years, Teller could never be sure whether his company was going to be welcome when he gathered with his colleagues, and whether his outstretched hand would be accepted.

Traits

Much of this book has been about the traits of the Martians, so what follows here is a summary.

Most of the Martians were rather liked by those who were in contact with them, with the exception of Edward Teller, who divided the people around him and about whom some damning characterizations have been aired. This was partly in response to his political stands and partly to the tactics with which he advanced them. Quite a few people felt that Eugene Wigner's overpolite behavior was both a shield, stopping others from getting close to him, and an affectation. Von Neumann generated substantive negative feeling only when he ran off with other people's problems and quickly solved them. Even Szilard generated some criticism, of course: Enrico Fermi, for example, accused him of not always telling the truth. Szilard may have been guilty of exaggerating some problems to advance his cause, but it may also be that these only seemed exaggerations to others because he saw farther ahead than his partners in the discussions. Einstein said of Szilard in 1930 that he "may be inclined to exaggerate the significance of reason in human affairs."[76] Von Kármán was generally liked by those with whom he came into contact, but he remained aloof from his surroundings. This aloofness was a characteristic trait of the Martians: it was as if they had indeed come from a different planet. Perhaps Teller was the most capable of developing loyal friendships, just as he was the most capable of losing them and developing enemies.

Abraham Pais, the Dutch–American physicist turned science historian, wrote about Wigner, the Martian he knew best: "I never felt that I fully understood who he was, and so it has been with colleagues of mine with whom I have discussed his personality." Pais added that "I have not been able to grasp the personalities not only of Wigner but also of Szilard and Teller."[77] Pais was of Jewish–Dutch origin, but the common European and Jewish roots did not help him in getting closer to the Martians, and he thought that this was because of their very different Hungarian origin.

Theodore von Kármán

Von Kármán was very clever, understood every problem, and attempted to solve them with his mathematical prowess. In this he was similar to von Neumann. Both enjoyed life; looked for such enjoyment; and looked down a little on others. Both had something of the Hungarian gentry in them. Von Kármán never married, yet liked to appear in the company of attractive women; in fact, he considered women as decorations rather than equal partners, with the possible exception of his mother and sister. Von Kármán and von Neumann would at times become so absorbed in their own thoughts that the people they were with ceased, in effect, to exist. They were both deeply concerned with their immediate families but nobody else, not even with friends who thought that they were close to them. Both fully devoted themselves to the defense of the United States, but in this, von Kármán was not ideological. He could have been devoted just as deeply to the defense of any other power, except Nazi Germany, because it had excluded him.

Lee Edson collaborated with von Kármán for years on his memoirs, and was a close observer of von Kármán's character.[78] He noted his sense of humor, which helped to carry him and the people around him over difficult situations. Even half a century later, the Nobel laureate Nicolaas Bloembergen remembered how von Kármán had eased the tension at a meeting on intelligence: the gathering had a heavy military presence, and von Kármán started by saying that there were three kinds of intelligence, human, animal, and military.[79]

Von Kármán was little known to the public—he had no interest in public relations. At the same time, he was not modest or humble about his accomplishments. When Edson met him for the first time, he found him "a gnome of a man with a Mona Lisa smile, sad blue eyes, and a head of wavy gray hair." Edson noticed his showmanship and story-telling skills, and quoted someone according to whom von Kármán's thick and mysterious Hungarian accent was "fabricated for 'commercial reasons.'" Edson enumerates various characteristics of von Kármán's, including impatience and tolerance; he welcomed change and innovation every-

(Left) Theodore von Kármán, American stamp;
(above) Theodore von Kármán, Hungarian stamp.

where, except in his own life; he enjoyed the company of rich, famous, and powerful people, but he was not a snob.[80]

Leo Szilard

Wigner was a good source for characterizing Szilard, describing him as "a vivid man about 5 feet 6 inches tall, a bit shorter even than I was. His face was a good, broad Hungarian face. His eyes were brown. His hair, like my own, was brown, poorly combed, and already receding from his forehead."[81] As did many others, Wigner found Szilard busy and mysterious: he appeared at one point then disappeared, only to reappear again a few days later at Wigner's front door with bold ideas and little patience.

Szilard approached the great physicists in Berlin and engaged them in conversation, while Wigner, being Szilard's friend, stood nearby and enjoyed Szilard's encounters. Wigner thought that Szilard was so little intimidated that "if he had seen the President of the United States at a meeting or the President of Soviet Russia, he would have promptly introduced himself and begun asking pointed questions."[82] This was exactly what Szilard would later do. According to George Klein, Szilard's most extraordinary quality was "his complete lack of shyness or humility when it came to following rationally drawn inferences to their ultimate conclusions."[83] Wigner wondered about the best adjectives to describe Szilard. He discarded "brash" and preferred "well-relaxed" and "unencumbered." Klein found Szilard to have "very broad intellectual interests that he could pull together instantly into all sorts of different combinations." Szilard was apt to making "humorous, provocative, cynical, poetic, or even withering" remarks, which could be lumped together as "Szilardisms." James Watson labeled some of his own ideas "Szilard ideas" without recognizing that they could be taken literally as well, because "szilárd" means "solid" in Hungarian.[84]

Szilard did not fully develop his ideas and so, with a few exceptions, did not arrive at decisive discoveries. Jacques Monod wondered about this and felt that perhaps Szilard's creative nature kept him from performing decisive work.[85] His name might have been associated with more significant achievements had he carried his ideas through; but then he would have been only one of the many distinguished scientists. He may have gone that way had he cared more about his ego than he did, but a meaningful idea meant more to him than his own fame and interests. For Szilard "science was much more than a profession, or even an avocation." For Szilard, science was "a mode of being."[86] Other scientists seldom come to realizations that rock the dogmas of their field. Szilard thrived on challenging the generally accepted, what others might have considered to be obvious.

It was typical of Szilard when visiting an establishment, for example, Monod's laboratory at the Pasteur Institute in Paris, to line people up outside his office and bring them in one by one to tell him about their research. Days later he would come back with generalizing and interconnecting observations. He did this at private parties as well; rather than taking part in the general discussions in the living room, he would set up one of the bedrooms as his headquarters and receive the guests individually, in the same manner as in the Pasteur Institute. Not everybody liked Szilard's techniques of quizzing and questioning at meetings and elsewhere; some thought him to be obnoxious and lazy.

Szilard preferred talking to people in one-to-one encounters to reading and liked to pump individuals for information. He did this selflessly and more often than not would return to the same person with useful suggestions. He could come up with excellent ideas for further work or for breaking an impasse because he was looking at every problem from many different angles, and would integrate the information he was collecting from many sources in his conversations.

Szilard's quick mind may have deterred some from cooperating with him. Thus, for example, a Denver colleague felt compelled to renege on a previous offer to Szilard of an appealing appointment. He told him, "Your mind is so much more powerful than mine that I find it impossible when I am with you to resist the tremendous polarizing forces of your ideas and outlook."[87] Some considered him tactless and intrusive in his relationships with people and their work. He could keep reason and emotion separate, a trait that could also be observed in his friendships. He was always ready to act upon even the wildest ideas to accomplish what he had set out to accomplish. If he could find no institution that would both take

him and be suitable for his operations, he would create one. Szilard's role in initiating the Salk Institute for Biological Studies to blend studies of science and social
policy was an example, and he derived enjoyment from its existence during the
last months of his life.

Szilard had simple tastes in food and in literature. When his friends praised
his *The Voice of the Dolphins*, he was not satisfied by their telling him that they liked
it; he would have rather them say that it was great literature. When they explained
to him that great literature was more complex and generated an emotional response,
he did not seem to understand. "Szilard generalized so aggressively because he tried
to explain almost everything—from moral values to paintings to music to immune systems—as quantitative statements about universal truth." Szilard was not
deterred from voicing his opinion about paintings, for example, although he had
no background for forming an expert opinion. He "judged one painting as better than another not because it is prettier or technically more complex, or somehow inspired, but simply because it 'reduces the entropy of the universe' more
efficiently."[88]

Szilard never let health issues interfere with his life. His bladder cancer was
an extreme example of this. Apparently, his bladder had been bleeding for half a
year before he agreed to be examined while visiting Stockholm in 1959.[89] However, before he let the doctor perform his tests, he examined the doctor for his
intelligence. The doctor finally determined that Szilard suffered from bladder
cancer and that an operation was indicated. After some hesitation, Szilard and
his medical doctor wife went to the library to study the possibilities. He then
decided not to have an operation. He moved to the Memorial Sloan-Kettering
Cancer Center in New York City, opted for radiation treatment, and directed it
himself. Otherwise, he continued his life on the fast track. He told his doctors
that "if worst comes to worst, I'll be dead ten years longer."[90]

He did not turn a blind eye to his illness and even considered the possibility
of suicide, which he went about in his usual innovative and factual manner. If
the need should arise, he wanted to die in the least uncomfortable way and in a
way that would not jeopardize his wife's receiving the insurance money. This
prompted him, together with Bela, to think about a "suicide kit" that would be
painless and leave no trace. They thought that they might produce something
saleable and patent it.[91] However, when he left the hospital he was cured, and when
he died a few years later the autopsy revealed no evidence of cancer in his urinary
tract, so he was successful in treating his cancer.

Szilard knew about academic pettiness and told Jonas Salk, concerning the
Salk vaccine: "Jonas, they'll never forgive you for having been right."[92] There were
frustrating experiences for Szilard, too, for example, having some writings rejected
by magazines, but he never complained of failures or refusals. He always used
action as the best and the only medicine, and it was magazine rejections that
prompted Szilard to produce *The Voice of the Dolphins*. Back in 1933, Paul Ehrenfest of the University of Leiden wrote to the British scientist Frederick G. Donnan

that Szilard "reacts to any difficulty which may arise with immediate action rather than depression or resignation."[93] These are chilling words from Ehrenfest, who soon after committed suicide.

Szilard was an ideological man. He could not have approved of Nazi Germany and Stalin's Russia, no matter what, but he could have found a lot of excuses for communism if practiced in its purist form, without Lenin's and Stalin's tyranny. As a human being, he was for truth in a most painstaking way, and he was a deeply democratic man. He tolerated opposing views as long as there was reasoning behind them. He helped the disfranchised, the underdog, and he was ready to go a long way in defending other people's rights. Szilard was aware of his merits and knew that no ordinary life would suffice for him. He always went to the top to deal with the people who were in charge of a situation.

Szilard dispensed his wisdom whether he was asked to do so or not. This is not an uncommon character trait, but most similar gurus dispense advice whether sound or not. Szilard virtually always dispensed sound advice and the recipients were often outstanding scientists and other professionals. However, Szilard would not always dispense wisdom that was practical in the circumstances; he invariably looked ahead, and advice that might sometimes have been sound from a longer-term perspective was not necessarily so under the current conditions.

The best minds appreciated Szilard the most. Salk put it succinctly: "Leo cared not to carry the torch but simply to light it; and when there were not others to carry, he did so himself."[94] James Watson said about him: "I still miss his unusual intelligence and wit. He was irreplaceable in the truest sense."[95] And Teller made the following comparison: "I cannot but think of that legendary, restless figure, Dr. Faust, who in Goethe's tragedy dies at the very moment when at last he declares he is content."[96]

Wigner called Szilard the most imaginative man that he ever knew, but it may have been more foresight than imagination. He could foresee developments, but not so much drastic changes. He foresaw the collapse of Weimar Germany, but not the collapse of the Soviet Union. He foresaw the coming wars and he did a tremendous amount of work to avoid them, but there is hardly any indication in his writings about the threat of terrorism.

Eugene P. Wigner

Wigner was a lonely man at the beginning at Princeton; he did not "Americanize" quickly, he did not "transplant easily," unlike von Neumann.[97] Nonetheless, both of von Neumann's wives were Hungarian, whereas Wigner's three marriages were all to American women. Wigner had two children with his second wife, a boy and a girl, and one daughter out of wedlock back in his Berlin days.[98] Frederick Seitz became his first graduate student in 1932, and they "formed a long-standing relationship."[99] It is noteworthy that Seitz did not use the word

Eugene P. Wigner, Hungarian stamp.

friendship and, apart from Szilard, von Neumann, and Teller, one wonders whether Wigner had any friends at all. Even within this very small group of friends they retained a considerable degree of formality; they addressed each other in the formal way by surnames rather than first names, and sometimes added "Úr" in the address, like Master Teller and Master Szilard (Teller Úr and Szilard Úr).[100]

Anecdotes abound about Wigner, especially about his legendary politeness. Freeman Dyson, world-renowned physicist and even more famous science writer, hardly knew Wigner although they lived near each other for many years.[101] Dyson tried to be friendly with Wigner, but they never got close. Dyson knew a Japanese sociologist who wrote about Japanese society; one of her papers was called "Politeness as a Tool of Repression" and he thought that this might be true not only of Japanese society but also of Wigner.

Szilard called Wigner "the conscience of the [Manhattan] Project."[102] He also called Wigner a fighter, but Wigner was sometimes less politely referred to by others as stubborn. This stubbornness manifested itself in political conservatism, as well as scientific conservatism in the eyes of younger physicists. According to a recent Nobel laureate and former Princeton colleague, David Gross, at some point "Wigner decoupled from the frontiers of physics."[103]

Philip Anderson at one time worked on ferroelectricity, and Wigner developed some ideas about ferroelectricity which Anderson thought "nonsensical."[104] This was about 1950, one year after Anderson had received his PhD degree, and he tried to explain to Wigner how ferroelectricity worked. Wigner responded to his explanation by essentially brushing him off with strongly over-polite behavior. Anderson thinks that Wigner was right in terms of the personal situation—that it was rude of Anderson to confront him in this way—but there was no way that Wigner was right about the science, where he was way out of his area of expertise.

In the late 1950s, they had one more encounter when Anderson purposely chose not to mention one of Wigner's papers, which Wigner took very negatively in his polite way. Wigner did not believe the BCS (Bardeen–Cooper–Schrieffer) theory of superconductivity, and he never accepted it. When Anderson finally understood this, it was a true disappointment to him: "Up until that point, Wigner had been very central in theoretical physics, but at about that time, in the 1950s, he put his feet down and refused to go any further. At that point, Wigner, as a person, seemed to become less relevant to physics."[105]

Steven Weinberg also had the impression that Wigner lost touch with modern physics at some point.[106] Once Weinberg gave a talk at a symposium in Wigner's honor, explaining how much he had learned from Wigner's approach to elementary particles and why his approach was superior to others. Wigner came up to him after his talk, and Weinberg's impression was that Wigner did not really understand what the talk had been about. From this encounter, Weinberg came to feel that what he had thought was Wignerism was not entirely Wignerism, but he allows for the possibility that by then Wigner may have already been ill. In any case, Weinberg has complicated feelings for Wigner as a person.

Whether Wigner remained relevant to modern physics or not, he certainly remained alert and interested. It was later, after the events related by Anderson and Weinberg, that Benoit Mandelbrot, the inventor of the fractal concept, showed him the mountainlike fractal structures. Wigner was puzzled, but did not let Mandelbrot explain them to him. In Mandelbrot's words, "He thought for a while, mumbling aloud, and he guessed it right."[107] This resembled the young Wigner of around 1930 to whom Victor Weisskopf had shown a paper relevant to the topic they were discussing. Wigner looked at the title of the paper but declined to read it; instead, he derived the solution to the issue that the paper was supposed to be addressing. When he was done he told Weisskopf that there was no need to read the paper because it either gave Wigner's solution or it was wrong.[108]

Although Anderson and Wigner never argued about politics, Anderson knew that they were on opposite sides, him being a liberal and Wigner a conservative. Anderson remembers one party where they had a discussion about the David Bohm affair. Wigner was the only member of the physics department who was not in favor of keeping Bohm when his tenure decision came up. Wigner's objection could hardly have been based on Bohm's achievements in science, so it had to be political. The department voted for Bohm's tenure, but the president of Princeton turned down their recommendation and fired him.

Wigner was a man with strong opinions wrapped in polite, but often transparent, words and body language. His body language was part of his deceiving behavior. Even when it was clear from his questions that he had seen to the nub of the ideas under discussion, and was preparing the most ruthless traps for his opponents, he liked to appear modest and apologetic.[109] People observed this for decades, including long after his retirement. Whether Wigner was generous and magnanimous in his general life outlook is difficult to assess. Another Weisskopf story relates that he had once read in one of Wigner's papers about a certain formula; the paper claimed that the formula had been derived by Gregory Breit, and the full citation was given. When Weisskopf looked up the reference, there was no derivation in it. So Weisskopf confronted Wigner, who told him that Breit could have derived the formula if he had thought of it.[110]

Wigner appeared genuinely worried when Szilard did not have a job, but he never understood the peculiarity of Szilard's expectations of a job. Wigner did not appear to be generous and magnanimous when judging his friends, namely, Szilard and Michael Polanyi. He did not think Szilard capable of holding a bona fide research position or university professorship until after Szilard had become quite well recognized in nuclear physics.[111] This is independent of the fact that Szilard himself did not truly want an ordinary job that would bog him down. When the question of nominating Polanyi for the Nobel Prize came up, by which time Wigner was already a Nobel laureate, he hesitated and waited to see if others would be willing to nominate Polanyi. When this happened he added his support, but not before.[112] However, in John C. Polanyi's words, Wigner managed to bring Michael Polanyi to Stockholm when he conspicuously mentioned Polanyi's influence on his career in his traditionally very short (two minute) speech during the Nobel banquet in 1963.[113]

John von Neumann

Stanislaw Ulam's comments regarding von Neumann are of special interest because Ulam was also a distinguished mathematician and he knew von Neumann very well. Ulam writes about him extensively in his memoirs.[114] He even began a book about von Neumann, but ended up writing his own memoirs. Von Neumann left no memoirs.

In many aspects von Neumann was similar to von Kármán. He liked to cultivate interactions with successful people regardless of their areas of activity.[115] He could be deep in thought while in the company of women and simply not be disturbed by their presence. He could appear as if he were staring at them, whereas

(Left) John von Neumann, Hungarian stamp; (right) John von Neumann, American stamp.

his gaze would actually be turned inwards. In 1953–1954 Mandelbrot was the last young scientist at the Institute for Advanced Study in Princeton sponsored by von Neumann.[116] Mandelbrot had sent him his thesis; von Neumann had found it interesting and invited him to the institute for a year. In order to push Mandelbrot's appointment through quickly, von Neumann had to cut some red tape by contacting Warren Weaver at the Rockefeller Foundation. Mandelbrot found von Neumann very encouraging. When, years later, in a crisis he went back to Warren Weaver for advice, he found out that von Neumann had asked Weaver to watch out for Mandelbrot because he might get into trouble and would need help. In spite of this experience, even Mandelbrot says that von Neumann was not a warm person. That does not mean, though, that he did not crave for warmth from others.

Von Neumann's daughter, Marina von Neumann (Whitman), lived her first dozen years with her mother, except for the summers which were spent with her father.[117] At the age of thirteen, the arrangement was reversed by prior agreement. Marina thinks that he would have liked more warmth from her than she felt capable of giving. Also, he probably suffered more from his first wife's leaving him than his quick return to Budapest for a second wife would imply. According to his daughter, for whom this was hearsay only, he begged his first wife not to leave, and would have rather lived in an arrangement that gave her complete freedom in her relationships than have her leave him. However, she just found it too heavy to be John von Neumann's wife.

Like Szilard, von Neumann was not given to complaining. However, he may have suffered privately from the lack of appreciation of his peers at the Institute for Advanced Study. Besides, some detested computers while von Neumann was very much involved in their development. His physicist colleagues disliked his strong involvement in military affairs. There were rumors that von Neumann had expected to be made director, but Oppenheimer was elected instead. One may wonder whether von Neumann would have really wanted to have such an administrative position, but he might have as he later accepted the position of commissioner of the Atomic Energy Commission. This was an ironic twist in the light of Oppenheimer's later difficulties over his security clearance with the same AEC. Oppenheimer and von Neumann had similar family and educational backgrounds, and could have become either close friends or no friends at all; they were certainly no close friends. Von Neumann was successful in Washington and became an insider, but he was not a happy man there. This is perhaps why he accepted an academic position at the University of California, but died before he could take it.[118]

Eugene Wigner was a keen observer of von Neumann, and one could hardly find a more genuine admirer, yet he made some observations that were not very flattering. When Wigner was having his difficulties with Princeton University in 1936 he turned to von Neumann, who promised to recommend him for jobs where he could.[119] Wigner, though, had expected some sympathy and consolation, even solidarity, from his friend, but none was forthcoming. This remained a lasting scar for Wigner.

What we call public relations today must have been on von Neumann's mind from early childhood. Wigner writes: "Jancsi was somewhat retiring. He participated in the pranks of the class, but a bit half-heartedly, just enough to avoid unpopularity."[120] For Wigner, in addition to their high school teacher, Rátz, and his later mentor, Polanyi, von Neumann was the one from whom he learned most, and learned such mathematics that the other two could not have provided. Von Neumann proved to be a good pedagogue for Wigner.[121] When he asked von Neumann to explain, say, Warring's theorem to him, von Neumann would ask him whether he knew Hilbert's third theorem, and if Wigner was not sure he would ask whether he knew D'Alambert's theorem, and so on. Von Neumann would then explain what Wigner wanted to know using knowledge that Wigner already possessed, even if he had had to skirt around the things that Wigner was not familiar with in a laborious way. Wigner "learned more mathematics from him than from anyone else."[122] Wigner found "the accuracy of his logic to be the most decisive character" of von Neumann's mind, and listed brilliance and retentiveness as other characteristics. Because of his broad interests and involvement in so many areas, he was called the "man of all science."[123]

Von Neumann was famous for his humor, which was typical Budapest humor, or, rather, Central European Jewish humor. Stanislaw Ulam certainly understood and shared it and noted that his friend liked brief verbal distractions from serious concentrated thought.[124] It is doubtful whether von Neumann's humor is easy to perceive outside the Central European Jewish frame of mind; nevertheless, it is worth taking the risk of presenting a sample. Arthur Koestler studied humor and illustrated some of his findings with stories from von Neumann.[125] A typical story is: "A convict was playing cards with his gaolers. On discovering that he cheated they kicked him out of the gaol."[126] Koestler introduced the concept of bisociation. Whereas thought association is made between thoughts on the same plane, bisociation refers to connections between thoughts from different planes. The unexpected relationship is the source of humor. Koestler argued that bisociation is also an important ingredient of scientific discovery in which, again, unexpected relationships turn up.

Von Neumann and Ulam had a common language, which was a rare intimacy for a Martian outside the Martians' circle. The two had their own codes for stories depicting human fallibilities. A case in point: the word "asparagus" became a code word for them to characterize attempts "to obtain an unduly large share of credit for scientific work or any other accomplishment of a joint or group character."[127] The origin was a Berlin story of a boarding house: the boarders were eating their dinner and one man was taking most of the asparagus, a delicacy, from the common platter. Seeing this, another boarder noted that the others also liked asparagus. The two mathematicians played with this story and developed it, planning to write "a twenty-volume treatise on 'Asparagetics through the Ages.'"

Another humorous feature of Ulam and von Neumann's interactions was the "Nebich Index."[128] First, what is "nebich?" It is an untranslatable Yiddish expression that is a combination of commiseration, scorn, drama, and ridicule. Ulam illuminates the expression with a story. The popular Swiss hero Wilhelm Tell waits to shoot the hated Austrian governor Gessler. Somebody says, "Through this street the Nebich must come." Gessler is a Nebich, he is hated and he will fall victim to people's scorn. If he came through a nebich street, it would mean that the street was insignificant and miserable. Ulam warned that to understand the meaning and usage of nebich might take years of apprenticeship, which is an exaggeration. Von Neumann's classic story was about a little boy who comes home from school in turn-of-the-century Budapest and tells his father about his failing grade. He had to compose an essay about the future of the Austro-Hungarian monarchy, and he just wrote three words, "Nebich, nebich, nebich." The father is most surprised for he considers this a perfect answer to the question posed by the teacher, so what might have gone wrong? The boy, as it turns out, misspelled nebich, and this is why he got the failing grade.

There were traits that von Neumann did not possess, but admired.[129] He looked up to powerful men, members of the military establishment, and to people who could influence events. He appreciated toughness and ruthlessness, traits he clearly lacked. He preferred to avoid controversy; in this he very much differed from Szilard and Teller and was similar to von Kármán. He was not eager to participate in debates and had a tendency to yield to forcefully expressed opinions.

By all accounts, and as I have already suggested, von Neumann was not a warm personality. He did not divulge his inner feelings to anyone; he did not need friendly advice; he did not display emotions. A crack in this behavior appeared towards the end of his life: while he was proud to have been asked to serve as commissioner of the AEC, he had his doubts whether he should accept it and he revealed these to Ulam.[130] Even when on his deathbed, he could not accept the inevitability of death—the fact that soon he would not be able to think. He felt he had a lot of unfinished business on earth.

Edward Teller

Teller was an amicable and friendly person throughout his years in Europe and when he was at George Washington University. Gamow characterized him as "helpful, willing and able to work on other people's ideas without insisting on everything having to be his own." Gamow thought that something must have changed in him at Los Alamos. However, Ulam's first impressions of Teller when they met at Los Alamos were consistent with Gamow's observation: "He was a warm person and clearly desired friendship with other physicists." According to Ulam, two factors may have especially contributed to the changes in Teller's personality and he observed similar changes in other physicists as well. One factor was that, however important their previous work may have been, the scientists at Los Alamos were thrown into a project that had tremendous importance and their responsibility took on historic proportion. This went with virtually unlimited funds for people whose research used to receive minuscule financial backing. The other factor may have been a certain feeling of frustration: they were thrown together with the most brilliant minds in their field and, because of their own brilliance, must have realized their own limitations more sharply than ever. Again, this may have been applicable to everyone, but people react in different ways to the pressures generated in such situations. Many, perhaps all, may have wanted to have their own stamp on the product of Los Alamos and this was clearly impossible. Ulam quotes Fermi's remark in his characteristic Italian accent when teasing Teller: "Edward-a how come-a the Hungarians have not-a invented anything?"[131] The result was, according to Ulam, various conflicts between Teller and some other scientists, including the person in charge of the theoretical work and Teller's former close friend, Hans Bethe.

Did Teller ever cheat or lie? Some say yes, but it is difficult to gather evidence. He was certainly never a person who shied away from bombastic statements. When he was campaigning for his Plowshare Program, in which he wanted to utilize nuclear energy for peaceful projects, he declared at the University of Alaska in 1959: "If your mountain is not in the right place, just drop us a card." He then published an article with the title "We're Going to Work Miracles," in which he elaborated on the projects to be accomplished in Alaska, but nothing came out of it.[132] He made unsubstantiated promises and painted pictures that were more optimistic than was really the case in negotiations over large appropriations. His attitude may have negatively influenced the fate of others.

Did Teller have the ability to manipulate others and did he do that? A benevolent example is his own description of how he fared better in his exams as an undergraduate than his knowledge would have justified. In this, we need to be magnanimous because the way he manipulated his examiner also displayed ability and intelligence. This is not to say that ability and intelligence condone manipulation of others, but here we are considering an examination where the student has to demonstrate knowledge that goes beyond a simple grasp of the factual material. It is also a question whether and how the student can present his knowledge and whether he can apply it under various conditions.

Teller describes an examination situation in which he was asked about the composition of the atmosphere. After having said that the atmosphere consisted of nitrogen, oxygen, and rare gases, he was asked about those rare gases and their proportions. Teller did not know the answer but he went on as if he did. He said: "There is helium and argon. If helium predominates, the atmosphere would be less dense. If argon were more abundant, the reverse would be true."[133] Although this response did not contain the answer it was logical, and while speaking Teller watched the examiners' facial expressions. When he was satisfied that he had read the right answer off the faces of the examiners, he did not wait for them to ask him again, but finished his exposition by posing the question himself about which of them predominates and then giving the correct answer right away (argon). Lest we tend to condemn Teller's method, the ingenuity he showed in circumventing the answer in this performance displayed considerable background knowledge, which is also part of learning.

Teller has been portrayed as fiercely arrogant and stubborn, sure of himself and winning all his debates. Learning more about him, though, reveals another trait: a great deal of uncertainty and a desire to please others, or at least to correspond to their expectations of him. Of course the people he wanted to please were not the ones with whom he was rude and to whom he appeared adamant. Even in the question of the SDI, in which to others he appeared so stubbornly convinced, he repeatedly longed for Hans Bethe's approval, inviting him to Los Alamos and briefing him about the project. Bethe, of course, had the necessary security clearance for this, but on each occasion he went away unconvinced.[134] According to the co-author of Teller's *Memoirs*, Bethe's turning away from Teller over the years hurt Teller more than losing anybody else's friendship.[135] Teller's insecurity can also be spotted in the differences between his private and public behavior. Donald Glaser was sitting next to Teller during a flight and they had an amicable and meaningful conversation.[136] However, when they got off the plane and there was audience, Teller started speaking loudly and was obviously putting on a show.

Holding grudges and spitefulness were also characteristic of Teller. When he suffered a heart attack in 1979 and may have thought he was dying, he dictated a memorandum, part of which was directed at belittling Stanislaw Ulam's role in solving the problem of the hydrogen bomb.[137] In our last correspondence, only weeks before his death, he did not miss the opportunity to lash out at Linus Pauling and especially at Robert Oppenheimer.[138]

Of all the Martians, my impression of Teller is that I have met his type most often in Hungary, although, of course, less brilliant examples of the species. He is very clever, argues in a convincing way, and has the capability to turn the argument around if it comes out that the facts are just the opposite to what he had supposed them to be. This is less opportunistic than it seems: scientific reasoning may sometimes follow such a process. It is less attractive when this approach is being applied in political arguments. When Teller and his young associates switched from the X-ray laser to the Brilliant Pebbles in the SDI program, they had to literally reverse some of their basic arguments in advancing the new concept, and they did so with no embarrassment.

Teller did everything with a zealot's conviction, as if he were on a mission. He was acting on the premise that the others might not have recognized the dangers, or the means of protecting the Free World from them. This was all right from his point of view because he could lead the way to save the world.[139] Teller was doing this in the conviction that he was right to try everything in his power to stop communism and the Soviet Union. Under the Reagan administration, he had acquired an unprecedented prestige and influence that made it possible for him to make claims that went unchecked, and to get carried away by his vision of deploying technological progress in the defense of his country.

Religion and Jewishness

For the Martians, Jewishness was not religion, neither was it ethnicity; it was more a cultural background, tradition, and belonging. All except Teller converted, but the religions they converted to had no greater importance for them than Judaism. We have already seen that Teller was advised, upon embarking on his life in America, to make friends not only with Jews and he considered himself successful in this. Their children did not receive religious training, and Wendy Teller was surprised when her father's first question about her date was "Is he Jewish?"[140]

Szilard did not believe in a personal God, but considered himself a religious man in that he believed that life had a meaning. Szilard agreed with Einstein that as long as you pray to God asking for something, it is not religion. This may have been rather characteristic of the Martians. They were not religious, especially not in the conventional sense. From their childhood they did not follow the prescriptions of Judaism, but they never denied their roots, they never turned away from their Jewishness. This is important in view of the fact that many Hungarian Jews are often rather secretive about their origin. This widespread attitude has two sources: the long history of attempts at assimilation and the long experience of persecution of Jews and anti-Semitism in Hungary.

Wigner repeatedly declared that Jewishness had little importance for him, but he meticulously considers everybody else's being Jewish or non-Jewish in his *Recollections*. He appeared tragicomically ignorant about his roots.[141] He never talked about the family's Jewishness with his father or mother. They celebrated Seder; he had Bar Mitzvah, and he went to the synagogue twice a year. He attended Jewish religion class, but "hardly in spirit." He "very rarely wore the yarmulke." The family never spoke Hebrew at home (not a very distinguishing feature in any case), never had Shabbat dinner on Friday, and did not keep kosher. Wigner hardly experienced anti-Semitism in his youth, but whatever experiences he did have he did everything to forget about. Thus his statement about his lack of anti-Semitic experiences should be taken with caution. He notes that he had succeeded in completely forgetting the anti-Semitic incidents to which he had been exposed.

In the von Neumann family, only the maternal grandfather observed Judaism.[142] When one of the von Neumann brothers asked their father why they considered themselves Jewish while observing no religion, the answer was, "tradition." The family converted to Catholicism in 1929, after the father's death, but they did this "for sake of convenience, not conviction." There is a story that von Neumann became a strict Catholic on his deathbed, having talks with a Benedictine monk and later with a Jesuit. Apparently, he was trying everything to change the course his body was taking against his will. Ulam found the experience heartbreaking.[143] However, according to his brother, the story about John von Neumann's second conversion is a legend: he invited the priests for their classical education.[144]

Wigner gave no sign of being afraid of death: "That I will die hardly bothers me." He was critical of the religions misleading people about the existence of life after death: "We are all guests in this world, and our culture commits a crime when it persuades us to think otherwise." He realized that the "optimism" of believing in life after death has so deeply penetrated human thinking that he referred to culture in this connection rather than to religion. He did not believe in Heaven and found it incompatible with science: "As a scientist, I must say that we have no heavenly data. So I am afraid that after death, we merely cease to exist."[145]

Wigner and von Neumann thus had very different attitudes toward death. However, von Neumann was fifty-three years old when he died and Wigner was ninety-two. Furthermore, von Neumann was at the peak of his political–societal career, if not necessarily of his scientific career, when he died, whereas Wigner had long before ceased to be a factor in scientific life and had made peace with the thought of ceasing to exist. We do not know about Teller's inner thoughts in this connection during the last period of his life, but he must have been prepared to die. It is also true that he was alert almost to the last minute, in contrast with Wigner who showed strong signs of Alzheimer's disease during the last period of his life. Szilard and von Kármán led their usual lives and died apparently without thinking about the imminence of death.

Yuval Ne'eman, the theoretical physicist/military leader/politician, assessed the Martians' relationship to Israel. He considers the development of the atomic bomb to "represent the defensive reaction of yet another Jewish group to Hitler's threat."[146] He likens it to the uprising of the Warsaw Ghetto, the Jewish maquis in the French Resistance, and Hannah Szenes' sacrifice.

Von Kármán was happy to advise the Israeli Defense Research and Development organization and provided it with free consultancy. Wigner visited Jerusalem during the mid-1930s, and was offered a permanent professorial position there, but he declined because of the scarcity of positions. In later years, Wigner regularly attended scientific meetings in Israel. Szilard and von Neumann were not much involved with Israel, although on one occasion von Neumann asked to be thoroughly briefed about Israel's problems and in his characteristic way promised to come back with a solution within twenty-four hours if he found one. He never came back. Exactly the same story can be found about Szilard in the literature.

Teller had the most extensive interactions with Israel from the mid-1960s. He participated in scheming about various plans that were analogous to those in the Plowshare Program in the United States. These included the possibilities of using nuclear energy for accomplishing enormous construction projects. As in America, they did not go beyond the drawing boards in Israel. Teller also actively interacted with Israeli politicians in other projects, like supporting the idea of establishing a second engineering school at Tel Aviv University, in addition to the Technion—the Israel Institute of Technology. When Teller lectured in Israel, there was always a huge audience.

Being Hungarian

The extent to which the Martians identified themselves as Hungarians bordered on nationalism, with the exception of Szilard. In the best tradition of the happy peacetime between 1867 and 1914, they felt no contradiction in being both Jewish and Hungarian. They somehow filtered out their experiences in the Hungary of the early 1920s. Again, Szilard was different; he did not forget and did not forgive, although he had experienced little of the harsh persecution before he left, except, of course, the incident at the Technical University. Von Kármán was no longer in Hungary by the time of the so-called White Terror of the early 1920s, but Wigner, von Neumann, and Teller got a taste of it. Nonetheless, they all had a feeling of belonging to Hungary.

Wigner liked to recite Hungarian poetry, von Neumann loved Budapest jokes and missed the coffeehouses, and Teller always distinguished between his home country and the communist political system. They had no first-hand experience of the growing anti-Semitism between the two wars, the anti-Jewish legislation, the deportation to Auschwitz and the ruthless role of the Hungarian authorities in it, and the killings in Budapest near the end of the war. Teller presided over the movement of Hungarian Americans to reelect President Reagan; one might have thought that he was by then above such particular alignments, but he was not. When he was dying, Teller asked his assistant to read Hungarian poetry for him, and passed away while listening to the epic poem *Toldi* in Hungarian by János Arany.[147] Wigner wrote in his memoirs: "After 60 years in the United States, I am still more Hungarian than American."[148]

After World War II, von Kármán was the first of them to visit Budapest. Wigner came back to Hungary in 1976 and made three more visits through 1987. Teller returned to Hungary in 1990, only after the political changes, and he came back a few more times. He truly indulged in the attention and friendliness of his Hungarian reception. Von Neumann never returned to Hungary; he died relatively young and there was no occasion for such a visit.

Szilard had an opportunity to visit in 1960, but refused. In contrast with Teller, Szilard did not find Hungary a relevant issue for him, and the story of his visit with James Byrnes in 1945 illustrated this. Whereas Szilard wanted to talk about the postwar Soviet behavior in general, Byrnes told Szilard, "Well, you come from Hungary—you would not want Russia to stay in Hungary indefinitely."[149] Byrnes "offended Szilard's sense of proportion" by reducing the problem, by reference to Szilard's origin, to Hungary. Szilard (prophetically as it turned out) was concerned with the possibility of an arms race between the two postwar super-powers rather than with the fate of Hungary in particular. In this, he viewed it as accidental that he happened to have come from Hungary; it had no relevance to the bigger issue.

It would be a mistake, though, to think that Szilard was exempt from having any benevolent Hungarian national feelings. In the section about family origin and education in the first chapter, we related a story about his grandfather in which he had honestly reported the children who had violated the order to the teacher, and included himself because he was one of the violators.[150] This could have been the whole story, but there was more to it. The incident happened during the proudest time in Hungarian history, the 1848 revolution, and the violation of discipline was that the children went out onto the street, Szilard's future grand-father included, to cheer the Hungarian soldiers who were marching by. Szilard was also fond of Imre Madách's *The Tragedy of Man*, an icon of Hungarian litera-ture that he referred to repeatedly throughout his career. He extracted from it some of his most remarkable and favorite life lessons, like "it is not necessary to succeed in order to persevere," and that even in the most pessimistic circumstances "there remains a narrow margin of hope." So, Szilard was deeply soaked in Hungarian culture, and it was he who answered Fermi's question about the extraterrestrial creatures by saying, "They are among us, but they call themselves Hungarians."[151]

One of the most important characteristics of where one belongs is the language one uses. The Martians liked to use the Hungarian language and conducted much of their correspondence with each other in Hungarian.[152] I can personally attest to the fact that both Wigner and Teller spoke excellent Hungarian. Wigner spoke English with a Hungarian accent and German intonation, while Teller's English was heavily accented by his Hungarian mother tongue. Some thought that von Kármán maintained his thick Hungarian accent artificially. Von Neumann's Hungarian accent was called "delightful." Herman Goldstine thought that he "carefully pre-served certain fixed mispronunciations": he once heard von Neumann pronounce "a word properly but then quickly corrected himself and again said it in his own style."[153] Szilard, too, had an accent that was characteristically Hungarian.[154]

*   *   *

If I had to choose epitaphs for the Martians, the easiest would be for Szilard: "light-ing the torch," for Wigner: "something must be reasonable," and for Teller: "pro-tect the free world with whatever means." I would find it more difficult for the other two. Perhaps for von Kármán it would be that he tried to reduce everything to an approximate mathematical formulation, and for von Neumann that he at-tempted to find a quick solution to even the most complex problems, so that he could move on to the next problem or simply continue to enjoy life. It was said of him that he "warmed both hands before the fire of life."[155]

Above: Participants in a theoretical physics meeting in Washington, D.C., 1946, with (sitting, from left) Leo Szilard (fourth), John von Neumann (seventh), and Edward Teller (eighth) and (standing, from left) Max Delbrück (eighth), James Franck (ninth), George Gamow (eleventh), Merle Tuve (twelfth), David Hawkins (far right), and (sitting, from left) Hermann Weyl (third), S. Spiegelman (fifth), Fritz London (sixth), Niels Bohr (ninth), George W. Beadle (tenth), and Carl F. Cori (twelfth). (Egon Weiss Collection; courtesy of Helen Weiss, Carlsbad, California.)

Below: Detail from above (left to right): Leo Szilard, S. Spiegelman, Fritz London, John von Neumann, Edward Teller, and Niels Bohr.

Above: John von Neumann and Edward Teller among the participants of the First Shelter Island meeting of theoretical physicists in 1947, including, from left to right: 1, Isidor Rabi; 2, Linus Pauling; 3, John Van Vleck; 4, Willis Lamb; 5, Gregory Breit; 8, George Uhlenbeck; 9, Julian Schwinger; 10, Teller; 13, von Neumann; 14, John Wheeler; 15, Hans Bethe; 16, Robert Serber; 17, Robert Marshak; 18, Abraham Pais; 19, Robert Oppenheimer; 20, David Bohm; 21, Richard Feynman; 22, Victor Weisskopf. (Courtesy of Marina Whitman.)

Below: Scientific Advisory Board of the U.S. Air Force, Cambridge, Massachusetts, 1952, including Theodore von Kármán (first row, fourth from the left) and John von Neumann (fourth row, first from the right); George Kistiakowsky is on von Neumann's right. (Air Force Photo, Cambridge Research Center; courtesy of Marina Whitman.)

Above: Leo Szilard with Laura Polanyi and others in the 1950s. (Courtesy of the Hungarian National Museum, Budapest.)

Below: Meeting of the Advisory Board to General Dynamics in 1953. (Right) Theodore von Kármán (second from the back), John A. Wheeler (fifth from the back), Edward Teller (partly hidden, third from the front); (left) Eugene P. Wigner (partly hidden, second from the back), George Gamow (fifth from the back), Richard L. Garwin (second from the front). (Courtesy of Richard L. Garwin.)

Right: Edward Teller in the limelight. (Courtesy of Wendy Teller, the Lawrence Livermore National Laboratory, and Paul Teller.)

Below: President Kennedy visits the Lawrence Berkeley National Laboratory in 1962. From left to right: Norris Bradbury, John Foster, Edwin McMillan, Glenn Seaborg, John Kennedy, Edward Teller, Robert McNamara, and Harold Brown. (Courtesy of Lawrence Berkeley National Laboratory.)

Above: John von Neumann, Robert Oppenheimer, Herman Goldstine, and Julian Bigelow in front of the computer at the Institute of Advanced Study in Princeton. (Photo by Alan W. Richards; courtesy of Marina Whitman.)

Left: Edward Teller speaking. (Courtesy of Wendy Teller and Paul Teller.)

Above: Leo Szilard and Alan Garen during a break at a scientific conference, c. 1953. (Photo by and courtesy of Karl Maramorosch.)

Below: Cold Spring Harbor, 1953 (left to right): Max Delbrück, Alan Garen, Leo Szilard, and James D. Watson. (Courtesy of James D. Watson.)

Above: Theodore von Kármán (front row, center) and John von Neumann (back row) among a group of scientists in Paris; also in the back row is Werner Heisenberg and fourth from the left in the front row is Carl Friedrich Weizsäcker. (Courtesy of Marina Whitman.)

Below: Leo Szilard and Alfred Hershey in Cold Spring Harbor, 1953. (Photo by and courtesy of Karl Maramorosch.)

Facing page, top: John von Neumann fielding questions from young people at an exhibition in the 1950s. (Courtesy of Marina Whitman.)

Facing page, bottom: John von Neumann and Werner Heisenberg in the 1950s. (Courtesy of Marina Whitman.)

Above: John von Neumann (sitting second from the left) as commissioner of the U.S. Atomic Energy Commission, with other members and staff of the AEC: AEC Chairman Lewis L. Strauss (sitting fourth from the left); Commissioner Willard F. Libby is between von Neumann and Strauss. (Courtesy of Marina Whitman.)

Facing page, top: John von Neumann receiving Medal of Freedom from President Dwight D. Eisenhower at the White House, 1956. (Courtesy of the Dwight D. Eisenhower Library, Abilene, Kansas.)

Facing page, bottom: Princeton physics faculty, 1962. Wigner is fourth from the left in the front row. (Courtesy of Robert Matthews.)

Right: Leo Szilard with (from left) Victor Weisskopf, G. Brock Chisholm, and Mark Oliphant at a Pugwash meeting. (Courtesy of the Archives of Fizikai Szemle, Budapest.)

Below: Leo Szilard and Jonas Salk in Cold Spring Harbor, 1953. (Photo by and courtesy of Karl Maramorosch.)

Facing page top: Theodore von Kármán lecturing at the Jet Propulsion Laboratory in Pasadena, California. (Courtesy of NASA.)

Facing page, bottom: Theodore von Kármán (center) with William H. Pickering (left), former director of the Jet Propulsion Laboratory (JPL), and Frank J. Malina, co-founder and first director of the JPL. (Courtesy of NASA.)

Above: Theodore von Kármán with Mici Teller. (Courtesy of Wendy Teller and Paul Teller.)

Left: Eugene P. Wigner in his Princeton office, holding a photograph of Einstein. (Courtesy of the late George Marx.)

Below: Eugene P. Wigner and Edward Teller at the Livermore National Laboratory. (Courtesy of the Lawrence Livermore National Laboratory.)

Facing page, top: Eugene P. Wigner and the Swedish queen at the Banquet of the Nobel Prize award ceremonies in Stockholm, 1963. (Courtesy of Martha Wigner Upton and the late George Marx.)

Facing page, bottom: Eugene P. Wigner and the author in Austin, Texas, 1969.

Facing page, top: Edward Teller with grandchildren. (Courtesy of Wendy Teller and Paul Teller.)

Facing page, bottom: Soviet President Mikhail Gorbachev, President Ronald Reagan, and Edward Teller at a White House reception, 1987. (Courtesy of Wendy Teller and the Ronald Reagan Library, Simi Valley, Calif.)

Above: Edward Teller and the author in the Tellers' home in Stanford, California, 1996. (Photo by and courtesy of Magdolna Hargittai.)

Right: Edward Teller at the bust of John von Neumann on the campus of the Budapest University of Technology and Economics. (Photo by and courtesy of János Philip.)

Greatness in Science

The Martians were scientists first and became players in defense and politics second. It is difficult to assess the degree of their greatness in science, yet it is an interesting question, on which the Martians also had opinions. Theodore von Kármán ranked scientists by the number of great ideas they had had.[1] He placed Isaac Newton, with five or six great ideas, above everybody else, then came Albert Einstein with four. He assigned all the other major scientists one, or at most two great ideas. He credited himself with three, perhaps three and a half, thus implicitly concluding that he was just below Newton and Einstein but above everybody else. Eugene Wigner, too, mused about greatness in science, and he also considered Newton and Einstein to be above everybody else. The next layer, for him, came from among his contemporaries, Max von Laue, Walther Nernst, Michael Polanyi, and Wolfgang Pauli. There was some indication that he placed himself in this group or not far below.[2]

Stanislaw Ulam was interested in von Neumann's place among the greatest mathematicians and thought that he may not have reached the height of Jules H. Poincaré or David Hilbert, but then they worked purely in theory and did not care about applications. They are "idolized more than von Neumann as mathematicians' mathematicians." Ulam noted that Norbert Wiener and von Neumann had intersecting lines in their interests in pure mathematics and applications, although their personalities were very different. Wiener was an eccentric, while von Neumann was "a really solid person."[3] Wiener had a sense of what was important and what was worth thinking about, and he had primarily one technique, the Fourier transform, which he used in many problems. Von Neumann had many different techniques at his disposal; he had received a very broad education and had a wide knowledge of the world.

Von Neumann remained a benchmark for Wigner throughout his life; he had known him from a very early age, and von Neumann showed more brilliance than Wigner. The fact that Wigner compared von Neumann with Einstein at all attests to how highly he thought of his former schoolmate.[4] Wigner accepted that Einstein was a world-famous genius in a class with Newton, but he pointed out that Einstein was "far slower" than von Neumann at deriving mathematical identities. But Wigner realized that Einstein's understanding was deeper than von Neumann's. Besides, von Neumann never produced "anything so original" as Einstein's special and general theories of relativity.

Wigner's contribution to science was especially profound: as a consequence, we now view the "principles of symmetry as the most fundamental part of our description of nature." The laws of nature "summarize the regularities that are independent of the initial conditions, symmetry principles play a similar role with respect to the laws of nature."[5] Wigner's achievement has deeply affected our understanding of nature, yet its popular appeal has remained limited. Wigner excelled in applications as well, especially in nuclear reactor design.

Perhaps von Neumann's most conspicuous contribution was the introduction of the stored program in computers, which revolutionized not only computation but also opened up the most versatile applications of the computer in the most diverse areas of human endeavor. However, this was more an innovation than a new insight into the secrets of nature. He also made contributions in other fields, from information theory to molecular biology, but none of these are sufficient to make him conspicuous in these areas when taken against the background of the other important discoveries of the twentieth century.

Szilard was the first to conceive of the nuclear chain reaction, and he also realized before anybody else how it could be applied. He predicted that once the nuclear chain reaction could be carried out, harvesting nuclear energy would become possible. After the accidental discovery of nuclear fission, the road was open to the nuclear chain reaction and the liberation of nuclear energy, both for peaceful purposes and for bombs of a strength heretofore never realized.

Von Kármán's science was primarily in the application of mathematics in aerodynamics, hydrodynamics, and aviation.

Teller participated in numerous discoveries and perhaps more effects carry his name—jointly with others—than the names of the other Martians. His scientific contribution to the realization of thermonuclear energy production under terrestrial conditions has not yet been unambiguously determined, partly because some of it is still classified and partly because of the controversy around the relative contributions made by him and by Stanislaw Ulam.

As a working definition we may consider that a genius is somebody who sees connections that his great scientist colleagues do not. The discovery of the quantum by Max Planck was a product of genius, for example. According to Wigner, von Neumann was the only genius among the Martians. Ulam found von Neumann "quick, brilliant, efficient, and enormously broad in scientific interests beyond mathematics . . . his virtuosity in following complicated reasoning and his insights were supreme; yet he lacked absolute self-confidence." According to Ulam, von Neumann felt that he lacked the power to come to new truths intuitively at the highest level, and Ulam believed that he may have lacked "the gift for a seemingly irrational perception of proofs or formulation of new theorems."[6] Ulam speculated that von Neumann may have lost his confidence by seeing others make contributions that could have been his had he been more daring.

In scientific research the proper choice of problems is of great importance, because to solve a very important problem may take as much effort and time as to solve a problem of secondary importance. Of course, it takes special talent to determine the degrees of importance of problems, and Ulam had the impression that von Neumann was not always able to correctly choose which problems to devote himself to.[7] Rather, he may have developed a habit of taking the line of least resistance; of course, what was of least resistance for von Neumann would have been formidable resistance for others.

It is often a question of compromise between the possible and the important in choosing a research project. For von Neumann, the "possible" may have been a determining factor over the "important," but it may also be that he just tried to solve the problems that came his way without giving too much consideration to their degrees of importance. There is no doubt that he solved important problems, but they did not give him the one big discovery. Von Neumann was an excellent example of the digging type of researcher, who takes up a multitude of challenges during his career.

Von Neumann and von Kármán were similar in that they were ready to attack virtually any problem that they came across, and von Neumann attacked problems that his colleagues might have preferred him to leave alone. Referring once more to the definition of genius, it is worth noting that Szilard often saw connections that others found hard to understand for quite some time. Szilard was also universally interested in problems; however, he was satisfied to give directions for their solution and mostly did not try to solve them himself. When he did, he often did not claim credit for his contribution. According to Monod, Szilard "was as generous with his ideas as a Maori chief with his wives."[8] There are hints in the literature that others won Nobel Prizes from ideas originating from Szilard. However, generating ideas is far from making discoveries, and caution is called for in assessing Szilard's contributions to other people's achievements.

Although Wigner called Szilard the most imaginative man he ever knew, among the Martians the most imaginative label might also be applied to Teller. He had tremendous numbers of ideas, and they did not all need to be good as long as there was a filter to weed out the useless ones. This has been compared to throwing darts at a target on the wall. The darts cover not only the target but also the wall, yet a few hit the bull's eye. Even a few bull's eyes suffice to make one into a great scientist.

To be a great scientist is, however, not the same as to be a genius. As there is no objective measure for genius, there is none for greatness in science, either. On one hand, there may be a scientist who opens up new vistas in science yet makes no significant discovery; this does not mean that such a scientist may not be great. On the other hand, great discoverers are not necessarily great scientists. There are many one-discovery scientists who make a truly important breakthrough and soon after disappear into oblivion. None of the Martians was such a one-discovery scientist, and one of the remarkable characteristics of their careers was that they maintained their presences at the frontiers of science for a long time.

There should be many one-discovery scientists among the Nobel laureates, because it was Alfred Nobel's intention, as expressed in his will, that the award be given for great discoveries and not necessarily to great scientists. As the award-giving organizations apply Nobel's will often rather liberally, there are quite a few great scientists among the laureates who may or may not have made great discoveries. Of the Martians, only Wigner became a Nobel laureate. His Nobel Prize was met with universal approval; the community of physicists considered his award long overdue. It is of interest to look briefly into the prize-winning potential of the other Martians' achievements. We will take into account their own evaluations, if such information is available, and the experience of the first one hundred years of the Nobel Prize in the sciences.[9] First, however, let me issue a caveat. I do not wish to idolize the Nobel Prize, but merely to use it as a reference, as the most prestigious award in science.

Von Kármán wrote in his memoirs that Prandtl deserved the Nobel Prize. He said of Prandtl that he "unraveled the puzzle of some natural phenomena of tremendous basic importance . . . but he never received the prize, apparently because the Nobel Committee didn't (and still doesn't) regard the science of mechanics as a sublime achievement of the human brain—certainly not as sublime as other branches of physics."[10] By implication, of course, von Kármán meant that he deserved it as well. Indeed, he could have received one in physics, for example, for the Kármán Vortex Streets; it was not merely an engineering discovery—it might also have been considered to be a discovery in an area of fundamental physics.

Szilard might have been considered for a Nobel Prize for the discovery of the Szilard–Chalmers effect, which is a simple method for separating isotopes. This might not appear as a major enough discovery for such an award, but it is difficult to quantify the requirements for a Nobel Prize. In addition to those given for the truly seminal discoveries, many others have been awarded for discoveries that could hardly warrant such a claim. For example, the discovery of yet another elementary particle may be argued as deserving of a Nobel Prize, but the opposite argument can be made just as strongly. The discovery of the nuclear chain reaction might have also been considered worthy of the prize; in this case, the award could have been made jointly with others whose contributions were important in the actual realization of the nuclear chain reaction.

Sometimes it is argued that Szilard was not considered to be a viable choice for the Nobel Prize because of the military application of the nuclear chain reaction. However, Otto Hahn received one in 1945 (for 1944), for his discovery of the fission of heavy nuclei. This happened only a few months after the Hiroshima and Nagasaki bombs that were a direct consequence of Hahn's discovery. Many felt that Hahn's award was given too soon after the war, and the Jewish refugee Lise Meitner conspicuously did not share the prize. The impression is unavoidable that the old German-oriented Swedish bias was still at work in this case, although in the years following World War II the Swedes quickly reoriented themselves.[11] Many of the participants in the Manhattan Project received the Nobel Prize in subsequent years for discoveries unrelated to the atomic bomb.

More significantly, Szilard might have shared the Nobel Peace Prize awarded to Linus Pauling for his struggle for arms control. The Nobel Peace Prize is awarded by a committee elected by the Norwegian parliament and Pauling was greatly admired in Norway, whereas Szilard was much less known there.[12] Also, as one of Szilard's biographers noted, he operated on the periphery of the arms control community.[13]

What might Szilard have thought about the Nobel Prize? Wigner received the Nobel Prize for Physics for 1963, the same year in which Pauling received his Nobel Peace Prize (for 1962). Szilard may have felt doubly let down, but if he was, he never showed any sign of it. Wigner sensed some resentment on Szilard's part, but Wigner's antenna may have been supersensitive to this. That the Nobel Peace Prize was on Szilard's mind is witnessed by his playful statement concerning the discovery of nuclear fission: "those of *us* who missed this discovery ought to be considered . . . for the next . . . Nobel Prize for Peace" (italics added).[14] On a different occasion he told Joseph Rotblat (again, playfully) that he, Szilard, should have received the Nobel Peace Prize for *not* having carried out the systematic search for suitable elements for the nuclear chain reaction immediately after having come to the idea of such a reaction.[15]

Von Neumann's activities were not primarily in areas where Nobel Prize categories exist, although lately the scope of the physics prizes has broadened. His innovation of the stored program feature of computers might or might not have been considered for such recognition had von Neumann lived longer. His chances would have sharply increased with the instigation of the "Bank of Sweden Prize in Economic Sciences in Memory of Alfred Nobel" in 1968. It has been awarded since 1969 and is known popularly as the Nobel Prize in Economics. In 1994, it was awarded for the pioneering analysis of equilibria in the theory of noncooperative games. One of the awardees was the Budapest-born Hungarian American John Harsanyi. The work selected for the distinction was a continuation of von Neumann's work; suffice it to mention his book *Theory of Games and Economic*

Behavior, co-authored with the Princeton economist Oskar Morgenstern. Other prizes in economics have also had relevance to von Neumann's work.[16]

Edward Teller also could have won a Nobel Prize either in Physics or in Chemistry. He could have shared prizes for his contributions to nuclear physics. His chemistry prize could have been a shared one, for example for the B.E.T. equation describing multilayer absorption, or for the Jahn–Teller effect. His absence from the roster of Nobel laureates, however, is not conspicuous. In our recorded conversation in 1996, he told us that it was the B.E.T. equation for which he should have won the Nobel Prize. However, later he asked us to delete this statement from the printed version of the conversation. Such a request was uncharacteristic of Teller, who usually insisted on having the full texts of his interviews published or nothing at all.[17]

One could also ask whether Teller might have won the Nobel Peace Prize. This is bound to be a controversial issue, and I feel that the paper is burning while I am writing these strokes on it, but this is a legitimate question. Controversial figures have won Nobel Peace Prizes because this award is given for well-defined deeds rather than for universally approved oeuvre, as many examples during the past decades have demonstrated. Teller was virtually alone among the leading physicists in pushing for the development of the American hydrogen bomb, which was finally given the green light by President Truman in January 1950. Teller's relentless struggle resulted in America gaining a minuscule advantage over the Soviets, which became clear by the mid-1950s when both superpowers possessed hydrogen bombs. The policy of MAD, mutually assured destruction, could be instituted. However senseless the policy of MAD sounds, it contributed to preserving peace between the superpowers for decades. To prove it otherwise, we should have experienced World War III, which, fortunately, did not happen. A sure sign of the positive role of MAD was the vigorous protest against SDI by those whose opposition stemmed from a fear of undermining the MAD-based peace.

Had They Lived . . .

Had the Martians stayed in Hungary, or in Germany, they would have ended up in Auschwitz or in Mauthausen, like Teller's uncle and Mici Teller's brother, Teller's childhood friend, and other friends and family members. During the period between the two world wars, there were two and a half decades of vicious anti-Semitic propaganda in Hungary, capped by a series of ever more restricting, paralyzing, dispossessing, and humiliating anti-Jewish legislation between 1939 and 1944. All this culminated in the deportation of half a million Jews, mostly from the countryside, to Auschwitz. The en mass deportation of the Jews from Budapest was prevented by the protest of the Allies and the king of Sweden; besides, the front was fast approaching. When the Hungarian Nazis came to power in October 1944, they instituted a bloody frenzy of killing in Budapest. People were herded to the banks of the Danube, shot, and pushed into the river, often after having been tortured, or they were killed in other ways. Conservative estimates put the number of victims in Budapest at 100,000.

The speed and brutality of the destruction of Hungarian Jewry was unprecedented even in the darkest years of World War II. It would have taken a miracle for the Martians to survive it, but had that happened they would have had to start their lives anew, having probably lost everything amidst a population that had gained materially from the murder of their Jewish compatriots. This financial motivation was a more important ingredient of anti-Semitism in Hungary than, for example, in Germany. The small number of surviving Jews, returning from hell, were met with animosity or worse by the people who had benefited from the loot of the deported and murdered Jews.[18]

Had the Martians survived all this, they would have been forced out of their homes in Budapest and sent to the countryside in 1951 by the Communist authorities. Teller's mother, sister, and nephew were kicked out of Budapest along with many thousands of ostensibly capitalist elements, who were stripped of their homes and means of livelihood. This lasted until after Stalin's death, at which time they could return to Budapest but received no support or compensation for their lost homes and belongings. Teller's nephew slipped out of Hungary when the borders were left temporarily unguarded in 1956, but Teller's mother and sister would not undertake the risky adventure of crossing the border illegally. They left Hungary in 1959, thanks to Szilard's intervention on their behalf with the Soviet and Hungarian delegates at a Pugwash meeting.

Suppose, however, that we disregard the almost certain physical annihilation of the Martians and consider what their chances would have been of leading a normal life under communism and Soviet domination through the decades after World War II in Hungary. Although the political situation and degree of repression changed, the pressure to conform continued for a long time, and that is what the Martians would have found hard to live with.

In Hungary under communism, it was not only in important international issues that there was no place for alternative opinions: there had to be a party line even in such trivial matters as the beauty of a poem or a song. Regimentation was not simply ensured by censorship, there was self-censorship as people tried to streamline their own thinking according to the supposed party line. The Martians might not have survived postwar Hungary, although they would have suffered different degrees of difficulty. It would have been hardest for Szilard; the others might have found some sort of accommodation. But here we presume that they would have been great scientists no matter what. This premise is faulty in the first place, because had they stayed in Hungary they would have been unable to fulfill their potentials, without which there would be no reason to contemplate their fates in these pages.

To let our imagination go yet farther, we might ask: How would the Martians have fared had they lived in the Soviet Union? This question is of interest because the Soviet Union was the counterpart of the United States in the Cold War. Also, in the 1920s and 1930s, at the time of the westward exodus of Jewish scientists from Central Europe, there was a trickle of emigration to the Soviet Union. We have seen one aborted example, that of Teller's friend, Laszlo Tisza. The only way we can handle this question is to consider the fate of some Soviet scientists.

The Martians could have been arrested and executed in the late 1930s. Supposing that they did not suffer this fate, they would have undoubtedly become involved in weapons projects. Many Soviet scientists participated in these programs. In World War II, which in the Soviet Union had the label of the Great Patriotic War, Stalin did everything to broaden his power base. It was a unique moment of Soviet history, in which he invoked nationalist feelings, Russian history, and even the Eastern Orthodox Church in his calling for the defense of Fatherland. The invading Germans were fighting not only communism but also the peoples of the Soviet Union. To resist the Nazis was a deep-felt patriotic duty for the scientists.[19] Even after the war, most physicists and other scientists worked for the Soviet nuclear program with devotion. Lev Landau was an exception because he worked for it from expediency, but work he did. Andrei Sakharov became a conspicuous exception of a different kind, whose opposition came out into the open. However, it happened after the end of the Stalin era and after he had completed his work on the Soviet hydrogen bomb.

It is an arbitrary guess to chart the hypothetical fate of the Martians. Under Stalin, Szilard would have been killed or at least exiled and condemned to disappear. Wigner could have become a purely theoretical physicist with proper academic recognition. Teller might have become a stellar project leader in the nuclear weapons project and a consultant to the government. He might have been respected by some and feared by more. Von Kármán and von Neumann might have become valued scientists working on classified projects, showered with all the perks the regime could offer.

Under the less restrictive regimes after Stalin, Szilard might have ended up in a psychiatric hospital, and the others may have followed the same paths as under Stalin. Teller's example is especially important because Sakharov may have been the Soviet Teller, as he was often so characterized, in his role as the key figure in creating the Soviet hydrogen bomb, but I doubt that Teller would have become another Sakharov. He was too much of a law-abiding citizen to turn against the powers-that-be in his country. All this, however, may be far from the mark, because until a person is under the conditions about which we are guessing, it is impossible to really know what that person's attitude will be. My guesses are based on their behavior under the Hungarian, German, and American conditions that they experienced, and not under the Soviet conditions that they did not.

When Edward Teller died in September 2003, the last Martian was gone and they suddenly became part of history. The change was abrupt, perhaps also because Teller lived an exceptionally long life, and it dawned on me that their time was a time of long ago.

The question of how the Martians live on could be asked instantly. Paradoxically, they live on strongly in the Hungarian national consciousness. Although they were forced out of Hungarian life in their youth and received hardly any recognition even at the peak of their international fame and activities, since their deaths they have been afforded full honors. In contrast, their memories may be fading in the United States, the country where they achieved the most. A case in point is that although Teller was instrumental in creating the second weapons laboratory, the Lawrence Livermore National Laboratory carries the name of Ernest Lawrence, who was also an important force in shepherding the idea over all the hurdles. But Lawrence had already had one national laboratory named after him, the Lawrence Berkeley National Laboratory in Berkeley, also in California.

Martin Summerfield, Theodore von Kármán's long-time associate, lamented the absence of von Kármán's name from the historiography of rocket science. He noted that Robert Goddard is considered to be the father of American rocket science, and suggested that a more accurate assignment of labels would see Goddard called the pioneer and von Kármán the father. He justified his suggestion by pointing out that Goddard had hardly any followers, whereas von Kármán created a large school, and his pupils, and the pupils of his pupils, are all around the world, heading laboratories and holding university chairs.[20]

The Martians also live on in the works written about them, and in the work of scientists who use, and refer to, the effects they discovered, of which there are quite a few. And, of course, the Martians live on in the history books. Although it is debatable that the Einstein letter initiated by Szilard was the triggering point in the American nuclear program, it is a real story and a romantically attractive one at that. Szilard and the other Martians continue to figure in the stories about American involvement in World War II.

They had additional roles in the Cold War era. In particular, Teller has been labeled the father of the hydrogen bomb, a title that he protested against vigorously. By the time my wife and I talked with him about it in 1996, he may have become resigned to accepting the label, which to us he clarified rather than protested. However, even such an oversimplifying label as this should be refined, and Teller should be called the father of the American hydrogen bomb rather than of the hydrogen bomb in general. The Martians also live on in the prizes, societies, and craters of the Moon that have been named after them, and as token villains (Teller as Dr. Strangelove, for some).

Isidor I. Rabi was very critical of Teller, declaring that "He is a danger to all that is important . . . it would have been a better world without Teller . . . he is an enemy of humanity."[21] Rabi also blamed Szilard for the delay in the start of the American atomic bomb program.[22] John A. Wheeler's assessment of Teller seems more objective: "I may have disagreed with his tactics but never with his goals."[23]

Conclusion

The Martians were exceptional individuals, and they constituted a group, however diverse they may have been as individuals. There were special circumstances that, combined with their personal qualities, contributed to the formation of this group. Reviewing their paths leads us to conclude that the emergence of another group of Martians is not to be expected any time soon. Hitler's accession to power was a focused event that ejected the Martians from Europe and took them to the United States, which was more than ready to receive them. Soon afterward, the discovery of nuclear fission, the demonstration of the feasibility of the nuclear chain reaction, and the looming German menace prompted the Martians to turn to the defense of the United States. They understood the dangers of the international situation and the physics involved better than most of their peers, and they were available, whereas most other scientists had already become involved in classified war-related work. There is no foreseeable scenario that would bring together similar conditions. However, in science the most important developments are not predictable. The Martians were catapulted into their mission by progress in science and the development of the world situation, and while we cannot anticipate something similar happening again, it cannot be excluded with any reasonable certainty, either.

Szilard was especially good at forecasting, but even he could not see some of the important developments that lay ahead. He envisioned the future with the Soviet Union as one of the two superpowers, and never hinted at its possible collapse. This is the more interesting because the Soviet Union's demise had been repeatedly predicted ever since its formation, but when this finally became a reality even the experts appeared genuinely surprised. Von Neumann was also living in the future as far as his computers were concerned, but curiously his imagination, too, had severe limitations. He did not foresee the economic and technological impacts of the computer, and in particular could not imagine that it would enter everyday life and become a common household item.[24] Sadly, he died too early to witness this development.

In reflecting on the greatness of the Martians as scientists we have to remember that it is an ambiguous attribute, because scientific discoveries are made, if not by this researcher then by another, sooner or later. This is a fundamental difference between scientific contributions and artistic creations. Had Beethoven not existed, his symphonies would have never been created by others. The Martians' scientific discoveries would have been made by others, rather sooner than later. Also, research contributions (except for a few truly seminal ones) tend to be forgotten, whereas artistic productions are attached to their creators' names forever. Michael Polanyi wrote to Szilard, referring to his writings: "Maybe . . . you will be remembered by these light-hearted fancies long after your contributions to science will have joined the melting pot of anonymity."[25]

The impact of the Martians on questions of war and peace and world political affairs is a different matter. Szilard's envisioning of the nuclear chain reaction that might lead to an explosion, the Szilard–Wigner–Teller trio's action in initiating Einstein's letter to President Roosevelt, thus setting the development of nuclear weaponry in motion, and Teller's contribution to inducing the United States to develop the hydrogen bomb, including von Neumann's and von Kármán's applications of computation, mathematics, and mechanics for modern warfare, decisively affected how the second half of the twentieth century played out. In these deeds the time element was more significant than it is in scientific discoveries: it was of overriding importance. Scientific excellence and creativity, political sagacity, and fierce dedication to democracy and freedom together carried the Martians to the place they hold today: among the important contributors to the history of the twentieth century.

Sampler of Quotable Martians

Some of the quotations may not have originated with the Martians but only have been used by them, and so it may be difficult to delineate these and trace their origins.

Theodore von Kármán

"Exaggerated concern about what others are doing can be foolish. It can paralyze effort, and stifle a good idea. One can find that in the history of science almost every problem has been worked on by somebody else. This should not discourage anyone from pursuing his own path."

T. von Kármán (with Lee Edson), *The Wind and Beyond: Theodore von Kármán, Pioneer in Aviation and Pathfinder in Space*, p. 35.

[The research seminars are] "the transmission belt of the newest scientific ideas."

The Wind, p. 47.

"In science you must be a radical in order to find a new truth."

The Wind, p. 71.

"Although some people think scientists make war, I find it easy to take the position that war makes scientists."

The Wind, p. 79.

"When dealing with pompous ignoramuses a plausible lie is better than a difficult truth."

The Wind, p. 88.

"Making records and being first are not enough from a long-range point of view."

The Wind, p. 254.

"You cannot preach international cooperation and disarmament from a position of weakness. My *Old Testament* faith tells me that to get one's point across it is best to have a big stick. You don't have to use it, but you're freer to talk without interference."

The Wind, p. 352.

"Nothing in my view is so pathetic as an idealistic man talking of situations which he doesn't have the strength to control."

The Wind, p. 352.

"Engineers are people who perpetuate the mistakes made in the previous generation."

Quoted in S. M. Ulam, *Adventures of a Mathematician.* University of California Press, Berkeley and Los Angeles, 1991, p. 71.

"Good judgment comes from experience, but experience comes from bad judgment."

The Wind, p. 224.

Following the thin song of mathematics and not the heavy voice of experience proved to be another victory for engineering science.

The Wind, p. 256 [slightly paraphrased].

"One should not be unduly limited by the facts; and one should never repeat a story without improving it."

Theodore von Kármán quoted in E. Teller (with Judith Shoolery), *Memoirs: A Twentieth-Century Journey in Science and Politics*, p. 134.

"Prophesy is not a scientific activity."

Quoted in the obituary by Solly Zuckerman in the London *Times* (www.aam314.vzz.net/Karman.html).

Leo Szilard

"The creative scientist has much in common with the artist and the poet. Logical thinking and an analytical ability are necessary attributes to a scientist, but they are far from sufficient for creative work. Those insights in science that have led to a breakthrough were not logically derived from preexisting knowledge: The creative processes on which the progress of science is based operate on the level of the subconscious."

>Quoted by Jonas Salk in his Foreword to W. Lanouette (with Bela Silard), *Genius in the Shadows: A Biography of Leo Szilard, The Man Behind the Bomb*, pp. xiii–xiv.

"It is easy to overestimate our own freedom from intimidation and to underestimate the courage of others."

>Quoted in H. S. Hawkins, G. Allen Greb, and G. Weiss Szilard, Eds., *Toward a Livable World: Leo Szilard and the Crusade for Nuclear Arms Control*, p. 107.

"The past is unimportant, the future is all."

>Quoted in Lanouette, *Genius*, p. 4.

"It is not necessary to succeed in order to persevere."

>Quoted in Lanouette, *Genius*, p. 23.

"An optimist is the one who thinks that the future is uncertain."

>A favorite saying of both Szilard and Wigner.

"If you want to succeed in this world you don't have to be much cleverer than other people; you just have to be one day earlier than most people."

>Quoted in S. R. Weart and G. Weiss Szilard, Eds., *Leo Szilard: His Version of the Facts. Selected Recollections and Correspondence*, p. 14.

"An expert is a man who knows what cannot be done."

>Quoted in Lanouette, *Genius*, p. 133.

"If you are an expert, you believe that you are in possession of the truth, and since you know so much, you are unwilling to make allowances for unforeseen developments."

>Quoted in Weart and Szilard, *Leo Szilard*, p. 229.

"Science is the art of the impossible."

>Quoted in Lanouette, *Genius*, p. 301.

"If I do not call a spade a spade I find it rather difficult to find a suitable name for it."
        Weart and Szilard, *Leo Szilard*, p. 156.

"If authority is not given to the best men in the field there does not seem to be any compelling reason to give it to the second-best man and one may give it to the third- or fourth- or fifth-best men, whichever of them appears to be most agreeable on purely subjective grounds."
        Weart and Szilard, *Leo Szilard*, p. 177.

"I would rather have roots than wings, but if I cannot have roots I shall have wings."
        Quoted in Lanouette, *Genius*, p. 395.

(On dying prematurely): "If worst comes to worst, I'll be dead ten years longer."
        Quoted in Lanouette, *Genius*, p. 404.

"The most important step in getting a job done . . . is the recognition of the problem."
        Quoted in Lanouette, *Genius*, p. 441.

"In life you must often choose between getting a job done or getting credit for it."
        Quoted in Lanouette, *Genius*, p. 441.

(On arms control): "Thinking up clever ideas is not enough. You also need power—political, legal, financial—to enforce your views."
        Quoted in Lanouette, *Genius*, p. 447.

"The mysteries of biology are no less deep than the mysteries of physics were one or two generations ago, and the tools are available to solve them provided only that we believe they can be solved."
        Quoted in Lanouette, *Genius*, p. 468.

(To Jonas Salk, about academic pettiness): "They will never forgive you for having been right."
        Quoted in Lanouette, *Genius*, p. 470.

"Confront scientists with a new idea, and most will say, 'It's not true!' Next they'll say, 'If true, it's not very important.' Finally, they'll say, "We knew it all along!'"
        Quoted in Lanouette, *Genius*, p. 470.

"It is better to be clear and wrong than to be right and confused."
    Quoted in Lanouette, *Genius*, p. 471.

"The most important property of man's brain is the ability to forget things."
    Quoted in Lanouette, *Genius*, p. 389.

"To make progress is not enough, for if the progress is not fast enough, something is going to overtake us."
    Quoted in Lanouette, *Genius*, p. 466.

"A man's clarity of judgment is never very good when he is involved."
    Weart and Szilard, *Leo Szilard*, p. 5.

"If I had to choose between being tactless and being untruthful, I would prefer to be tactless."
    Weart and Szilard, *Leo Szilard*, p. 5.

"Great achievement in the field of science requires a certain kind of sensitivity, and sensitivity leads to shyness."
    Weart and Szilard, *Leo Szilard*, p. 12.

"In science the greatest thoughts are the simplest thoughts."
    Weart and Szilard, *Leo Szilard*, p. 12.

"It is not a good thing for a scientist to be dependent on laying golden eggs."
    Albert Einstein to Leo Szilard upon Szilard's graduation in Berlin; quoted in Weart and Weiss Szilard, *Leo Szilard*, p. 12.

"The development of Western civilization was not brought about by humanity's yearning for civilization but rather arose in a more mechanical way."
    Weart and Szilard, *Leo Szilard*, p. 23.

(Referring to H. G. Wells): "The forecast of writers may prove to be more accurate than the forecast of the scientists."
    Weart and Szilard, *Leo Szilard*, p. 38.

"Don't be driven by conscience to 'finish up' dull projects, but plunge into work on your next appealing idea."
    Quoted in Lanouette, *Genius*, p. 393.

"The one thing that most scientists are really afraid of is to make a fool of themselves."
    Weart and Szilard, *Leo Szilard*, p. 83.

"I have been asked whether I would agree that the tragedy of the scientist is that he is able to bring about great advances in our knowledge, which mankind may then proceed to use for purposes of destruction. My answer is that this is not the tragedy of the scientist; it is the tragedy of mankind."

Weart and Szilard, *Leo Szilard*, p. 229.

"[I]t will appear to many people premature to take some action until it will be too late to take any action."

Quoted in R. Molander and R. Nichols, *Who Will Stop the Bomb? A Primer on Nuclear Proliferation*, p. 111.

"Not everyone is as fortunate as Christ. To sacrifice yourself and do some good, that takes luck."

Leo Szilard quoting Albert Einstein, in Weart and Szilard, *Leo Szilard*, p. 12.

"As long as you pray to God and ask for something, you are not a religious man."

Leo Szilard quoting Albert Einstein, in Weart and Szilard, *Leo Szilard*, p. 12.

"I do not believe that atomic armaments give us security. I think that atomic bombs give us insecurity."

Quoted in Hawkins et al., *Toward a Livable World*, p. 114.

"No man can speak for a purpose in public on major issues without impunity for long. He will soon end up speaking for a purpose not only in public but also in private. And how much longer will it take until he will not only speak for a purpose but also think for a purpose. For a while he may succeed in deceiving others—in the end he will succeed in deceiving himself."

Quoted in Hawkins et al., *Toward a Livable World*, p. 126.

"Scientists are, by and large, addicted to the truth, to thinking the truth and to stating the truth. Not until a scientist becomes an administrator will he find himself in a conflict of loyalties with his loyalty to truth taking second place."

Quoted in Hawkins et al., *Toward a Livable World*, p. 127.

"When scientists talk to each other, we ask ourselves only whether it is true what our fellow scientists say, while if statesmen speak to each other, the first question is not 'Is it true what he says?' but rather 'Why does he say it?'"

Quoted in Hawkins et al., *Toward a Livable World*, p. 141.

The main aim of the scientist is to clarify. The main aim of the politician is to persuade."

Quoted in Hawkins et al., *Toward a Livable World*, p. 196.

"If we want to have peace, we have to make peace not atoms."
Quoted in Hawkins et al., *Toward a Livable World*, p. 144.

"Maybe there is a shortage of scientists and engineers in America as well as in the rest of the world but, my God, what a shortage of statesmen!"
Quoted in Hawkins et al., *Toward a Livable World*, p. 147.

"It is not safe to generalize, even from one case."
Szilard quoting Michael Polanyi, quoted in Hawkins et al., *Toward a Livable World*, p. 163.

(Referring to the McCarthy period): "Even when things were at their worst the majority of Americans were free to say what they thought for the simple reason that they never thought what they were not free to say."
Quoted in Hawkins et al., *Toward a Livable World*, p. 164.

"Why make the same mistakes when you can so easily make new ones?"
Quoted in Hawkins et al., *Toward a Livable World*, p. 167.

"Unjustified distrust is responsible for far more misfortunes in this world than is unjustified trustfulness."
Quoted in Hawkins et al., *Toward a Livable World*, p. 194.

Ten Commandments
by Leo Szilard
(Translated by Jacob Bronowski, in Weart and Szilard, *Leo Szilard*, p. vi)
1. *Recognize the connections of things and the laws of conduct of men, so that you may know what you are doing.*
2. *Let your acts be directed towards a worthy goal, but do not ask if they will reach it; they are to be models and examples, not means to an end.*
3. *Speak to all men as you do to yourself, with no concern for the effect you make, so that you do not shut them out from your world; lest in isolation the meaning of life slips out of sight and you lose the belief in the perfection of the creation.*
4. *Do not destroy what you cannot create.*
5. *[Untranslatable pun.]*
6. *Do not covet what you cannot have.*
7. *Do not lie without need.*
8. *Honor children. Listen reverently to their words and speak to them with infinite love.*
9. *Do your work for six years; but in the seventh, go into solitude or among strangers, so that the recollection of your friends does not hinder you from being what you have become.*

10. *Lead your life with a gentle hand and be ready to leave whenever you are called.*

Lanouette, *Genius*, p. 203, gives the English translation of Szilard's fifth commandment as "Touch no dish except that you are hungry." (In Szilard's original German, "Rühre kein Gericht an, es sei denn, dass Du hungrig bist.")

Eugene P. Wigner

"[I]n national politics the truth is often less popular than a clever lie."
> E. P. Wigner (with Andrew Szanton), *The Recollections of E. P. Wigner as Told to Andrew Szanton*, p. 154.

"Stupidity is a general human property."
> Attributed to Eugene P. Wigner by Edward Teller, *Memoirs*, p. 65.

"The only absolute laws are the laws of science."
> *Recollections*, p. 161.

"We are all guests in this world, and our culture commits a crime when it persuades us to think otherwise."
> *Recollections*, p. 317.

"As a scientist, I must say that we have no heavenly data. So I am afraid that after death, we merely cease to exist."
> *Recollections*, p. 318.

"[T]he subject [of Nazi crimes] should be raised regularly to prevent it from recurring."
> *Recollections*, p. 182.

"People do not build their beliefs on a foundation of reason. They begin with certain beliefs, then find reasons to justify them."
> *Recollections*, p. 295.

"A full professor knows nothing about everything, an associate professor knows something about a little, and an assistant professor knows it better."
> Wigner's version of a well-known saying, quoted in J. Walsh, "A Conversation with Eugene Wigner," *Science* 1973, 181, 527–533, p. 532.

"Conflicts do not arise logically, but emotionally; they are caused by incompatible ambitions and desires, whether between nations or within a single country."
> E. P. Wigner, *Symmetries and Reflections: Scientific Essays,* p. 243.

"Our intellect is our servant, our desires are the matters of our actions. Man will always satisfy his desires if they seem easy to satisfy."
  Symmetries, p. 265.

"[T]he way we die—whether fighting evil or, having abandoned our friends and been abandoned by them in turn, delivered to our enemies—is a decisive element when we consider the success of the whole life."
  Symmetries, p. 266.

"May I, may we all, be able to live up to the principles which we profess when strong and not in immediate danger."
  Symmetries, p. 265.

"[S]ome of the great physicists were appointed as great physicists more nearly by the government which gave them big accelerators than appointed by Providence by giving them a devoted interest in knowledge, an appreciation of the true problems and mysteries, and the humility necessary to search for the solution of these patiently."
  Symmetries, p. 279.

"The promise of future science is to furnish a unifying goal to mankind rather than merely the means to an easy life, to provide some of what the human soul needs in addition to bread alone."
  Symmetries, p. 280.

"Emigration is in many ways very stimulating. . . . In a foreign country you have to excel."
  Walsh, "A Conversation with Eugene Wigner," p. 532.

John von Neumann

"It is not enough for a European to be rich, he also needs a bank account in Switzerland."
  Quoted in N. Macrae, *John von Neumann: The Scientific Genius Who Pioneered the Modern Computer, Game Theory, Nuclear Deterrence, and Much More*, p. 89.

"The only way science could progress was by scholars picking up each other's work and improving it."
  Quoted in Macrae, *John von Neumann*, p. 171.

"It is just as foolish to complain that people are selfish and treacherous as it is to complain that the magnetic field does not increase unless the electric field has a curl. Both are laws of nature."
Quoted in Wigner, *Symmetries*, p. 261.

(On the elegant Gothic chapel in Princeton): "This is our one-million-dollar protest against materialism."
Quoted in Ulam, *Adventures*, p. 71.

"Cars are no good for transportation anymore, but they make marvelous umbrellas."
Quoted in Ulam, *Adventures*, p. 71.

"There probably is a God. Many things are easier to explain if there is than if there isn't."
Quoted in Macrae, *John von Neumann*, p. 379.

"So long as there is the possibility of eternal damnation for nonbelievers it is more logical to be a believer at the end."
Quoted in Macrae, *John von Neumann*, p. 379.

Edward Teller

Although we cannot change the past, we can know it. We can change the future, but we cannot know it.
Memoirs, pp. 99–100 (paraphrased).

"The eyes of childhood are magnifying lenses."
Memoirs, p. 5.

"When God created the scientist, he gave him comfort, security, and an appetite for knowledge, and the Devil created a colleague for the scientist."
Memoirs, pp. 115–116.

"I like activity. In fact, I believe that there is no other way in which to enjoy life in a consistent manner."
Quoted by Judith Shoolery, personal communication, 2004.

"I hate doubt, and yet I am certain that doubt is the only way to approach anything worth believing in."
Quoted by Judith Shoolery, personal communication, 2004.

"I believe in good. It is an ephemeral and elusive quality. It is the center of my beliefs, but it cannot be strengthened by talking about it."

Quoted by Judith Shoolery, personal communication, 2004.

"I believe in evil. It is the property of all those who are certain of truth. Despair and fanaticism are only differing manifestations of evil."

Quoted by Judith Shoolery, personal communication, 2004.

"I believe in excellence. It is a basic need of every human soul. All of us can be excellent, because, fortunately, we are exceedingly diverse in our ambitions and talents."

Quoted by Judith Shoolery, personal communication, 2004.

"Total security has never been available to anyone. To expect it is unrealistic; to imagine that it can exist is to invite disaster."

Quoted by Judith Shoolery, personal communication, 2004.

"I believe that no endeavor that is worthwhile is simple in prospect; if it is right, it will be simple in retrospect."

Quoted by Judith Shoolery, personal communication, 2004.

"We must learn to live with contradictions, because they lead to deeper and more effective understanding."

E. Teller, "Science and Morality," *Science* 1998, 280, 1200–1201, p. 1200.

"Attempts have been made to add laws to quantum mechanics to eliminate uncertainty. Such attempts have not only been unsuccessful; they have not even appeared to lead to any interesting results."

"Science and Morality," p. 1200.

NOTES

Preface

1. E. Teller (with Judith Shoolery), *Memoirs: A Twentieth-Century Journey in Science and Politics*. Perseus, Cambridge, Mass., 2001, p. v.

2. G. Marx, *The Voice of the Martians*. Akadémiai Kiadó, Budapest, 1997.

3. Tibor Frank, László Kovács, Rezső Kunfalvi, Ferenc Nagy, Gábor Palló, Gyula Radnai, and others.

4. W. O. McCagg, Jr., *Jewish Nobles and Geniuses in Modern Hungary*. East European Monographs, Boulder; distributed by Columbia University Press, New York, 1986; originally appeared in 1972.

5. Ibid., pp. 208–222.

6. I. Hargittai, *Candid Science* book series, Volumes I–VI; I. Hargittai, *The Road to Stockholm: Nobel Prizes, Science, and Scientists*. Oxford University Press, Oxford, 2002; I. Hargittai, *Our Lives: Encounters of a Scientist*. Akadémiai Kiadó, Budapest, 2004.

7. The Hungarian article was a compilation of excerpts from E. P. Wigner, "The Limits of Science." *Proceedings of the American Philosophical Society* 1950, 94, no. 5 (October); I. Hargittai, "Tudományok határán" (On the limits of science). *Élet és Irodalom* 1964, no. 51, 6 [December 19].)

8. T. von Kármán (with Lee Edson), *The Wind and Beyond: Theodore von Kármán, Pioneer in Aviation and Pathfinder in Space*. Little, Brown, Boston, 1967; W. Lanouette (with Bela Silard), *Genius in the Shadows: A Biography of Leo Szilard, The Man Behind the Bomb*. University of Chicago Press, 1992; E. P. Wigner (with Andrew Szanton), *The Recollections of E. P. Wigner as Told to Andrew Szanton*. Plenum Press, New York, 1992; N. Macrae, *John von Neumann: The Scientific Genius Who Pioneered the Modern Computer, Game Theory, Nuclear Deterrence, and Much More*. American Mathematical Society, Providence, R.I., 1999; Teller, *Memoirs*.

9. Quoted in G. Herken, *Cardinal Choices: Presidential Science Advising from the Atomic Bomb to SDI.* Stanford University Press, Palo Alto, Calif., 2000, p. 15.

Introduction

1. N. Macrae, *John von Neumann: The Scientific Genius Who Pioneered the Modern Computer, Game Theory, Nuclear Deterrence, and Much More.* American Mathematical Society, Providence, R.I., 1999, pp. 39–41.

2. E. Chargaff, *Heraclitean Fire: Sketches from a Life before Nature.* Rockefeller University Press, New York, 1978, pp. 8–9.

3. *Nobel Lectures Including Presentation Speeches and Laureates' Biographies: Physics 1942–1962.* World Scientific, Singapore, 1998, pp. 20–21.

4. A. Pais, *The Genius of Science: A Portrait Gallery of Twentieth-Century Physicists.* Oxford University Press, Oxford, 2000, pp. 264–279; J. S. Rigden, *Rabi: Scientist and Citizen.* Basic Books, New York, 1987, p. 17.

5. I. Hargittai, *Our Lives: Encounters of a Scientist.* Akadémiai Kiadó, Budapest, 2004, pp. 67–70.

6. In Hungarian, "Véreim, Magyarok!"

Chapter 1

1. In addition to the biographers of the individual Martians, for Eugene P. Wigner I used E. Czeizel, *Tudósok, gének, dilemmák: A magyar származású Nobel-díjasok családfaelemzése* (Scientists, genes, dilemmas: genealogical analysis of Nobel laureates of Hungarian origin). Galenus, Budapest, 2002. Dr. Czeizel's new book is about a dozen more famous Hungarian scientists, including the rest of the Martians, and he kindly made his findings available to me before publication: E. Czeizel, *Tudósok, gének, tanulságok: A magyar természettudós géniuszok családfaelemzése* (Scientists, genes, lessons: Genealogical analysis of Hungarian geniuses in science). Galenus, Budapest, 2006.

2. The dual monarchy of Austria–Hungary in 1867–1918 was a personal union, with Franz Joseph I (1830–1916) being emperor of Austria and king of Hungary.

3. http://209.132.68.98/pdf/theodore-vonKármán_fbifile_part1a.pdf.

4. According to John von Neumann's brother, Nicolas A. Vonneuman, it was a German publisher rather than von Neumann himself who first introduced the "von Neumann" way of writing his name. See N. A. Vonneuman's comments in the third appendix to the Hungarian translation of the book by H. H. Goldstine, *The Computer from Pascal to von Neumann*, entitled *A számitógép Pascaltól Neumannig*, Műszaki Könyvkiadó. Budapest, 2003, pp. 332–335. Nicholas Vonneuman combined von and Neumann in creating a simpler surname in the United States.

5. S. M. Ulam, *Adventures of a Mathematician.* University of California Press, Berkeley, 1991, p. 11.

6. T. von Kármán (with Lee Edson), *The Wind and Beyond: Theodore von Kármán, Pioneer in Aviation and Pathfinder in Space.* Little, Brown, Boston, 1967, p. 20.

7. Ibid., pp. 15–16.

8. Ibid., pp. 23–24.

9. E. Czeizel, "Szilárd Leó családfája" (The genealogy of Leo Szilard), *Fizikai Szemle* (Budapest) 1998, 2, 42–44.

10. W. Lanouette (with Bela Silard), *Genius in the Shadows: A Biography of Leo Szilard, The Man Behind the Bomb.* University of Chicago Press, Chicago, 1992.

11. S. R. Weart and G. Weiss Szilard, Eds., *Leo Szilard: His Version of the Facts. Selected Recollections and Correspondence.* MIT Press, Cambridge, Mass., 1978, p. 3.

12. Weart and Szilard, *Leo Szilard,* p. 5.

13. Ibid., pp. 4–8.

14. Czeizel, *Tudósok, gének, tanulságok.*

15. N. A. Vonneuman, *John von Neumann as Seen by His Brother.* Private edition by N. A. Vonneuman, 1987.

16. Nicholas Kurti is quoted in a story about Vámbéry in chapter 5.

17. E. Teller (with Judith Shoolery), *Memoirs: A Twentieth-Century Journey in Science and Politics.* Perseus, Cambridge, Mass., 2001, p. 33.

18. Judith Shoolery, personal communication, Half Moon Bay, California, February 2004.

19. Some biographers refer to those in this second category as technical high schools, but this is an exaggeration because the difference between the two directions was only in an emphasis on certain subjects.

20. J. Lukacs, *Budapest 1900: A Historical Portrait of a City and Its Culture.* Grove Press, New York, 1988, pp. 145–146.

21. Ibid., pp. 145–146.

22. Von Kármán *The Wind,* p. 20.

23. The Abel Prize of Norway is internationally the highest prize in mathematics; in 1941, when Peter Lax was 15 years old, he and his family left Hungary for the United States.

24. Von Kármán, *The Wind,* pp. 21–22.

25. E. P. Wigner (with Andrew Szanton), *The Recollections of E. P. Wigner as Told to Andrew Szanton.* Plenum Press, New York, 1992, p. 57.

26. J. von Neumann, letter to Leopold Fejér, July 17, 1929; in *Neumann János és a "magyar titok" a dokumentumok tükrében* (John Neumann and the 'Hungarian secret' as reflected by documents) (Ferenc Nagy, comp.). Országos Műszaki Információs Központ és Könyvtár, Budapest, 1987, pp. 223–224.

27. See, e.g., T. Frank, "George Pólya and the Heuristic Tradition." *Revista Brasileira de História da Matemática* 2004, 4 (7), 19–36. The Stanford competitions were administered until 1965.

28. Teller, *Memoirs,* pp. 21–38.

29. G. Radnai, "Szilárd Leó iskolái" (Leo Szilard's schools). *Fizikai Szemle* 1998, no. 2, 61–62.

30. G. Klein, *The Atheist and the Holy City: Encounters and Reflections.* MIT Press, Cambridge, Mass., 1992, p. 21.

31. Wigner, *Recollections,* p. 45.

32. N. Macrae, *John von Neumann: The Scientific Genius Who Pioneered the Modern Computer, Game Theory, Nuclear Deterrence, and Much More.* American Mathematical Society, Providence, R.I., 1999, p. 72.

33. E. P. Wigner, "City Hall Speech–Stockholm, 1963." In E. P. Wigner, *Symmetries and Reflections: Scientific Essays.* Indiana University Press, Bloomington, 1967, pp. 262–263.

34. L. Kovács, *Eugene Wigner and His Hungarian Teachers*. Savaria University Press, Szombathely, Hungary, 2002, pp. 19–27.

35. Ibid, pp. 28–36.

36. Wigner, *Recollections*, p. 55.

37. Macrae, *John von Neumann*, p. 72.

38. Lukacs, *Budapest 1900*, p. 188.

39. Ibid., p. 189.

40. Ibid.

41. Ibid., p. 14.

42. Ibid., p. 85.

43. Ibid., p. 91.

44. "Isten vele, Mihály." I heard the story repeatedly from my stepfather (József Pollák, 1901–1973), who belonged to the generation of the Martians. He could not study in Hungary, and lived for years in Italy and France in the 1920s.

45. I. Hargittai, "Beszélgetés Marx Györggyel" (Conversation with George Marx), *Magyar Tudomány* 2003, 48 (7), 883–889, p. 884.

46. Ibid., p. 885.

47. Ulam, *Adventures*, p. 111.

48. George Klein interview, in I. Hargittai, *Candid Science II: Conversations with Famous Biochemical Scientists*. Imperial College Press, London, 2002, pp. 416–441, p. 425.

49. Wigner, *Recollections*, pp. 221–222.

50. W. Laqueur, *Generation Exodus: The Fate of Young Jewish Refugees from Nazi Germany*. Brandeis University Press, Hanover, N.H., 2001, p. xiii.

51. See, e.g., I. Hargittai and M. Hargittai, *In Our Own Image: Personal Symmetry in Discovery*. Kluwer Academic/Plenum Press, New York, 2000, pp. 12–14.

52. M. Polanyi, *Pesti Futár* 1929, pp. 37–38 (English translation by I. Hargittai).

53. Von Kármán, *The Wind*, pp. 26–34.

54. Today it is the Budapest University of Technology and Economics, the result of a recent name change, but for a long time it was called the Budapest Technical University. There are several versions of the name in English, for example, "the King Joseph Institute of Technology" in *Leo Szilard: His Version of the Facts*. The Hungarian name used to be Királyi József Nádor Műszaki Egyetem. In the English translation, Institute of Technology is accurate, but King Joseph is not. What stands before the name Joseph is not a noun (king) but an adjective (royal), and the Joseph after whom the school was named was Archduke Joseph (1776–1847) of the Habsburgs, the palatine of Hungary, acting as surrogate for the king.

55. *A Magyar Tudományos Akadémia tagjai* (Members of the Hungarian Academy of Sciences), vol. 1. MTA, Budapest, 2003, pp. 89–90.

56. Von Kármán, *The Wind*, pp. 26–34.

57. E. Rácz, "Kármán és Magyarország" (Kármán and Hungary). *Fizikai Szemle* 1984, 190–191.

58. Von Kármán, *The Wind*, pp. 26–34.

59. *Mérnök és Építészeti Egylet Közlönye*, Budapest, 1906 (Communications of the Association of Engineers and Architects).

60. Von Kármán, *The Wind*, pp. 26–34.

61. Ibid., pp. 91–95.

62. In addition to von Kármán's *The Wind*, I used Czeizel's *Tudósok génék, tanulságok*.

63. The respective FBI files can now be examined at http://209.132.68.98/pdf/theodore-vonKármán_fbifile_part1a.pdf.

64. Előd Abody (formerly Anderlik), letter to Theodore von Kármán, January 10, 1947. I thank Dr. Tamás Lajos, Budapest, for a copy of this letter received from Tibor Frank. The original is in the California Institute of Technology Archives.

65. Rácz, "Kármán."

66. Radnai, "Szilárd."

67. Weart and Szilard, *Leo Szilard*, p. 5.

68. Charles H. Townes interview, in B. Hargittai and I. Hargittai, *Candid Science V: Conversations with Famous Scientists*. Imperial College Press, London, 2005, pp. 94–137.

69. Weart and Szilard, *Leo Szilard*, p. 5.

70. F. Szabadváry, "Szilárd Leó tanulmányai a Budapesti József Nádor Műegyetemen" (Leo Szilard's studies at the Budapest Palatine Joseph Technical University), *Fizikai Szemle* 1998, p. 63.

71. Weart and Szilard, *Leo Szilard*, p. 5.

72. Ulam, *Adventures*, p.70.

73. Lanouette, *Genius*, p. 46.

74. There are busts of von Kármán, Wigner, and von Neumann in the university garden, but no busts of Szilard or Teller.

75. Lanouette, *Genius*, pp. 50–51.

76. R. W. Clark, *Einstein: The Life and Times*. World Publishing Company, New York, 1971, p. 322.

77. The story is documented in Nagy, *Neumann János*.

78. Ibid., p. 69. In the German translation of the title of his dissertation, the word "general" was absent.

79. Ibid., pp. 64–65.

80. Ibid., pp. 106–107; letter of January 14, 1936, by Neumann to Ortvay.

81. Ibid., pp. 123–124; letter of March 2, 1938, by Ortvay to Neumann.

82. Ibid., pp. 119–120; letter of April 30, 1937, by Neumann to Ortvay.

83. Clarence Larson's video interview with Edward Teller in 1984, unpublished.

84. Teller, *Memoirs*, p. 38.

85. Ibid., p. 37.

86. Ibid., p. 38.

Chapter 2

1. T. von Kármán (with Lee Edson), *The Wind and Beyond: Theodore von Kármán, Pioneer in Aviation and Pathfinder in Space*. Little, Brown, Boston, 1967, p. 34.

2. Ibid., p. 35.

3. Ferenc Molnar was one of the great generation of Hungarians, who, like the Martians, achieved world fame after emigrating to America. His works include *Carousel* and other well-known plays.

4. P. Germain, "Kármán professzor jelentősebb eredményei a hidrodinamikában" (Professor Kármán's significant results in hydrodynamics). *Fizikai Szemle* 1984, 191–192.

5. Von Kármán, *The Wind*, pp. 42–43.

6. Ibid., p. 44.

7. Ibid., p. 47.

8. Ibid., p. 48. The mathematician was Ernst Zermelo, quoted in von Kármán, *The Wind*, p. 50.

9. Ibid., pp. 60–75.

10. Ibid., p. 62.

11. William H. Pickering interview, in B. Hargittai and I. Hargittai, *Candid Science V: Conversations with Famous Scientists*. Imperial College Press, London, 2005, pp. 218–227.

12. G. V. R. Born, *The Born Family in Göttingen and Beyond*. Institut für Wissenschaftgeschichte, Göttingen, 2002. I am grateful to Gustav Born for this book; Max Born might have shared the Physics Prize with his pupil, Werner Heisenberg, who received it in 1933 for the creation of quantum mechanics.

13. Privatdozent roughly corresponded to assistant professor or associate professor in modern terms, but with no assurance of becoming full professor. Specific heat of a substance is the amount of heat needed to increase the temperature of one gram of that substance by one degree (centigrade or kelvin). Its SI unit is J/gK. M. Born, *My Life and My Views*. Charles Scribner's Sons, New York, 1968, pp. 25–27.

14. When Abraham Pais summarized Born's oeuvre, he singled out his contributions to relativity theory, the dynamics of crystal lattices, optics, and quantum physics. A. Pais, *The Genius of Science: A Portrait Gallery of Twentieth-Century Physicists*. Oxford University Press, Oxford, 2000, pp. 30–47. See also, Nevill Mott's introduction, "The Scientific Work of Max Born," to M. Born, *My Life: Recollections of a Nobel Laureate*. Charles Scribner's Sons, New York, 1975, pp. ix–xi.

15. Born, *My Life*, pp. 140–142.

16. Otto Toeplitz, Richard Courant, and Hermann Weyl; von Kármán, *The Wind*, p. 69.

17. Born, *My Life*, p. 141.

18. Von Kármán, *The Wind*, p. 69.

19. Ibid., pp. 70–71.

20. Ibid., p. 71.

21. Ibid.

22. N. T. Greenspan, *The End of the Certain World. The Life and Science of Max Born: The Nobel Physicist Who Ignited the Quantum Revolution*. Basic Books, New York, 2005, pp. 115–116.

23. Von Kármán, *The Wind*, p. 83.

24. Ibid., pp. 96–120.

25. Ibid., p. 97.

26. *Flugwissenschaftliche Vereinigung Aachen* (FVA).

27. Von Kármán, *The Wind*, p. 97.

28. Ibid., pp. 99, 101.

29. *Reichsverkehrsministerium*.

30. Von Kármán, *The Wind*, p. 120.

31. Ibid., pp. 135–138.

32. Ibid., p. 138.

33. http://209.132.68.98/pdf/theodore-vonKármán_fbifile_part1a.pdf.

34. T. Frank, "Theodore von Kármán: A Global Life." In *Modelling Fluid Flow: The State of the Art* (J. Vad, T. Lajos, and R. Schilling, Eds.). Springer-Verlag, Berlin, 2004, pp. 79–89.

35. Incidentally, the Technical University and Humbolt University were on different sides of the Berlin Wall for forty years, so what was a short walk for Szilard was impossible to do for a long time.

36. Nicholas Kurti interview by I. Hargittai, London, 1994, unpublished.

37. Sidney Altman interview, in I. Hargittai, *Candid Science II: Conversations with Famous Biochemical Scientists.* Imperial College Press, London, 2002, pp. 338–349.

38. W. Lanouette (with Bela Silard), *Genius in the Shadows: A Biography of Leo Szilard, The Man Behind the Bomb.* University of Chicago Press, 1992, p. 57.

39. E. P. Wigner (with Andrew Szanton), *The Recollections of E. P. Wigner as Told to Andrew Szanton.* Plenum Press, New York, 1992, p. 98.

40. R. Peierls, *Bird of Passage: Recollections of a Physicist.* Princeton University Press, Princeton, N.J., 1985.

41. O. Frisch, *What Little I Remember.* Cambridge University Press, 1979.

42. Lanouette, *Genius,* p. 60.

43. The second law of thermodynamics has a variety of formulations. One of them is that the entropy of a closed system increases with time.

44. S. R. Weart and G. Weiss Szilard, Eds., *Leo Szilard: His Version of the Facts. Selected Recollections and Correspondence.* MIT Press, Cambridge, Mass., 1978, p. 11.

45. Maxwell's Demon operates a partition dividing two volumes of a gas in such a way as to make the volume of gas containing the fast molecules hotter than it was at the start and the other volume cooler. This would be in violation of the second law.

46. L. E. Kay, *Who Wrote the Book of Life? A History of the Genetic Code.* Stanford University Press, Palo Alto, Calif., 2000, pp. 64–65.

47. H. H. Goldstine, *The Computer from Pascal to von Neumann.* Princeton University Press, Princeton, N.J., 1972, pp. 279–280.

48. Lanouette, *Genius,* p. 64.

49. T. Frank, "Ever Ready to Go: The Multiple Exiles of Leo Szilard." *Physics in Perspective* 2005, 7, 204–252.

50. C. W. Chu, "A Theoretical Alchemist." In *Proceedings of the International Symposium on Frontiers of Science, 2002, Beijing, in Celebration of the 80th Birthday of C. N. Yang* (Hwa-Tung Nieh, Ed.). World Scientific, Singapore, 2003, pp. 514–517.

51. J. D. Watson (with A. Berry), *DNA: The Secret of Life.* Heinemann, London, 2003, p. 58.

52. V. Telegdi, "Szilard as Inventor: Accelerators and More." *Physics Today* 2000, October, 25–28.

53. Lanouette, *Genius,* p. 173.

54. Ibid., p. 66.

55. Ibid., p. 67.

56. H. F. Mark, *From Small Organic Molecules to Large: A Century of Progress.* American Chemical Society, Washington, D.C., 1993.

57. Edward Teller interview, in M. Hargittai and I. Hargittai, *Candid Science IV: Conversations with Famous Physicists*. Imperial College Press, London, 2004, pp. 404–423.

58. Lanouette, *Genius*, p. 89.

59. Ibid., p. 82–89.

60. This relatively mild example of Szilard's correcting Einstein is described by Herman Mark in Mark, *Small Organic Molecules*, p. 29.

61. Lanouette, *Genius*, p. 89.

62. G. Dannen, "The Einstein-Szilard Refrigerators." *Scientific American* 1997, January, pp. 90–95. Kóródi's original name was Kornfeld. His sister, Klára Kornfeld, was the mother of Peter Lax.

63. Weart and Szilard, *Leo Szilard*, p. 12.

64. For this and the remainder of the paragraph, see Lanouette, *Genius*, p. 85.

65. Ibid, p. 100.

66. Ibid., pp. 82–87.

67. Ibid., p. 92.

68. E. Ruska, Nobel lecture. In *Nobel Lectures Including Presentation Speeches and Laureates' Biographies: Physics 1981–1990*. World Scientific, Singapore, 1993, pp. 355–380.

69. D. Gabor, Nobel lecture. In *Nobel Lectures Including Presentation Speeches and Laureates' Biographies: Physics 1971–1980*. World Scientific, Singapore, 1992, pp. 11–44.

70. Lanouette, *Genius*, p. 96.

71. Weart and Szilard, *Leo Szilard*, p. 13.

72. Szanton/Wigner, *Recollections*, pp. 63–81.

73. Ibid., p. 66.

74. Eugene P. Wigner conversations, in M. Hargittai and I. Hargittai, *Candid Science IV*, pp. 2–19.

75. Wigner, *Recollections*, p. 75.

76. Mark, *Small Organic Molecules*.

77. The new technique was gas-phase electron diffraction, which was then taken to the United States by Linus Pauling directly from Mark's laboratory, with Mark's assistance. It was the experimental technique I have used during much of my own research career.

78. Wigner, *Recollections*, pp. 76–81.

79. Ibid., p. 78.

80. E. P. Wigner, "City Hall Speech–Stockholm, 1963." In E. P. Wigner, *Symmetries and Reflections: Scientific Essays*. Indiana University Press, Bloomington, 1967, pp. 262–263.

81. Wigner, *Recollections*, pp. 83–84.

82. Ibid., p. 87.

83. A. Calaprice, Ed., *The Expanded Quotable Einstein*. Princeton University Press, Princeton, N.J., 2000, pp. 241, 245.

84. Wigner, *Recollections*, p. 92.

85. Ibid., pp. 96–97.

86. Ibid., pp. 101–102.

87. Eugene P. Wigner conversations, in M. Hargittai and I. Hargittai, *Candid Science IV*, pp. 2–19.

88. M. Chayut, "From the Periphery: The Genesis of Eugene P. Wigner's Application of Group Theory to Quantum Mechanics." *Foundations of Chemistry* 2001, 3, 55–78.

89. Wigner, *Recollections*, pp. 101–102.

90. Ulam, *Adventures*, p. 112.

91. Wigner, *Recollections*, pp. 115–125.

92. Ibid., p. 116–117.

93. Ibid., p. 117.

94. E. Wigner, group theory book in German: E. Wigner, *Gruppentheorie und ihre Anwendung auf die Quantenmechanik der Atomspektren*. Vieweg, Braunschweig, 1931. English translation: E. P. Wigner, *Group Theory and Its Application to the Quantum Mechanics of Atomic Spectra*. Academic Press, New York, 1959.

95. Wigner, *Recollections*, pp. 124–125.

96. Steven Weinberg interview, in M. Hargittai and I. Hargittai, *Candid Science IV*, pp. 20–31, pp. 29–30.

97. Gerard 't Hooft interview, in M. Hargittai and I. Hargittai, *Candid Science IV*, pp. 110–141, p. 121.

98. E. Vogt, "Eugene Paul Wigner: A Towering Figure of Modern Physics," *Physics Today* December 1995, 40–44; D. J. Gross, "Symmetry in Physics: Wigner's Legacy," *Physics Today* December 1995, 46–50.

99. E. P. Wigner, Nobel lecture. In *Nobel Lectures Including Presentation Speeches and Laureates' Biographies: Physics 1963–1970*. World Scientific, Singapore, 1998, pp. 6–17; Gross, "Symmetry in Physics," pp. 46–50.

100. Wigner, Nobel lecture, pp. 6–17, pp. 6–7.

101. E. P. Wigner, "Symmetry in Nature." In *Proceedings of the Robert A. Welch Foundation Conferences on Chemical Research: XVI. Theoretical Chemistry* (W. O. Milligan, Ed.). The Robert A. Welch Foundation, Houston, Tx., 1973, pp. 231–260.

102. Wigner, *Recollections*, p. 125.

103. Steven Weinberg interview, in M. Hargittai and I. Hargittai, *Candid Science IV*, p. 29.

104. Wigner, *Recollections*, p. 120.

105. J. von Neumann, E. Wigner, "Zur Erklärung einiger Eigenschaften der Spektren aus der Quantenmechanik des Drehelektrons." Parts I, II, III, *Zeitschrift für Physik* 1928, 47, 203; 49, 73; 51, 844.

106. Wigner, *Recollections*, pp. 127–129.

107. Ibid., p. 154.

108. N. Macrae, *John von Neumann: The Scientific Genius Who Pioneered the Modern Computer, Game Theory, Nuclear Deterrence, and Much More*. American Mathematical Society, Providence, R.I., 1999, pp. 96–98.

109. Goldstine, *Computer*, pp. 172–173, 175.

110. Macrae, *John von Neumann*, pp. 146–147.

111. Ibid., pp. 129–132.

112. J. von Neumann, *Mathematische Grundlagen der Quantenmechanik*. Springer-Verlag, Berlin, 1932.

113. Macrae, *John von Neumann*, p. 146.

114. E. Teller (with Judith Shoolery), *Memoirs: A Twentieth-Century Journey in Science and Politics*. Perseus, Cambridge, Mass., 2001, p. 47.

115. P. L. Rose, *Heisenberg and the Nazi Atomic Bomb Project: A Study of German Culture*. University of California Press, Berkeley, 1998, pp. 284–285, 309.

116. M. Frayn, *Copenhagen*. Methuen Drama, London, 1998.

117. J. Medawar and D. Pyke, *Hitler's Gift: Scientists Who Fled Nazi Germany*. Piatkus, London, 2000, pp. 148, 160.

118. I. Buruma, *Wages of Guilt: Memories of War in Germany and Japan*. Vintage, London, 1995, p. 143.

119. Teller, *Memoirs*, pp. 244–245.

120. Buruma, *Wages of Guilt*, p. 143.

121. Teller, *Memoirs*, p. 433.

122. G. Gorelik, "Lev Landau, Prosocialist Prisoner of the Soviet State." *Physics Today* May 1995, 11–15, 86.

123. Vitaly L. Ginzburg interview, in I. Hargittai and M. Hargittai, *Candid Science VI: Conversations with Famous Scientists*. Imperial College Press, London, in press.

124. Edward Teller interview, in M. Hargittai and I. Hargittai, *Candid Science IV*, pp. 404–423.

125. Laszlo Tisza interview, in M. Hargittai and I. Hargittai, *Candid Science IV*, pp. 390–403.

126. Tisza's colleague at MIT, Wolfgang Ketterle, was one of the co-recipients of the 2001 Nobel Prize in Physics for this achievement. Wolfgang Ketterle interview, in M. Hargittai and I. Hargittai, *Candid Science IV*, pp. 368–389.

127. Laszlo Tisza interview, in M. Hargittai and I. Hargittai, *Candid Science IV*, pp. 390–403.

128. Alexei A. Abrikosov interview, in B. Hargittai and I. Hargittai, *Candid Science V*, pp. 176–197.

129. Kenneth S. Pitzer interview, in I. Hargittai, *Candid Science: Conversations with Famous Chemists*. Imperial College Press, London, 2000, pp. 438–447.

130. For a discussion, see, e.g., I. Hargittai and M. Hargittai, *Symmetry Through the Eyes of a Chemist*, 2nd ed., Plenum Press, New York, 1995, pp. 280–285.

131. For the story of this discovery, see B. Davis, "Brunauer, Emmett and Teller (The Personalities behind the BET Method." *Energeia* 1994, 5(6), 1, 4–5; 1995, 6(1), 1, 3–4. See also B. H. Davis, "B, E, & T: The scientists behind surface science." *CHEMTECH* 1991, January, 19–25.

132. Teller, *Memoirs*, p. 113.

133. In 1972, he was asked to give one of the main lectures at a prestigious theoretical chemistry meeting, E. Teller, "Lasers in Chemistry." In *Proceedings of the Robert A. Welch Foundation Conferences on Chemical Research: XVI. Theoretical Chemistry* (W. O. Milligan, Ed.). The Robert A. Welch Foundation, Houston, Tx., 1973, pp. 205–228.

134. The episode is described identically in Teller's *Memoirs*, p. 65, and in Wigner, *Recollections*, p. 123.

135. Teller, *Memoirs*, p. 77.

Chapter 3

1. Quoted on the back cover of the book by J. Medawar and D. Pyke, *Hitler's Gift: Scientists Who Fled Nazi Germany*. Piatkus, London, 2000.

2. E. P. Wigner (with A. Szanton), *The Recollections of Eugene P. Wigner as told to Andrew Szanton*. Plenum Press, New York, 1992, pp. 154–157.

3. T. von Kármán (with Lee Edson), *The Wind and Beyond: Theodore von Kármán, Pioneer in Aviation and Pathfinder in Space*. Little, Brown, Boston, 1967, pp. 142–146.

4. H. Pry, "Kármán aacheni munkássága" (Kármán's activities in Aachen). *Fizikai Szemle* 1984, 192–194.

5. Von Kármán, *The Wind*, pp. 120–121.

6. Ibid., p. 146.

7. Quoted in H. Krebs, in collaboration with Roswitha Schmid, *Otto Warburg: Cell Physiologist, Biochemist, and Eccentric*. Clarendon Press, Oxford, 1981, p. 91, after H. Fraenkel and R. Manvell, *Hermann Göring*. Verlag für Literatur und Zeitgeschehn GmbH, Hannover, 1964, p. 125.

8. Krebs, *Otto Warburg*, p. 59.

9. Von Kármán, *The Wind*, pp. 216–223.

10. Ibid., pp. 222–223.

11. William H. Pickering interview, in B. Hargittai and I. Hargittai, *Candid Science V: Conversations with Famous Scientists*. Imperial College Press, London, 2005, pp. 218–227.

12. Von Kármán, *The Wind*, p. 115.

13. Ibid., pp. 120–121.

14. Ibid., pp. 131–133.

15. Ibid., p. 133.

16. Ibid., p. 173.

17. Ibid., pp. 190–198.

18. Ibid., p. 196.

19. Ibid., p. 200.

20. See, e.g., G. Pendle, *Strange Angel: The Otherworldly Life of Rocket Scientist John Whiteside Parsons*. Harcourt, Orlando, Fla., 2005, p. 82.

21. Von Kármán, *The Wind*, p. 189.

22. Ibid., pp. 154–155.

23. Ibid., pp. 202–215.

24. Ibid., pp. 207–208.

25. Ibid., p. 211.

26. http://209.132.68.98/pdf/theodore-vonKármán_fbifile_part1a.pdf.

27. W. Lanouette (with Bela Silard), *Genius in the Shadows: A Biography of Leo Szilard, The Man Behind the Bomb*. University of Chicago Press, 1992, p. 104.

28. *Leo Szilard: His Version of the Facts. Selected Recollections and Correspondence.* (S. R. Weart and G. Weiss Szilard, Eds.). MIT Press, Cambridge, Mass., 1978, pp. 13–14.

29. See, e.g., M. Perutz, "Enemy Alien." In *I Wish I'd Made You Angry Earlier: Essays on Science and Scientists* (M. Perutz, Ed.). Oxford University Press, Oxford, 1998, pp. 73–106.

30. H. E. Armstrong, "Foreign Scientists in Britain. Professor Kapitza's Recall to Russia." *Times* (London), May 7, 1935. Armstrong was highly critical of the British scientists who expressed their shock over Kapitza's detention in Russia against his will in 1934, but he managed to insert a reminder of the dissatisfaction he had expressed earlier about British universities employing foreign scientists.

31. H. E. Armstrong, "Physical Chemistry in the University of Manchester." *Nature* 1933, 132, 67.

32. Quoted in S. M. Ulam, *Adventures of a Mathematician*. University of California Press, Berkeley, 1991, p. 121.

33. Lanouette, *Genius*, p. 112.

34. Ibid., p. 114.

35. Weart and Szilard, *Leo Szilard*, p. 14.

36. Arno Penzias interview, in M. Hargittai and I. Hargittai, *Candid Science IV: Conversations with Famous Physicists*. Imperial College Press, London, 2004, pp. 272–285.

37. Weart and Szilard, *Leo Szilard*, p. 14.

38. Lanouette, *Genius*, p. 118.

39. Today it exists as the Society for the Protection of Science and Learning.

40. G. A. Olah, *A Life of Magic Chemistry: Autobiographical Reflections of a Nobel Prize Winner*. Wiley-Interscience, New York, 2001, p. 65.

41. Lanouette, *Genius*, pp. 120–122.

42. "Nationalism and Academic Freedom." *Nature* 1933, 131, 853–855, p. 854.

43. T. Frank, "Ever Ready to Go: The Multiple Exiles of Leo Szilard." *Physics in Perspective* 2005, 7, 204–252.

44. Lanouette, *Genius*, pp. 108–109.

45. Ibid., p. 108.

46. Weart and Szilard, *Leo Szilard*, p. 36.

47. The letters from Volmer, Einstein, Ehrenfest, and Schrödinger are quoted in Lanouette, *Genius*, pp. 124, 125, 125–126, and, 126, respectively.

48. F. Crick, *What Mad Pursuit: A Personal View of Scientific Discovery*. Basic Books, 1988, p. 19.

49. Lanouette, *Genius*, pp. 106, 127.

50. P. de Kruif, *Microbe Hunters*. Harcourt Brace, New York, 1926.

51. N. Bohr, "Light and Life." *Nature* 1933, 131, 421, 457; H. G. Wells, *The Science of Life: A Summary of Contemporary Knowledge About Life and its Possibilities*. Amalgamated Press, 1929.

52. E. Rutherford is being quoted in a report "Atomic Transmutation." *Nature* 1933, 132, 432–433, p. 433.

53. Lanouette, *Genius*, pp. 133–143.

54. E. Teller (with Judith Shoolery), *Memoirs: A Twentieth-Century Journey in Science and Politics*. Perseus, Cambridge, Mass., 2001, p. 110.

55. A. Calaprice, Ed., *The Expanded Quotable Einstein*. Princeton University Press, Princeton, N.J., 2000, p. 174, referring to the source, *Einstein on Peace* (O. Nathan and H. Norden, Eds.). Simon and Schuster, New York, 1960, p. 290.

56. Teller, *Memoirs*, p. 110.

57. Weart and Szilard, *Leo Szilard*, p. 17.

58. Nikolai N. Semenov interview, in I. Hargittai, *Candid Science: Conversations with Famous Chemists*, Imperial College Press, London, 2000, pp. 466–475.

59. Lanouette, *Genius*, p. 135.

60. See, e.g., I. Hargittai, *The Road to Stockholm: Nobel Prizes, Science, and Scientists*. Oxford University Press, Oxford, 2002, pp. 169–183.

61. H. G. Wells, *The World Set Free: A Story of Mankind.* Macmillan, London, 1914.

62. Weart and Szilard, *Leo Szilard*, p. 17.

63. Lanouette, *Genius*, p. 145.

64. L. Szilard and T. A. Chalmers, "Chemical Separation of the Radioactive Element from Its Bombarded Isotope in the Fermi Effect." *Nature* 1934, 134, 462.

65. F. Sherwood Rowland, personal communication, Lindau, Germany, 2005.

66. Lanouette, *Genius*, pp. 147–148.

67. Ibid., p. 170.

68. See, e.g., David Shoenberg interview, in M. Hargittai and I. Hargittai, *Candid Science IV*, pp. 688–697.

69. This happened when it was still possible for a foreign national to become FRS, rather than foreign member of the Royal Society as is the case today.

70. See more on Kapitsa in *Kapitza in Cambridge and Moscow: Life and Letters of a Russian Physicist* (J. W. Boag, P. E. Rubinin, and D. Shoenberg, Eds.). North-Holland, Amsterdam, 1990. Note the two different transliterations of Kapitsa's name.

71. Lanouette, *Genius*, pp. 141–143.

72. Ibid., p. 159.

73. Wigner, *Recollections*, pp. 159–160.

74. See, e.g., Philip Anderson interview, in M. Hargittai and I. Hargittai, *Candid Science IV*, pp. 586–601.

75. L. Hoddeson and V. Daitch, *True Genius: The Life and Science of John Bardeen, The Only Winner of Two Nobel Prizes in Physics.* Joseph Henry Press, Washington, D.C., 2002, pp. 51–55, 108.

76. Wigner, *Recollections*, p. 171.

77. A. Pais, *The Genius of Science: A Portrait Gallery of Twentieth-Century Physicists.* Oxford University Press, Oxford, 2000, pp. 339–340.

78. Wigner, *Recollections*, pp. 171–174.

79. R. Serber (with R. P. Crease), *Peace & War: Reminiscences of a Life on the Frontier of Science.* Columbia University Press, New York, 1998, p. 19.

80. Wigner, *Recollections*, p. 179.

81. Pais, *Genius of Science*, pp. 339–340.

82. H. Weyl, *Symmetry.* Princeton University Press, Princeton, N.J., 1952.

83. N. Macrae, *John von Neumann: The Scientific Genius Who Pioneered the Modern Computer, Game Theory, Nuclear Deterrence, and Much More.* American Mathematical Society, Providence, R.I., 1999, pp. 157–161.

84. T. Frank, "Double Divorce: The Case of Mariette and John von Neumann." *Nevada Historical Society Quarterly* Summer 1991, 360–363.

85. Wigner, *Recollections*, p. 134.

86. Macrae, *John von Neumann*, p. 159.

87. E. Regis, *Who Got Einstein's Office? Eccentricity and Genius at the Institute for Advanced Study.* Perseus Publishing, Cambridge, Mass., 1987.

88. Macrae, *John von Neumann*, pp. 169, 178.

89. Ibid., p. 172.

90. Ibid., p. 171.

91. Ibid., p. 180.

92. Teller, *Memoirs*, pp. 96–108.

93. Ibid., pp. 116–117.

94. G. Gamow, *My World Line: An Informal Autobiography*. Viking Press, New York, 1970. This is an unfinished autobiography with a Foreword by Stanislaw M. Ulam.

95. Teller, *Memoirs*, pp. 117–123.

96. Gamow, *My World Line*, pp. 108–123.

97. This was in an interview in writing for the *New York Post* after the Oppenheimer hearing. I thank Judith Shoolery for a copy of Gamow's original handwritten answers to Fern Marja's questions.

98. Teller, *Memoirs*, p. 137.

99. Ibid., p. 119.

100. Ibid., pp. 117–123.

101. Edward Teller interview, in M. Hargittai and I. Hargittai, *Candid Science IV*, pp. 404–423.

102. See, e.g., I. Hargittai, "The Great Soviet Resonance Controversy." In I. Hargittai, *Candid Science*, pp. 8–13.

103. Teller, *Memoirs*, pp. 132–134.

104. Ibid., pp. 143–145.

105. V. F. Weisskopf, *The Privilege of Being a Physicist*, W. H. Freeman, New York, 1989; John A. Wheeler interview, in M. Hargittai and I. Hargittai, *Candid Science IV*, pp. 424–439.

106. Teller, *Memoirs*, pp. 143–145.

107. Ibid., p. 145.

108. Ibid., pp. 149–150.

109. *The Public Papers and Addresses of Franklin D. Roosevelt*, with a Special Introduction and Explanatory Notes by President Roosevelt (Samuel I. Rosenman, comp.), 1940 vol.: *War—And Aid to Democracies*. MacMillan, New York, 1941, pp. 184–187, as quoted in Teller, *Memoirs*, pp. 149–150.

Chapter 4

1. A. H. Compton, *Atomic Quest: A Personal Narrative*. Oxford University Press, New York, 1956, p. 55.

2. S. R. Weart and G. Weiss Szilard, Eds., *Leo Szilard: His Version of the Facts. Selected Recollections and Correspondence*. MIT Press, Cambridge, Mass., 1978, p. 177.

3. T. von Kármán (with Lee Edson), *The Wind and Beyond: Theodore von Kármán, Pioneer in Aviation and Pathfinder in Space*. Little, Brown, Boston, 1967, p. 224.

4. L. Edson, Introduction, "Collaboration with a Genius," to von Kármán, *The Wind*, p. 5.

5. Von Kármán, *The Wind*, pp. 123, 157–164.

6. Ibid., pp. 216–234.

7. There was a Hungarian pioneer of jet propulsion, Albert Fonó, whose suggestion for such torpedoes was turned down by the Austro-Hungarian military leadership during World War I. He patented a jet propulsion motor in 1928. Fonó, in his obituary of von Kármán [A. Fonó, "Kármán Tódor (1881–1963)." *Fizikai Szemle* 1963, 230–231], men-

tioned that von Kármán recognized Fonó's pioneering work and never considered himself to be the inventor of the supersonic jet, whereas according to Fonó, it was indeed von Kármán who developed it into a science.

8. Von Kármán, *The Wind*, p. 225.

9. Ibid., p. 224.

10. Ibid., pp. 233–234.

11. Ibid., pp. 229–230.

12. There is a whole section on the importance of naming of new discoveries in I. Hargittai, *The Road to Stockholm: Nobel Prizes, Science, and Scientists*. Oxford University Press, Oxford, 2002, pp. 184–191.

13. Von Kármán, *The Wind*, p. 233.

14. John W. Parsons, whose life was cut tragically short in an explosion, is the subject of a recent book: G. Pendle, *Strange Angel: The Otherworldly Life of a Rocket Scientist John Whiteside Parsons*. Harcourt, Orlando, Fla., 2005.

15. Von Kármán, *The Wind*, p. 238.

16. Ibid., pp. 243–244.

17. Ibid., pp. 247–248.

18. Ibid., pp. 255–256.

19. Ibid., p. 254.

20. Ibid., pp. 256–265.

21. Ibid., pp. 267–268.

22. Norman Ramsey interview (by M. Hargittai), in M. Hargittai and I. Hargittai, *Candid Science IV: Conversations with Famous Physicists*. Imperial College Press, London, 2004, pp. 316–343; von Kármán, *The Wind*, pp. 265–271.

23. Von Kármán, *The Wind*, pp. 265–271.

24. Ibid., p. 279.

25. W. Lanouette (with Bela Silard), *Genius in the Shadows: A Biography of Leo Szilard, The Man Behind the Bomb*. University of Chicago Press, 1992, p. 175.

26. L. L. Strauss, *Men and Decisions*. Popular Library, New York, 1963.

27. Ibid., pp. 174–176.

28. The letter is reproduced in full in Weart and Szilard, *Leo Szilard: His Version*, p. 62 (document 22).

29. E. Teller (with Judith Shoolery), *Memoirs: A Twentieth-Century Journey in Science and Politics*. Perseus Publishing, Cambridge, Mass., 2001, p. 142.

30. Weart and Szilard, *Leo Szilard*, pp. 113–114 (document 70, including footnote on p. 114).

31. L. Szilard, "The Sensitive Minority among Men of Science." In *Leo Szilárd Centenary Volume* (G. Marx, Ed.). Eötvös Physical Society, Budapest, 1998, pp. 176–184, p. 176.

32. Teller, *Memoirs*, p. 142.

33. Weart and Szilard, *Leo Szilard*, p. 56.

34. E. P. Wigner (with A. Szanton), *The Recollections of Eugene P. Wigner as Told to Andrew Szanton*. Plenum Press, New York, 1992, p. 199. Wigner says that Einstein "grasped the situation" within ten minutes. In a 1973 interview, he said that "Einstein understood it in half a minute." J. Walsh, "A Conversation with Eugene Wigner." *Science* 1973, 181, 527–533.

35. Walsh, "A Conversation with Eugene Wigner," p. 530.

36. See, e.g., G. Herken, *Cardinal Choices: Presidential Science Advising from the Atomic Bomb to SDI*, revised and expanded edition. Stanford University Press, Palo Alto, Calif., 2000, p. 15.

37. Weart and Szilard, *Leo Szilard*, p. 84.

38. Ibid., pp. 94–96. The letter is reprinted here courtesy of the Albert Einstein Archives, The Jewish National & University Library, © The Hebrew University of Jerusalem, Israel.

39. Lanouette, *Genius*, p. 210.

40. Hans Bethe on Szilard's contribution, in M. Palevsky, *Atomic Fragments: A Daughter's Questions*. University of California Press, Berkeley, 2000, p. 23.

41. A. Calaprice, Ed., *The Expanded Quotable Einstein*. Princeton University Press, Princeton, N.J., 2000, p. 377, referring to the source, Z. Rosenkranz, *Albert through the Looking Glass: The Personal Papers of Albert Einstein*. Jewish National and University Library, Jerusalem, 1998, pp. 66–67.

42. Wigner, *Recollections*, pp. 203–204.

43. Walsh, "A Conversation with Eugene Wigner," p. 530.

44. Weart and Szilard, *Leo Szilard*, pp. 119–126.

45. H. G. Wells, *The World Set Free: A Story of Mankind*. Macmillan, London, 1914.

46. R. Polenberg, Ed., *In the Matter of J. Robert Oppenheimer: The Security Clearance Hearing*. Cornell University Press, Ithaca, N.Y., 2002, p. 156.

47. Weart and Szilard, *Leo Szilard*, p. 117.

48. Lanouette, *Genius*, p. 248.

49. Ibid., pp. 223–227.

50. Weart and Szilard, *Leo Szilard*, pp. 115–116.

51. Leo Szilard to Vannevar Bush on August 11, 1943, quoted in T. Frank, "Ever Ready to Go: The Multiple Exiles of Leo Szilard." *Physics in Perspective* 2005, 7, 204–252, p. 225.

52. Weart and Szilard, *Leo Szilard*, p. 178.

53. Frank, "Ever Ready to Go," 204–252.

54. Compton, *Atomic Quest*, p. 120.

55. L. M. Groves, *Now It Can Be Told: The Story of the Manhattan Project*, Harper, New York, 1962. Groves was promoted to general ostensibly to command higher authority, but also as a sweetener, as he was not initially very eager to accept the assignment.

56. E. Teller, Introduction. In Groves, *Now It Can Be Told*, pp. iii–ix, p. viii.

57. Compton, *Atomic Quest*, p. 113.

58. Teller, Introduction, p. v.

59. S. Goldberg, "Groves and the Scientists: Compartmentalization and the Building of the Bomb," *Physics Today* 1995, August, 38–43; S. Goldberg, *Fighting to Build the Bomb: The Private Wars of General Leslie R. Groves*, Steerforth Press, South Royalton, Vt., 1995.

60. A. C. Brown and C. B. MacDonald, Eds., *The Secret History of the Atomic Bomb*. Dial Press, New York, 1977.

61. H. Thayer, *Management of the Hanford Engineer Works in World War II: How the Corps, DuPont and the Metallurgical Laboratory Fast Tracked the Original Plutonium Works*. ASCE Press, New York, 1996.

62. L. M. Groves, *Now It Can Be Told: The Story of the Manhattan Project*. Da Capo Press, New York, 1983 (first published in 1962), pp. 44–45.

63. P. M. Stern (with H. P. Green), *The Oppenheimer Case: Security on Trial.* Harper & Row, New York, 1969, p. 43.

64. O. Frisch, *What Little I Remember.* Cambridge University Press, Cambridge, 1979; R. Peierls, *Bird of Passage: Recollections of a Physicist.* Princeton University Press, Princeton, N.J., 1985.

65. Frank, "Ever Ready to Go," p. 222.

66. D. C. Cassidy, *J. Robert Oppenheimer and the American Century.* Pi Press, New York, 2005, pp. 218–219.

67. Also in hindsight, C. P. Snow dismissed any possible impact of Einstein's letter on subsequent events; see C. P. Snow, *Variety of Man*, Charles Scribner's Sons, New York, 1966, pp. 118–119.

68. Lanouette, *Genius*, p. 235.

69. Weart and Weiss Szilard, *Leo Szilard: His Version*, pp. 189–192.

70. Lanouette, *Genius*, pp. 256–257.

71. Ibid., p. 236.

72. Weart and Szilard, *Leo Szilard*, p. xvii.

73. Lanouette, *Genius*, pp. 306, 308.

74. H. Bethe, "Szilard Worked First to Build the Bomb and Then to Oppose It." *Physics Today* 1993, September, 63–64.

75. Groves, *Now It Can Be Told*, 1962; Szilard fared better than some others: Groves sidestepped some controversial issues and entirely ignored certain people with whom he did not get along, according to R. S. Norris, *Racing for the Bomb: General Leslie R. Groves, The Manhattan Project's Indispensable Man*, Steerforth Press, South Royalton, Vt., 2002, p. 522.

76. Groves, *Now It Can Be Told*, 1962, p. 45.

77. Ibid., p. 420.

78. Lanouette, *Genius*, p. 245.

79. Compton, *Atomic Quest*, p. 143.

80. Ibid., p. 139.

81. Lanouette, *Genius*, pp. 249–250.

82. See, e.g., R. Rhodes, *The Making of the Atomic Bomb.* Simon & Schuster, New York, 1986, pp. 504–506.

83. R. Kunfalvi, "Emlékeim Szilárd Leóról: Beszélgetés D. Hawkins professzorral" (My recollections of Leo Szilard: Conversation with Professor D. Hawkins). *Fizikai Szemle* 1976, 353–356. David Hawkins of the University of Colorado at Boulder was a young philosopher during World War II and did office work for Robert Oppenheimer at Los Alamos. He told about a group of people who dealt with various patent issues related to the atomic bombs that were expected to become important after the war. A young lawyer, who was also an army officer, used to complain to Hawkins about the difficulties Szilard caused them. When Hawkins met Szilard and asked him about the patent issues, Szilard told him the quoted story.

84. Lanouette, *Genius*, pp. 260–262.

85. Herken, *Cardinal Choices*, p. 3.

86. Lanouette, *Genius*, p. 262.

87. Weart and Szilard, *Leo Szilard*, pp. 181–188.

88. Lanouette, *Genius*, pp. 269–273.

89. Compton, *Atomic Quest*, p. 242.

90. Weart and Szilard, *Leo Szilard*, pp. 211–212 (document 107).

91. S. A. Goudsmit, *Alsos*. Tomash Publishers and American Institute of Physics, San Franciso, 1983.

92. Weart and Szilard, *Leo Szilard*, pp. 211–212 (document 107).

93. Lanouette, *Genius*, p. 276.

94. I experienced this when visiting Hiroshima in the 1990s. Being a Hungarian scientist, I was wondering whether I would be received with any hostile sentiments; but it was the opposite: the people I came across remembered Szilard in a most appreciative way.

95. Lanouette, *Genius*, pp. 278–279.

96. H. DeWolf Smyth, *Atomic Energy for Military Purposes: The Official Report on the Development of the Atomic Bomb under the Auspices of the United States Government, 1940–1945*. Princeton University Press, Princeton, N.J., 1945.

97. Lanouette, *Genius*, pp. 278–279.

98. Weart and Szilard, *Leo Szilard*, p. 163 (document 97).

99. See "Leo Szilard, Interview: President Truman Did Not Understand." In *U.S. News & World Report* 1960, August 15, pp. 68–71; www.peak.org/~danneng/decision/usnews.html.

100. L. W. Alvarez, *Alvarez: Adventures of a Physicist*. Basic Books, New York, 1987, p. 150.

101. H. W. French, "100,000 People Perished, but Who Remembers?" *The New York Times*, March 14, 2002, p. A4. I am grateful to Maurice Goldhaber for this reference.

102. Compton, *Atomic Quest*, p. 228.

103. Philip Anderson interview, in M. Hargittai and I. Hargittai, *Candid Science IV*, pp. 586–601.

104. Palevsky, *Atomic Fragments*, p. 31.

105. I. Hargittai, "'You are pleasantly disagreeable': Eugene P. Wigner Remembers." *Chemical Intelligencer* 1999, 5 (3), 50–52. It is based on a video recording of March 4, 1986, by Clarence Larson.

106. John A. Wheeler interview, in M. Hargittai and I. Hargittai, *Candid Science IV*, pp. 424–439, p. 435.

107. N. Bohr and J. A. Wheeler, "The Mechanism of Nuclear Fission." *Physical Review* 1939, 56, 426–450.

108. Wigner, *Recollections*, p. 192.

109. Ibid., p. 198.

110. Weart and Szilard, *Leo Szilard: His Version of the Facts*, p. 83.

111. Teller, *Memoirs*, p. 146.

112. The NBS was the predecessor of today's National Institute of Science and Technology (NIST).

113. Wigner, *Recollections*, pp. 203–204.

114. Ibid., p. 207.

115. Compton, *Atomic Quest*, p. 55.

116. Wigner, *Recollections*, p. 212.

117. Frank, "Ever Ready to Go," pp. 204–252.

118. Ibid., pp. 212–218.

119. Compton, *Atomic Quest*, p. 55.

120. In full, E. I. du Pont de Nemours and Company.

121. Alvin Weinberg, "Eugene Wigner, the First Nuclear Engineer." In *Eugene Paul Wigner Centennial* (G. Marx, Ed.). Roland Eötvös Physical Society, Budapest, 2002, pp. 144–159.

122. Compton, *Atomic Quest*, p. 167.

123. Walsh, "Conversation with Eugene W

igner," 527–533.

124. E. P. Wigner, "Twentieth Birthday of the Atomic Age." In E. P. Wigner, *Symmetries and Reflections: Scientific Essays of Eugene P. Wigner*. Indiana University Press, Bloomington, 1967, pp. 238–244.

125. Compton, *Atomic Quest*, pp. 168–169.

126. Ibid., p. 169.

127. Weart and Szilard, *Leo Szilard*, p. 149.

128. Compton, *Atomic Quest*, pp. 168–169.

129. Groves, *Now It Can Be Told*, 1962, p. 51.

130. Ibid., p. 59.

131. Wigner, *Recollections*, p. 249.

132. I. Hargittai, "'You are pleasantly disagreeable'," pp. 50–52.

133. John A. Wheeler interview, in M. Hargittai and I. Hargittai, *Candid Science IV*, pp. 426–427.

134. Alvarez, *Alvarez*, p. 150.

135. Palevsky, *Atomic Fragments*, p. 28.

136. Luis Alvarez interview, in B. Hargittai and I. Hargittai, *Candid Science V: Conversations with Famous Scientists*. Imperial College Press, London, 2005, pp. 198–217.

137. Maurice Goldhaber interview, in M. Hargittai and I. Hargittai, *Candid Science IV*, pp. 214–231.

138. Compton, *Atomic Quest*, p. 226.

139. N. Macrae, *John von Neumann: The Scientific Genius Who Pioneered the Modern Computer, Game Theory, Nuclear Deterrence, and Much More*. American Mathematical Society, Providence, R.I., 1999, pp. 191–197.

140. Ibid., p. 194.

141. Ibid., p. 202.

142. Ibid., p. 205.

143. S. M. Ulam, *Adventures of a Mathematician*. University of California Press, Berkeley and Los Angeles, 1991, p. 141.

144. Macrae, *John von Neumann*, p. 208.

145. Ibid.

146. Ibid., p. 238.

147. Teller, *Memoirs*, pp. 173–177.

148. Edward Teller dictated a twenty-page memorandum in George A. (Jay) Keyworth's office on September 20, 1979, after suffering a heart attack that he ascribed to the strained political atmosphere in the wake of the Three Mile Island nuclear plant accident. I am grateful to Richard L. Garwin for a copy of this memorandum.

149. R. Serber (with R. P. Crease), *Peace & War: Reminiscences of a Life on the Frontiers of Science.* Columbia University Press, New York, 1998.

150. Macrae, *John von Neumann*, p. 238.

151. H. H. Goldstine, *The Computer from Pascal to von Neumann.* Princeton University Press, Princeton, N.J., 1972, pp. 180–182.

152. Quoted in Macrae, *John von Neumann*, p. 210.

153. Ibid., pp. 230–232.

154. Ibid., p. 245; this a reference to G. H. Hardy's *A Mathematician's Apology,* reprint edition, Cambridge University Press, Cambridge, 1992.

155. Teller, *Memoirs*, pp. 151–154.

156. Ibid., p. 151.

157. Ibid., p. 157.

158. Teller memorandum, September 20, 1979.

159. Teller, *Memoirs*, pp. 157–160.

160. Ibid., pp. 151–154.

161. Ibid., p. 210.

162. Ibid., p. 172.

163. Ibid., pp. 176–177.

164. A. Koestler, *Darkness at Noon*, Macmillan, New York, 1941; Edward Teller interview, in M. Hargittai and I. Hargittai, *Candid Science IV*, pp. 404–423; Teller, *Memoirs*, pp. 181–183.

165. Edward Teller interview, in M. Hargittai and I. Hargittai, *Candid Science IV*, p. 109.

166. Teller, *Memoirs*, p. 183.

167. Ibid., p. 188.

168. Ibid., p. 206.

169. Ibid., p. 209.

170. See Edward Teller in the NOVA documentary *Genius Behind the Bomb: Leo Szilard.* Helen Weiss Productions, Washington, D.C., 1992.

171. Teller, *Memoirs*, pp. 215–216.

172. Ibid., p. 217.

173. Ibid., p. 219.

Chapter 5

1. The future Nobel Peace Prize winner Joseph Rotblat.

2. Nicholas Kurti interview by I. Hargittai in London, 1994, unpublished.

3. The story is authentically described in Lord Alder and R. Dalby, *The Dervish of Windsor Castle: The Life of Arminius Vambery.* Bachman & Turner, London, 1979, p. 318. I thank Tibor Frank for this reference.

4. S. M. Ulam, *Adventures of a Mathematician.* University of California Press, Berkeley, 1991, p. 49.

5. H. S. Hawkins, G. A. Greb, and G. Weiss Szilard, Eds., *Toward a Livable World: Leo Szilard and the Crusade for Nuclear Arms Control.* MIT Press, Cambridge, Mass., 1987.

6. T. von Kármán (with Lee Edson), *The Wind and Beyond: Theodore von Kármán, Pioneer in Aviation and Pathfinder in Space.* Little, Brown, Boston, 1967, pp. 273–274.

7. Ibid., pp. 284–295.

8. E. L. Feinberg, "Soviet Science in Danger." *Physics Today* May 1992, 30–38, p. 31.

9. Von Kármán, *The Wind*, p. 291.

10. E. Teller (with Judith Shoolery), *Memoirs: A Twentieth-Century Journey in Science and Politics.* Perseus, Cambridge, Mass., 2001, pp. 224–226.

11. Von Kármán, *The Wind*, p. 289–294.

12. Ibid., pp. 298–299.

13. Ibid., pp. 301–307.

14. Ibid., pp. 308–311.

15. T. Hager, *Force of Nature: The Life of Linus Pauling.* Simon & Schuster, New York, 1995, pp. 351–354.

16. Von Kármán, *The Wind*, pp. 301–307.

17. Ibid., pp. 305–306.

18. Ibid., p. 307.

19. Ibid., pp. 322–323.

20. William H. Pickering interview, in B. Hargittai and I. Hargittai, *Candid Science V: Conversations with Famous Scientists.* Imperial College Press, London, 2005, pp. 218–227.

21. Von Kármán, *The Wind*, p. 324.

22. Ibid., p. 333.

23. Ibid., pp. 351, 352.

24. W. Lanouette (with Bela Silard), *Genius in the Shadows: A Biography of Leo Szilard, The Man Behind the Bomb.* University of Chicago Press, 1992, p. 284.

25. Ibid., pp. 290, 294; *Congressional Record*, November 14, 1945, pp. A4877–A4878; *The New York Times*, November 9, 1945.

26. Ibid., p. 296.

27. Ibid., p. 298.

28. Ibid., pp. 348–349.

29. See, e.g., I. Hargittai, *Our Lives: Encounters of a Scientist.* Akadémiai Kiadó, Budapest, 2004, p. 146.

30. A. Novick, "Phenotypic Mixing." In *Phage and the Origins of Molecular Biology*, expanded ed.(J. Cairns, G. S. Stent, and J. D. Watson, Eds.). Cold Spring Harbor Laboratory Press, Cold Spring Harbor, N.Y., 1992, pp. 133–141.

31. Lanouette, *Genius*, p. 315.

32. L. E. Kay, *Who Wrote the Book of Life? A History of the Genetic Code.* Stanford University Press, Palo Alto, Calif., 2000, p. 167.

33. B. Schechter, *My Brain Is Open: The Mathematical Journeys of Paul Erdős.* Oxford University Press, Oxford, 1998, p. 190.

34. Barton J. Bernstein quoting Dennis Gabor in Hawkins et al., *Toward a Livable World*, p. xxii.

35. E. Schrödinger, *What Is Life? The Physicist's Approach to the Subject—With an Epilogue of Determinism and Free Will.* Cambridge University Press, 1944.

36. See, e.g., Gunther Stent interview, in B. Hargittai and I. Hargittai, *Candid Science V*, pp. 480–527.

37. See, e.g., a set of fascinating papers in Cairns et al., *Phage*.

38. Walter Gilbert interview, in I. Hargittai, *Candid Science II: Conversations with Famous Biochemical Scientists.* Imperial College Press, London, 2002, pp. 98–113.

39. I. Hargittai, *The Road to Stockholm: Nobel Prizes, Science, and Scientists.* Oxford University Press, Oxford, 2002, pp. 169–183.

40. V. Telegdi, "Szilard as Inventor: Accelerators and More." *Physics Today* 2000, October, 25–28, p. 28.

41. Quoted in D. A. Grandy, *Leo Szilard: Science as a Mode of Being.* University Press of America, Lanham, Maryland, 1996, p. 166, from *International Science and Technology*, May 1962, 36.

42. James D. Watson interview, in I. Hargittai, *Candid Science II*, pp. 2–15; François Jacob interview, in I. Hargittai, *Candid Science II*, pp. 84–97; Rita Levi-Montalcini interview, in I. Hargittai, *Candid Science II*, pp. 364–375; George Klein interview, in I. Hargittai, *Candid Science II*, pp. 416–441.

43. Monod's Nobel lecture. In *Nobel Lectures including Presentation Speeches and Laureates' Biographies: Physiology or Medicine 1963–1970.* World Scientific, Singapore, pp. 188–209.

44. Kay, *Book of Life*, p. 201.

45. Marshall W. Nirenberg interview, in I. Hargittai, *Candid Science II*, pp. 130–141, p. 140.

46. James D. Watson interview, in I. Hargittai, *Candid Science II*, pp. 2–15.

47. François Jacob interview, in I. Hargittai, *Candid Science II*, p. 91.

48. Kay, *Book of Life*, p. 167. The quotation here is from the Szilard application.

49. Novick, "Phenotypic Mixing," pp. 133–141, p. 140.

50. D. M. Blow, "Max Ferdinand Perutz OM CH CBE." *Biographical Memoirs of Fellows of the Royal Society* 2004, 50, 227–256, and references therein, including some unpublished manuscripts by Max Perutz.

51. Max Perutz interview, in I. Hargittai, *Candid Science II*, pp. 280–295.

52. Lanouette, *Genius*, p. 333.

53. Ibid., p. 366.

54. See note to document 1, in Hawkins et al., *Toward a Livable World*, p. 20.

55. Lanouette, *Genius*, pp. 320–322.

56. Ibid., p. 364.

57. Ibid., pp. 325–326.

58. Ibid., p. 357.

59. B. J. Barton, in Hawkins et al., *Toward a Livable World*, p. xlv.

60. He mentions this in an interview, excerpts from which are included in a NOVA documentary, *Genius behind the Bomb: Leo Szilard.* Helen Weiss Productions, Washington, D.C., 1992.

61. J. W. Boag, P. E. Rubinin, and D. Shoenberg, Eds., *Kapitza in Cambridge and Moscow: Life and Letters of a Russian Physicist.* North-Holland, Amsterdam, 1990.

62. Hawkins et al., *Toward a Livable World*, pp. 279–287.

63. Lanouette, *Genius*, p. 416.

64. Hawkins et al., *Toward a Livable World*, pp. 279–287.

65. Matthew Meselson interview, in I. Hargittai and M. Hargittai, *Candid Science VI: Conversations with Famous Scientists.* Imperial College Press, London, in press.

66. Lanouette, *Genius*, p. 428.

67. Leo Szilard's letter of March 27, 1963, to Eugene P. Wigner from Hotel Dupont Plaza, Washington. Archives of *Fizikai Szemle*, Budapest.

68. Lanouette, *Genius*, pp. 327–368.

69. L. Szilard, "The Sensitive Minority among Men of Science." In *Leo Szilard Centenary Volume* (G. Marx, Ed.). Eötvös Physical Society, Budapest, 1998, pp. 176, 184, pp. 176, 182.

70. Matthew Meselson interview, in Hargittai and Hargittai, *Candid Science VI*.

71. Szilard, "The Sensitive Minority," p. 183.

72. See "Leo Szilard, Interview: President Truman Did Not Understand." *U.S. News & World Report* 1960, August 15, pp. 68–71; http://www.peak.org/~danneng/decision/usnews.html. The quote is on p. 7 of the web document.

73. See, e.g., the Szilard–Teller debate in 1960, referred to in Lanouette, *Genius*, p. 411.

74. Vitaly L. Ginzburg interview in I. Hargittai and M. Hargittai, *Candid Science VI*, in press (the original conversation was in Russian); it is known from other sources that the person Ginzburg referred to was Lev D. Landau.

75. Lanouette, *Genius*, p. 357.

76. J. Rotblat, "The Early Days of Pugwash." *Physics Today* 2001, 54 (6), June, 50–55.

77. Szilard, "The Sensitive Minority among Men of Science," pp. 176–184.

78. Lanouette, *Genius*, p. 410.

79. Ibid., p. 357.

80. Ibid., p. 433.

81. John F. Kennedy to Leo Szilard, May 27, 1960, addressed to the Memorial Hospital at 68th Street and York Avenue. Thanks to the late George Marx for a copy of this document.

82. In the 1990s, Representative William Richardson of New Mexico, went on a self-appointed mission to North Korea, and it proved to be a pivotal point for his subsequent career as energy secretary in the Clinton Administration.

83. Lanouette, *Genius*, p. 433.

84. Tibor Frank is quoting Szilard in a letter of November 14, 1963 to Kennedy. T. Frank, "Ever Ready to Go: The Multiple Exiles of Leo Szilard." *Physics in Perspective* 2005, 7, 204–252.

85. Lanouette, *Genius*, pp. 456–458.

86. Ibid., pp. 437–438.

87. Ibid., pp. 454, 461.

88. Ibid., p. 455.

89. E. P. Wigner (with Andrew Szanton), *The Recollections of E. P. Wigner as Told to Andrew Szanton*. Plenum Press, New York, 1992, pp. 267–270.

90. Teller, *Memoirs*, p. 269.

91. K. Z. Morgan and K. M. Peterson, *The Angry Genie: One Man's Walk through the Nuclear Age*. University of Oklahoma Press, Norman, 1999, p. 66.

92. Wigner, *Recollections*, p. 269.

93. Ibid., pp. 270–271.

94. Ibid., p. 261.

95. David Gross interview, in I. Hargittai and M. Hargittai, *Candid Science VI*, in press.

96. Wigner, *Recollections*, pp. 287–297.

97. Eugene P. Wigner conversations, in M. Hargittai and I. Hargittai, *Candid Science IV: Conversations with Famous Physicists.* Imperial College Press, London, 2004, pp. 2–19. Note, though, that one of the lines crosses the Danube under the river, so it has to be deep underground.

98. Maurice Goldhaber interview, in M. Hargittai and I. Hargittai, *Candid Science IV*, pp. 214–231.

99. A. M. Weinberg, *Reflections on Big Science.* MIT Press, Cambridge, Mass., 1967, p. 139.

100. N. Macrae, *John von Neumann: The Scientific Genius Who Pioneered the Modern Computer, Game Theory, Nuclear Deterrence, and Much More.* American Mathematical Society, Providence, R.I., 1999, p. 334.

101. Kay, *Book of Life*, p. 104; S. J. Heims, *John von Neumann and Norbert Wiener: From Mathematics to the Technologies of Life and Death.* MIT Press, Cambridge, Mass., 1980, p. 247.

102. H. H. Goldstine, *The Computer from Pascal to von Neumann.* Princeton University Press, 1972, p. 224.

103. Macrae, *John von Neumann*, pp. 333–336.

104. Ibid., pp. 341, 347.

105. Ibid., p. 347.

106. Ibid., pp. 352–353.

107. Ibid., p. 354.

108. Ibid., p. 357.

109. H. F. York, *The Advisors: Oppenheimer, Teller, and the Superbomb.* W. H. Freeman, San Francisco, 1976, p. 95.

110. Macrae, *John von Neumann*, pp. 358–362.

111. Ibid., pp. 367–368.

112. Teller, *Memoirs*, pp. 220–221.

113. Ibid., p. 223.

114. Ibid., p. 234.

115. Ibid., pp. 235–238.

116. Ibid., p. 251.

117. Hwa-Tung Nieth, Ed., *In Celebration of the 80th Birthday of C. N. Yang: Proceedings of the International Symposium on Frontiers of Science, 2002 Beijing.* World Scientific, Singapore, 2003.

118. Teller, *Memoirs*, p. 258.

119. Ibid., pp. 253–254.

120. Ibid., pp. 259–260.

121. Ibid., p. 269.

122. Ibid., p. 360.

123. H. Brown and M. May, "Edward Teller in the Public Arena." *Physics Today* 2004, 51–53, p. 53.

124. Teller, *Memoirs*, p. 289.

125. Ibid., p. 279.

126. Ibid., pp. 280–282.

127. P. M. Stern (with H. P. Green), *The Oppenheimer Case: Security on Trial.* Harper & Row, New York, 1969, p. 138.

128. Glenn T. Seaborg interview, in I. Hargittai, *Candid Science III: More Conversations with Famous Chemists*. Imperial College Press, London, 2003.

129. G. T. Seaborg, *A Chemist in the White House: From the Manhattan Project to the End of the Cold War*. American Chemical Society, Washington, D.C., 1998, p. 18.

130. The whole letter of October 14, 1949, by Seaborg to Oppenheimer is quoted in Seaborg, *Chemist in the White House*, pp. 41–42.

131. It surfaced only in the Oppenheimer hearings in 1954, as mentioned in York, *The Advisors*, p. 48, footnote 2. The way York is restating Seaborg's position is not quite the same as what Seaborg found worthy of highlighting in his book, *Chemist in the White House*, from which I quote in the main text. According to York, "In essence, Seaborg's letter says he would have to know a lot more about the matter before he could agree to oppose going ahead with the super."

132. The two recommendations (majority and minority) of the GAC are reproduced in full, for example, in Seaborg, *A Chemist in the White House*, pp. 42–43.

133. Ibid., p. 43.

134. Stern, *Oppenheimer Case*, p. 146, footnote.

135. York, *The Advisors*, p. 54.

136. L. L. Strauss, *Men and Decisions*. Popular Library, New York, 1963, p. 212.

137. Vitaly L. Ginzburg interview, in I. Hargittai and M. Hargittai, *Candid Science VI*, in press.

138. Kenneth S. Pitzer interview, in I. Hargittai, *Candid Science: Conversations with Famous Chemists*. Imperial College Press, London, 2000, pp. 438–447, p. 443.

139. D. Holloway, *Stalin and the Bomb: The Soviet Union and Atomic Energy, 1939–1956*. Yale University Press, New Haven, Conn., 1994, p. 318.

140. York, *The Advisors*, p. 34.

141. A. B. Kojevnikov, *Stalin's Great Science: The Times and Adventures of Soviet Physicists*. Imperial College Press, London, 2004.

142. York, *The Advisors*, pp. 45–67.

143. L. W. Alvarez, *Alvarez: Adventures of a Physicist*. Basic Books, New York, 1987.

144. York, *The Advisors*, pp. 64–67.

145. Strauss, *Men and Decisions*, pp. 229, 230.

146. York, *The Advisors*, p. 66.

147. Stern, *Oppenheimer Case*, p. 147.

148. York, *The Advisors*, pp. 64–67.

149. D. Acheson, *Present at Creation: My Years in the State Department*. W. W. Norton, New York, 1969.

150. Teller, *Memoirs*, p. 294.

151. E. Teller, *Bulletin of the Atomic Scientists* 1950, 6 (3), 71, quoted in York, *The Advisors*, p. 71.

152. H. Urey, *Bulletin of the Atomic Scientists* 1950, 6 (3), 72–73, quoted in York, *The Advisors*, p. 71.

153. Quoted in Strauss, *Men and Decisions*, pp. 235–236.

154. H. Bethe, "Edward Teller: A Long Look Back" (review of Teller's *Memoirs*). *Physics Today* 2001, November, 55–56.

155. Ulam, *Adventures*, pp. 209–224.

156. John A. Wheeler interview (by M. Hargittai), in M. Hargittai and I. Hargittai, *Candid Science IV*, pp. 424–439, p. 428.

157. Wolfgang Panofsky interview (by M. Hargittai), in I. Hargittai and M. Hargittai, *Candid Science VI*, in press.

158. Teller, *Memoirs*, pp. 295–299.

159. Ulam, *Adventures*, pp. 209–224.

160. Teller, *Memoirs*, p. 299–303.

161. Stanislav Ulam doubted that this claim would be valid if the multiplications by all schoolchildren were taken into account.

162. Edward Teller dictated a twenty-page memorandum in George A. (Jay) Keyworth's office on September 20, 1979, after he had suffered a heart attack that he ascribed to the strained political atmosphere in the wake of the Three Mile Island nuclear plant accident. I am grateful to Richard L. Garwin for a copy of this memorandum.

163. Teller, *Memoirs*, p. 316.

164. Ulam, *Adventures*, p. 219.

165. Teller memorandum, September 20, 1979.

166. Ulam, *Adventures*, pp. 209–224.

167. Ibid., p. 220.

168. Teller, *Memoirs*, p. 318.

169. Ulam, *Adventures*, pp. 209–224.

170. Teller, *Memoirs*, p. 320.

171. Richard Garwin interview, in I. Hargittai and M. Hargittai, *Candid Science VI*, in press.

172. Teller memorandum, September 20, 1979.

173. Vitaly L. Ginzburg interview, in I. Hargittai and M. Hargittai, *Candid Science VI*, in press.

174. Ulam, *Adventures*, pp. 310–311.

175. Richard Garwin interview, in I. Hargittai and M. Hargittai, *Candid Science VI*, in press.

176. York, *The Advisors*, p. 129.

177. Teller, *Memoirs*, pp. 330–342.

178. York, *The Advisors*, p. 129.

179. Harold Agnew interview, in B. Hargittai and I. Hargittai, *Candid Science V: Conversations with Famous Scientists*. Imperial College Press, London, 2005, pp. 300–315.

180. Edward Teller interview, in M. Hargittai and I. Hargittai, *Candid Science IV*, pp. 404–423.

181. Teller, *Memoirs*, p. 341.

182. Ibid., pp. 343–354.

183. Ibid., pp. 399, 400.

184. J. Shepley and C. Blair, Jr., *The Hydrogen Bomb*. McKay, New York, 1954.

185. Teller, "The Work of Many People." *Science*, 1955, February 25, 267–275.

186. Teller, *Memoirs*, p. 466.

187. Ibid., pp. 420–421.

188. Ibid., p. 431.

189. Ibid., pp. 442–443.

190. A. Latter and E. Teller, *Our Nuclear Future*. Criterion Books, New York, 1958.

191. Teller, *Memoirs*, p. 443.

192. Wolfgang Panofsky interview (by M. Hargittai), in I. Hargittai and M. Hargittai, *Candid Science VI*, in press.

193. Teller, *Memoirs*, p. 492.

194. Ibid., p. 455.

195. Ibid., p. 515.

196. Kojevnikov, *Stalin's Great Science*, p. 297.

197. Donald Glaser interview, in I. Hargittai and M. Hargittai, *Candid Science VI*, in press.

198. Teller, *Memoirs*, p. 465.

199. Ibid., p. 466.

200. J. W. Boag, P. E. Rubinin, and D. Shoenberg, Eds., *Kapitza in Cambridge and Moscow: Life and Letters of a Russian Physicist*. North-Holland, Amsterdam, 1990, p. 390.

201. Teller, *Memoirs*, p. 468.

202. Ibid., p. 469.

203. E. Teller, with W. Teller and W. Talley, *Conversations on the Dark Secrets of Physics*. Plenum Press, London, 1991; E. Teller, *The Constructive Uses of Nuclear Explosives*. McGraw-Hill, New York, 1968.

204. Teller, *Memoirs*, p. 501.

205. Ibid., p. 504.

206. Ibid., pp. 507–508.

207. Ibid., pp. 510–511.

208. Ibid., pp. 519–524.

209. E. Teller, *Pursuit of Simplicity*. Pepperdine Press, Malibu, Calif., 1980; E. Teller, *Better a Shield than a Sword*. Free Press, New York, 1986.

210. Judith Shoolery, personal communication, in Half Moon Bay, California, February 2004.

211. Teller, *Memoirs*, pp. 525–531.

212. See Peter Goodchild, *Edward Teller: The Real Dr. Strangelove*. Weidenfeld & Nicolson, London, 2004, p. 348.

213. C. H. Townes, *How the Laser Happened: Adventures of a Scientist*. Oxford University Press, New York, 1999.

214. Teller, *Memoirs*, p. 531.

215. A. Penzias, "Sakharov and SDI." In *Andrei Sakharov: Facets of a Life* (B. L. Altshuler, Ed.). Editions Frontiers, Gif-sur-Yvette, France, 1991, pp. 507–513.

216. Teller, *Memoirs*, p. 534.

217. Ibid., p. 535, footnote.

218. S. A. Blumberg and L. G. Panos, *Edward Teller: Giant of the Golden Age of Physics*. Charles Scribner's Sons, New York, 1990, p. 259.

219. Teller, *Memoirs*, p. 535, footnote.

220. W. J. Broad, *Teller's War: The Top-Secret Story behind the Star Wars Deception*. Simon & Schuster, New York, 1992, p. 41.

221. Ibid., pp. 193–194.

222. Townes, *How the Laser Happened*, p. 166.

223. Ibid., p. 168.

224. Charles H. Townes interview, in B. Hargittai and I. Hargittai, *Candid Science V*, pp. 94–137.

225. Teller, *Memoirs*, p. 541.

Chapter 6

1. In characterizing Fermi, Emilio Segrè's book about him is especially helpful. Segrè was his pupil, friend, and close observer. E. Segrè, *Enrico Fermi: Physicist*. University of Chicago Press, 1972.

2. M. Palevsky, *Atomic Fragments: A Daughter's Questions*. University of California Press, Berkeley, 2000, p. 8.

3. E. P. Wigner, "Enrico Fermi." In *Symmetries and Reflections: Scientific Essays* (W. J. Moore and M. Scriven, Eds.). Indiana University Press, Bloomington, 1967, pp. 252–256, quote on pp. 254–255. Reprinted from the *Yearbook of the American Philosophical Society*, 1955, pp. 435–439.

4. Segrè, *Enrico Fermi*, pp. 79–80.

5. E. Fermi, E. Amaldi, O. D'Agostino, B. Pontecorvo, F. Rasetti, and E. Segrè, "Artificial Radioactivity Produced by Neutron Bombardment. Part II." *Proceedings of the Royal Society of London*, Series A, 1935, 149, 522–558.

6. Segrè, *Enrico Fermi*, p. 86.

7. Ibid., p. 36.

8. Donald Glaser interview, in I. Hargittai and M. Hargittai, *Candid Science VI: Conversations with Famous Scientists*. Imperial College Press, London, in press.

9. Segrè, *Enrico Fermi*, p. 56.

10. Ibid., pp. 88–89.

11. E. Fermi, Nobel lecture. In *Nobel Lectures Including Presentation Speeches and Laureates' Biographies: Physics 1922–1941*. World Scientific, Singapore, 1998, pp. 414–421. The footnote is on p. 417.

12. Segrè, *Enrico Fermi*, pp. 61–62.

13. Ibid., p. 93.

14. Ibid., pp. 102–103.

15. Ibid., pp. 102–103.

16. S. R. Weart and G. Weiss Szilard, Eds., *Leo Szilard: His Version of the Facts. Selected Recollections and Correspondence*. MIT Press, Cambridge, Mass., 1978, p. 54.

17. Ibid., p. 54.

18. W. Lanouette (with Bela Silard), *Genius in the Shadows: A Biography of Leo Szilard, The Man Behind the Bomb*. University of Chicago Press, 1992, pp. 181–182.

19. Segrè, *Enrico Fermi*, pp. 107–108.

20. Ibid., pp. 149–161.

21. Lanouette, *Genius*, p. 180.

22. Ibid., pp. 217–219.

23. Ibid., p. 218.

24. Quoted in V. L. Telegdi, "Enrico Fermi in America." *Physics Today* 55 (6), June 2002, pp. 38–43, p. 43.

25. Lanouette, *Genius*, p. 352.

26. P. M. Stern (with H. P. Green), *The Oppenheimer Case: Security on Trial.* Harper & Row, New York, 1969; D. C. Cassidy, *J. Robert Oppenheimer and the American Century.* Pi Press, New York, 2005; G. Herken, *Brotherhood of the Bomb: The Tangled Lives and Divided Loyalties of Robert Oppenheimer, Ernest Lawrence, and Edward Teller.* Henry Holt, New York, 2002; S. S. Schweber, *In the Shadow of the Bomb: Bethe, Oppenheimer, and the Moral Responsibility of the Scientist.* Princeton University Press, Princeton, N.J., 2000; J. Conant, *109 East Palace: Robert Oppenheimer and the Secret City of Los Alamos.* Simon & Schuster, New York, 2005; K. Bird and M. J. Sherwin, *American Prometheus: The Triumph and Tragedy of J. Robert Oppenheimer.* Knopf, New York, 2005.

27. The acclaimed movie *Gentleman's Agreement* (Twentieth Century Fox Film Corporation, 1947), which exposes such discrimination, plays as late as the years following World War II.

28. Schweber, *In the Shadow of the Bomb*, p. 54.

29. Cassidy, *J. Robert Oppenheimer*, p. 32.

30. Quoted in Stern, *Oppenheimer Case*, p. 251.

31. Ibid., p. 23.

32. F. Camon, *Conversations with Primo Levi* (J. Shepley, trans.). Marlboro Press, Marlboro, Vt., 1989, pp. 45–46.

33. Cassidy, *J. Robert Oppenheimer*, p. 95.

34. The essence of the Born–Oppenheimer approximation is the following: since the relatively heavy nuclei move much more slowly than do electrons, the latter are assumed to move about a fixed nuclear arrangement. Accordingly, the internal motion of the nuclei is ignored in this approximation. It has great utility in many of today's approaches in molecular physics and theoretical chemistry. See, e.g., I. Hargittai and M. Hargittai, *Symmetry Through the Eyes of a Chemist*, 2nd ed. Plenum Press, New York, 1995.

35. M. Born, *My Life: Recollections of a Nobel Laureate.* Charles Scribner's Sons, New York, 1975, p. 229; A. Pais, *Inward Bound*, Oxford University Press, New York, 1988, p. 367.

36. H. Bethe, "J. Robert Oppenheimer, 1904–1967." Royal Society of London *Biographical Memoirs of Fellows* 1968, 14, 391–416, p. 391.

37. I. Hargittai, *The Road to Stockholm: Nobel Prizes, Science, and Scientists.* Oxford University Press, Oxford, 2002, pp. 61–64.

38. Cassidy, *J. Robert Oppenheimer*, pp. 172–173.

39. L. R. Groves, *Now It Can Be Told: The Story of the Manhattan Project.* Harper, New York, 1962, pp. 61–63.

40. Stern, *Oppenheimer Case*, p. 285.

41. Cassidy, *J. Robert Oppenheimer*, p. 225.

42. E. Teller (with Judith Shoolery), *Memoirs: A Twentieth-Century Journey in Science and Politics.* Perseus Publishing, Cambridge, Mass., 2001, p. 163.

43. There was, though, an accusation of his spying for the Soviet Union in the letter that triggered his security hearings; see later in the chapter.

44. Stern, *Oppenheimer Case*, p. 46.

45. Ibid., p. 48.

46. Ibid., pp. 62–63.

47. M. Born, *My Life and My Views.* Charles Scribner's Sons, New York, 1968, p. 40.

48. Stern, *Oppenheimer Case*, p. 120.

49. Ibid., p. 74.

50. Teller, *Memoirs*, quoting many of his letters to Maria Goeppert-Mayer.

51. Lanouette, *Genius*, p. 293.

52. Stern, *Oppenheimer Case*, pp. 97–103.

53. Ibid., pp. 127–128.

54. Ibid., pp. 179, 309.

55. Ibid., p. 204.

56. See, for example, Philip Anderson interview, in M. Hargittai and I. Hargittai, *Candid Science IV: Conversations with Famous Physicists.* Imperial College Press, London, 2004, pp. 586–601.

57. A. Penzias, "Sakharov and SDI." In *Andrei Sakharov: Facets of Life* (B. L. Altshuler, Ed.). Editions Frontiers, Gif-sur-Yvette, France, 1991, pp. 507–513.

58. See, e.g., Freeman Dyson's comments in this respect: Freeman Dyson interview (by M. Hargittai), in M. Hargittai and I. Hargittai, *Candid Science IV*, pp. 440–477.

59. Stern, *Oppenheimer Case*, p. 205.

60. Ibid., pp. 214–220.

61. Ibid., p. 221.

62. Ibid., p. 333.

63. Teller, *Memoirs*, appendix, pp. 570–602, pp. 571–572.

64. Teller, *Memoirs.* Chapter 30 contains Teller's comments on his testimony in the matter of J. R. Oppenheimer.

65. Herken, *Brotherhood of the Bomb*, p. 249.

66. Teller, *Memoirs*, appendix, p. 600.

67. Teller, *Memoirs*, chapter 30.

68. Quoted in Stern, *Oppenheimer Case*, p. 340.

69. See, for example, Teller, *Memoirs*, p. 601.

70. Quoted in Stern, *Oppenheimer Case*, p. 381.

71. A. Pais, *Einstein Lived Here.* Oxford University Press, New York, 1994, p. 241. Yet this did not necessarily mean that Einstein sympathized much with Oppenheimer. When Einstein first heard about the proposed hearing, he burst into laughter and said, "The trouble with Oppenheimer is that he loves a woman who doesn't love him—the United States government." [According to Robert Serber's memoirs, quoting Abraham Pais in R. Serber (with R. P. Crease), *Peace & War: Reminiscences of a Life on the Frontiers of Science.* Columbia University Press, New York, 1998, pp. 183–184.]

72. H. H. Goldstine, *The Computer from Pascal to von Neumann.* Princeton University Press, Princeton, N.J., 1972, p. 318.

73. Gertrud Weiss, according to B. J. Bernstein, in *Toward a Livable World: Leo Szilard and the Crusade for Nuclear Arms Control* (H. S. Hawkins, G. A. Greb, and G. Weiss Szilard, Eds.). MIT Press, Cambridge, Mass., 1987, p. xliii.

74. Letter from John A. Wheeler to Edward Teller, July 2, 1954. I thank Judith Shoolery for a copy of this letter.

75. J. S. Rigned, *Rabi: Scientist and Citizen.* Basic Books, New York, 1987, p. 230.

76. Quoted in Lanouette, *Genius*, p. 431.

77. A. Pais, *The Genius of Science: A Portrait Gallery of Twentieth-Century Physicists.* Oxford University Press, Oxford, 2000, p. 346.

78. T. von Kármán (with Lee Edson), *The Wind and Beyond: Theodore von Kármán, Pioneer in Aviation and Pathfinder in Space.* Little, Brown, Boston, 1967, pp. 3–13.

79. Nicolaas Bloembergen, personal communication, Lindau, Germany, June 2005.

80. Von Kármán, *The Wind*, pp. 6–9.

81. E. P. Wigner (with A. Szanton), *The Recollections of Eugene P. Wigner as Told to Andrew Szanton.* Plenum Press, New York, 1992, pp. 93–94.

82. Ibid., p. 95.

83. G. Klein, *The Atheist and the Holy City: Encounters and Reflections.* MIT Press, Cambridge, Mass., 1992, p. 22.

84. Klein, *The Atheist*, p. 22; James D. Watson interview, in I. Hargittai, *Candid Science II: Conversations with Famous Biochemical Scientists.* Imperial College Press, London, 2002, pp. 2–15, p. 15.

85. Lanouette, *Genius*, p. 389.

86. Monod's expression made its way into the subtitle of a book about Szilard, viz., D. A. Grandy, *Leo Szilard: Science as a Mode of Being.* University Press of America, Lanham, New York, 1996.

87. Lanouette, *Genius*, p. 392.

88. Ibid., p. 471.

89. Klein, *The Atheist*, pp. 30–36.

90. Quoted in Lanouette, *Genius*, p. 404.

91. Ibid., p. 407.

92. Ibid., p. 470.

93. Ehrenfest to Donnan on August 22, 1933, quoted in T. Frank, "Ever Ready to Go: The Multiple Exiles of Leo Szilard." *Physics in Perspective* 2005, 7, 204–252, p. 216.

94. Quoted in Lanouette, *Genius*, p. 480.

95. James D. Watson interview, in Hargittai, *Candid Science II*, pp. 2–15.

96. Quoted in Lanouette, *Genius*, p. 479.

97. F. Seitz, "Eugene Wigner (1902–1995)." *Nature* 1995, 373, 288.

98. A. Pais, *The Genius of Science*, p. 338. Abraham Pais met her in Princeton in the 1980s and she was present at the memorial service for Wigner in Princeton in 1995.

99. Seitz, "Eugene Wigner (1902–1995)," 288.

100. Edward Teller interview, in M. Hargittai and I. Hargittai, *Candid Science IV*, pp. 404–423.

101. Freeman Dyson interview, in M. Hargittai and I. Hargittai, *Candid Science IV*, pp. 440–474.

102. Weart and Szilard, *Leo Szilard*, p. 148.

103. David Gross interview, in I. Hargittai and M. Hargittai, *Candid Science VI*, in press.

104. Philip Anderson interview, in M. Hargittai and I. Hargittai, *Candid Science IV*, pp. 586–601.

105. Ibid., p. 591.

106. Steven Weinberg interview, in M. Hargittai and I. Hargittai, *Candid Science IV*, pp. 20–31.

107. Benoit Mandelbrot interview, in M. Hargittai and I. Hargittai, *Candid Science IV*, pp. 496–523, p. 516; see, e.g., B. Mandelbrot, *The Fractal Geometry of Nature*. W. H. Freeman, New York, 1983.

108. V. Weisskopf, *The Joy of Insight: Passions of a Physicist*. Basic Books/HarperCollins, New York, 1991, p. 43.

109. Frank Wilczek interview, in I. Hargittai and M. Hargittai, *Candid Science VI*, in press.

110. Weisskopf, *The Joy of Insight*, p. 43.

111. See Frank, "Ever Ready to Go," 204–252.

112. G. Pallo, "Kép a falon: A Wigner-Polányi kapcsolat" (Picture on the wall: The Wigner-Polanyi connection). *Fizikai Szemle* 2002 (10–11), 293–296.

113. John C. Polanyi interview, in I. Hargittai, *Candid Science III: More Conversations with Famous Chemists*. Imperial College Press, London, 2003, pp. 278–391; Wigner, *Symmetries*, pp. 262–263.

114. S. M. Ulam *Adventures of a Mathematician*. University of California Press, Berkeley, 1991, pp. 4–5.

115. Ibid., p. 71.

116. Benoit Mandelbrot interview, in M. Hargittai and I. Hargittai, *Candid Science IV*, pp. 496–523.

117. Interview with Marina Whitman (née von Neumann) by M. Hargittai, Ann Arbor, Michigan, July, 24, 2005.

118. N. Macrae, *John von Neumann: The Scientific Genius Who Pioneered the Modern Computer, Game Theory, Nuclear Deterrence, and Much More*. American Mathematical Society, Providence, R.I., 1999, p. 371.

119. Wigner, *Recollections*, p. 174.

120. Ibid., p. 258.

121. Interview of Eugene P. Wigner by István Kardos, September 1972, broadcast on Hungarian Television, March 1973. Published records (in Hungarian) in *Valóság*, 1973 (2), pp. 73–81.

122. E. P. Wigner, *Symmetries*, pp. 260–261.

123. S. S. Schweber, "A Short History of Shelter Island I." In *Shelter Island II: Proceedings of the 1983 Shelter Island Conference on Quantum Field Theory and the Fundamental Problems of Physics* (R. Jackiw, N. N. Khuri, S. Weinberg, and E. Witten, Eds.). MIT Press, Cambridge, Mass., 1985, pp. 302–343, p. 315.

124. Ulam, *Adventures*, p. 194.

125. See, e.g., D. Cesarani, *Arthur Koestler: The Homeless Mind*. Heinemann, London, 1998.

126. A. Koestler, *The Act of Creation*. Macmillan, New York, 1964, pp. 35–36.

127. Ulam, *Adventures*, p. 170.

128. Ibid., pp. 19–195. Note that I am using "nebich" rather than Ulam's spelling, "nebech."

129. Ibid., pp. 231–232.

130. Ibid., p. 238.

131. Ibid., pp. 151 (Gamow quote and Ulam quote), 164 (Fermi quote).

132. W. J. Broad, *Teller's War: The Top-Secret Story behind the Star Wars Deception*. Simon

& Schuster, New York, 1992, p. 47, quoting D. O'Neill, "Project Chariot: How Alaska Escaped Nuclear Excavation." *The Bulletin of the Atomic Scientists*, December 1989, 33; Broad, *Teller's War*, p. 47, quoting Edward Teller from *Popular Science* March 1960, p. 97.

133. Teller, *Memoirs*, p. 488.

134. Broad, *Teller's War*, pp. 126–127, 182.

135. Judith Shoolery, personal communication, Half Moon Bay, California, February 2004.

136. Donald Glaser interview, in I. Hargittai and M. Hargittai, *Candid Science VI*, in press.

137. This was on September 20, 1979, in George A. (Jay) Keyworth's office. I am grateful to Richard L. Garwin for a copy of this memorandum. (Teller ascribed his heart attack to the strained political atmosphere that prevailed in the wake of the Three Mile Island nuclear plant accident.)

138. I. Hargittai, "Utolsó levélváltásaim Teller Edével" (Last correspondence with Edward Teller). *Magyar Tudomány* 2003, 48, 1554–1558.

139. Broad, *Teller's War*, pp. 281–282.

140. Quoted in S. A. Blumberg and G. Owens, *Energy and Conflict: The Life and Times of Edward Teller*. G. P. Putnam's Sons, New York, 1976, p. 427.

141. Wigner, *Recollections*, pp. 33–34.

142. N. A. Vonneuman, *John von Neumann as Seen by His Brother*. Private edition by N. A. Vonneuman, 1987, p. 17.

143. Ulam, *Adventures*, pp. 243–245.

144. Vonneuman, *John von Neumann as Seen by His Brother*, p. 17.

145. Quoted in Wigner, *Recollections*, pp. 317–318.

146. Yuval Ne'eman interview, in M. Hargittai and I. Hargittai, *Candid Science IV*, pp. 32–63; Y. Ne'eman, "Edward Teller, the Hungarian, American and Jew, too." *Acta Physica Hungarica New Series, Heavy Ion Physics* 1998, 7, 155–165, p. 159.

147. We know about his last moments from Mrs. Margit Grigori. See I. Hargittai, "Last correspondence," 1554–1558.

148. Wigner, *Recollections*, p. 313.

149. Quoted in Weart and Szilard, *Leo Szilard*, pp. 181–188, p. 184.

150. Ibid., p. 9.

151. Quoted in F. Crick, *Life Itself: Its Origin and Nature*. Simon and Schuster, New York, 1981, pp. 13–14.

152. When my wife and I visited the Tellers in Stanford in 1996, the conversation we recorded with Edward Teller (see M. Hargittai and I. Hargittai, *Candid Science IV*) was in English at our request. The social chat was in Hungarian. When we remarked that they (Mici and Edward) spoke Hungarian very well (by then it was seventy years since he had left Hungary), they told us that they not only spoke in Hungarian a great deal, but invariably argued in it, and for arguing you must speak the language well. They also told us that there was a time in her childhood when their daughter Wendy thought that she would not be able to become a mother because parents were supposed to speak Hungarian and she did not.

153. H. H. Goldstine, *The Computer from Pascal to von Neumann*. Princeton University Press, Princeton, N.J., 1972, p. 176.

154. There is some original footage in the NOVA documentary *The Man Behind the Bomb: Leo Szilard.* Helen Weiss Productions, Washington, D.C., 1992.

155. Goldstine, *Computer*, p. 177.

Epilogue

1. T. von Kármán (with Lee Edson), *The Wind and Beyond: Theodore von Kármán, Pioneer in Aviation and Pathfinder in Space.* Little, Brown, Boston, 1967, p. 4.

2. E. P. Wigner (with A. Szanton), *The Recollections of Eugene P. Wigner as Told to Andrew Szanton.* Plenum Press, New York, 1992, pp. xv–xvi.

3. S. M. Ulam, *Adventures of a Mathematician.* University of California Press, Berkeley, 1991, pp. 82–97, pp. 82, 96.

4. Wigner, *Recollections*, pp. 169–170.

5. D. J. Gross, "Symmetry in Physics: Wigner's Legacy." *Physics Today* December 1995, 46–50, p. 49.

6. Ulam, *Adventures*, p. 76.

7. Ibid., p. 78.

8. Quoted in W. Lanouette (with Bela Silard), *Genius in the Shadows: A Biography of Leo Szilard, The Man Behind the Bomb.* University of Chicago Press, 1992, p. 320.

9. I. Hargittai, *The Road to Stockholm: Nobel Prizes, Science, and Scientists.* Oxford University Press, Oxford, 2002.

10. Von Kármán, *The Wind*, p. 40.

11. I. Hargittai, *The Road to Stockholm*, pp. 15–20.

12. One of Pauling's former postdoctoral fellows, Otto Bastiansen, was a dedicated admirer of both Pauling's science and his politics. Bastiansen, at different times, served in all the leading roles of Norwegian scientific life: chairman of the Research Council, rector of Oslo University, and president of the Norwegian Academy of Science and Letters. See more on him in I. Hargittai, *Our Lives: Encounters of a Scientist.* Akadémiai Kiadó, Budapest, 2004, pp. 83–92.

13. B. J. Bernstein, Introduction. In *Toward a Livable World: Leo Szilard and the Crusade for Nuclear Arms Control* (H. S. Hawkins, G. A. Gerb, and G. Weiss Szilard, Eds.). MIT Press, Cambridge, Mass., 1987, p. xxiii.

14. Ibid., p. xxvii.

15. Joseph Rotblat relates this in a brief segment of the NOVA documentary *The Man Behind the Bomb: Leo Szilard.* Helen Weiss Productions, Washington, D.C., 1992.

16. J. von Neumann and O. Morgenstern, *The Theory of Games and Economic Behavior.* Princeton University Press, Princeton, N.J., 1944; the 1989 prize went to the Norwegian Trygve Haavelmo and the 1992 prize to the American Gary S. Gray.

17. On at least one more occasion Teller asked an interviewer to delete something from a recorded conversation. In 1962 Eric Goldman asked him whether he would favor reinstating Oppenheimer's security clearance and Teller was speechless. Teller asked the interviewer to remove the question and his conspicuous silence before airing the interview. Goldman complied, but the incident leaked out and made quite a stir. The case is de-

scribed in P. M. Stern (with H. P. Green), *The Oppenheimer Case: Security on Trial.* Harper & Row, New York, 1969, p. 454.

18. I. Hargittai, *Our Lives*, pp. 211–216.

19. Vitaly L. Ginzburg interview, in I. Hargittai and M. Hargittai, *Candid Science VI: Conversations with Famous Scientists*, Imperial College Press, London, in press.

20. M. Summerfield, "Kármán Tódor a Jet Propulsion Lab megalapitója" (Theodore von Kármán, the Founder of the Jet Propulsion Lab). *Fizikai Szemle* 1984, p. 195; D. A. Clary, *Rocket Man: Robert H. Goddard and the Birth of the Space Age.* Hyperion, New York, 2003.

21. I. I. Rabi is quoted in S. A. Blumberg and G. Owens, *Energy and Conflict: The Life and Times of Edward Teller.* G. P. Putnam's Sons, New York, 1976, p. 1.

22. Rabi had a biting tongue, but only praise for the Swedes when they awarded him the 1944 physics Nobel Prize. Others criticized the institution of the Nobel Prize for conducting business as usual while all the horror was going on in the rest of Europe. See I. Hargittai, *Road to Stockholm*, p. 25.

23. John A. Wheeler interview (by M. Hargittai), in M. Hargittai and I. Hargittai, *Candid Science IV: Conversations with Famous Physicists.* Imperial College Press, London, 2004, pp. 424–439, p. 429.

24. Marina von Neumann Whitman, address at the John von Neumann Centennial meeting in Budapest, 2003; I am grateful to Dr. Whitman for the text of her speech.

25. See Bernstein in Hawkins et al., *Toward a Livable World*, p. lvii.

SELECT BIBLIOGRAPHY

Acheson, D., *Present at the Creation: My Years in the State Department*. W. W. Norton, New York, 1969.

Alvarez, L. W., *Alvarez: Adventures of a Physicist*. Basic Books, New York, 1987.

Badash, L., *Kapitza, Rutherford, and the Kremlin*. Yale University Press, New Haven, 1985.

Bernstein, J., *Hitler's Uranium Club: The Secret Recordings at Farm Hall*. American Institute of Physics, Woodbury, New York, 1996.

Bernstein, J., *Oppenheimer: Portrait of an Enigma*. Ivan R. Dee, Chicago, 2004.

Bird, K. and Sherwin, M. J., *American Prometheus: The Triumph and Tragedy of J. Robert Oppenheimer*. Alfred A. Knopf, New York, 2005.

Blumberg, S. A. and Owens, G., *Energy and Conflict: The Life and Times of Edward Teller*. G. P. Putnam's Sons, New York, 1976.

Blumberg, S. A. and Panos, L. G., *Edward Teller: Giant of the Golden Age of Physics*. Charles Scribner's Sons, New York, 1990.

Boag, J.W., Rubinin, P.E., and Shoenberg, D. (eds.), *Kapitza in Cambridge and Moscow: Life and Letters of a Russian Physicist*. North-Holland, Amsterdam, 1990.

Bongard-Levin, G. M. and Zakharov, V. E., *Rossiiskaya nauchnaya emigratsiya: Dvadtsat' portretov* (in Russian, "Russian scientific emigration: Twenty portraits"). URSS, Moscow, 2001.

Born, G. V. R., *The Born Family in Göttingen and Beyond*. Institut für Wissenschaftsgeschichte, Göttingen, 2002.

Born, M., *My Life and My Views*. Charles Scribner's Sons, New York, 1968.

Born, M., *My Life: Recollections of a Nobel Laureate*. Charles Scribner's Sons, New York, 1978.

Broad, W. J., *Teller's War: The Top-Secret Story Behind the Star Wars Deception*. Simon and Schuster, New York, 1992.

Brown, A., *The Neutron and the Bomb: A Biography of Sir James Chadwick*. Oxford University Press, Oxford, 1997.

Brown, A. C. and MacDonald C. B. (eds.), *The Secret History of the Atomic Bomb*. Dial Press, New York, 1977.

Buruma, I., *The Wages of Guilt: Memories of War in Germany and Japan*. Vintage, London, 1995.

Calaprice, A., *The Expanded Quotable Einstein*. Princeton University Press, 2000.

Cassidy, D. C., *J. Robert Oppenheimer and the American Century*. Pi Press, New York, 2005.

Childs, H., *An American Genius: The Life of Ernest Orlando Lawrence, Father of the Cyclotron*. E. P. Dutton, New York, 1968.

Clark, R. W., *Einstein: The Life and Times*. World Publishing Company, New York, 1971.

Clary, D. A., *Rocket Man: Robert H. Goddard and the Birth of the Space Age*. Hyperion, New York, 2003.

Compton, A. H., *Atomic Quest: A Personal Narrative*. Oxford University Press, New York, 1956.

Conant, J., *Tuxedo Park: A Wall Street Tycoon and the Secret Palace of Science That Changed the Course of World War II*. Simon and Schuster, New York, 2002.

Conant, J., *109 East Palace: Robert Oppenheimer and the Secret City of Los Alamos*. Simon and Schuster, New York, 2005.

Cornwell, J., *Hitler's Scientists: Science, War and the Devil's Pact*. Viking, New York, 2003.

Crick, F., *Life Itself: Its Origin and Nature*. Simon and Schuster, New York, 1981.

Czeizel, E., *Tudósok, Gének, Dilemmák: A magyar származású Nobel-díjasok családfaelemzése* (Scientists, genes, dilemmas: Geneological analysis of Nobel laureates of Hungarian extraction). Galenus Kiadó, Budapest, 2002.

Dyson, F., *Weapons of Hope*. Harper & Row, New York, 1985.

Eigen, M. and Winkler, R., *Laws of the Game: How the Principles of Nature Govern Chance*. Princeton University Press, 1993.

Fermi, L., *Illustrious Immigrants: The Intellectual Migration from Europe 1930–41*. University of Chicago Press, 1968.

Fermi, L., *Atoms in the Family: My Life with Enrico Fermi*. University of New Mexico Press, Albuquerque, 1982.

Frayn, M., *Copenhagen*. Methuen Drama, London, 1998.

Frisch, O., *What Little I Remember*. Cambridge University Press, 1979.

Gamow, G., *My World Line: An Informal Autobiography*. Viking Press, New York, 1970.

Ginzburg, V. L., *O fizike i astrofizike* (About physics and astrophysics). Byuro Kvantum, Moscow, 1995.

Ginzburg, V. L., *O nauke, o sebe i o drugikh* (About science, myself, and others). Fizmatlit, Moscow, 2003.

Goldstine, H. H., *The Computer from Pascal to von Neumann*. Princeton University Press, 1972.

Goodchild, P., *Edward Teller: The Real Dr. Strangelove*. Weidenfeld & Nicolson, London, 2004.

Gorn, M. H., *The Universal Man: Theodore von Kármán's Life in Aeronautics*. Smithsonian Institution Press, Washington, D.C., 1992.

Goudsmit, S. A., *Alsos*. Tomash Publishers and American Institute of Physics, 1983.

Grandy, D. A., *Leo Szilard: Science as a Mode of Being*. University Press of America, Lanham, Md., 1996.

Greenspan, N. T., *The End of the Certain World. The Life and Science of Max Born: The Nobel Physicist Who Ignited the Quantum Revolution*. Basic Books, New York, 2005.

Groves, L. R., *Now It Can Be Told: The Story of the Manhattan Project*. Harper, New York, 1962.

Hager, T., *Force of Nature: The Life of Linus Pauling*. Simon and Schuster, New York, 1995.

Hargittai, B. and Hargittai, I., *Candid Science V: Conversations with Famous Scientists*. Imperial College Press, London, 2005.

Hargittai, I., *Candid Science: Conversations with Famous Chemists*. Imperial College Press, London, 2000.

Hargittai, I., *Candid Science III: More Conversations with Famous Chemists*. Imperial College Press, London, 2003.

Hargittai, I., *Our Lives: Encounters of a Scientist*. Akadémiai Kiadó, Budapest, 2004.

Hargittai, I., *The Road to Stockholm: Nobel Prizes, Science, and Scientists*. Oxford University Press, Oxford, 2002.

Hargittai, I., *The Tragedy of Edward Teller*. Hungarian Academy of Sciences, Budapest, 2005.

Hargittai, I. and Hargittai, M., *In Our Own Image: Personal Symmetry in Discovery*. Plenum-Kluwer, New York, 2000.

Hargittai, I. and Hargittai, M., *Candid Science VI: More Conversations with Famous Scientists*. Imperial College Press, London, in press.

Hargittai, M. and Hargittai, I., *Candid Science IV: Conversations with Famous Physicists*. Imperial College Press, London, 2004.

Hawkins, H. S., Greb, G. A., and Weiss Szilard, G. (Eds.), *Toward a Livable World: Leo Szilard and the Crusade for Nuclear Arms Control*. MIT Press, Cambridge, Mass., 1987.

Heims, S. J., *John von Neumann and Norbert Wiener: From Mathematics to the Technologies of Life and Death*. MIT Press, Cambridge, Mass., 1980.

Herken, G., *Brotherhood of the Bomb: The Tangled Lives and Loyalties of Robert Oppenheimer, Ernest Lawrence, and Edward Teller*. Henry Holt, New York, 2002.

Herken, G., *Cardinal Choices: Presidential Science Advising from the Atomic Bomb to SDI*. Stanford University Press, 2000.

Herken, G., *The Winning Weapon: The Atomic Bomb in the Cold War 1945–1950*. Alfred A. Knopf, New York, 1981.

Hoddeson, L. and Daitch, L., *True Genius. The Life and Science of John Bardeen: The Only Winner of Two Nobel Prizes in Physics*. Joseph Henry Press, Washington, D.C., 2002.

Holloway, D., *Stalin and the Bomb: The Soviet Union and Atomic Energy 1939–1956*. Yale University Press, New Haven, 1994.

Isaacs, J. and Downing, T., *Cold War: For 45 Years the World Held Its Breath*. Bantam Press, London, 1998.

Kármán, T. von (with L. Edson), *The Wind and Beyond. Theodore von Kármán: Pioneer in Aviation and Pathfinder in Space*. Little, Brown, Boston, 1967.

Kay, L. E., *Who Wrote the Book of Life? A History of the Genetic Code*. Stanford University Press, Palo Alto, Calif., 2000.

Kevles, D. J., *The Physicists: The History of a Scientific Community in Modern America*. Alfred A. Knopf, New York, 1978.

Klein, G., *The Atheist and the Holy City: Encounters and Reflections.* MIT Press, Cambridge, Mass., 1992.

Koestler, A., *Darkness at Noon.* Macmillan, New York, 1941.

Koestler, A., *The Act of Creation.* Macmillan, New York, 1964.

Kojevnikov, A. B., *Stalin's Great Science: The Times and Adventures of Soviet Physicists.* Imperial College Press, London, 2004.

Kovács, L., *Eugene P. Wigner and His Hungarian Teachers.* Studia Physica Savariensia, Vol. IX. Szombathely, 2002.

Kovács, L., *Neumann János és magyar tanárai* (in Hungarian, "John von Neumann and his Hungarian teachers"). Studia Physica Savariensia, Vol. X. Szombathely, 2003.

Kovács, L., *László Rátz and John von Neumann: A Gifted Teacher and His Brilliant Pupil.* University of Manitoba, Winnipeg, 2003.

Krebs, H. (with R. Schmid), *Otto Warburg: Cell Physiologist, Biochemist, and Eccentric.* Clarendon Press, Oxford, 1981.

Lanouette, W. (with Bela Silard), *Genius in the Shadows: A Biography of Leo Szilard, The Man behind the Bomb.* University of Chicago Press, 1992.

Laqueur, W., *Generation Exodus: The Fate of Young Jewish Refugees from Nazi Germany.* Brandeis University Press, Hanover, N.H., 2001.

Lobikov, E. A., *Sovremennaya Fizika i Atomnii Projekt* (In Russian, "Modern Physics and the Atomic Project"). Institut kompyuternikh issledovanii, Moscow-Izhevsk, 2002.

Lukacs, J., *Budapest 1900: A Historical Portrait of a City and Its Culture.* Grove Press, New York, 1988.

Macrae, N., *John von Neumann: The Scientific Genius Who Pioneered the Modern Computer, Game Theory, Nuclear Deterrence, and Much More.* American Mathematical Society, Providence, R.I., 1999.

McCagg, W. O., Jr., *Jewish Nobles and Geniuses in Modern Hungary.* Columbia University Press, New York, 1986.

Marx, G., *The Voice of the Martians.* Akadémiai Kiadó, Budapest, 1997.

Marx, G. (ed.), *Leo Szilárd Centenary Volume.* Eötvös Physical Society, Budapest, 1998.

Marx, G. (ed.), *Eugene Paul Wigner Centennial.* Roland Eötvös Physical Society, Budapest, 2002.

Medawar, J. and Pyke, D., *Hitler's Gift: Scientists Who Fled Nazi Germany.* Piatkus, London, 2000.

Molander, R. and Nichols, R., *Who Will Stop the Bomb? A Primer on Nuclear Proliferation.* Facts on File Publications, New York, 1985.

Morgan, K. Z. and Peterson, K. M., *The Angry Genie: One Man's Walk through the Nuclear Age.* University of Oklahoma Press, Norman, 1999.

Nagy, F., *Neumann János és a "magyar titok" a dokumentumok tükrében* (in Hungarian, "János Neumann and the 'Hungarian secret' as reflected by documents"). Országos Műszaki Információs Központ és Könyvtár, Budapest, 1987.

Nieh, H.-T. (ed.), *In Celebration of the 80th Birthday of C. N. Yang: Proceedings of the International Symposium on Frontiers of Science, 2002, Beijing.* World Scientific, Singapore, 2003.

Nobel Foundation Directory, Stockholm, continuously updated.

Norris, R. S., *Racing for the Bomb: General Leslie R. Groves, The Manhattan Project's Indispensable Man.* Steerforth Press, South Royalton, Vt., 2002.

North, O. L., *Taking the Stand: The Testimony of Lieutenant Colonel Oliver L. North.* Pocket Books, New York, 1987.

Oppenheimer, J. R., *The Open Mind.* Simon and Schuster, New York, 1955.

Ottaviani, J., Johnston, J., Lieber, S., Locke, V., Mireault, B., Parker, J. (with C. Kemple, E. Newell, R. Thompson), *Fallout: J. Robert Oppenheimer, Leo Szilard, and the Political Science of the Atomic Bomb.* G. T. Labs, Ann Arbor, Mich., 2001.

Pais, A., *Einstein Lived Here.* Oxford University Press, New York, 1994.

Pais, A., *The Genius of Science: A Portrait Gallery of Twentieth-Century Physicists.* Oxford University Press, Oxford, 2000.

Palevsky, M., *Atomic Fragments: A Daughter's Questions.* University of California Press, Berkeley, 2000.

Parker, B., *Einstein: The Passion of a Scientist.* Prometheus Books, Amherst, New York, 2003.

Peierls, R., *Bird of Passage: Recollections of a Physicist.* Princeton University Press, 1985.

Polenberg, R. (ed.), *In the Matter of J. Robert Oppenheimer: The Security Clearance Hearing.* Cornell University Press, Ithaca, 2002.

Radnai, G. and Kunfalvi, R., *Physics in Budapest: A Survey.* North-Holland, Amsterdam, 1988.

Regis, E., *Who Got Einstein's Office? Eccentricity and Genius at the Institute for Advanced Study.* Perseus, Cambridge, Massachusetts, 1987.

Reményi Gyenes, I., *Ismerjük Őket? Zsidó származású nevezetes magyarok arcképcsarnoka.* (Do we know them? Portrait gallery of famous Hungarians of Jewish extraction). Ex Libris Kiadó, Budapest, 1997.

Rhodes, R., *The Making of the Atomic Bomb.* Simon and Schuster, New York, 1986.

Rhodes, R., *Dark Sun: The Making of the Hydrogen Bomb.* Simon and Schuster, New York, 1995.

Rigden, J. S., *Rabi: Scientist and Citizen.* Basic Books, New York, 1987.

Rose, P. L., *Heisenberg and the Nazi Atomic Bomb Project: A Study in German Culture.* University of California Press, Berkeley, 1998.

Schweber, S. S., *In the Shadow of the Bomb: Bethe, Oppenheimer, and the Moral Responsibility of the Scientist.* Princeton University Press, 2000.

Segrè, E., *Enrico Fermi: Physicist.* University of Chicago Press, 1970.

Segrè, E., *A Mind Always in Motion: The Autobiography of Emilio Segrè.* University of California Press, Berkeley, 1993.

Serafini, A., *Linus Pauling: A Man and His Science.* Paragon House, New York, 1989.

Serber, R. (with R. P. Crease), *Peace & War: Reminiscences of a Life on the Frontier of Science.* Columbia University Press, New York, 1998.

Snow, C. P., *Variety of Men.* Charles Scribner's Sons, New York, 1966.

Stern, P. M. (with H. P. Green), *The Oppenheimer Case: Security on Trial.* Harper & Row, New York, 1969.

Strauss, L. L., *Men and Decisions.* Popular Library, New York, 1963.

Szilard, L., *The Voice of the Dolphins and Other Stories.* Simon and Schuster, New York, 1961.

Teller, E., *Better a Shield Than a Sword: Perspectives on Defense and Technology.* Free Press, New York, 1987.

Teller, E., Teller, W., and Talley, W., *Conversations on the Dark Secrets of Physics*. Plenum Press, New York, 1991.

Teller, E. (with Judith Shoolery), *Memoirs: A Twentieth-Century Journey in Science and Politics*. Perseus, Cambridge, Mass., 2001.

Thayer, H., *Management of the Hanford Engineer Works in World War II: How the Corps, DuPont and the Metallurgical Laboratory Fast Tracked the Original Plutonium Works*. ASCE Press, New York, 1996

Thompson, K. W., *The Presidency and Science Advising, Vol. V*. University Press of America, Lanham, Md., 1988.

Townes, C. H., *How the Laser Happened: Adventures of a Scientist*. Oxford University Press, Oxford, 1999.

Ulam, S. M., *Adventures of a Mathematician*. University of California Press, Berkeley, 1991.

Wagner, F. S., *Wigner Jenő: Az atomkor egyik megalapitója*. (In Hungarian, "Eugene P. Wigner: One of the Founders of the Atomic Age.") Studia Physica Savariensia, Vol. X. Szombathely, 1998.

Wali, K. C., *Chandra: A Biography of S. Chandrasekhar*. University of Chicago Press, 1990.

Weart, S. R. and Weiss Szilard, G. (eds.), *Leo Szilard: His Version of the Facts. Selected Recollections and Correspondence*. MIT Press, Cambridge, Mass., 1978.

Weinberg, A. M., *Reflections on Big Science*. MIT Press, Cambridge, Mass., 1967.

Weisskopf, V. F., *The Privilege of Being a Physicist*. W. H. Freeman, New York, 1989.

Weisskopf, V., *The Joy of Insight: Passions of a Physicist*. Basic Books, New York, 1991.

Wells, H. G., *The World Set Free: A Story of Mankind*. Macmillan, London, 1914.

Welsome, E., *The Plutonium Files: America's Secret Medical Experiments in the Cold War*. Dial Press, New York, 1999.

Weyl, H., *Symmetry*. Princeton University Press, 1952.

Wheeler, J. A. (with K. Ford), *Geons, Black Holes, and Quantum Foam: A Life in Physics*. W. W. Norton, New York, 2000.

Wigner, E. P. (with A. Szanton), *The Recollections of Eugene P. Wigner as Told to Andrew Szanton*. Plenum Press, New York, 1992.

Wigner, E. P., *Symmetries and Reflections: Scientific Essays*. Indiana University Press, Bloomington, 1967.

York, H. F., *The Advisors: Oppenheimer, Teller, and the Superbomb*. W. H. Freeman, San Francisco, 1976.

Theodore von Kármán

1881, March 11 Born Tódor Kármán, Budapest

1891–1899 *Minta* Gimnázium

1903 Graduates from the Palatine Joseph Budapest Technical University

1903–1906 Assistant at the Budapest Technical University

1906–1908 Doctoral studies in Göttingen

1908 Visits Paris and observes pioneering flight

1912 Interlude in Banska Stiavnica, Mining College

1913 Becomes professor at and director of Aeronautical Institute, Technical University, Aachen, Germany

1914–1918 World War I, Head of Research in the Austro-Hungarian Army Aviation Corps

1918–1919 Official in the Ministry of Education in revolutionary Hungary

1919 Back to Aachen

1922 Organizes First International Applied Mechanics Congress in Innsbruck, Austria

1926 First visit to the United States at Caltech

1930 Moves permanently to the United States and becomes head of the Guggenheim Aeronautical Laboratory at Caltech

1933 Founds the U.S. Institute of Aeronautical Sciences, from which the Jet Propulsion Laboratory (JPL) evolved

1936 Becomes a naturalized U.S. citizen

1938 Member of the National Academy of Sciences (NAS) of the U.S.A.

1938 Member of the NAS committee advising the U.S. Army Air Corps

1944 Co-founder of the present NASA JPL

1944 Chairs the Army Air Corps Scientific Advisory Group

1946 Medal for Merit (U.S. presidential award)

1946 Foreign member of the Royal Society (London)

1946 Scientific Advisory Board to the Chief of Staff of the U.S. Air Force

1948 Franklin Gold Medal

1949 Professor emeritus at Caltech

1951 Launches the Advisory Group for Aeronautical Research and Development (AGARD), serving as its chairman until his death

1955 Appointed to the Pontifical Academy of Sciences by Pope Pius XII

1956 Initiates the International Council of Aeronautical Sciences (ICAS)

1960 Initiates the International Academy of Aeronautics and becomes its president

1962 Presides over the First International Symposium on the Basic Environmental Problems of Man in Space

1963 First recipient of the U.S. National Medal of Science (from President John F. Kennedy)

1963, May 7 Dies in Aachen, Germany

Leo Szilard

1898, February 11 Born Leó Spitz, Budapest

1900 Name change, to Leó Szilárd

1908–1916 Főreálgimnázium, Budapest District VI

1916–1917, 1918–1919 Budapest Technical University

1917–1918 In the Austro-Hungarian Army

1919, December Departure for Germany

1920, January Technical University Berlin, starts attending the physics colloquia at Berlin University

1920, Fall Berlin University

1922 PhD from Berlin University

1923–1927 Kaiser Wilhelm Institute for Chemistry in Berlin-Dahlem, University of Berlin, various appointments

1926 Begins filing patents for various innovations and inventions, several jointly with Albert Einstein

1927 Appointed Privatdozent at Berlin University

1931 First visit to the United States

1933, March 30 Departs from Germany for England, via Vienna

1933–1934 Develops the ideas of nuclear chain reaction and critical mass; files patent for nuclear chain reaction

1938 Moves to the United States

1939 Organizes Albert Einstein's letter to President Roosevelt and thus initiates U.S. atomic bomb project

1942 Moves to Chicago, works as chief physicist at Metallurgical Laboratory of the Manhattan Project

1942, December 2 World's first nuclear reactor starts operation

1943 Becomes a naturalized U.S. citizen

1945 Tries, unsuccessfully, to prevent the deployment of atomic bombs against Japan

1946 Appointed professor at the University of Chicago

1947 Shifts his main scientific interest from physics to biology
1951 Marries Gertrud (Trude) Weiss
1954 Fellow of the American Academy of Arts and Sciences
1957 Pugwash meetings start with Szilard's active participation
1959–1960 Fights bladder cancer, with success
1960 U.S. Atoms for Peace Award
1961 Member of the National Academy of Sciences of the U.S.A.; receives honorary doctorate from Brandeis University
1962 Founds Council for a Livable World
1964 Moves to the Salk Institute, La Jolla, California
1964, May 30 Dies in La Jolla, California

Eugene P. Wigner

1902, November 17 Born Jenő Pál Wigner, Budapest
1915 Conversion to Lutheran religion
1915–1919 Lutheran Gimnázium, Budapest
1919 Maturation from the Lutheran Gimnázium
1920–1921 Chemical engineering studies at the Budapest Technical University
1921–1925 Chemical engineering studies at the Technische Hochschule Berlin; from his junior year he works at the Kaiser Wilhelm Institute in Berlin-Dahlem; diploma work under Herman F. Mark and his doctoral dissertation under Michael Polanyi
1925–1926 Chemical engineer at the Mauthner Leather Company, Budapest
1926–1927 Research Assistant to Karl Weissenberg at the University of Berlin, then assistant to Richard Becker
1927 Assistant to David Hilbert in Göttingen
1928–1930 Berlin
1930–1933 Visiting lecturer, Princeton University
1933–1936 Visiting professor of physics, Princeton University
1936–1938 Professor of physics, University of Wisconsin
1936 Marries Amelia Frank, who dies in 1937
1937 Becomes a naturalized U.S. citizen
1938–1971 Thomas D. Jones Professor of Physics, Princeton University
1941–1977 Marries Mary Wheeler; they have two children, David and Martha; Mary Wheeler dies in 1977
1942–1945 Participant in the Manhattan Project at the University of Chicago
1945 Member of the National Academy of Sciences of the U.S.A.
1946 Medal for Merit (U.S. presidential award)
1946–1947 Director of Clinton Laboratories in Oak Ridge, Tennessee
1952–1957 Member, General Advisory Committee, U.S. Atomic Energy Commission
1958 Enrico Fermi Award
1963 Nobel Prize in Physics
1968 U.S. National Medal of Science (from President Lyndon B. Johnson)
1970 Foreign member of the Royal Society (London)

1971 Retirement
1979 Marries Eileen Hamilton
1995, January 1 Dies in Princeton, New Jersey

John von Neumann

1903, December 28 Born János Neumann, Budapest
1921 Matriculation from the Lutheran Gimnázium, Budapest
1921 Mathematics studies, University of Budapest
1921–1923 Technical University Berlin
1923–1925 Chemical engineering studies at the Eidgenössische Technische Hochschule (ETH), Zurich
1926 PhD in mathematics (with minors in physics and chemistry), University of Budapest
1927–1929 Privatdozent, University of Berlin
1929 Privatdozent, University of Hamburg
1929–1937 Marries Mariette Kövesi
1930–1933 Visiting professor, Princeton University
1932 Publishes *Mathematische Grundlagen der Quantenmechanik*, Springer, Berlin
1933–1957 Research professor of mathematics, Institute for Advanced Study, Princeton
1935 Daughter, Marina, is born
1937 Becomes a naturalized U.S. citizen
1937 Member of the National Academy of Sciences of the U.S.A.
1939 Marries Klári Dán
1940–1957 Member, Scientific Advisory Committee, Ballistic Research Laboratory, Aberdeen, Maryland
1943–1955 Consultant, Los Alamos National Laboratory
1944 Publishes (jointly with Oskar Morgenstern) *Theory of Games and Economic Behavior*, Princeton University Press
1947 Medal for Merit (U.S. presidential award)
1951–1953 President, American Mathematical Society
1952–1954 Member, General Advisory Committee, U.S. Atomic Energy Commission
1955–1957 Commissioner, U.S. Atomic Energy Commission
1956 Enrico Fermi Award (the second Fermi award; the first was given to Fermi in 1954)
1956 Medal of Freedom (U.S. presidential award)
1957, February 8 Dies in Washington, D.C.

Edward Teller

1908, January 15 Born Ede Teller, Budapest
1926 Enters and leaves Budapest Technical University
1926–1928 University student, Karlsruhe, Munich
1928–1930 PhD under Werner Heisenberg in Leipzig
1930–1933 Works as an assistant in Göttingen

1934–1935 Copenhagen, London

1931 Marries Mici (Auguszta) Harkányi-Schütz; they have two children, Paul and Susan Wendy

1935–1946 George Washington University, Washington, DC

1941 Becomes a naturalized U.S. citizen

1942–1946 Manhattan Project (1942–1943, Chicago, 1943–1946, Los Alamos National Laboratory)

1946–1952 University of Chicago

1948 Member of the National Academy of Sciences of the U.S.A.

1949–1952 Works for shorter and longer periods at Los Alamos

1954, April–June The hearings and judgments by the Security Board of the AEC in the matter of J. Robert Oppenheimer

1952–2003 Livermore (later Lawrence Livermore) National Laboratory, Livermore, California

1953–1975 University of California

1962 Enrico Fermi Award

1975–2003 Hoover Institution, Stanford University

1982 U.S. National Medal of Science (from President Ronald Reagan)

2003 Presidential Medal of Freedom (from President George W. Bush)

2003, September 9 Dies in Stanford, California

Hungarian History

1867 Compromise between Hungary and the Habsburgs

1867–1918 Austria–Hungary: Franz Joseph I, Emperor of Austria (1848–1916) and King of Hungary (1867–1916)

1918, October Bourgeois democratic revolution

1919, March–August Communist dictatorship

1920, June 4 Treaty of Trianon

1920 *Numerus clausus* (first anti-Jewish legislation in Europe)

1920–1944, October 15 Miklós (Nicholas) Horthy, regent (head of state) of Hungary

1938 First anti-Jewish law

1939 Second anti-Jewish law

1941 Third anti-Jewish law

1944, March 19 Germany occupies Hungary

1944, May–June Concentration and deportation of Jews from the provinces, most of them to Auschwitz and extermination

1944, October 15 Hungarian Nazi (Arrow-cross) takeover

1945, April Liberation of Hungary from the Nazis by the Red Army; Soviet occupation begins

1945–1948 Democracy and multi-party system

1948–1989 One-party, communist system

1956, October 23–November 4 Revolution, then suppression of the revolution

1990 Multiparty system reintroduced, first democratic elections

Other History

1914–1918 First World War

1918–1933 Democratic "Weimar Republic" in Germany

1919 Treaty of Versailles, ratified by the League of Nations in 1920

1929 Stock market crash, worldwide depression begins

1933–1945 Adolf Hitler chancellor of Germany

1933–1945 Franklin D. Roosevelt president of the United States of America

1938 Munich Agreement: Great Britain and France sell out Czechoslovakia to Hitler

1938, December Discovery of nuclear fission

1939, September 1 Germany attacks Poland, World War II begins

1939–1945 World War II

1939, October President Roosevelt receives Einstein's August letter

1941, December 7 Japan attacks the United States at Pearl Harbor, Hawaii

1941, December 8 United States enters World War II

1942, June Manhattan Project begins; in September Leslie R. Groves becomes its head

1942, December 2 First nuclear reactor, in Chicago

1943, May Los Alamos Laboratory begins operation

1945–1952 Harry S Truman president of the United States

1945, July 17 Atomic device test in Alamogordo

1945, May 9 VE Day

1945, August 6 and 11 Hiroshima and Nagasaki atomic bombs, respectively

1945, August 15 VJ Day

1949, August First Soviet atomic explosion

1950, January 27 The Americans learn from the British about Klaus Fuchs's espionage

1950, January 31 President Truman directs the Atomic Energy Commission "to continue its work on all forms of atomic weapons, including the so-called hydrogen or super-bomb."

1950, February 9 Senator Joseph R. McCarthy makes his first charges about Communist infiltration of the State Department; his anti-Communist witch-hunt becomes known as "McCarthyism," and lasts until 1954, when he is censured by his fellow senators

1950, March Secret directive by President Truman to intensify work on the hydrogen bomb

1950, June 25 North Korea invades South Korea

1952 Opening of the second U.S. weapons laboratory in Livermore, California

1952, November 1 The United States explodes the world's first hydrogen bomb

1953–1960 Dwight D. Eisenhower president of the United States

1953, March 5 Stalin dies

1953, August Explosion of the first Soviet thermonuclear device

1954, January Secretary of State John F. Dulles announces policy of Mutually Assured Destruction (MAD)

1954, April–May Oppenheimer hearings; April 28, Edward Teller testifies

1957 Soviet Sputnik

1961–1963 John F. Kennedy president of the United States

1962 Cuban missile crisis

1963 President Kennedy assassinated

1963–1968 Lyndon B. Johnson president of the United States

1964 N. S. Khrushchev removed from power in Moscow

1969–1974 Richard M. Nixon president of the United States

1974–1976 Gerald Ford president of the United States

1977–1980 Jimmy Carter president of the United States

1981–1988 Ronald Reagan president of the United States

1983, March 23 President Reagan announces the Strategic Defense Initiative (SDI)

1985–1991 Mikhail Gorbachev leader of the Soviet Union

1991, December 26 Dissolution of the Soviet Union; end of Cold War

1989–1992 George H. W. Bush president of the United States

1993–2000 William Clinton president of the United States

2001– George W. Bush president of the United States

INDEX

Wiesner, Jerome, 151, 153
Wigner, Eugene. *See also* Martians
    Adamson and, 101
    Breit and, 78
    on the Briggs Committee, 103
    Budapest Technical University, 16, 29
    chemistry, 51, 115, 118
    childhood, xxi, 9, 52
    City Hall speech, 52
    civil defense, 155
    during the Cold War, 154–156
    on the deployment of atomic bombs, 120
    Du Pont engineers and, 119
    Einstein and, 53, 98, 116, 230
    engineering, 118
    family, 116, 117
    GAC and, 155
    in Germany, 44, 50–57, 198
    group theory, 37, 53, 54
    emigration, 79–80
    Jewishness, 225
    at Mauthner tannery in Budapest, 53
    Polanyi and, 79, 115, 219
    Nobel lecture, 55
    nuclear fission, 115
    patenting, 154
    personal traits, 115, 155, 156, 216–219, 236
    politics, 217, 218
    post-war activities, 128, 147, 154, 155
    at Princeton University, 56
    quantum theory, 53
    scientific conservatism, 217, 218
    solid-state physics, 79
    Szilard and, 52, 74, 213, 214, 216, 219, 231
    symmetry studies, 54, 55
    teachers, 16
    teaching, 56, 79, 80
    Teller and, 63
    von Neumann and, 52, 54, 56, 220, 221, 230
    Wigneritis, 154
    in World War II, 115–121
Wilson, Robert, 115
Wind and Beyond, The (von Kármán)
World Set Free, The (Wells), 102

York, Herbert, 158, 166, 174
Young, Gale, 117, 154

Zacharias, Jerrold, 204